FULL METAL PANIC. 03

Original Author **SHOUJI GATOU**
Art **RETSU TATEO**
Character Creation **SHIKIDOUJI**

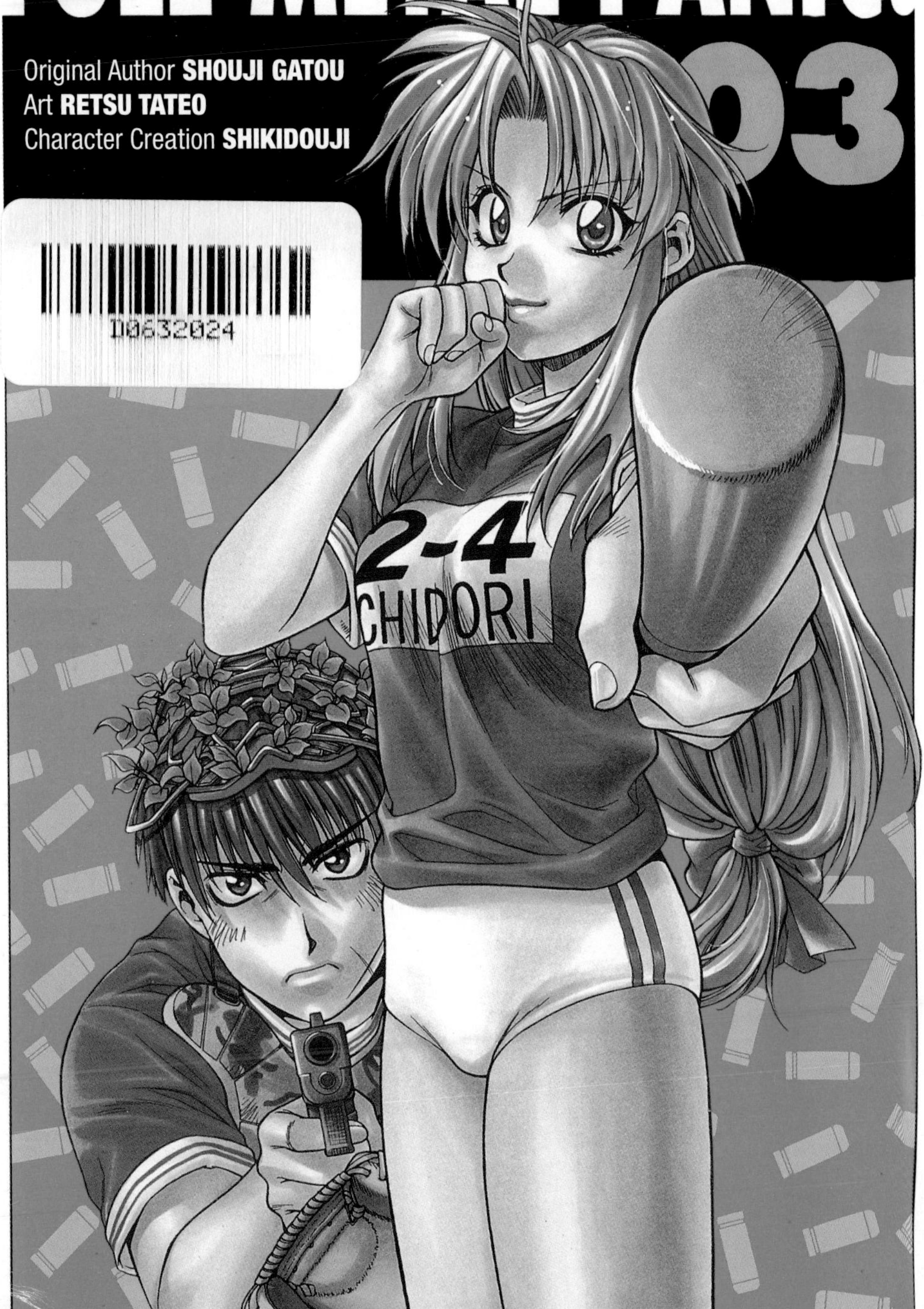
2-4
CHIDORI

FULL METAL PANIC!

CONTENTS

MISSION:15 Suspicion, confusion and aggravation
at the basketball tournament?! 3

MISSION:16 A mystery? Just who is this exchange student?! 33

MISSION:17 Together under one roof?! 57

MISSION:18 The miracle animal mission!! 81

MISSION:19 Holidays are for romance?!. 109

MISSION:20 I ain't afraid of no ghost!
Deserted island search team!! 139

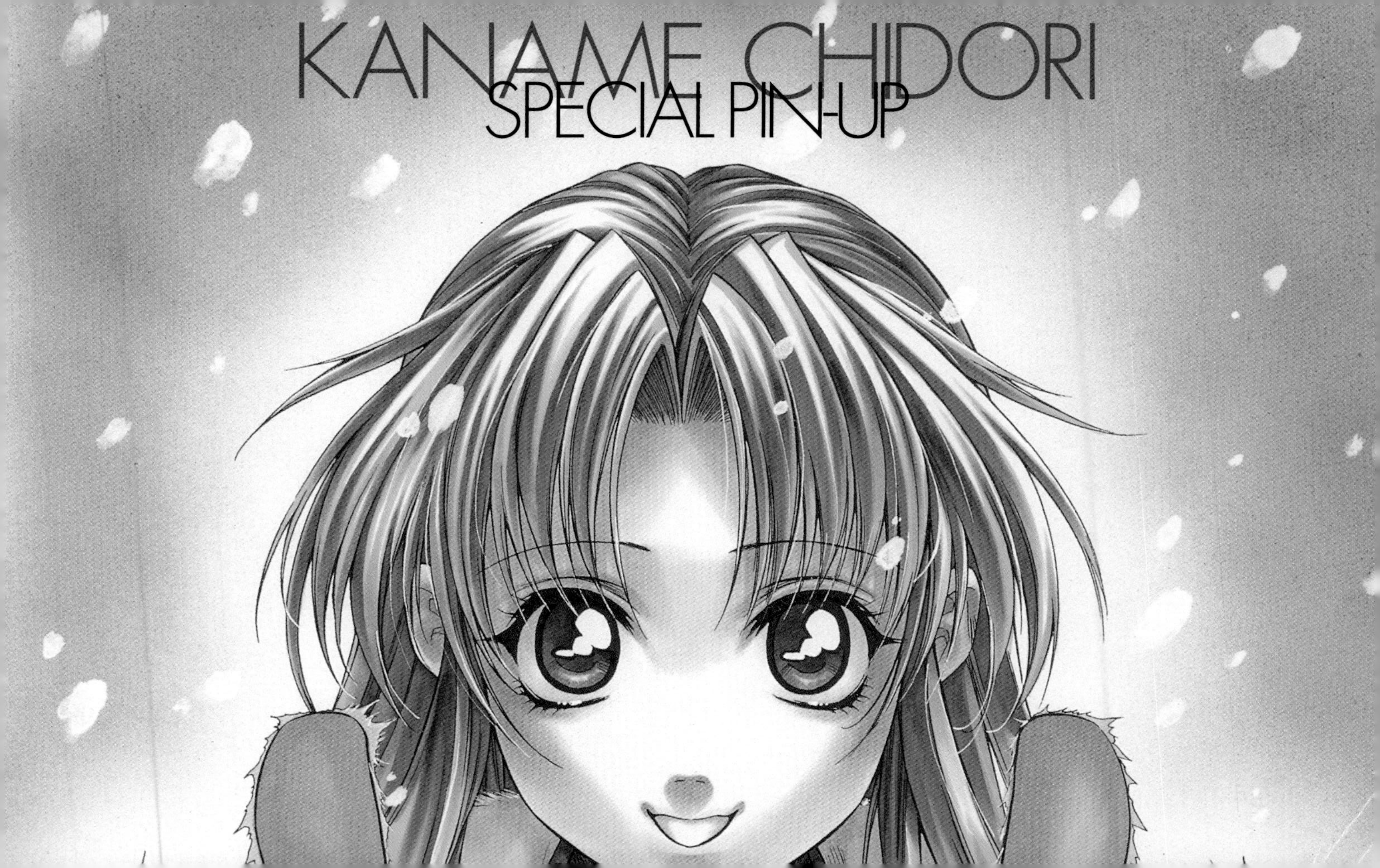
KANAME CHIDORI
SPECIAL PIN-UP

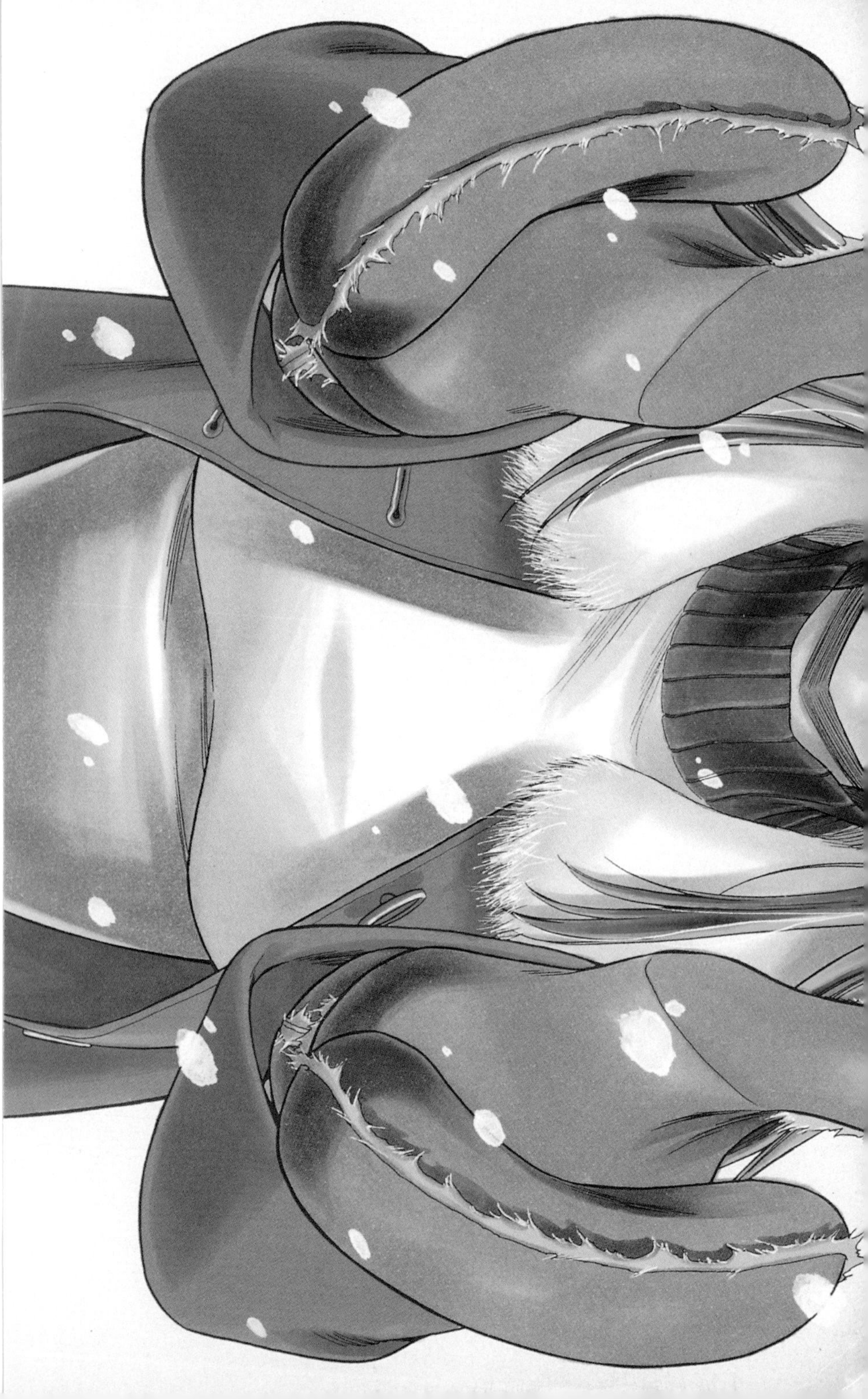

MISSION:15 [redacted]
Suspicion, confusion and aggravation at the basketball tournament?!

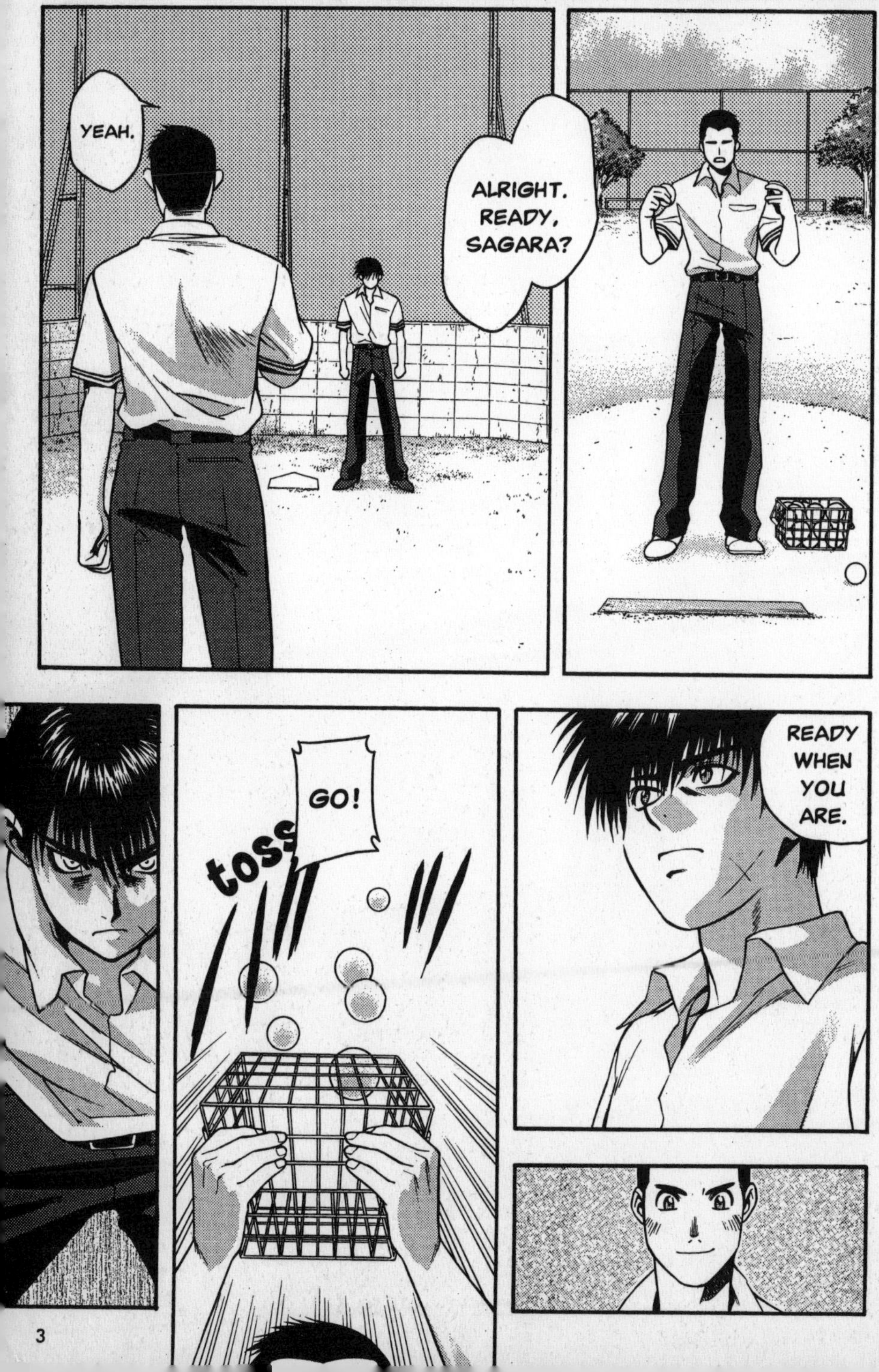

ALRIGHT. READY, SAGARA?
YEAH.
READY WHEN YOU ARE.
GO!
toss

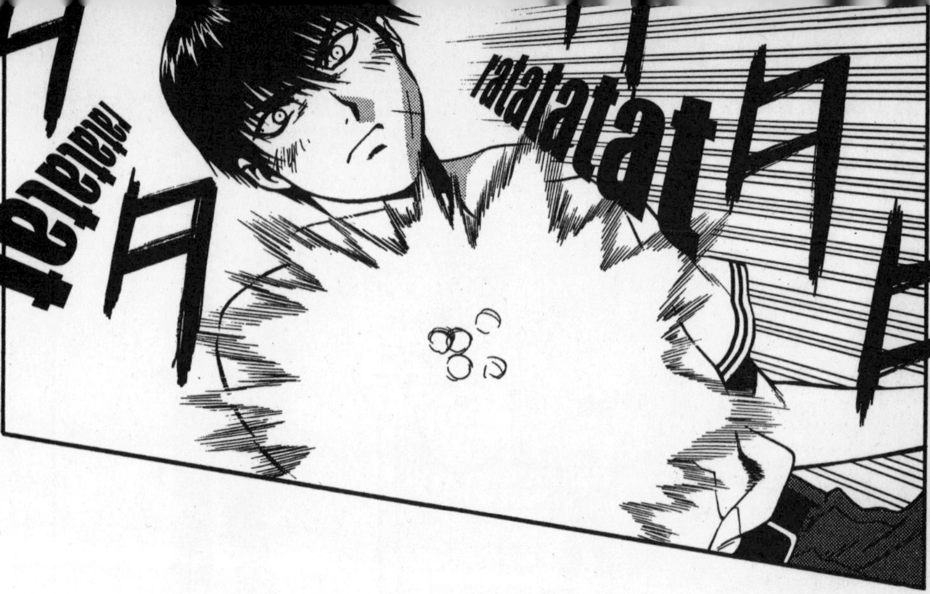
ratatatat
ratatat

MISSION:15 Suspicion, confusion and aggravation at the basketball tournament?!

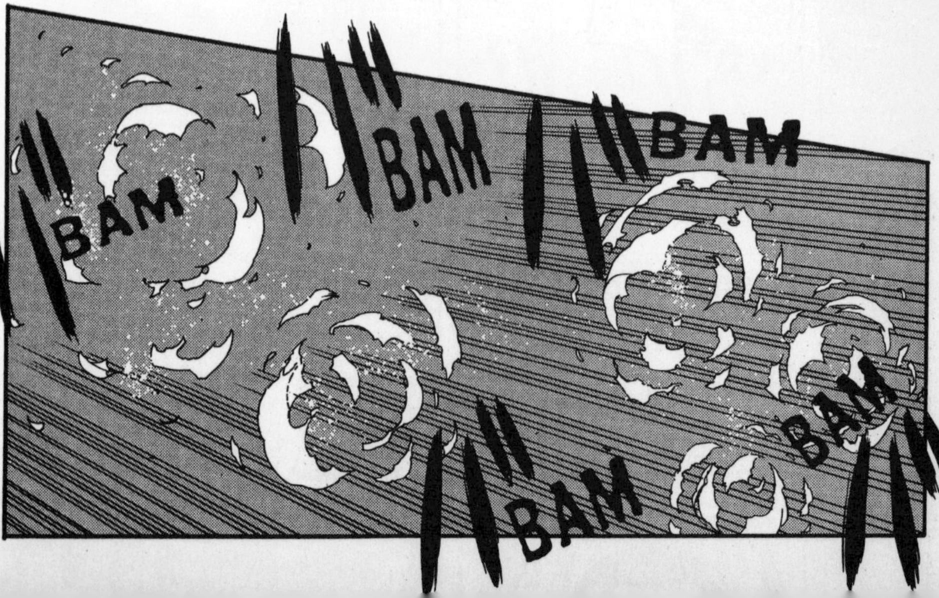
BAM
BAM
BAM
BAM
BAM

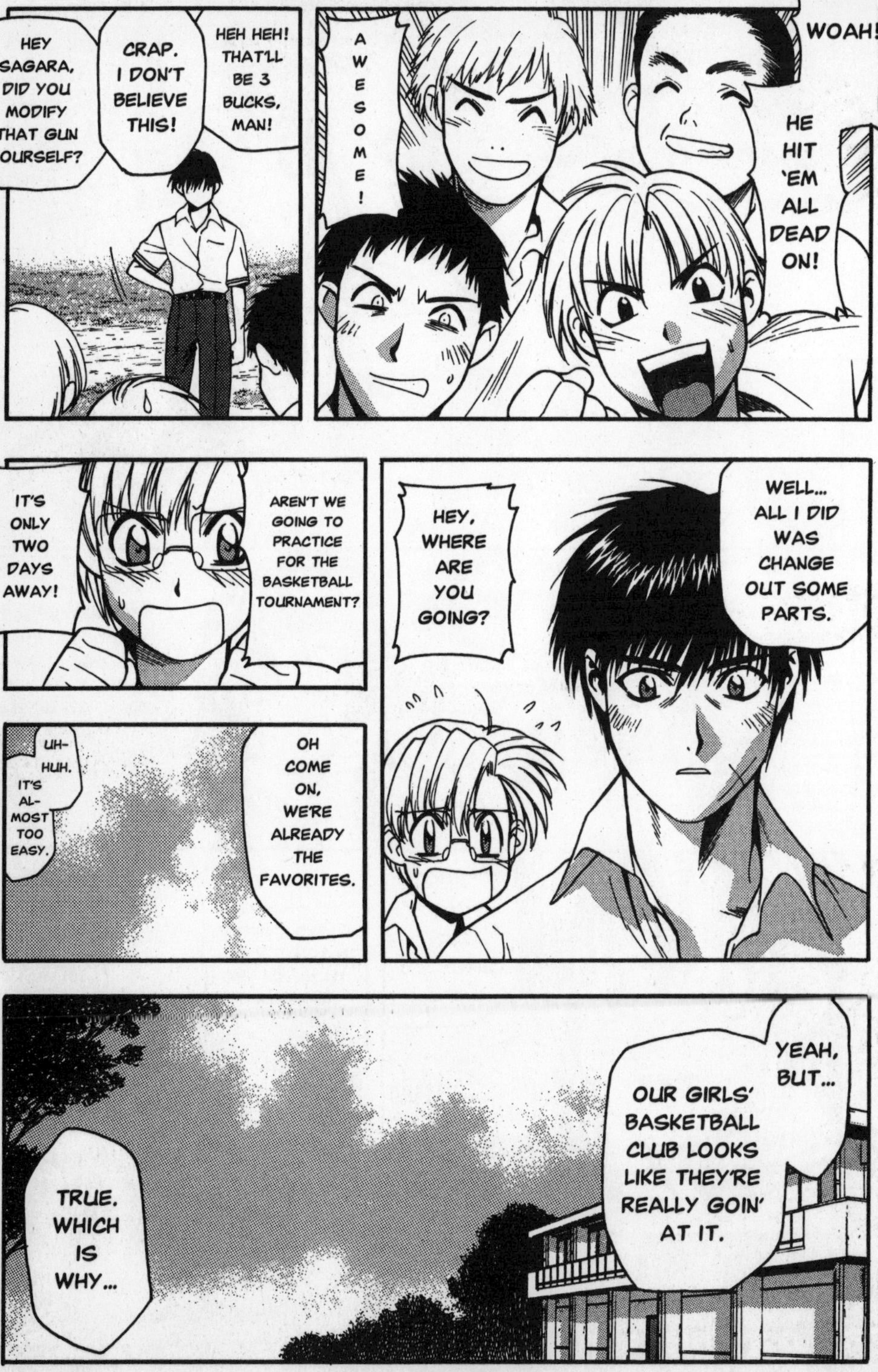
WOAH!
HE HIT 'EM ALL DEAD ON!
AWESOME!
HEH HEH! THAT'LL BE 3 BUCKS, MAN!
CRAP. I DON'T BELIEVE THIS!
HEY SAGARA, DID YOU MODIFY THAT GUN YOURSELF?
WELL... ALL I DID WAS CHANGE OUT SOME PARTS.
HEY, WHERE ARE YOU GOING?
AREN'T WE GOING TO PRACTICE FOR THE BASKETBALL TOURNAMENT?
IT'S ONLY TWO DAYS AWAY!
OH COME ON, WE'RE ALREADY THE FAVORITES.
UH-HUH. IT'S AL-MOST TOO EASY.
YEAH, BUT...
OUR GIRLS' BASKETBALL CLUB LOOKS LIKE THEY'RE REALLY GOIN' AT IT.
TRUE. WHICH IS WHY...

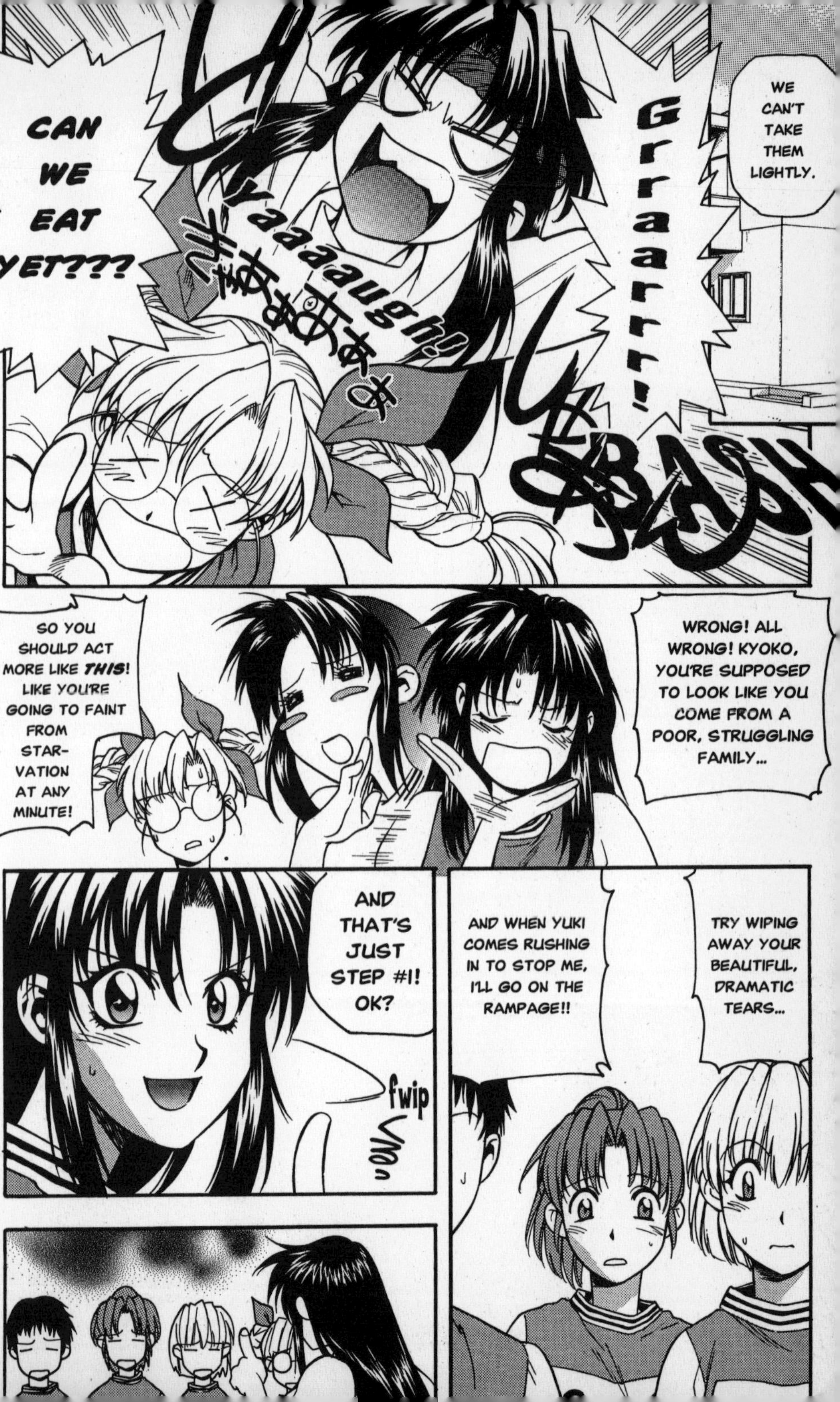
WE CAN'T TAKE THEM LIGHTLY.
Grrarrr!
BASH
Yaaaaaugh!!
CAN WE EAT YET???
WRONG! ALL WRONG! KYOKO, YOU'RE SUPPOSED TO LOOK LIKE YOU COME FROM A POOR, STRUGGLING FAMILY...
SO YOU SHOULD ACT MORE LIKE THIS! LIKE YOU'RE GOING TO FAINT FROM STAR-VATION AT ANY MINUTE!
TRY WIPING AWAY YOUR BEAUTIFUL, DRAMATIC TEARS...
AND WHEN YUKI COMES RUSHING IN TO STOP ME, I'LL GO ON THE RAMPAGE!!
AND THAT'S JUST STEP #1! OK?
fwip

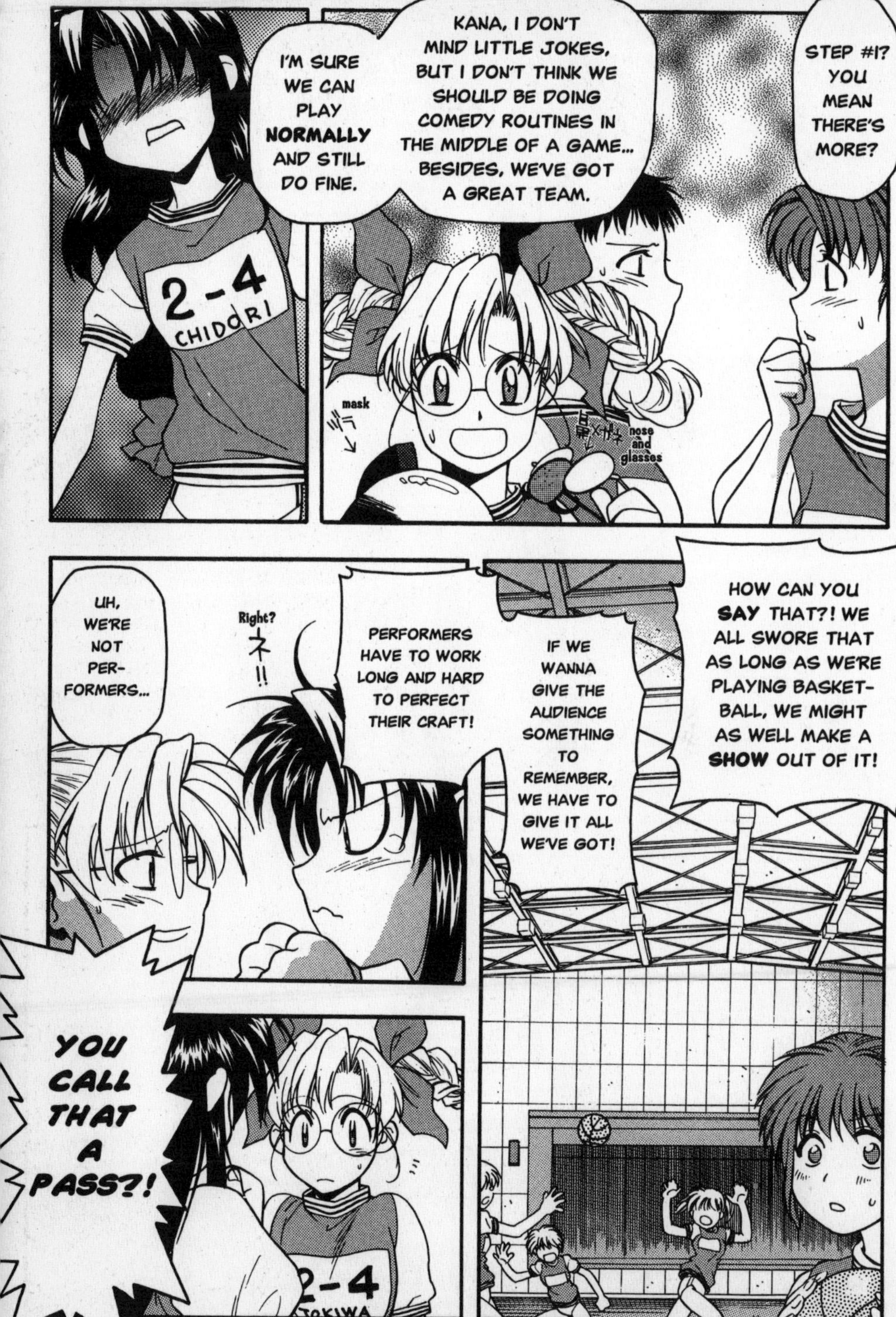
STEP #1? YOU MEAN THERE'S MORE?
KANA, I DON'T MIND LITTLE JOKES, BUT I DON'T THINK WE SHOULD BE DOING COMEDY ROUTINES IN THE MIDDLE OF A GAME... BESIDES, WE'VE GOT A GREAT TEAM.
nose and glasses
mask
I'M SURE WE CAN PLAY **NORMALLY** AND STILL DO FINE.
2-4 CHIDORI
HOW CAN YOU **SAY** THAT?! WE ALL SWORE THAT AS LONG AS WE'RE PLAYING BASKET-BALL, WE MIGHT AS WELL MAKE A **SHOW** OUT OF IT!
IF WE WANNA GIVE THE AUDIENCE SOMETHING TO REMEMBER, WE HAVE TO GIVE IT ALL WE'VE GOT!
PERFORMERS HAVE TO WORK LONG AND HARD TO PERFECT THEIR CRAFT!
Right? ネ!!
UH, WE'RE NOT PER-FORMERS...
YOU CALL THAT A PASS?!
2-4 TOKIWA

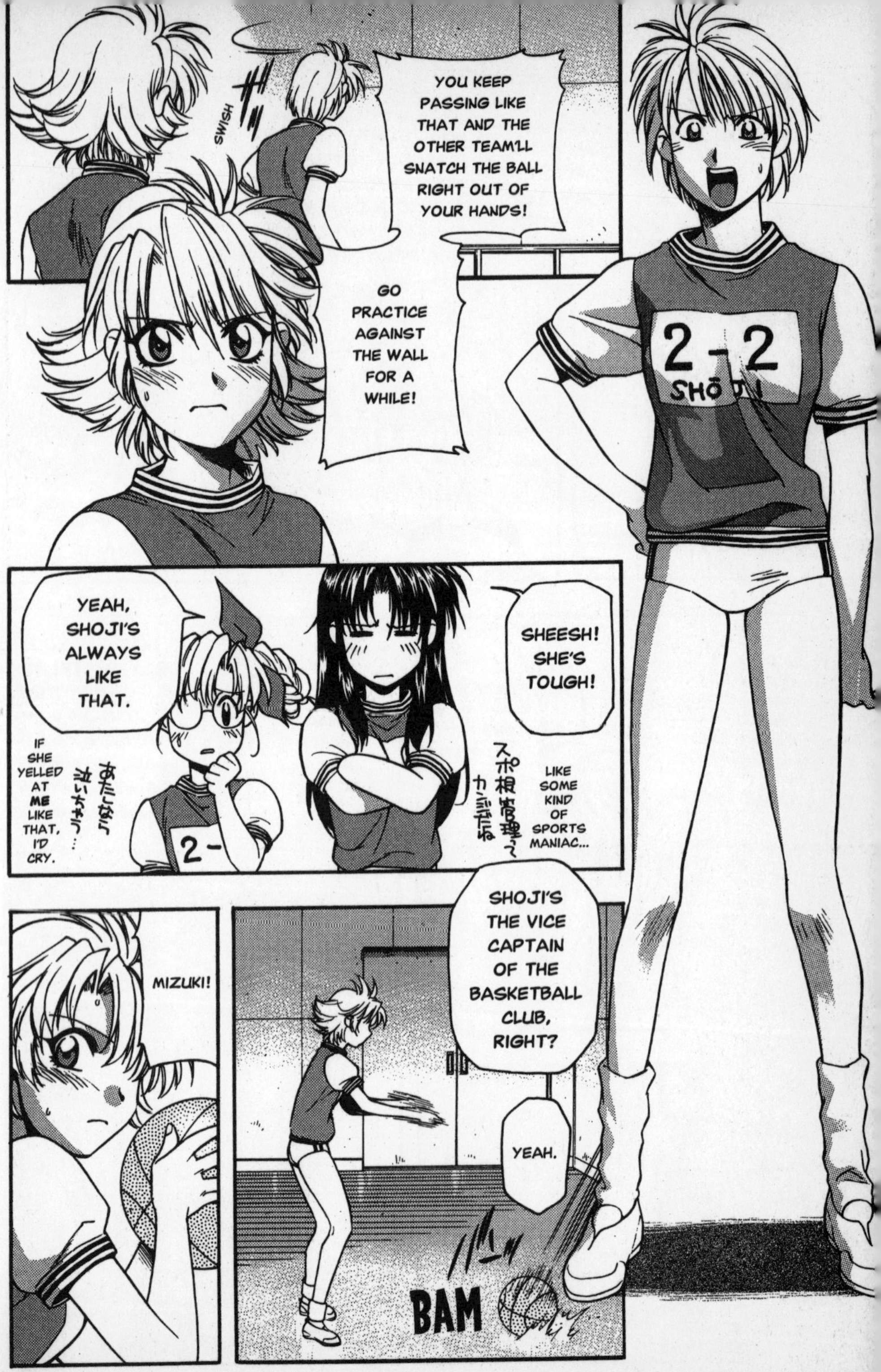
YOU KEEP PASSING LIKE THAT AND THE OTHER TEAM'LL SNATCH THE BALL RIGHT OUT OF YOUR HANDS!
SWISH
GO PRACTICE AGAINST THE WALL FOR A WHILE!
SHEESH! SHE'S TOUGH!
スポ根管理ってカンジだね
LIKE SOME KIND OF SPORTS MANIAC...
YEAH, SHOJI'S ALWAYS LIKE THAT.
あたしなら泣いちゃう…
IF SHE YELLED AT ME LIKE THAT, I'D CRY.
SHOJI'S THE VICE CAPTAIN OF THE BASKETBALL CLUB, RIGHT?
YEAH.
BAM
MIZUKI!

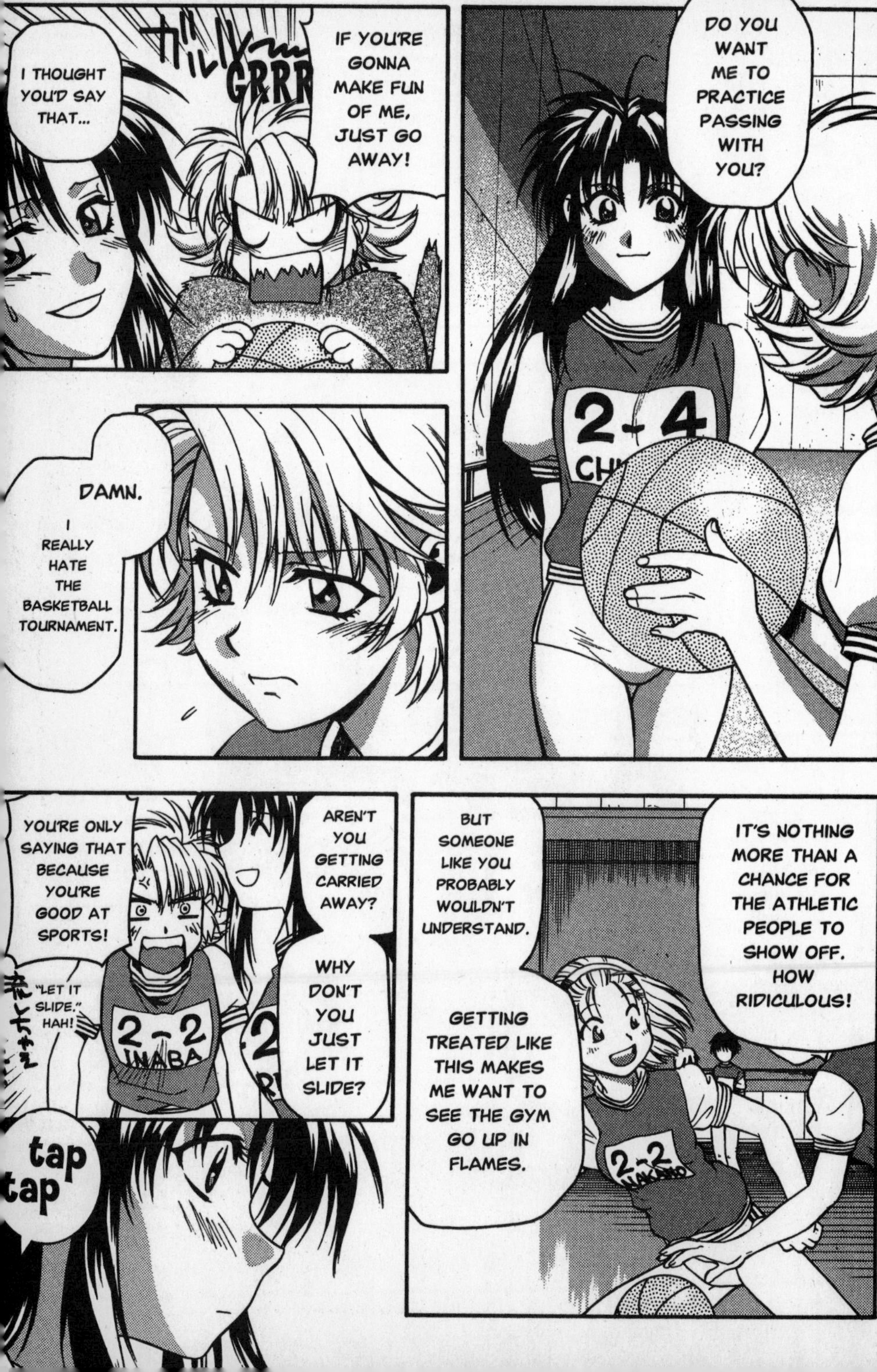
DO YOU WANT ME TO PRACTICE PASSING WITH YOU?
2-4 CHI
IF YOU'RE GONNA MAKE FUN OF ME, JUST GO AWAY!
GRRR
I THOUGHT YOU'D SAY THAT...
DAMN.
I REALLY HATE THE BASKETBALL TOURNAMENT.
IT'S NOTHING MORE THAN A CHANCE FOR THE ATHLETIC PEOPLE TO SHOW OFF. HOW RIDICULOUS!
BUT SOMEONE LIKE YOU PROBABLY WOULDN'T UNDERSTAND.
GETTING TREATED LIKE THIS MAKES ME WANT TO SEE THE GYM GO UP IN FLAMES.
2-2 NAKANO
AREN'T YOU GETTING CARRIED AWAY?
WHY DON'T YOU JUST LET IT SLIDE?
YOU'RE ONLY SAYING THAT BECAUSE YOU'RE GOOD AT SPORTS!
"LET IT SLIDE." HAH!
2-2 INABA
tap tap

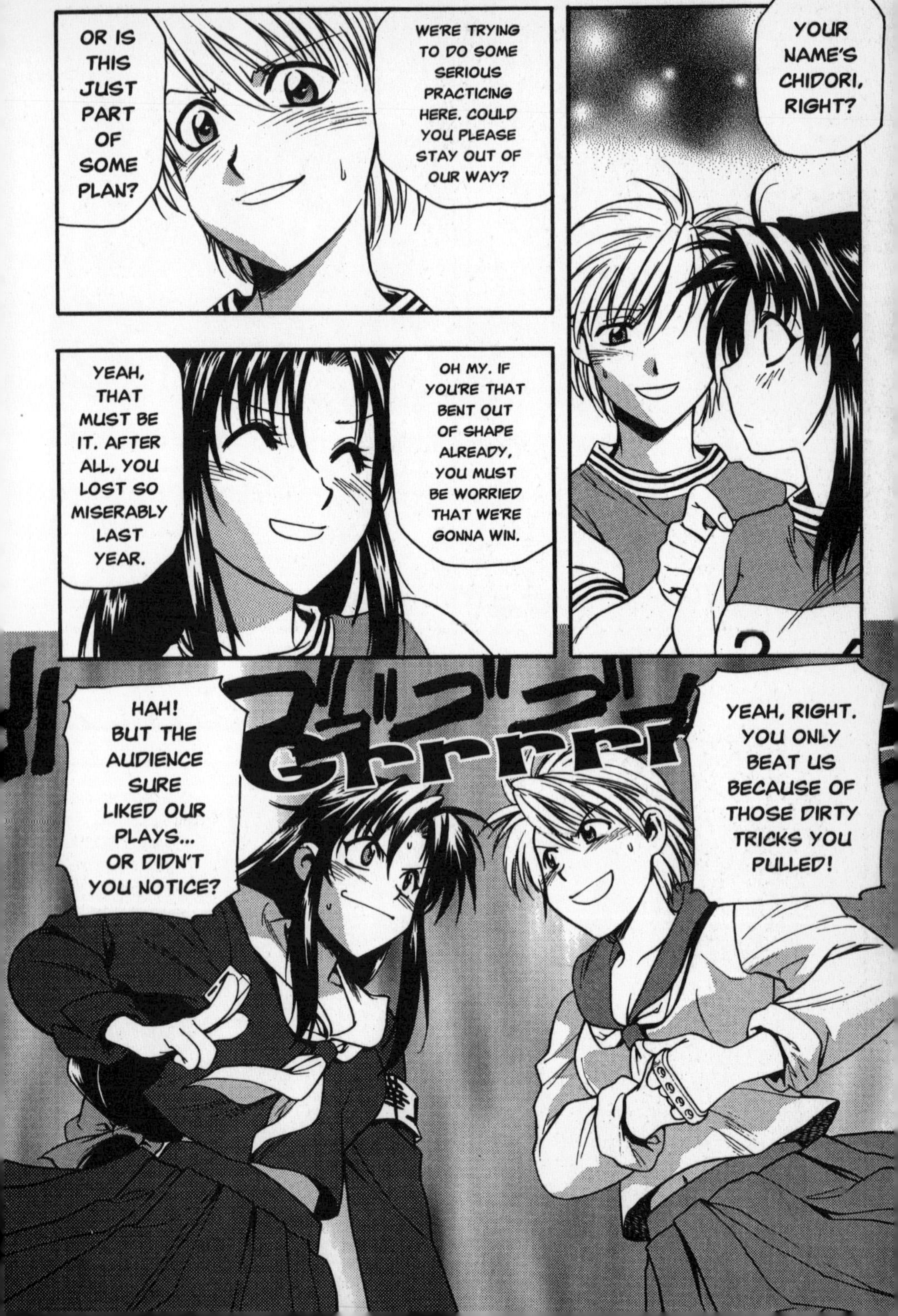
YOUR NAME'S CHIDORI, RIGHT?
WE'RE TRYING TO DO SOME SERIOUS PRACTICING HERE. COULD YOU PLEASE STAY OUT OF OUR WAY?
OR IS THIS JUST PART OF SOME PLAN?
OH MY. IF YOU'RE THAT BENT OUT OF SHAPE ALREADY, YOU MUST BE WORRIED THAT WE'RE GONNA WIN.
YEAH, THAT MUST BE IT. AFTER ALL, YOU LOST SO MISERABLY LAST YEAR.
YEAH, RIGHT. YOU ONLY BEAT US BECAUSE OF THOSE DIRTY TRICKS YOU PULLED!
Grrrrr!
HAH! BUT THE AUDIENCE SURE LIKED OUR PLAYS... OR DIDN'T YOU NOTICE?

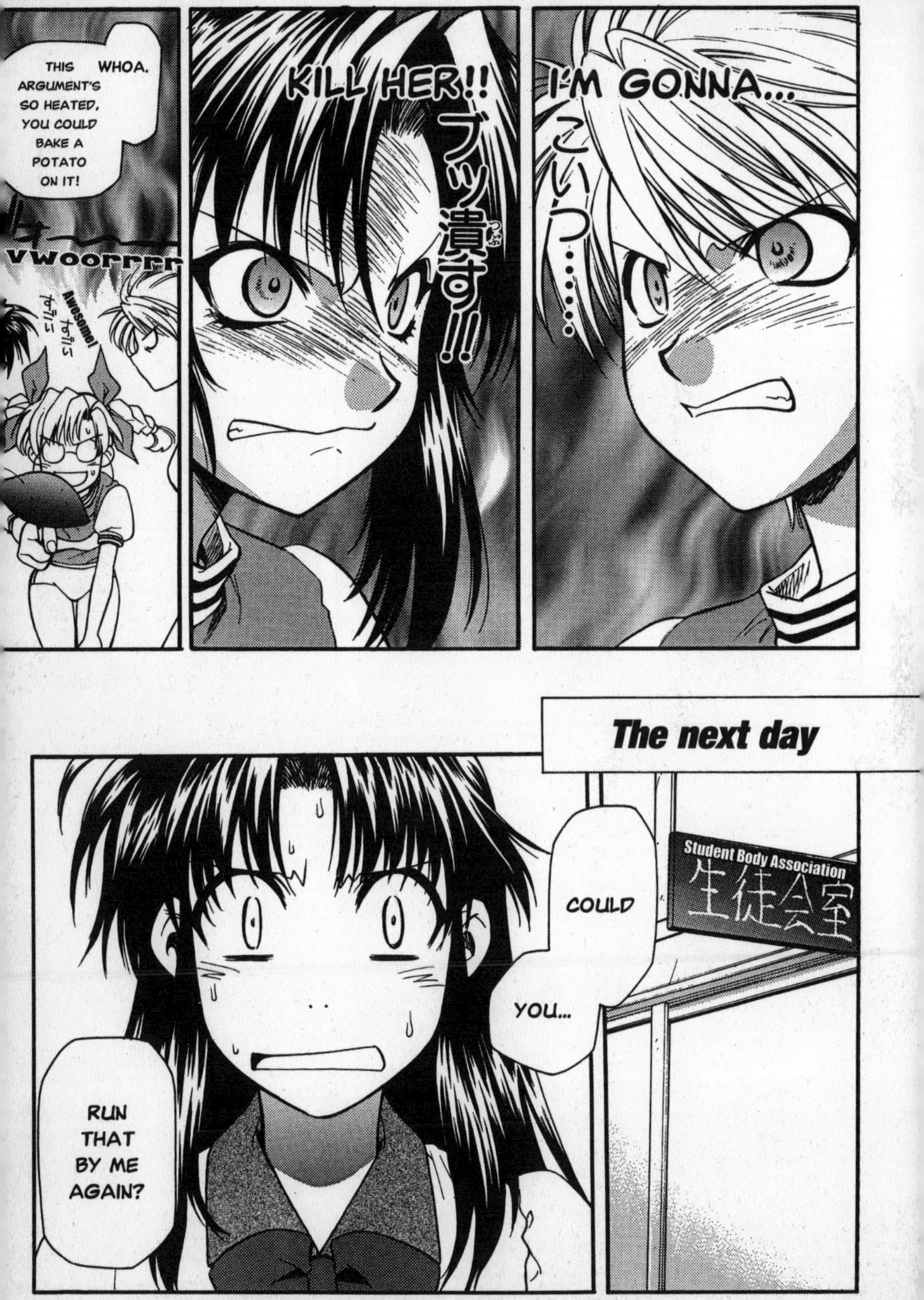
I'M GONNA...
こいつ……
KILL HER!!
ブッ潰す!!
WHOA. THIS ARGUMENT'S SO HEATED, YOU COULD BAKE A POTATO ON IT!
VWOORRRRR
Awesome!
すごい すごい
The next day
COULD
YOU...
Student Body Association
生徒会室
RUN THAT BY ME AGAIN?

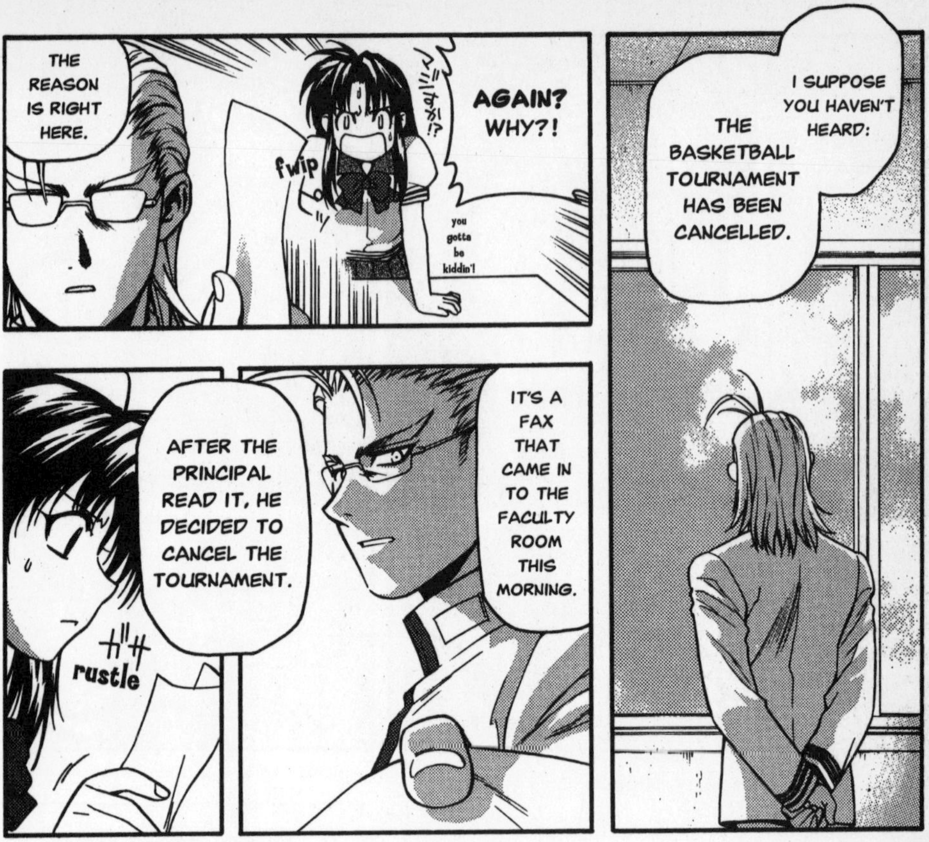
I SUPPOSE YOU HAVEN'T HEARD:
THE BASKETBALL TOURNAMENT HAS BEEN CANCELLED.
AGAIN? WHY?!
you gotta be kiddin'!
fwip
THE REASON IS RIGHT HERE.
IT'S A FAX THAT CAME IN TO THE FACULTY ROOM THIS MORNING.
AFTER THE PRINCIPAL READ IT, HE DECIDED TO CANCEL THE TOURNAMENT.
rustle

To those involved in the basketball tournament:

I am a female student in the 11th grade. I've been bad at sports ever since I was little, and everyone makes fun of me for it. I want to stay out of the tournament this year, but the class and my parents won't let me. But if I'm forced to be in it, I think I'll die! So I'm begging you, please cancel the tournament—or I'll DIE!

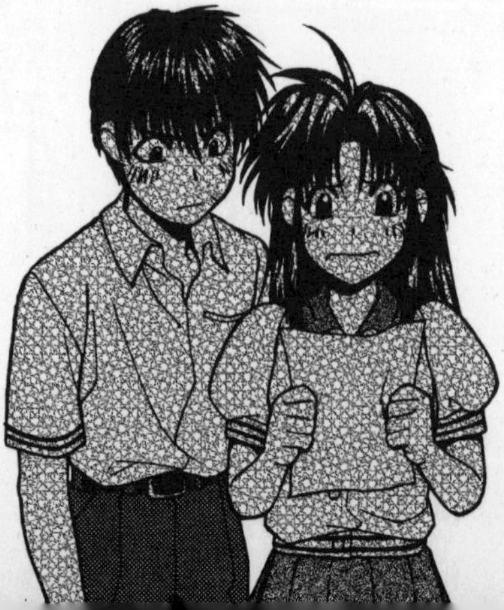

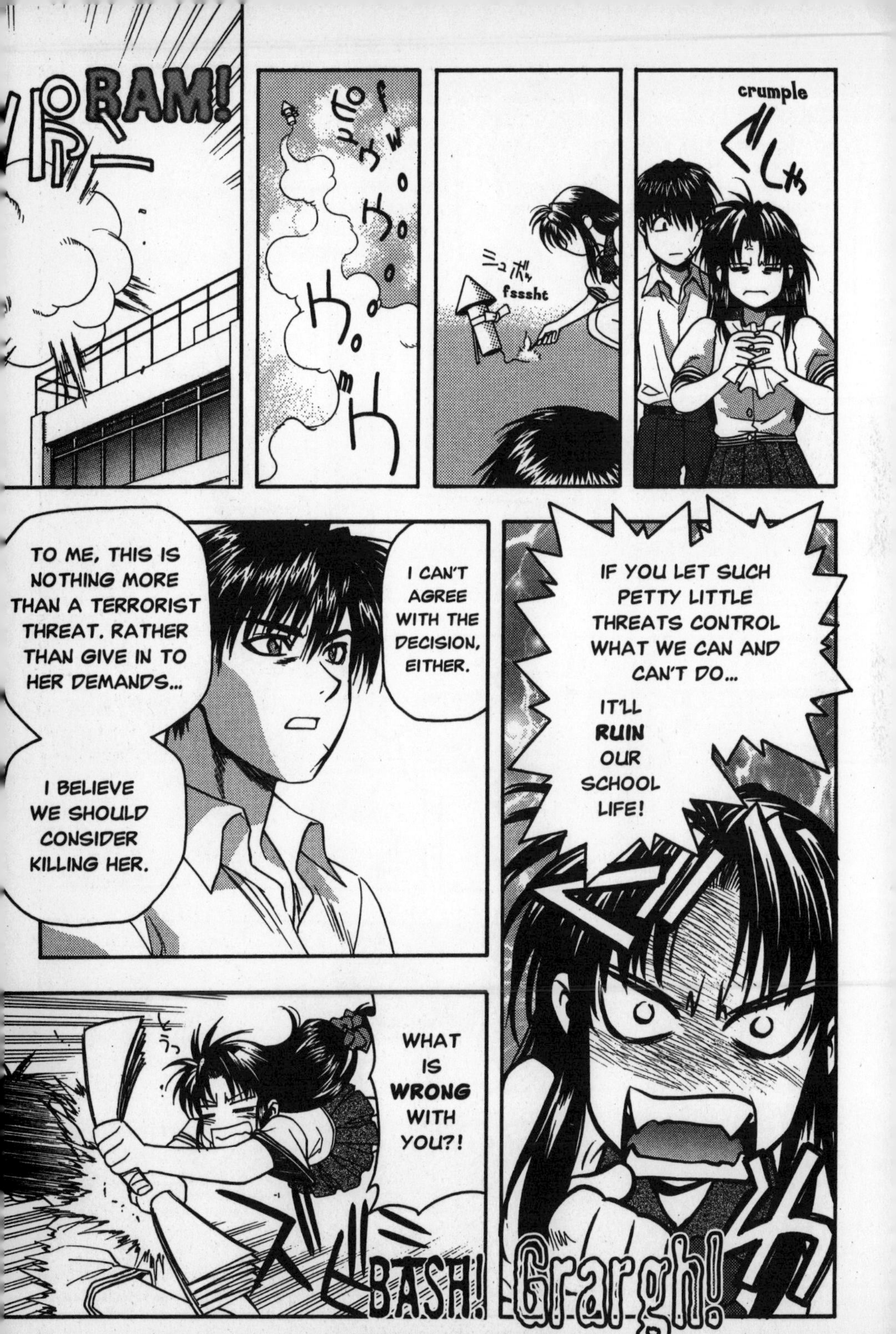
crumple
ぐしゃ
シュボッ
fsssht
fwooooom
RAM!
IF YOU LET SUCH PETTY LITTLE THREATS CONTROL WHAT WE CAN AND CAN'T DO...
IT'LL **RUIN** OUR SCHOOL LIFE!
Grargh!
I CAN'T AGREE WITH THE DECISION, EITHER.
TO ME, THIS IS NOTHING MORE THAN A TERRORIST THREAT. RATHER THAN GIVE IN TO HER DEMANDS...
I BELIEVE WE SHOULD CONSIDER KILLING HER.
WHAT IS **WRONG** WITH YOU?!
BASH!

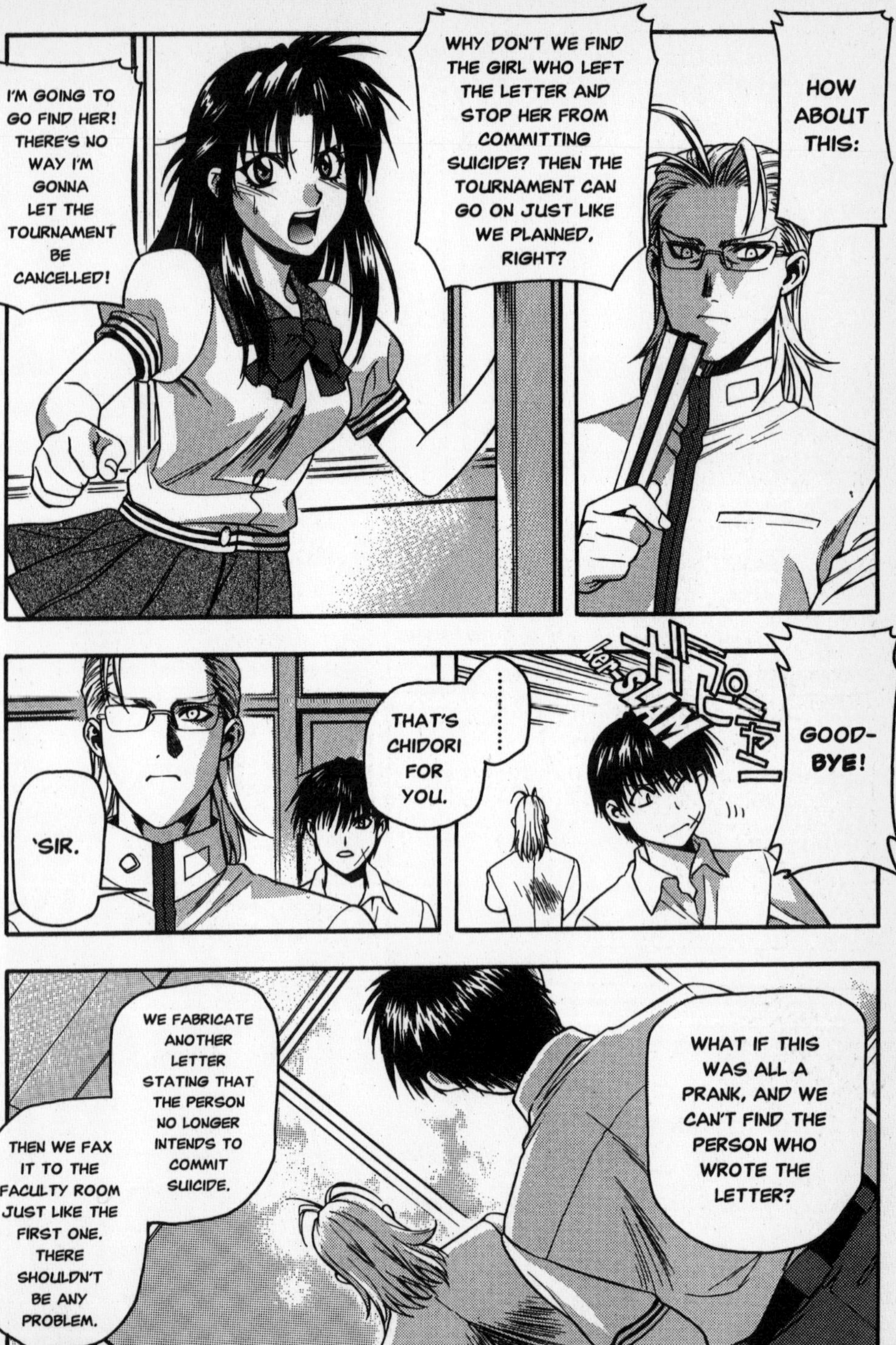
HOW ABOUT THIS:
WHY DON'T WE FIND THE GIRL WHO LEFT THE LETTER AND STOP HER FROM COMMITTING SUICIDE? THEN THE TOURNAMENT CAN GO ON JUST LIKE WE PLANNED, RIGHT?
I'M GOING TO GO FIND HER! THERE'S NO WAY I'M GONNA LET THE TOURNAMENT BE CANCELLED!
GOOD-BYE!
ker-SLAM
......
THAT'S CHIDORI FOR YOU.
'SIR.
WHAT IF THIS WAS ALL A PRANK, AND WE CAN'T FIND THE PERSON WHO WROTE THE LETTER?
WE FABRICATE ANOTHER LETTER STATING THAT THE PERSON NO LONGER INTENDS TO COMMIT SUICIDE.
THEN WE FAX IT TO THE FACULTY ROOM JUST LIKE THE FIRST ONE. THERE SHOULDN'T BE ANY PROBLEM.

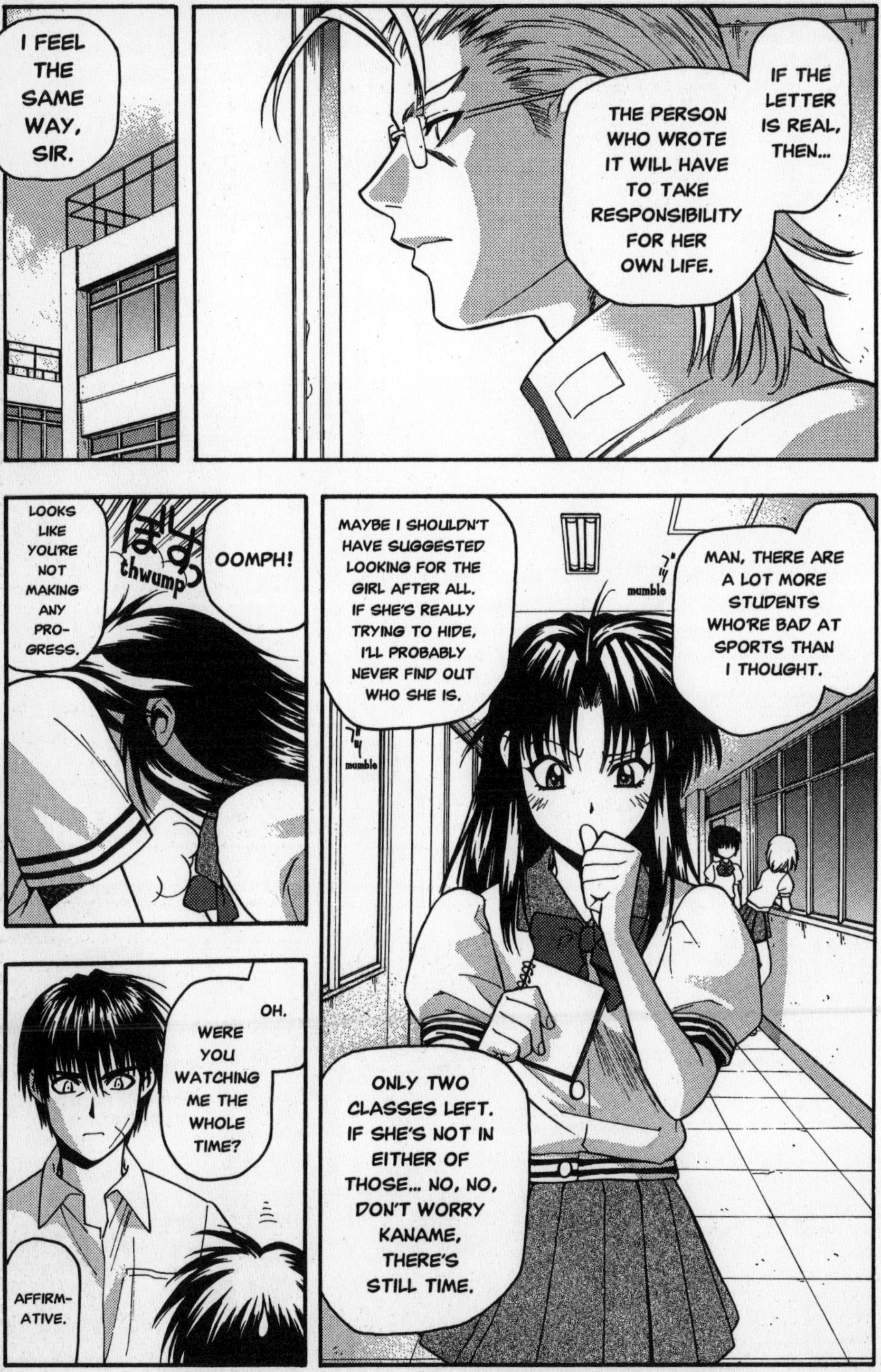
IF THE LETTER IS REAL, THEN...
THE PERSON WHO WROTE IT WILL HAVE TO TAKE RESPONSIBILITY FOR HER OWN LIFE.
I FEEL THE SAME WAY, SIR.
MAN, THERE ARE A LOT MORE STUDENTS WHO'RE BAD AT SPORTS THAN I THOUGHT.
mumble
MAYBE I SHOULDN'T HAVE SUGGESTED LOOKING FOR THE GIRL AFTER ALL. IF SHE'S REALLY TRYING TO HIDE, I'LL PROBABLY NEVER FIND OUT WHO SHE IS.
mumble
ONLY TWO CLASSES LEFT. IF SHE'S NOT IN EITHER OF THOSE... NO, NO, DON'T WORRY KANAME, THERE'S STILL TIME.
OOMPH!
thwump
LOOKS LIKE YOU'RE NOT MAKING ANY PRO-GRESS.
OH. WERE YOU WATCHING ME THE WHOLE TIME?
AFFIRM-ATIVE.

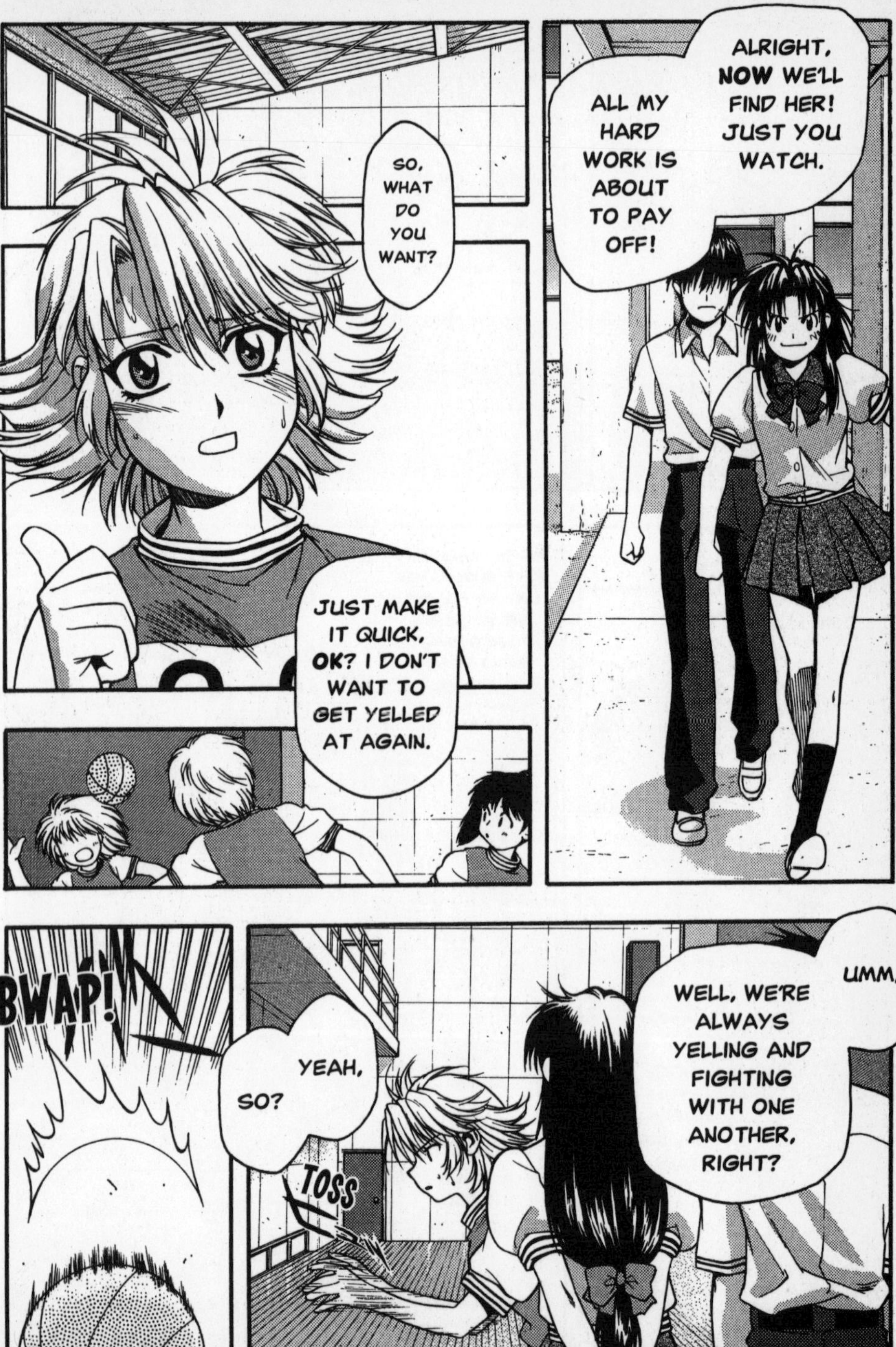
ALRIGHT, NOW WE'LL FIND HER! JUST YOU WATCH.
ALL MY HARD WORK IS ABOUT TO PAY OFF!
SO, WHAT DO YOU WANT?
JUST MAKE IT QUICK, OK? I DON'T WANT TO GET YELLED AT AGAIN.
UMM,
WELL, WE'RE ALWAYS YELLING AND FIGHTING WITH ONE ANOTHER, RIGHT?
YEAH,
SO?
TOSS
BWAP!

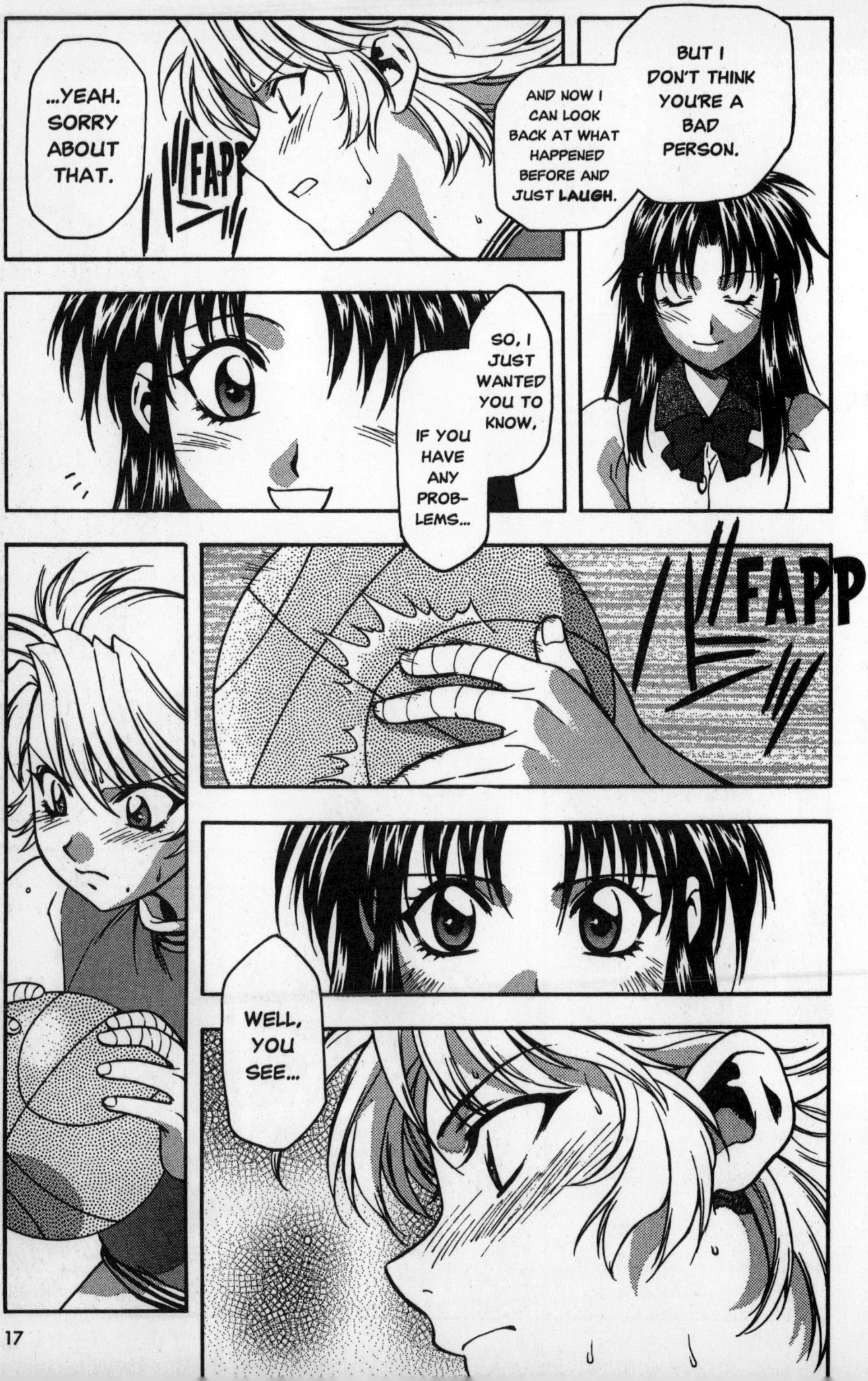
BUT I DON'T THINK YOU'RE A BAD PERSON.
AND NOW I CAN LOOK BACK AT WHAT HAPPENED BEFORE AND JUST **LAUGH**.
FAPP
...YEAH. SORRY ABOUT THAT.
SO, I JUST WANTED YOU TO KNOW,
IF YOU HAVE ANY PROB-LEMS...
FAPP
WELL, YOU SEE...

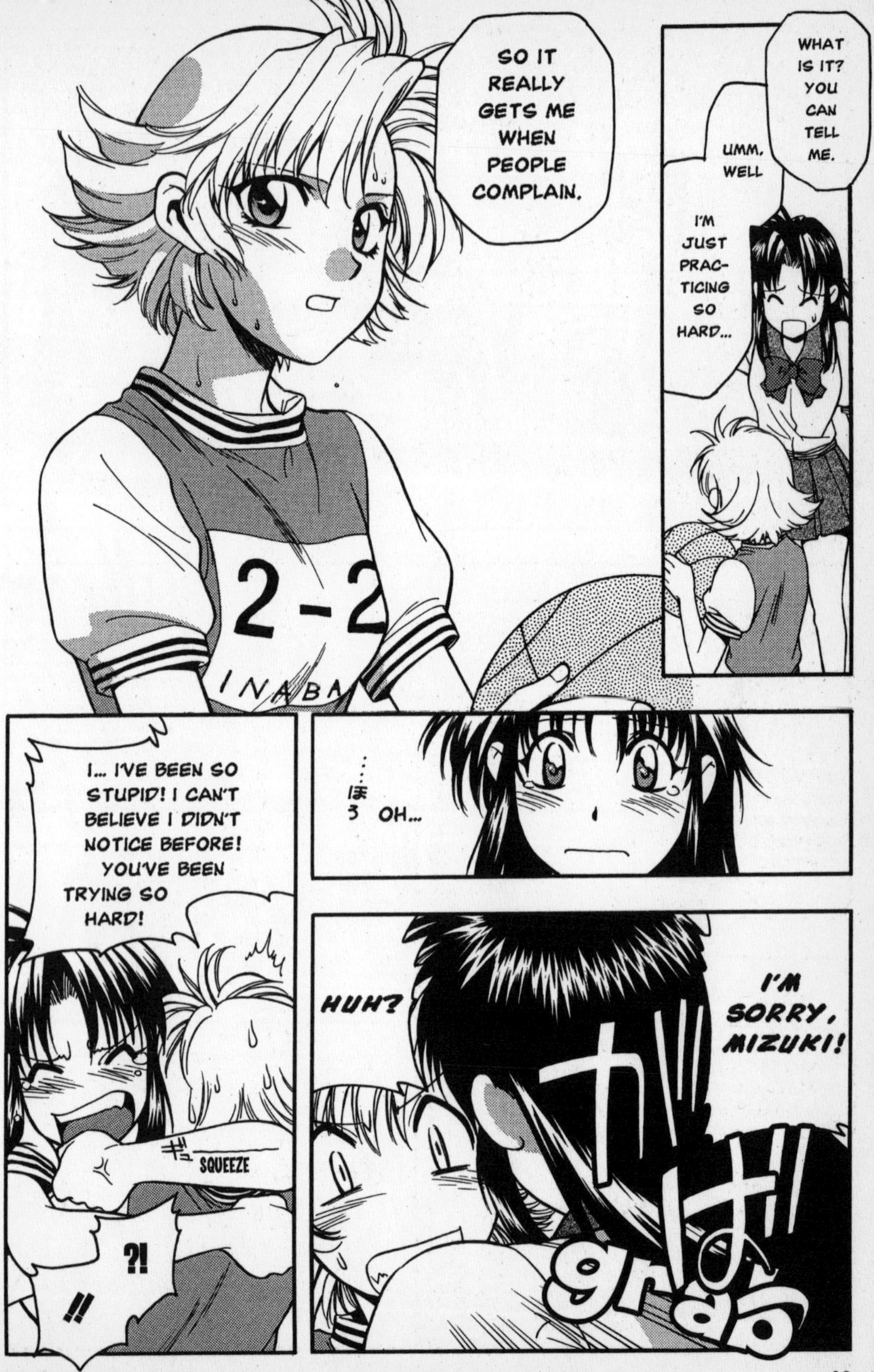
WHAT IS IT? YOU CAN TELL ME.
UMM, WELL
I'M JUST PRACTICING SO HARD...
SO IT REALLY GETS ME WHEN PEOPLE COMPLAIN.
INABA
2-2
……ほう OH...
HUH?
I'M SORRY, MIZUKI!
ガバッ
grab
I... I'VE BEEN SO STUPID! I CAN'T BELIEVE I DIDN'T NOTICE BEFORE! YOU'VE BEEN TRYING SO HARD!
ギュ SQUEEZE
?!
!!

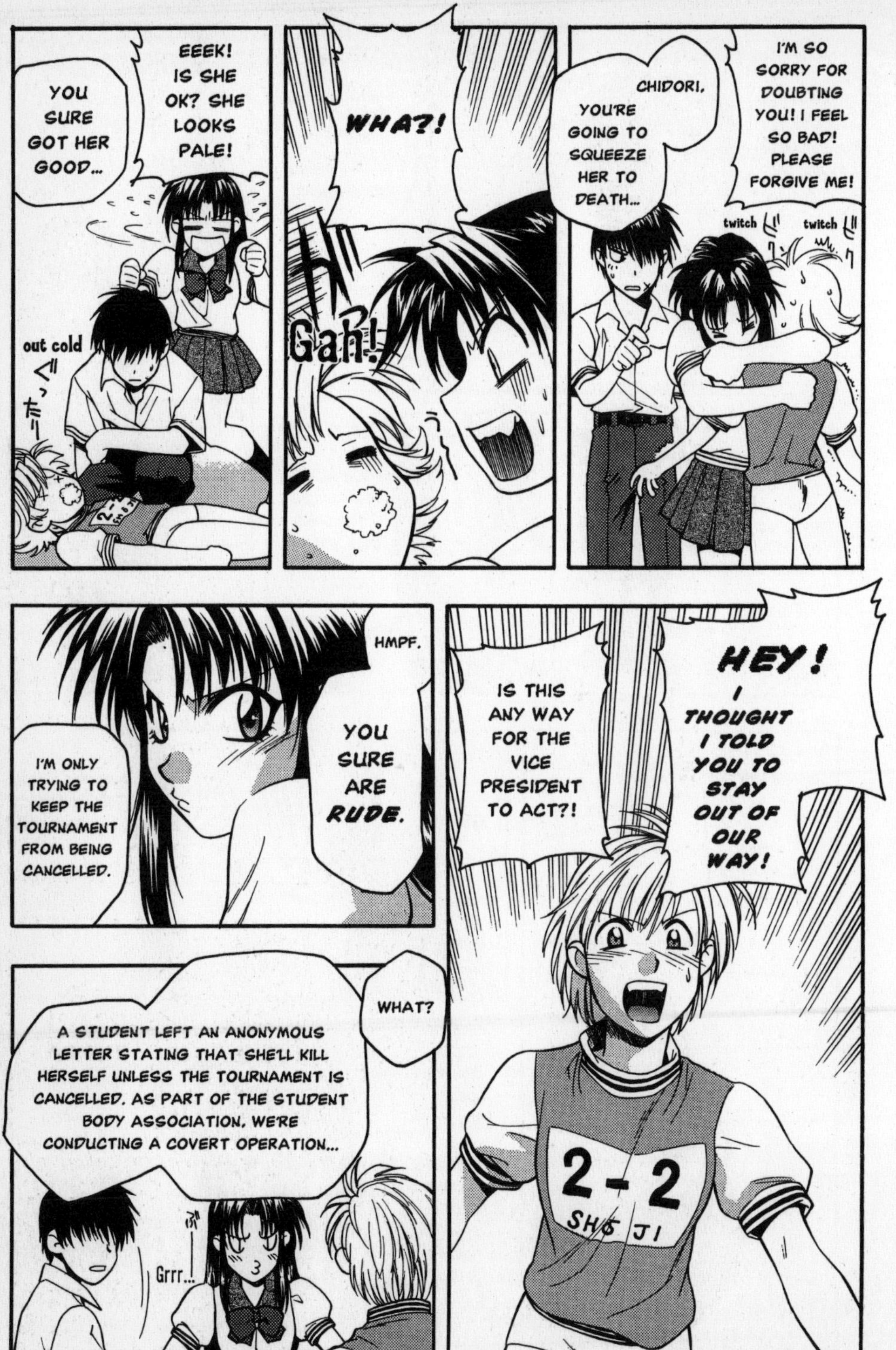
I'M SO SORRY FOR DOUBTING YOU! I FEEL SO BAD! PLEASE FORGIVE ME!
CHIDORI, YOU'RE GOING TO SQUEEZE HER TO DEATH...
twitch
twitch
WHA?!
Gah!
EEEK! IS SHE OK? SHE LOOKS PALE!
YOU SURE GOT HER GOOD...
out cold
HEY! I THOUGHT I TOLD YOU TO STAY OUT OF OUR WAY!
IS THIS ANY WAY FOR THE VICE PRESIDENT TO ACT?!
2-2
SHOJI
HMPF.
YOU SURE ARE RUDE.
I'M ONLY TRYING TO KEEP THE TOURNAMENT FROM BEING CANCELLED.
WHAT?
A STUDENT LEFT AN ANONYMOUS LETTER STATING THAT SHE'LL KILL HERSELF UNLESS THE TOURNAMENT IS CANCELLED. AS PART OF THE STUDENT BODY ASSOCIATION, WE'RE CONDUCTING A COVERT OPERATION...
Grrr...

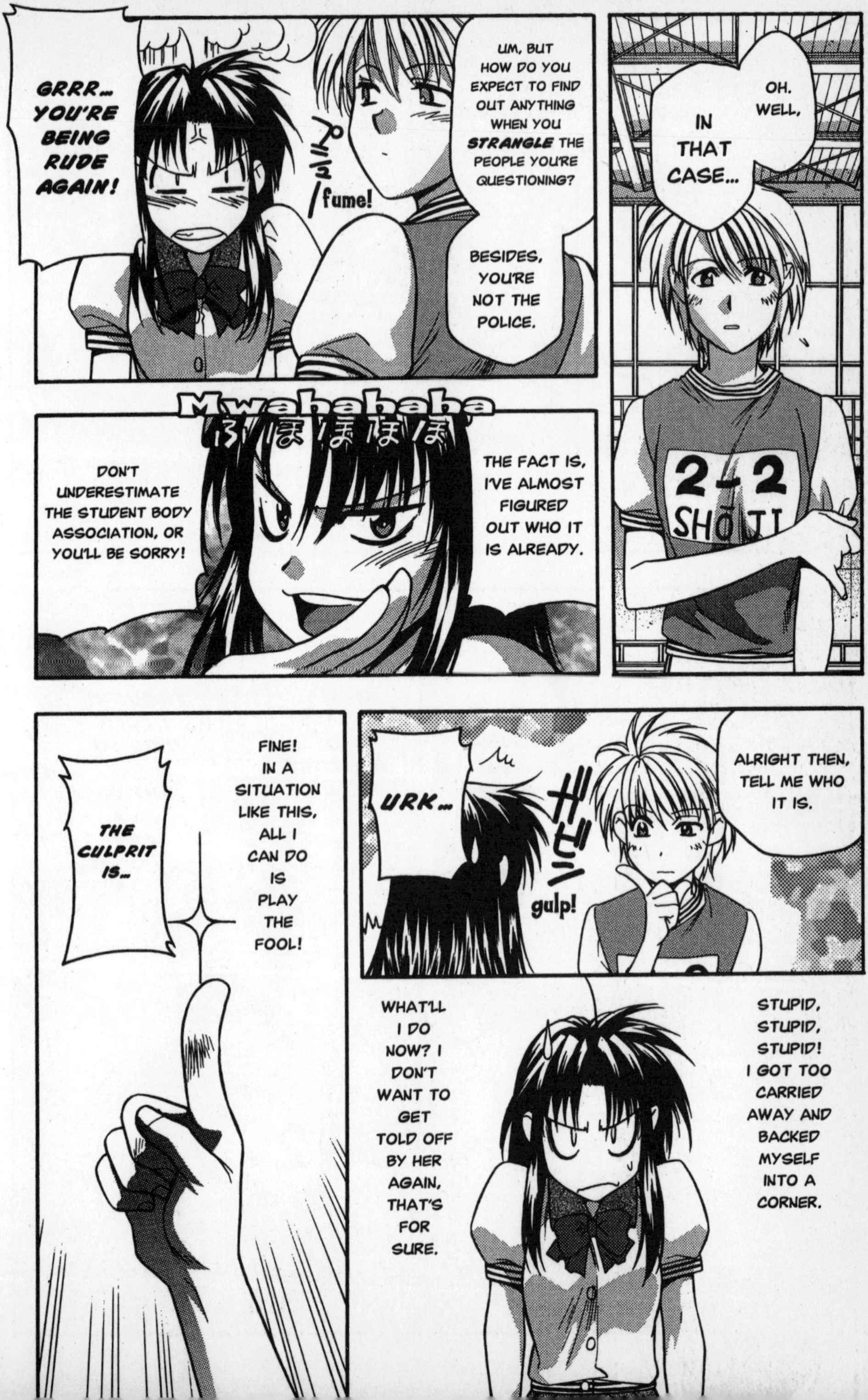
OH. WELL,
IN THAT CASE...
UM, BUT HOW DO YOU EXPECT TO FIND OUT ANYTHING WHEN YOU STRANGLE THE PEOPLE YOU'RE QUESTIONING?
BESIDES, YOU'RE NOT THE POLICE.
fume!
GRRR... YOU'RE BEING RUDE AGAIN!
Mwahahaha
THE FACT IS, I'VE ALMOST FIGURED OUT WHO IT IS ALREADY.
DON'T UNDERESTIMATE THE STUDENT BODY ASSOCIATION, OR YOU'LL BE SORRY!
2-2
SHŌJI
ALRIGHT THEN, TELL ME WHO IT IS.
gulp!
URK...
STUPID, STUPID, STUPID! I GOT TOO CARRIED AWAY AND BACKED MYSELF INTO A CORNER.
WHAT'LL I DO NOW? I DON'T WANT TO GET TOLD OFF BY HER AGAIN, THAT'S FOR SURE.
FINE! IN A SITUATION LIKE THIS, ALL I CAN DO IS PLAY THE FOOL!
THE CULPRIT IS...

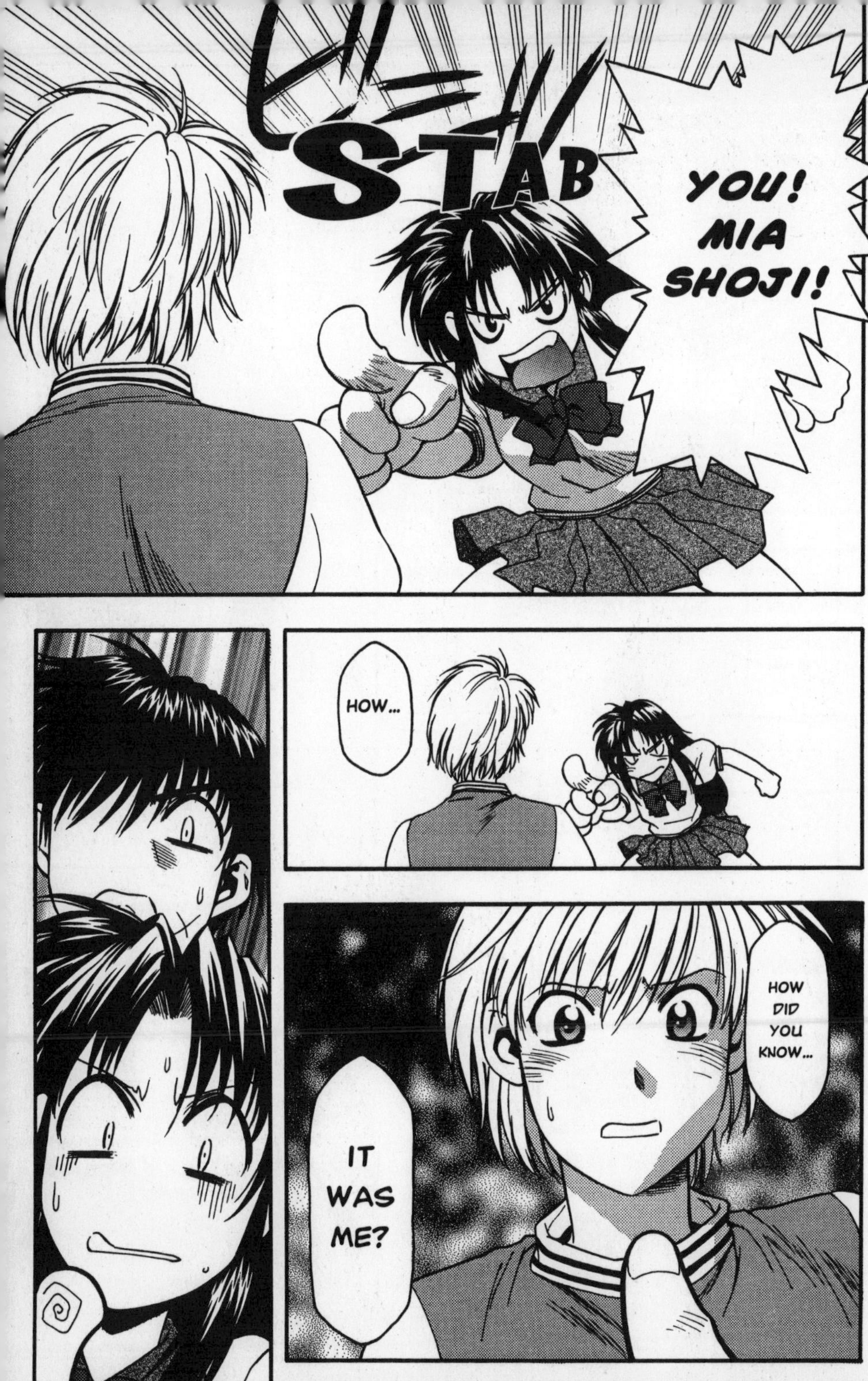
STAB
YOU! MIA SHOJI!
HOW...
HOW DID YOU KNOW...
IT WAS ME?

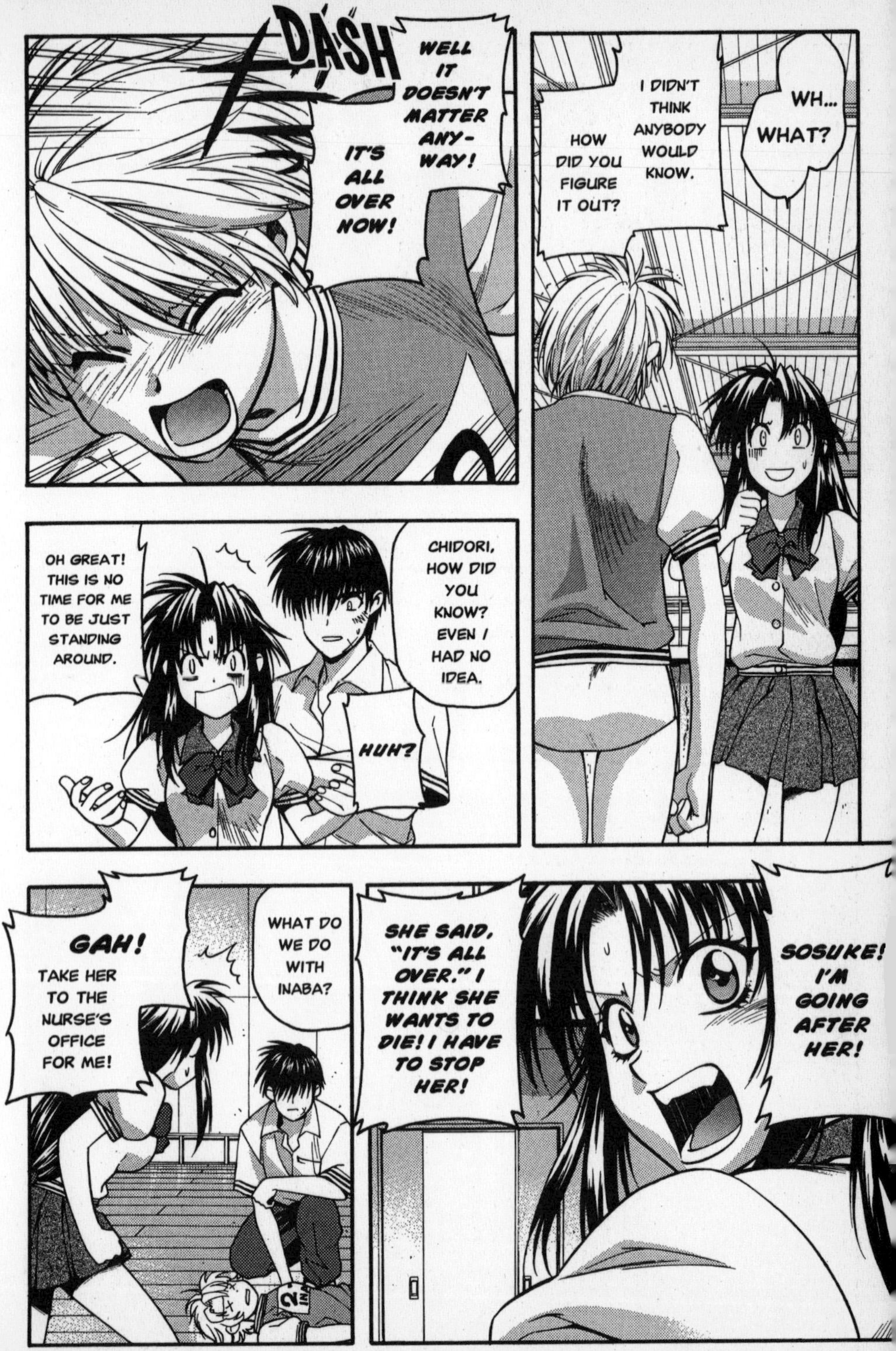
WH... WHAT?
I DIDN'T THINK ANYBODY WOULD KNOW.
HOW DID YOU FIGURE IT OUT?
DASH
WELL IT DOESN'T MATTER ANYWAY!
IT'S ALL OVER NOW!
CHIDORI, HOW DID YOU KNOW? EVEN I HAD NO IDEA.
OH GREAT! THIS IS NO TIME FOR ME TO BE JUST STANDING AROUND.
HUH?
SOSUKE! I'M GOING AFTER HER!
SHE SAID, "IT'S ALL OVER." I THINK SHE WANTS TO DIE! I HAVE TO STOP HER!
WHAT DO WE DO WITH INABA?
GAH! TAKE HER TO THE NURSE'S OFFICE FOR ME!

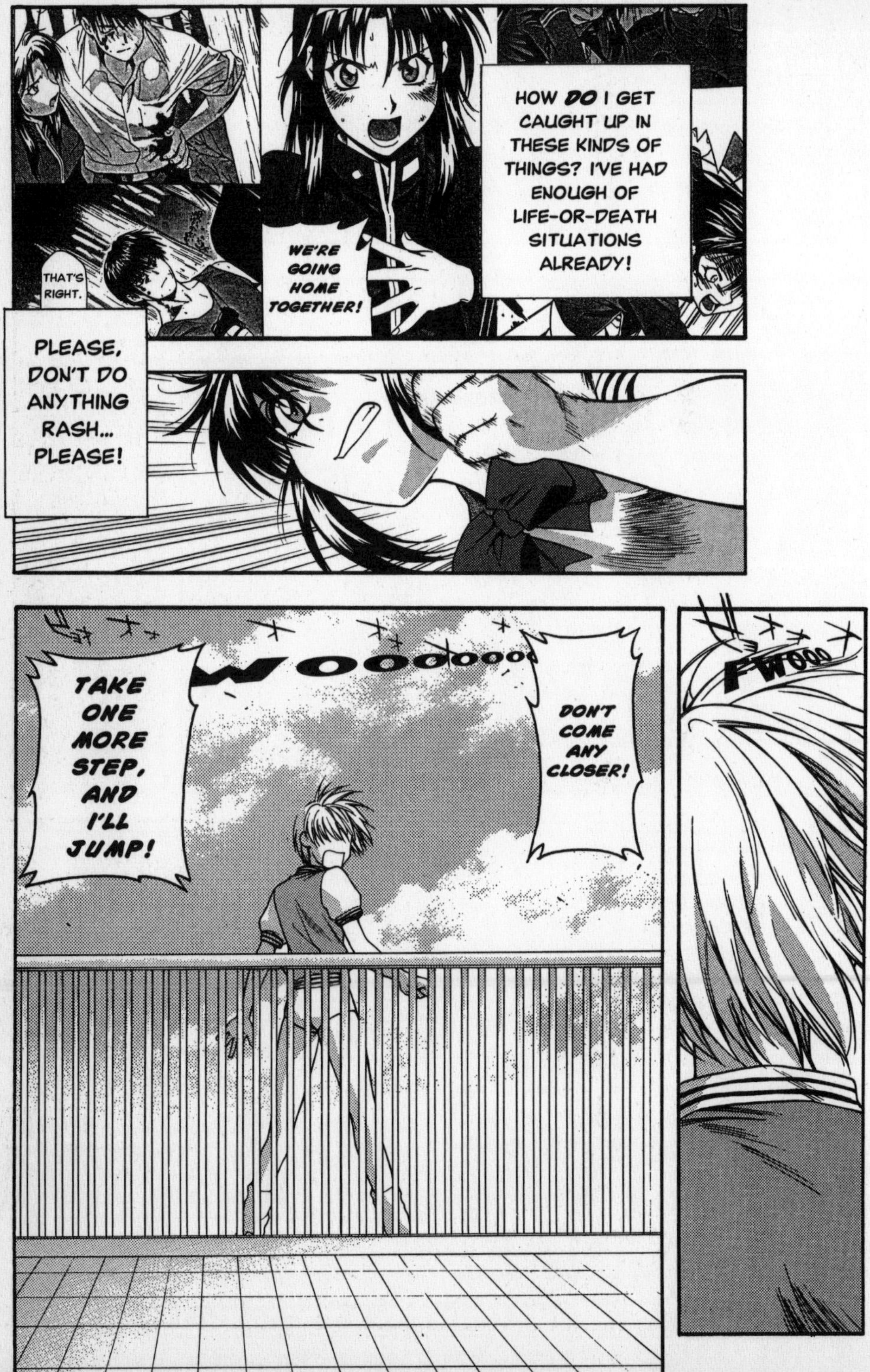
HOW DO I GET CAUGHT UP IN THESE KINDS OF THINGS? I'VE HAD ENOUGH OF LIFE-OR-DEATH SITUATIONS ALREADY!
WE'RE GOING HOME TOGETHER!
THAT'S RIGHT.
PLEASE, DON'T DO ANYTHING RASH... PLEASE!
FWOO
WOOOOOO
DON'T COME ANY CLOSER!
TAKE ONE MORE STEP, AND I'LL JUMP!

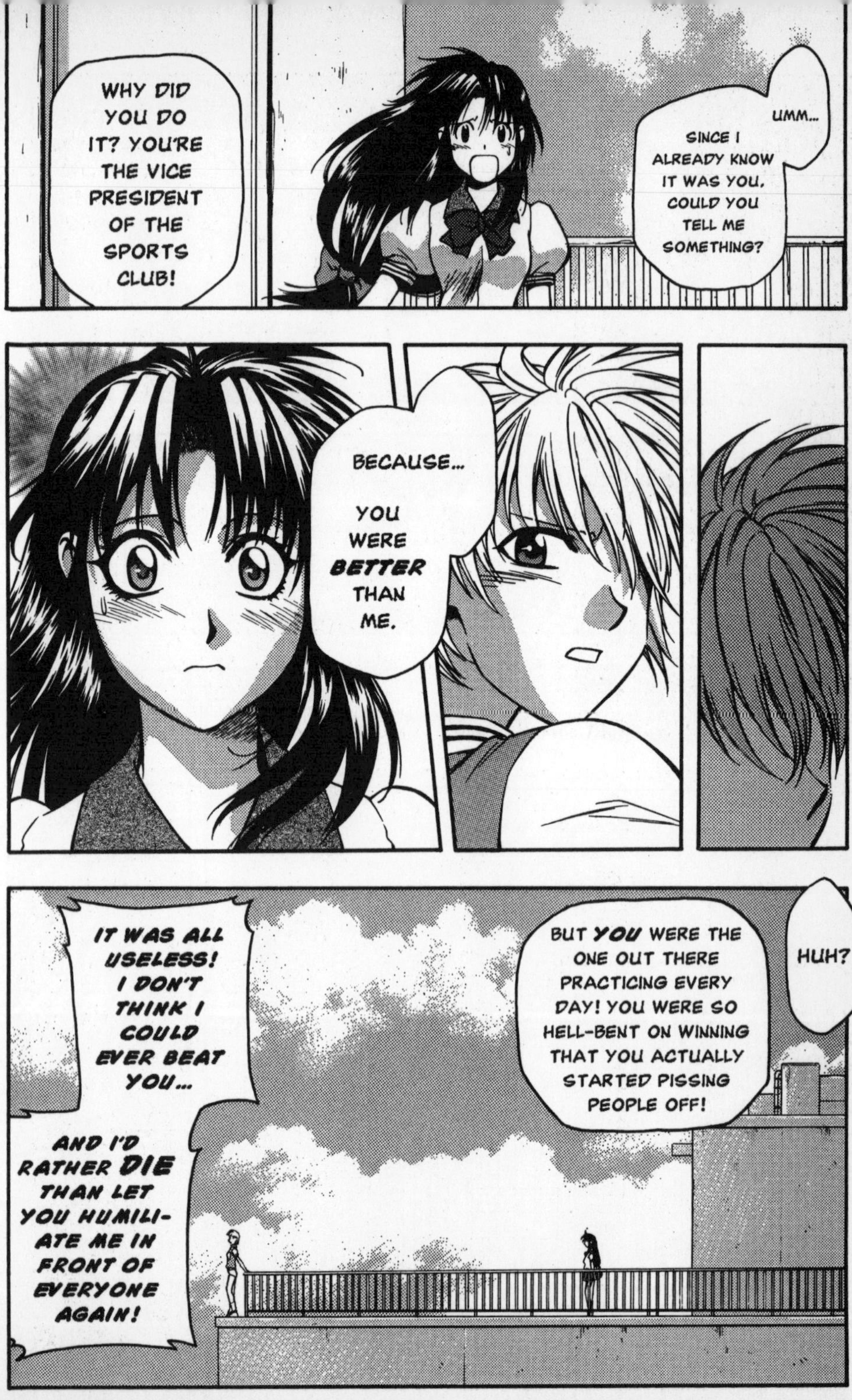
UMM...
SINCE I ALREADY KNOW IT WAS YOU, COULD YOU TELL ME SOMETHING?
WHY DID YOU DO IT? YOU'RE THE VICE PRESIDENT OF THE SPORTS CLUB!
BECAUSE... YOU WERE BETTER THAN ME.
HUH?
BUT YOU WERE THE ONE OUT THERE PRACTICING EVERY DAY! YOU WERE SO HELL-BENT ON WINNING THAT YOU ACTUALLY STARTED PISSING PEOPLE OFF!
IT WAS ALL USELESS! I DON'T THINK I COULD EVER BEAT YOU...
AND I'D RATHER DIE THAN LET YOU HUMILI-ATE ME IN FRONT OF EVERYONE AGAIN!

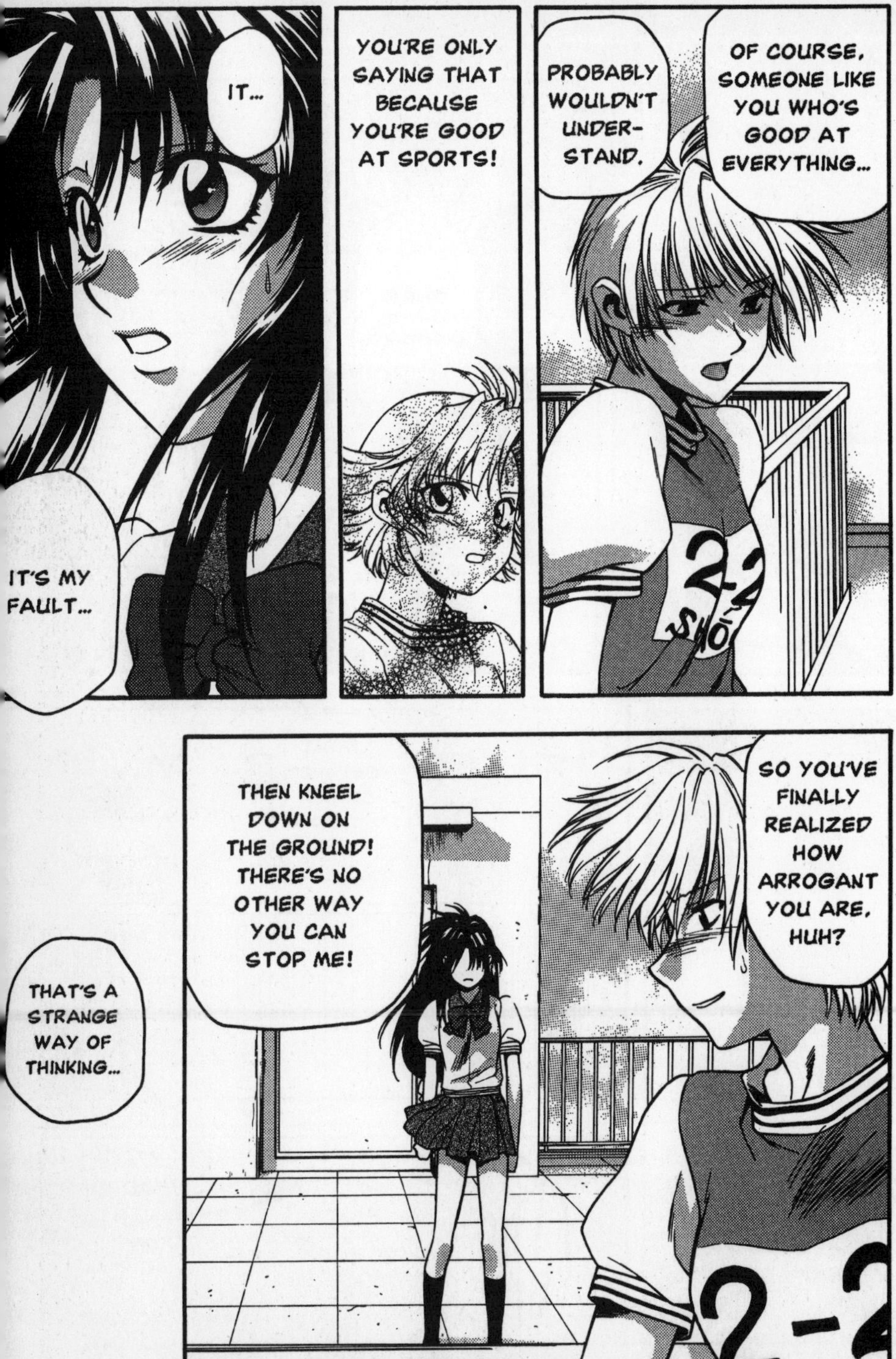
OF COURSE, SOMEONE LIKE YOU WHO'S GOOD AT EVERYTHING...
PROBABLY WOULDN'T UNDER-STAND.
YOU'RE ONLY SAYING THAT BECAUSE YOU'RE GOOD AT SPORTS!
IT...
IT'S MY FAULT...
2-2
SO YOU'VE FINALLY REALIZED HOW ARROGANT YOU ARE, HUH?
THEN KNEEL DOWN ON THE GROUND! THERE'S NO OTHER WAY YOU CAN STOP ME!
THAT'S A STRANGE WAY OF THINKING...

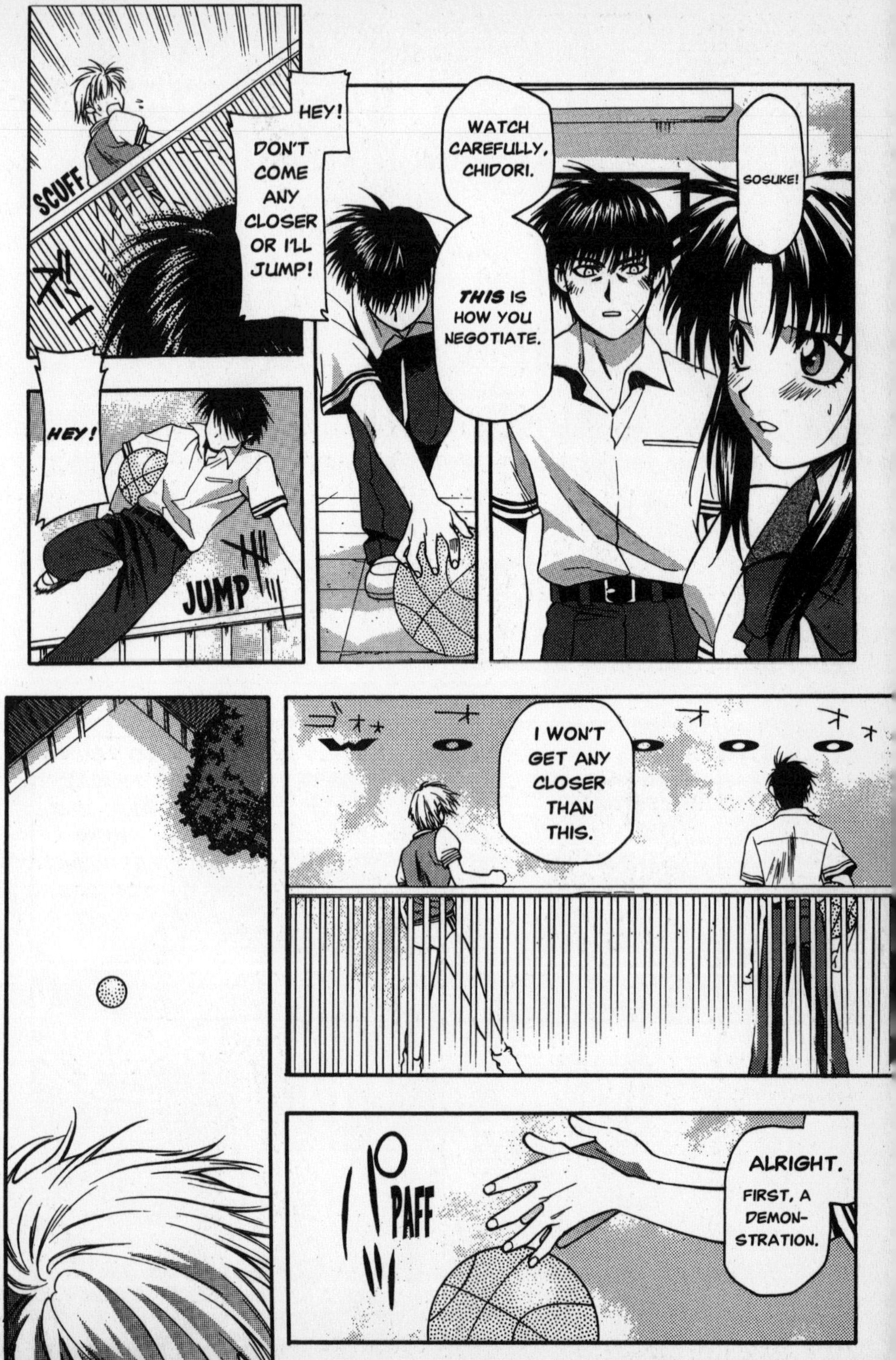
SOSUKE!
WATCH CAREFULLY, CHIDORI.
THIS IS HOW YOU NEGOTIATE.
HEY!
DON'T COME ANY CLOSER OR I'LL JUMP!
SCUFF
HEY!
JUMP
I WON'T GET ANY CLOSER THAN THIS.
ALRIGHT.
FIRST, A DEMONSTRATION.
PAFF

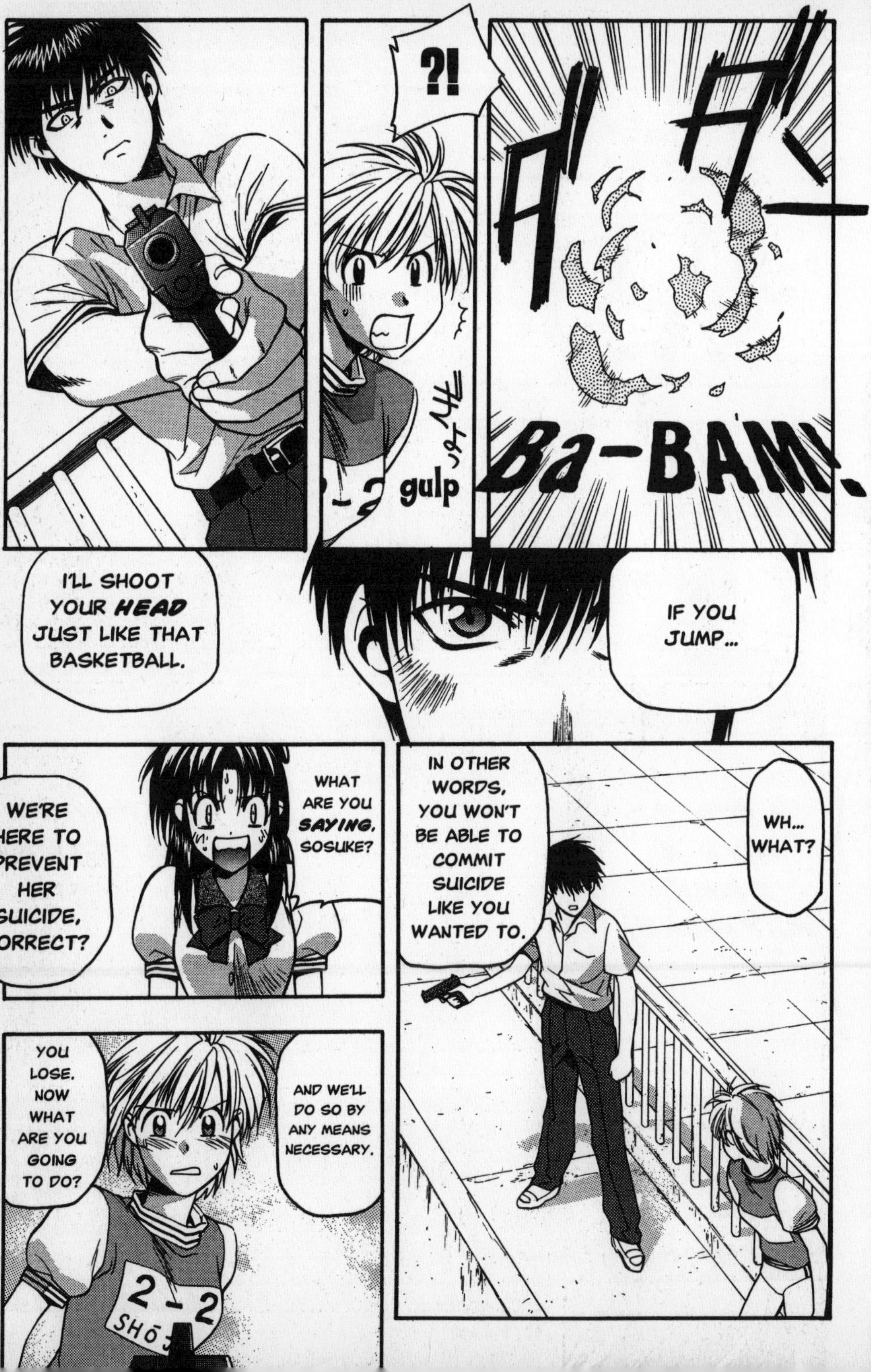
Ba-BAM!
?!
gulp
IF YOU JUMP...
I'LL SHOOT YOUR HEAD JUST LIKE THAT BASKETBALL.
WH... WHAT?
IN OTHER WORDS, YOU WON'T BE ABLE TO COMMIT SUICIDE LIKE YOU WANTED TO.
WHAT ARE YOU SAYING, SOSUKE?
WE'RE HERE TO PREVENT HER SUICIDE, CORRECT?
AND WE'LL DO SO BY ANY MEANS NECESSARY.
YOU LOSE. NOW WHAT ARE YOU GOING TO DO?

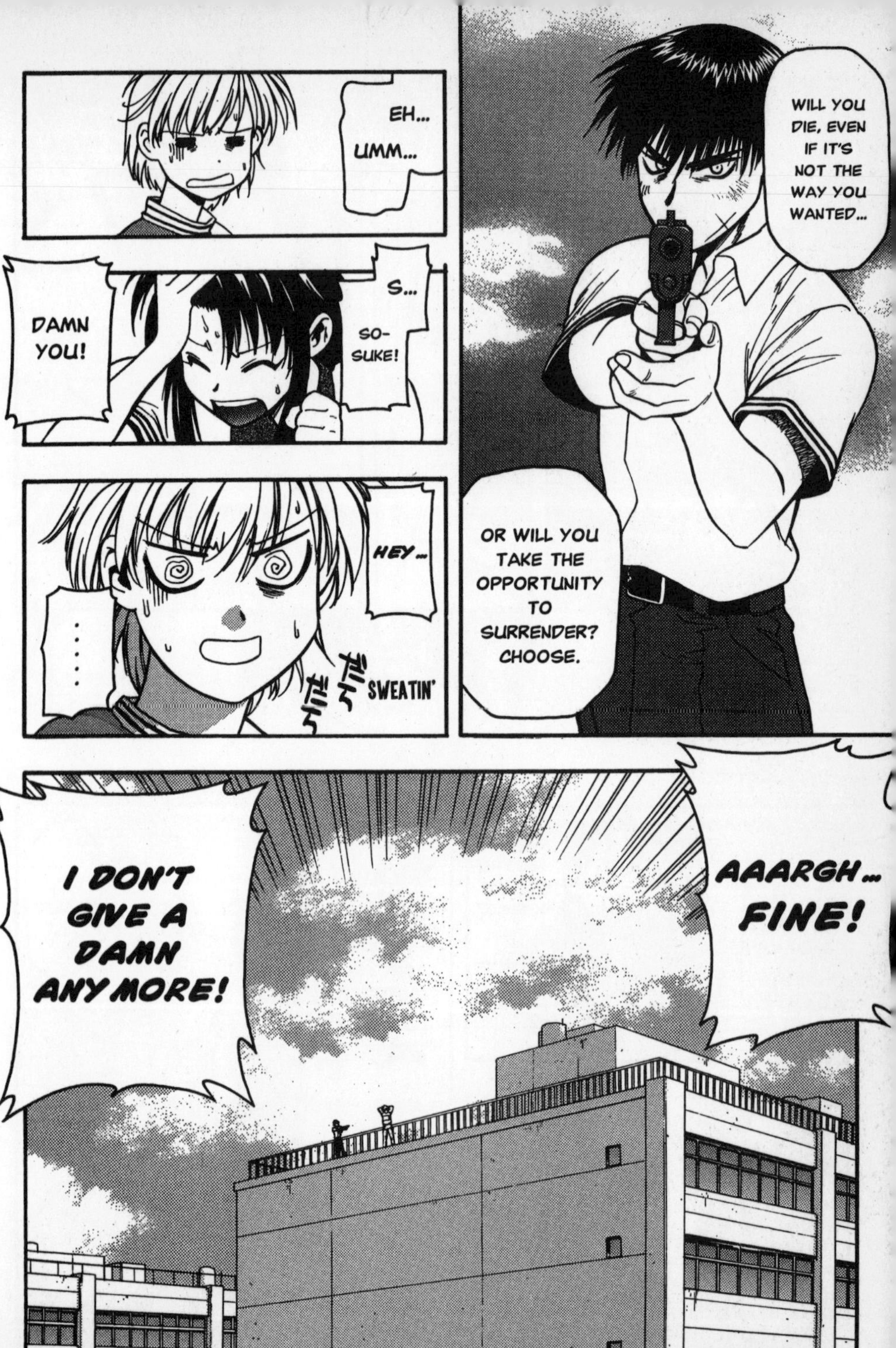
WILL YOU DIE, EVEN IF IT'S NOT THE WAY YOU WANTED...
OR WILL YOU TAKE THE OPPORTUNITY TO SURRENDER? CHOOSE.
EH... UMM...
S... SO-SUKE!
DAMN YOU!
HEY...
......
SWEATIN'
AAARGH... FINE!
I DON'T GIVE A DAMN ANYMORE!

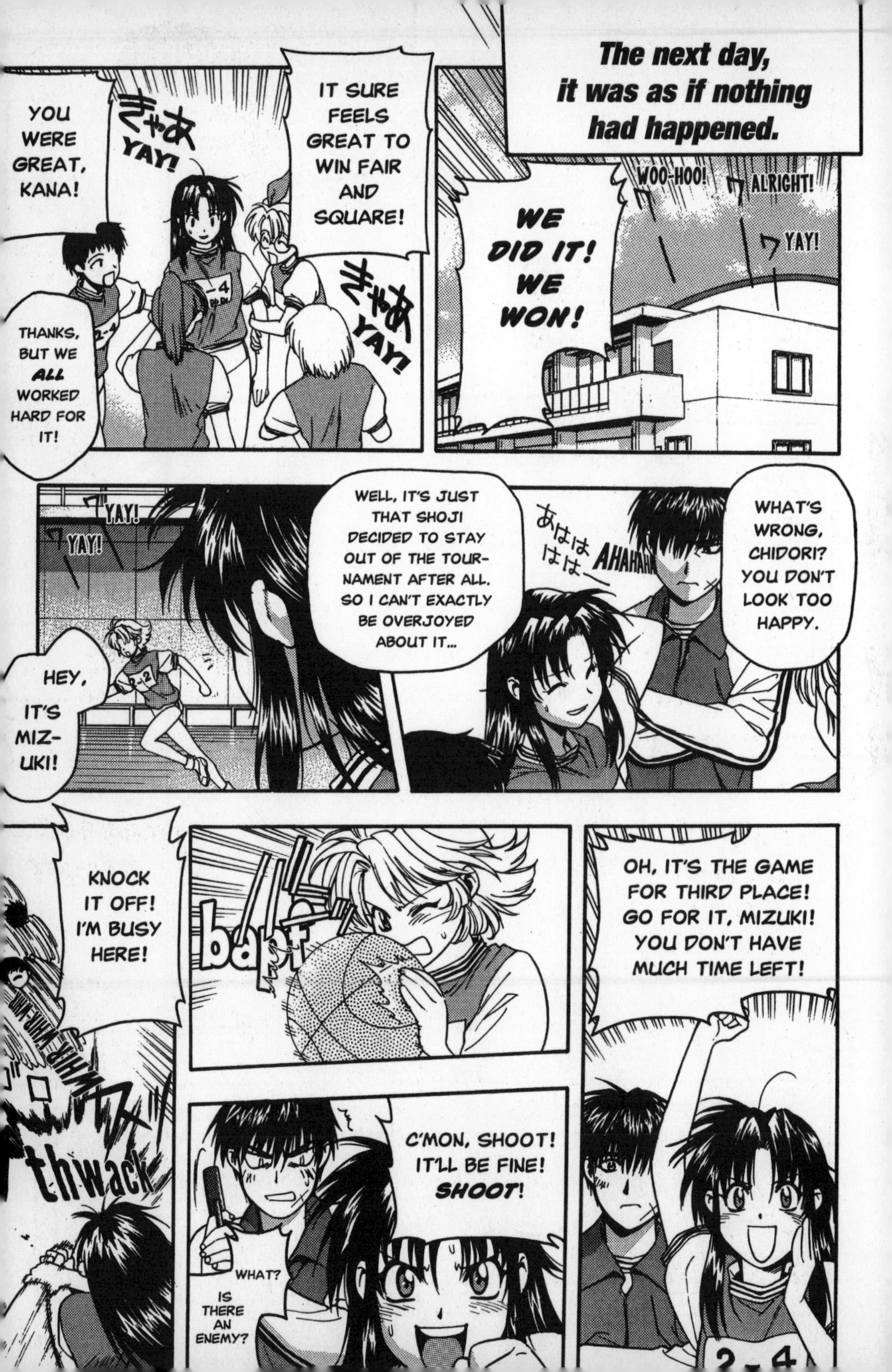
The next day, it was as if nothing had happened.
WOO-HOO!
ALRIGHT!
YAY!
WE DID IT! WE WON!
IT SURE FEELS GREAT TO WIN FAIR AND SQUARE!
きゃあ YAY!
YOU WERE GREAT, KANA!
きゃあ YAY!
THANKS, BUT WE ALL WORKED HARD FOR IT!
WHAT'S WRONG, CHIDORI? YOU DON'T LOOK TOO HAPPY.
あははは AHAHAHA
WELL, IT'S JUST THAT SHOJI DECIDED TO STAY OUT OF THE TOURNAMENT AFTER ALL. SO I CAN'T EXACTLY BE OVERJOYED ABOUT IT...
YAY!
YAY!
HEY, IT'S MIZUKI!
OH, IT'S THE GAME FOR THIRD PLACE! GO FOR IT, MIZUKI! YOU DON'T HAVE MUCH TIME LEFT!
KNOCK IT OFF! I'M BUSY HERE!
C'MON, SHOOT! IT'LL BE FINE! SHOOT!
WHAT? IS THERE AN ENEMY?
thwack

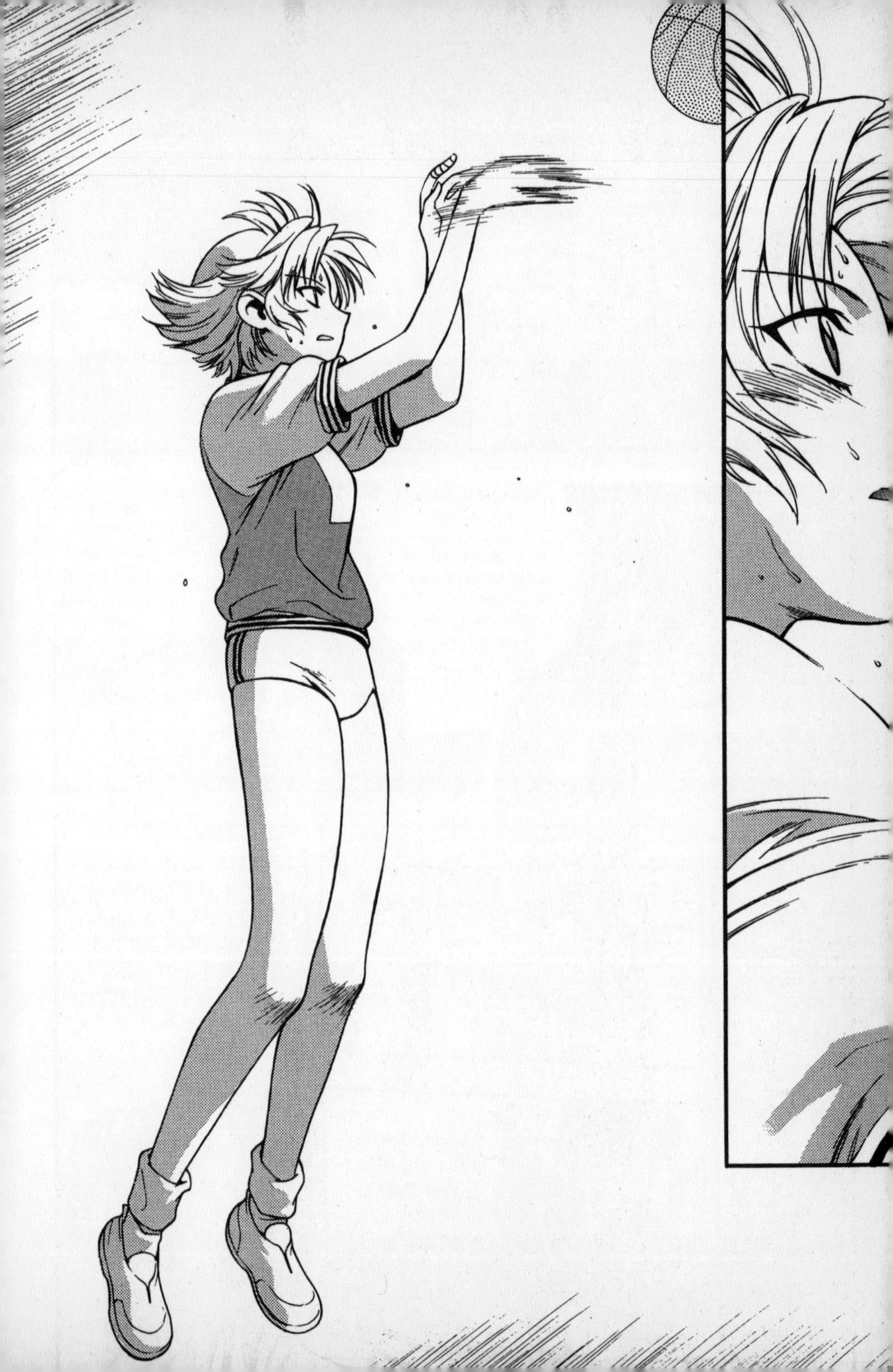

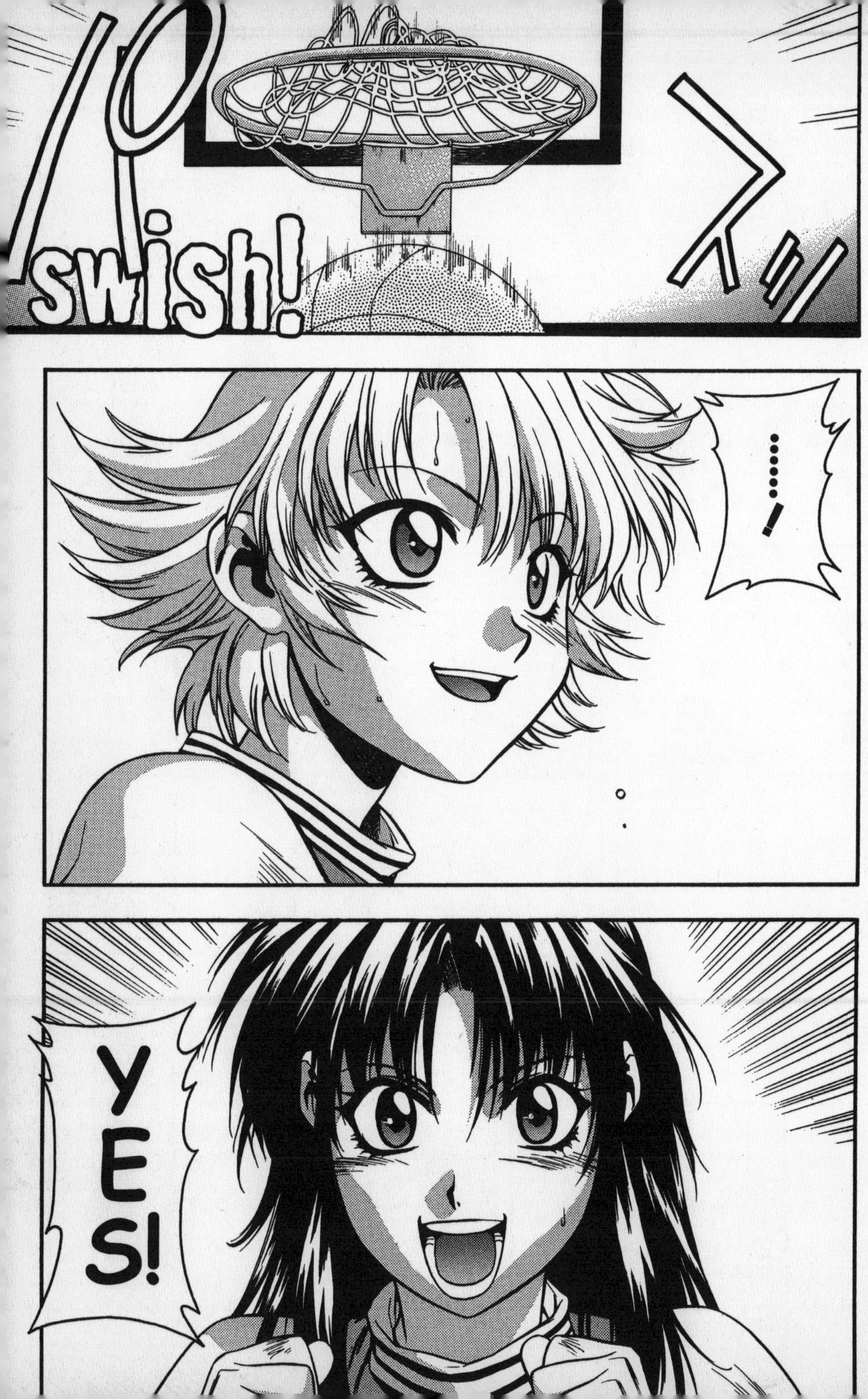
スッ
swish!
……!
YES!

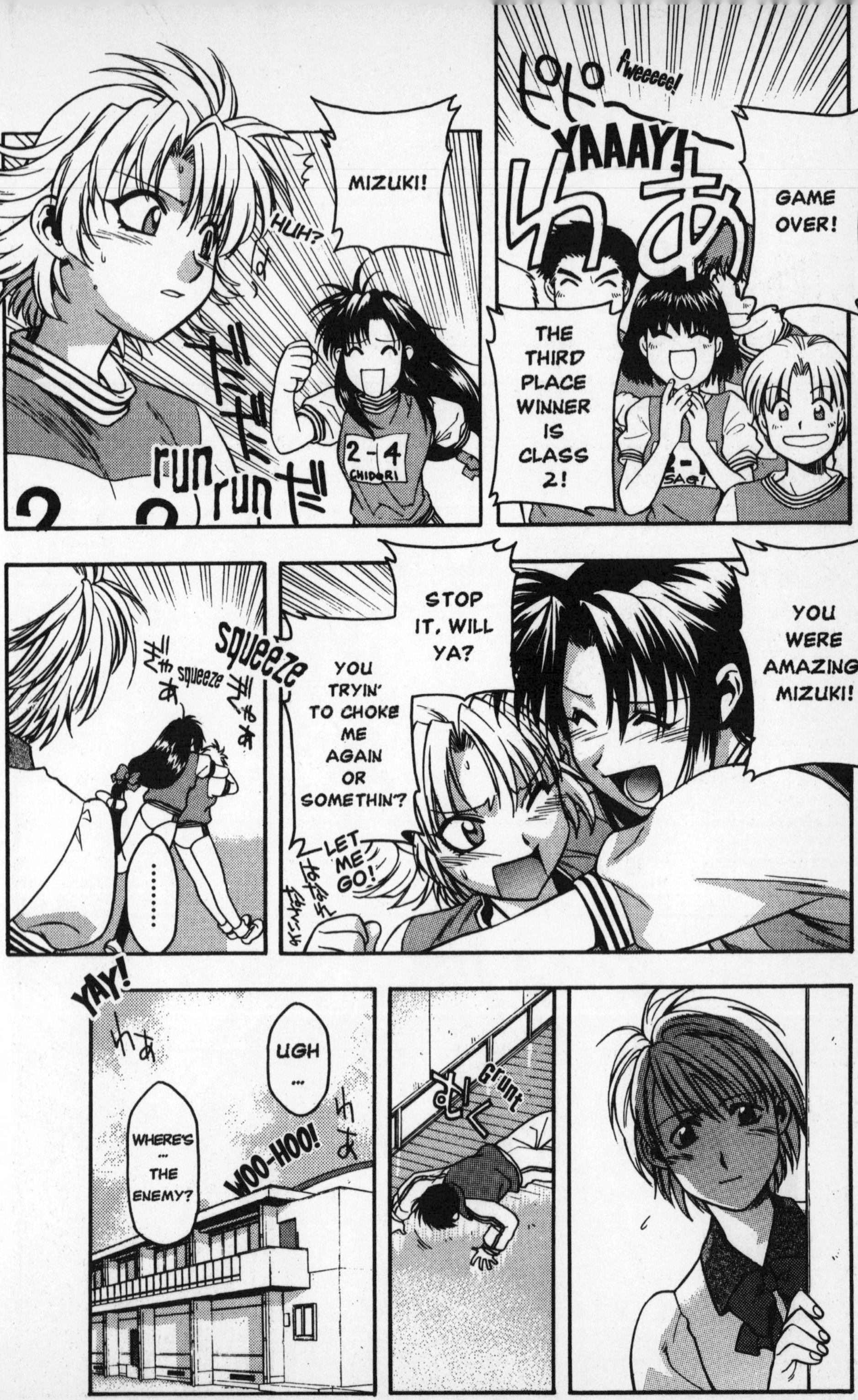
fweeeee!
YAAAY!
GAME OVER!
THE THIRD PLACE WINNER IS CLASS 2!
MIZUKI!
HUH?
2-4
CHIDORI
run
run
YOU WERE AMAZING, MIZUKI!
STOP IT, WILL YA?
YOU TRYIN' TO CHOKE ME AGAIN OR SOMETHIN'?
LET ME GO!
squeeze
squeeze
......
grunt
YAY!
UGH ...
WHERE'S ... THE ENEMY?
WOO-HOO!

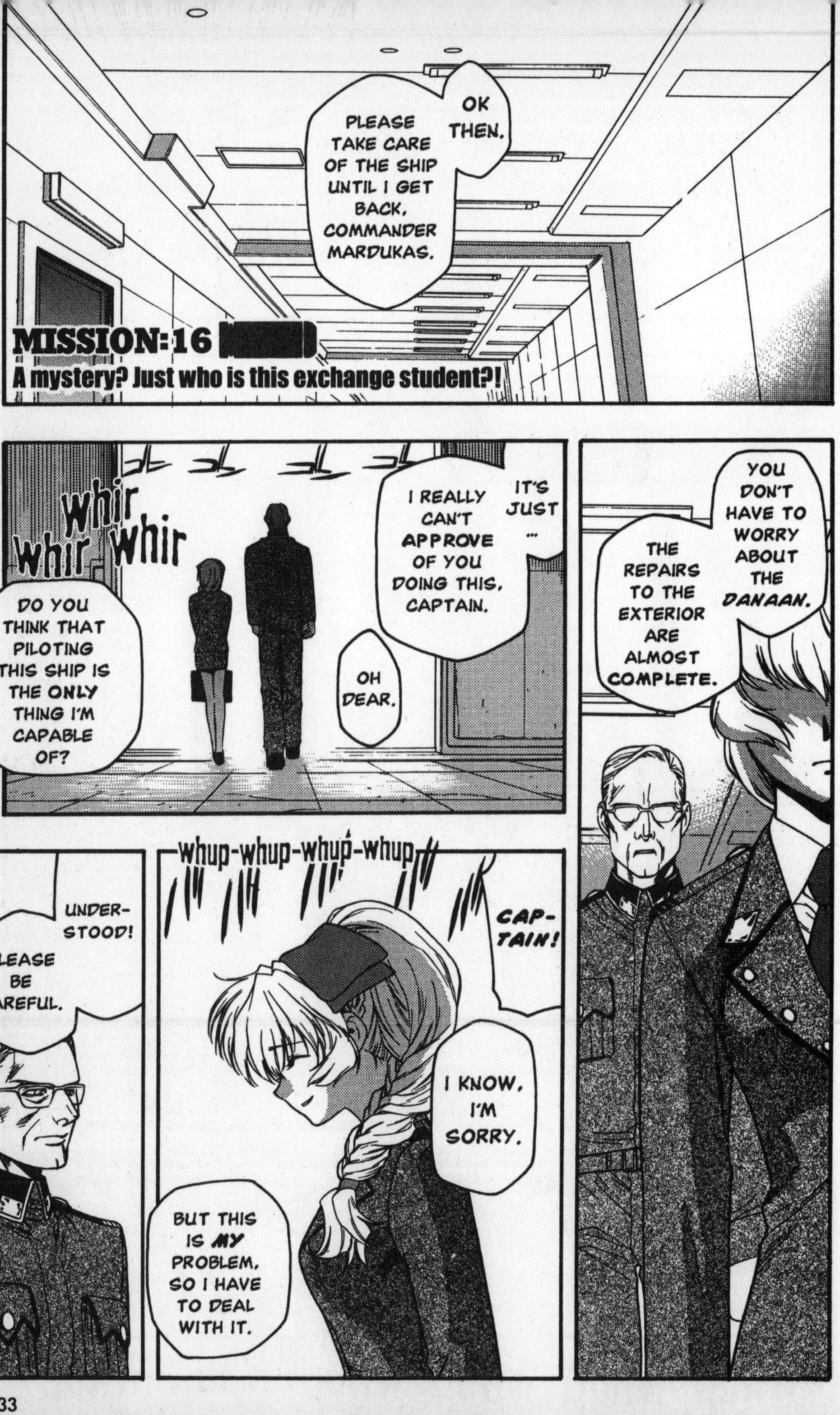
OK THEN.
PLEASE TAKE CARE OF THE SHIP UNTIL I GET BACK, COMMANDER MARDUKAS.
MISSION:16
A mystery? Just who is this exchange student?!
YOU DON'T HAVE TO WORRY ABOUT THE *DANAAN.*
THE REPAIRS TO THE EXTERIOR ARE ALMOST COMPLETE.
IT'S JUST ...
I REALLY CAN'T APPROVE OF YOU DOING THIS, CAPTAIN.
whir whir whir
OH DEAR.
DO YOU THINK THAT PILOTING THIS SHIP IS THE ONLY THING I'M CAPABLE OF?
whup-whup-whup-whup
CAP-TAIN!
I KNOW, I'M SORRY.
BUT THIS IS *MY* PROBLEM, SO I HAVE TO DEAL WITH IT.
UNDER-STOOD!
PLEASE BE CAREFUL.

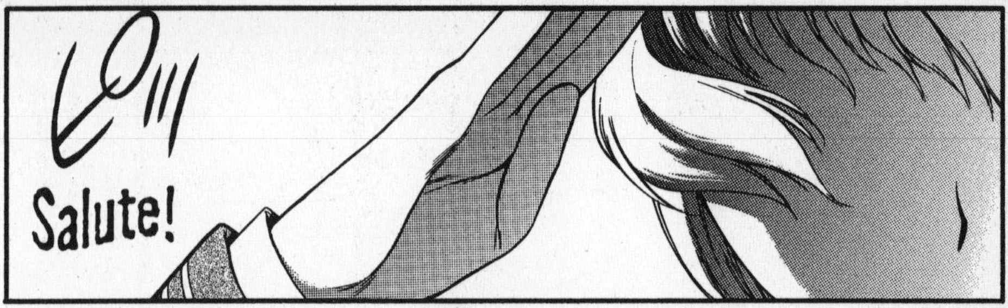
Salute!

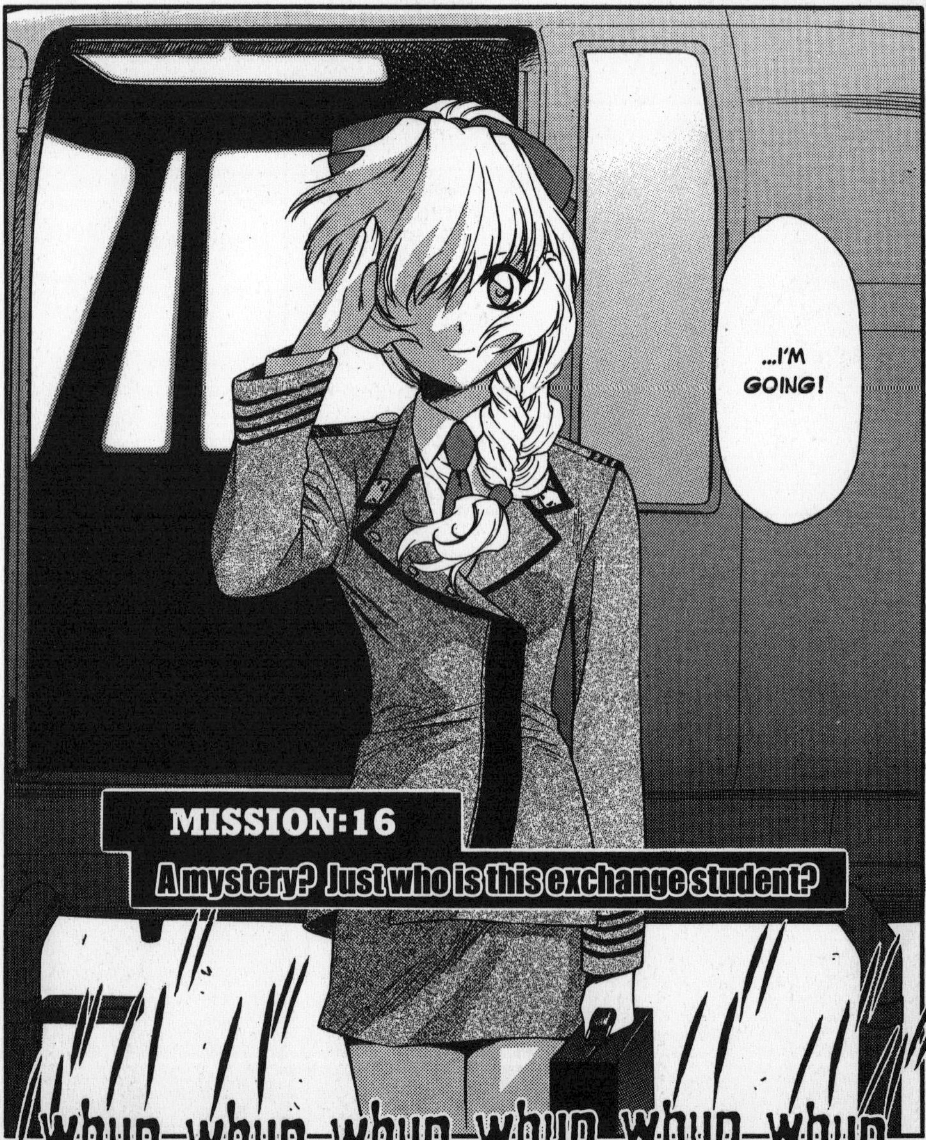
...I'M GOING!
MISSION:16
A mystery? Just who is this exchange student?
whup whup whup whup whup whup

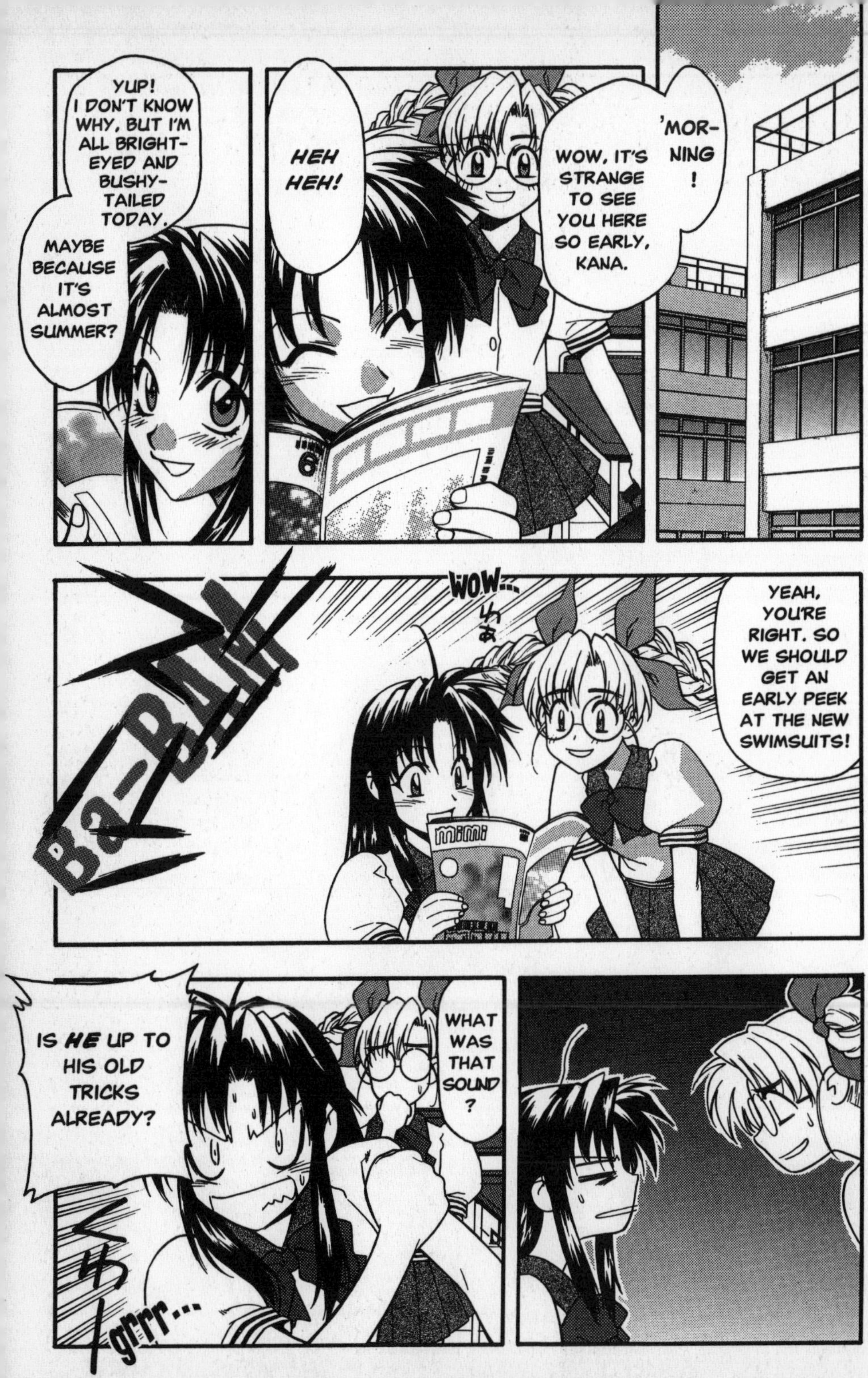
'MOR-NING!
WOW, IT'S STRANGE TO SEE YOU HERE SO EARLY, KANA.
HEH HEH!
YUP! I DON'T KNOW WHY, BUT I'M ALL BRIGHT-EYED AND BUSHY-TAILED TODAY.
MAYBE BECAUSE IT'S ALMOST SUMMER?
YEAH, YOU'RE RIGHT. SO WE SHOULD GET AN EARLY PEEK AT THE NEW SWIMSUITS!
WOW...
mimi
BA-BAM
WHAT WAS THAT SOUND?
IS HE UP TO HIS OLD TRICKS ALREADY?
grrr...

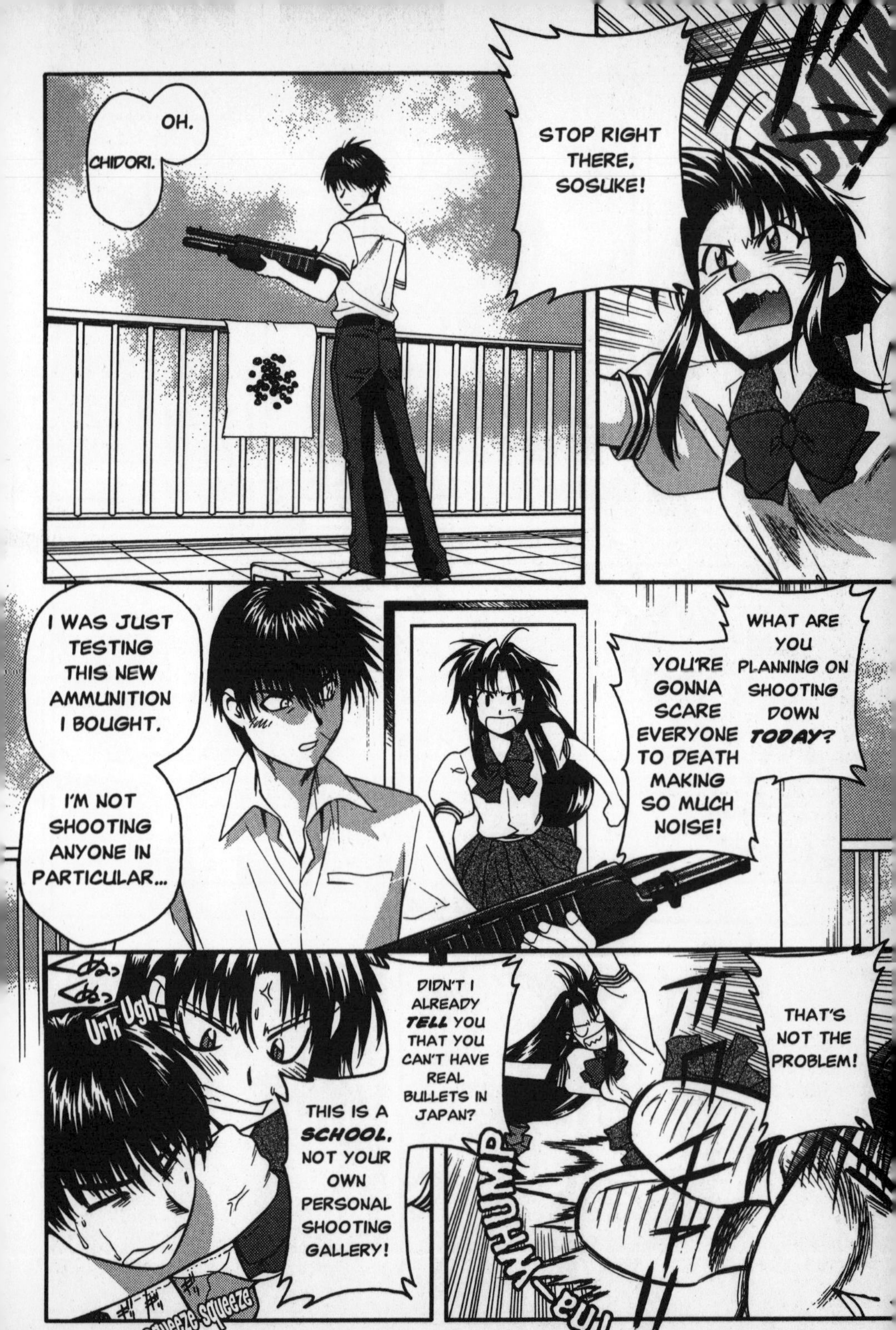

STOP RIGHT THERE, SOSUKE!
OH.
CHIDORI.
WHAT ARE YOU PLANNING ON SHOOTING DOWN TODAY?
YOU'RE GONNA SCARE EVERYONE TO DEATH MAKING SO MUCH NOISE!
I WAS JUST TESTING THIS NEW AMMUNITION I BOUGHT.
I'M NOT SHOOTING ANYONE IN PARTICULAR...
THAT'S NOT THE PROBLEM!
Tha-WHUMP
DIDN'T I ALREADY TELL YOU THAT YOU CAN'T HAVE REAL BULLETS IN JAPAN?
THIS IS A SCHOOL, NOT YOUR OWN PERSONAL SHOOTING GALLERY!
Urk Ugh
squeeze squeeze

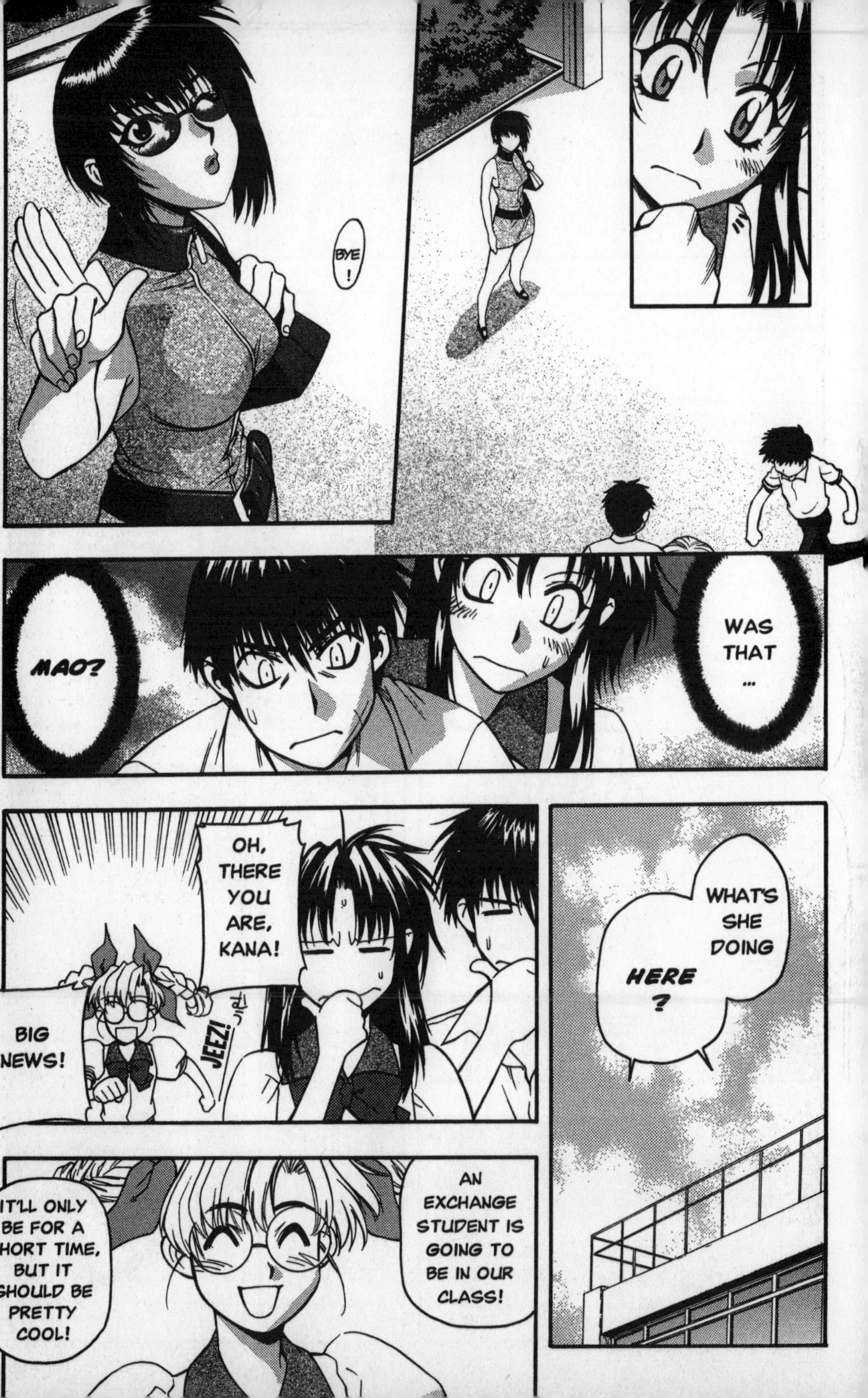
BYE!
WAS THAT ...
MAO?
WHAT'S SHE DOING HERE?
OH, THERE YOU ARE, KANA!
JEEZ!
BIG NEWS!
AN EXCHANGE STUDENT IS GOING TO BE IN OUR CLASS!
IT'LL ONLY BE FOR A SHORT TIME, BUT IT SHOULD BE PRETTY COOL!

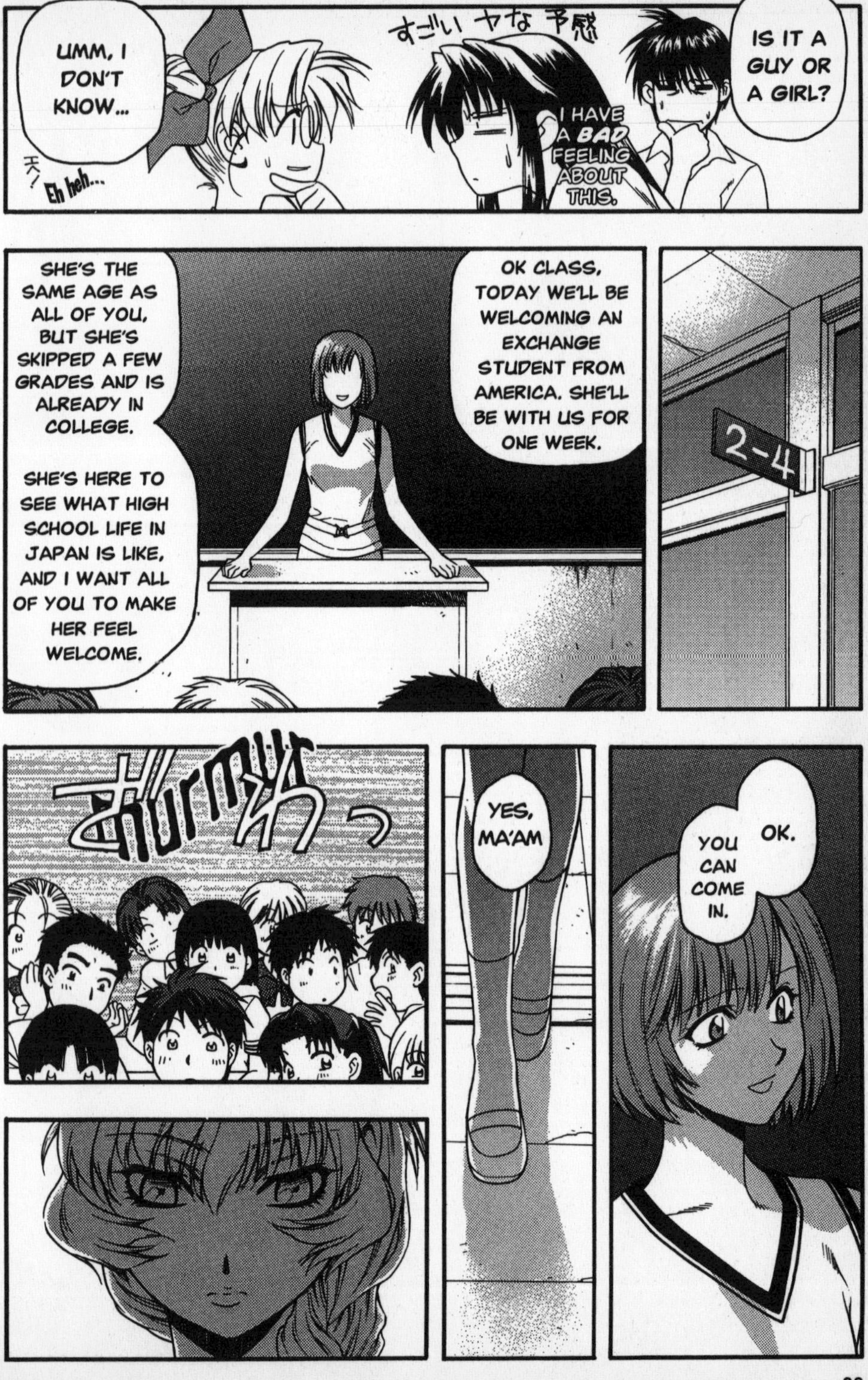
IS IT A GUY OR A GIRL?
すごい ヤな 予感
I HAVE A BAD FEELING ABOUT THIS.
UMM, I DON'T KNOW...
Eh heh...
2-4
OK CLASS, TODAY WE'LL BE WELCOMING AN EXCHANGE STUDENT FROM AMERICA. SHE'LL BE WITH US FOR ONE WEEK.
SHE'S THE SAME AGE AS ALL OF YOU, BUT SHE'S SKIPPED A FEW GRADES AND IS ALREADY IN COLLEGE.
SHE'S HERE TO SEE WHAT HIGH SCHOOL LIFE IN JAPAN IS LIKE, AND I WANT ALL OF YOU TO MAKE HER FEEL WELCOME.
OK.
YOU CAN COME IN.
YES, MA'AM

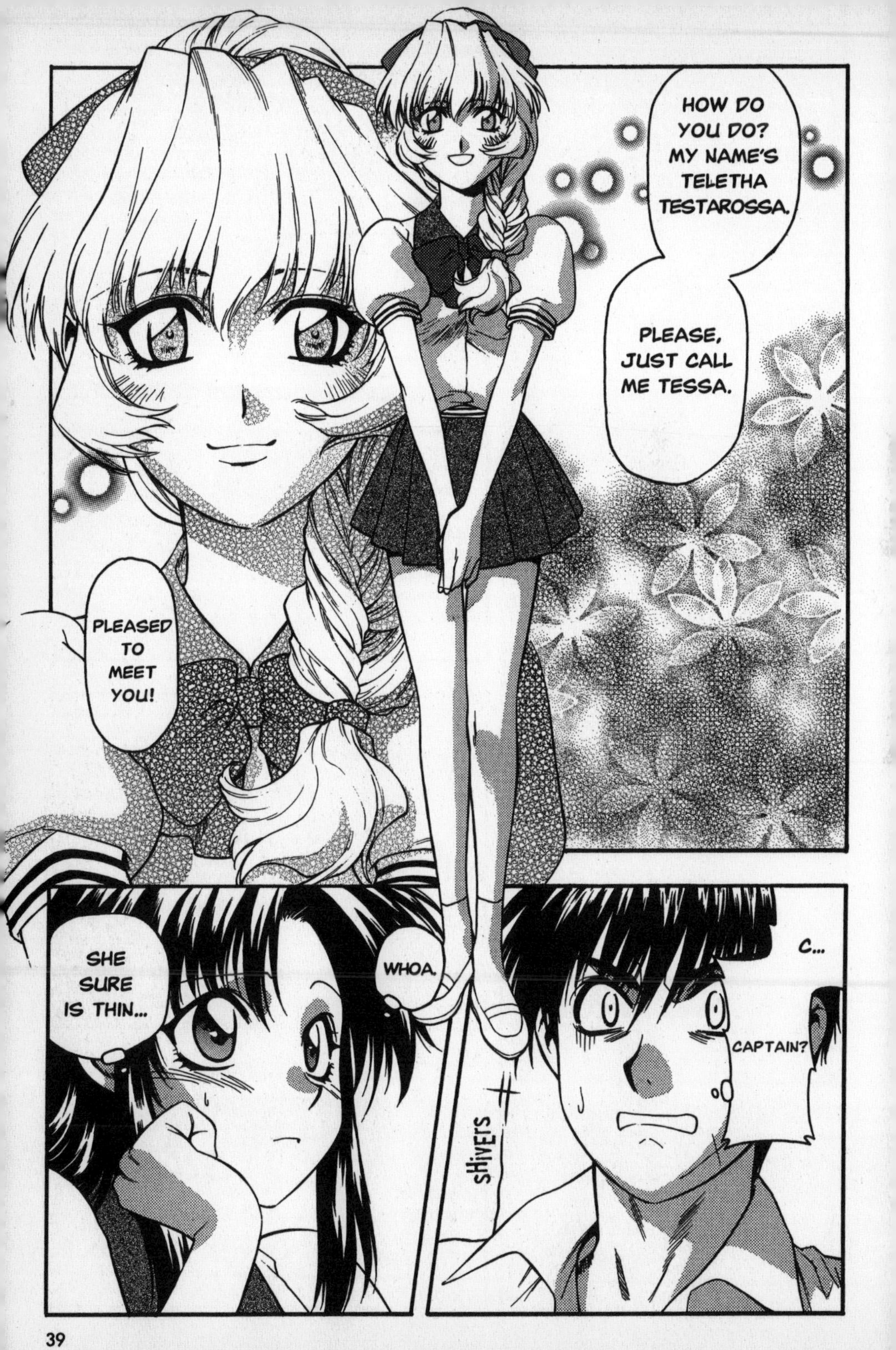
HOW DO YOU DO? MY NAME'S TELETHA TESTAROSSA.
PLEASE, JUST CALL ME TESSA.
PLEASED TO MEET YOU!
C...
CAPTAIN?
SHIVERS
WHOA.
SHE SURE IS THIN...

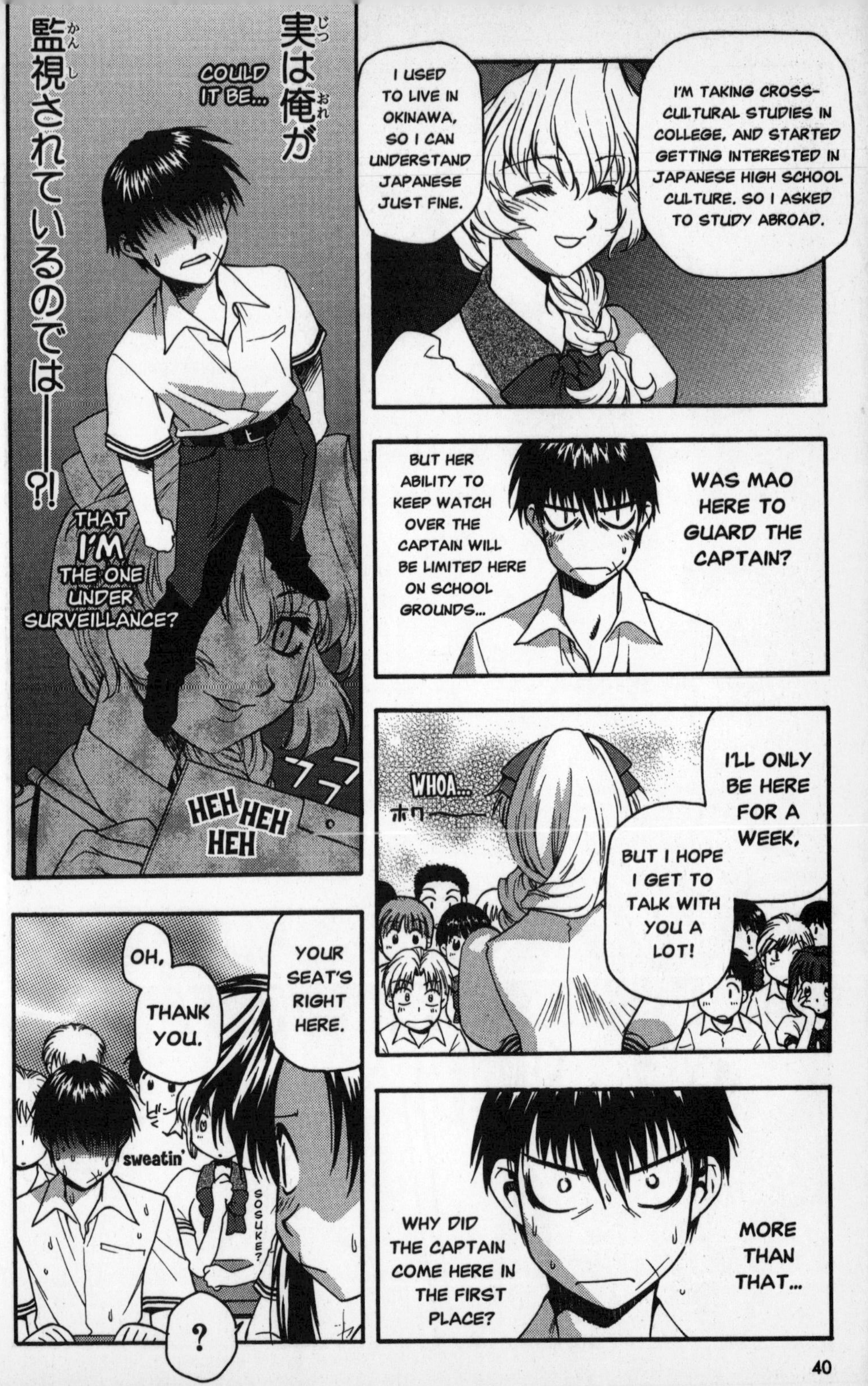
I'M TAKING CROSS-CULTURAL STUDIES IN COLLEGE, AND STARTED GETTING INTERESTED IN JAPANESE HIGH SCHOOL CULTURE. SO I ASKED TO STUDY ABROAD.
I USED TO LIVE IN OKINAWA, SO I CAN UNDERSTAND JAPANESE JUST FINE.
WAS MAO HERE TO GUARD THE CAPTAIN?
BUT HER ABILITY TO KEEP WATCH OVER THE CAPTAIN WILL BE LIMITED HERE ON SCHOOL GROUNDS...
I'LL ONLY BE HERE FOR A WEEK,
BUT I HOPE I GET TO TALK WITH YOU A LOT!
WHOA...
ホワ〜〜
実は俺が監視されているのでは――?!
COULD IT BE...
THAT I'M THE ONE UNDER SURVEILLANCE?
HEH HEH HEH
MORE THAN THAT...
WHY DID THE CAPTAIN COME HERE IN THE FIRST PLACE?
YOUR SEAT'S RIGHT HERE.
OH, THANK YOU.
SOSUKE?
sweatin'
?

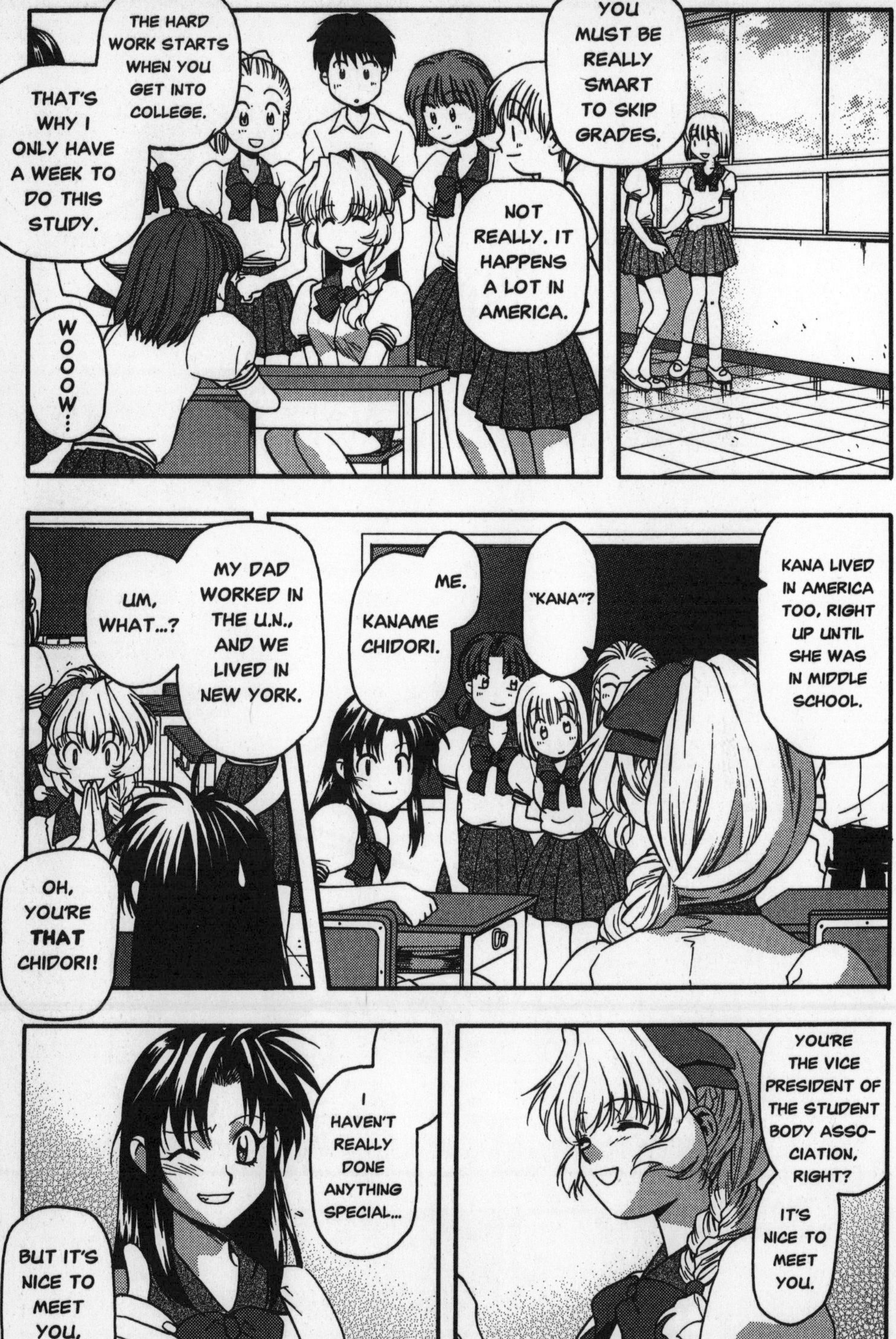
YOU MUST BE REALLY SMART TO SKIP GRADES.
NOT REALLY. IT HAPPENS A LOT IN AMERICA.
THE HARD WORK STARTS WHEN YOU GET INTO COLLEGE.
THAT'S WHY I ONLY HAVE A WEEK TO DO THIS STUDY.
WOOOOW...
KANA LIVED IN AMERICA TOO, RIGHT UP UNTIL SHE WAS IN MIDDLE SCHOOL.
"KANA"?
ME. KANAME CHIDORI.
MY DAD WORKED IN THE U.N., AND WE LIVED IN NEW YORK.
UM, WHAT...?
OH, YOU'RE **THAT** CHIDORI!
YOU'RE THE VICE PRESIDENT OF THE STUDENT BODY ASSOCIATION, RIGHT?
IT'S NICE TO MEET YOU.
I HAVEN'T REALLY DONE ANYTHING SPECIAL...
BUT IT'S NICE TO MEET YOU, TOO.

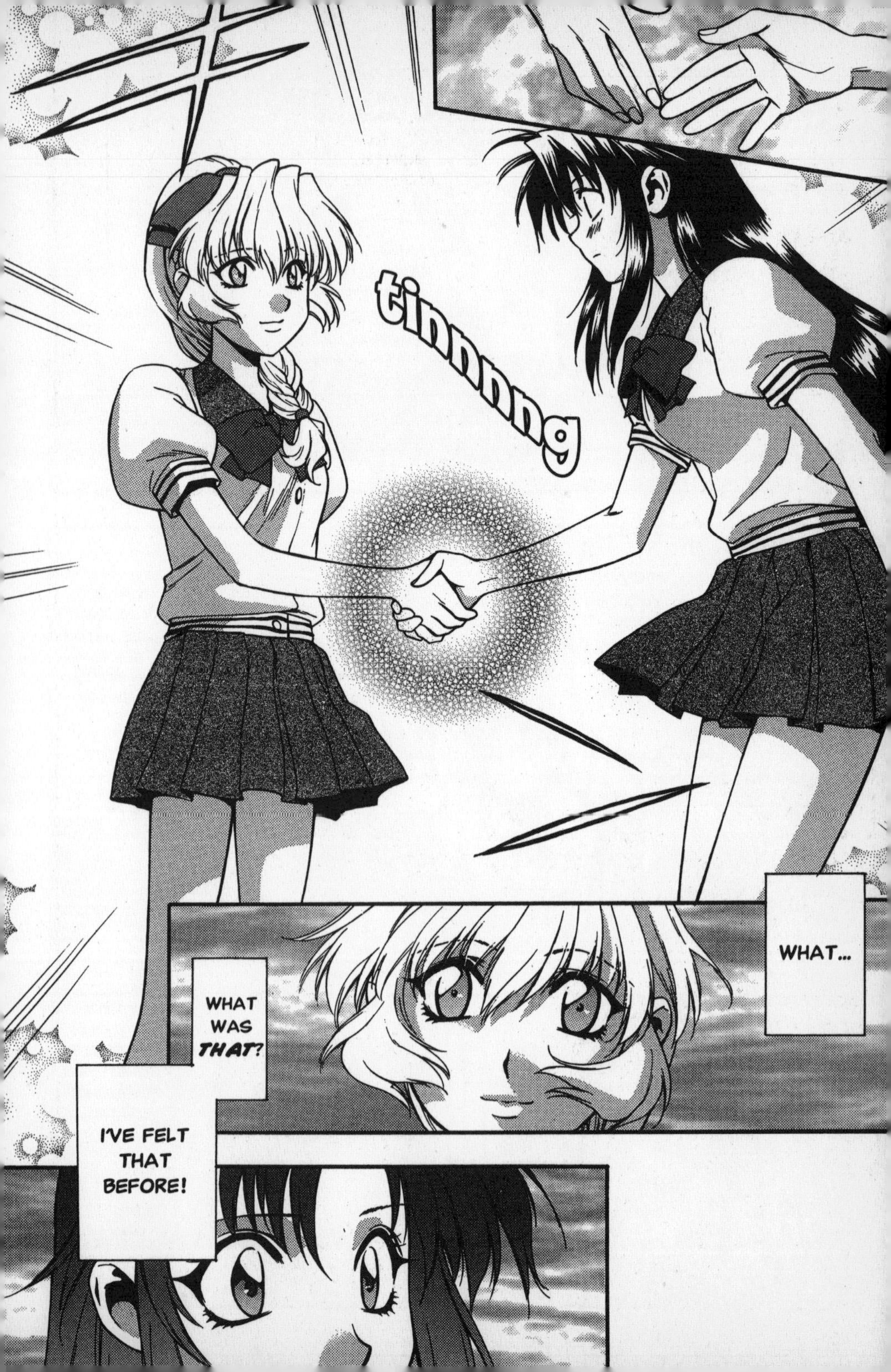
tinnnnng
WHAT...
WHAT WAS *THAT*?
I'VE FELT THAT BEFORE!

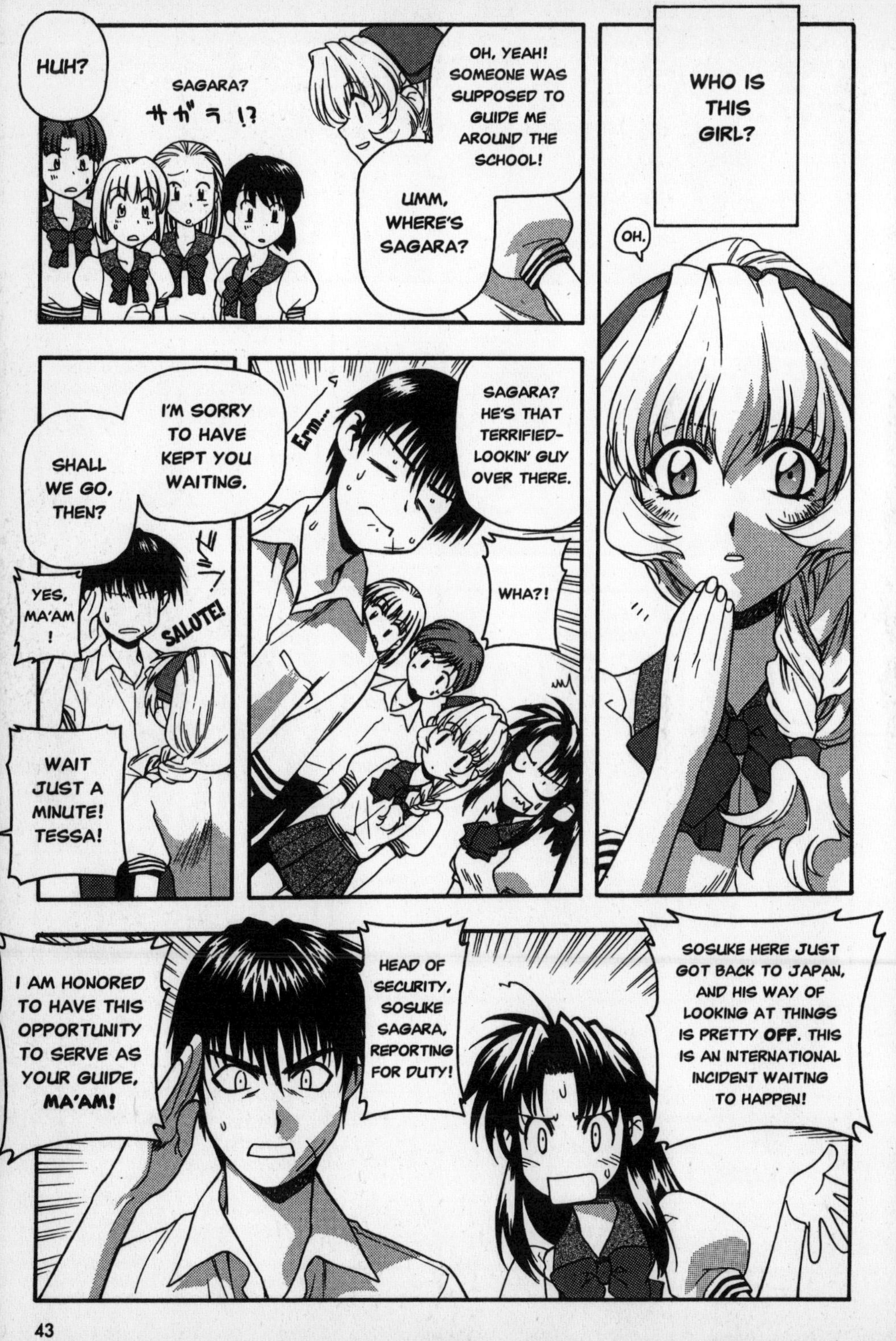

WHO IS THIS GIRL?
OH.
OH, YEAH! SOMEONE WAS SUPPOSED TO GUIDE ME AROUND THE SCHOOL!
UMM, WHERE'S SAGARA?
HUH?
SAGARA?
サガラ!?
SAGARA? HE'S THAT TERRIFIED-LOOKIN' GUY OVER THERE.
Erm...
WHA?!
I'M SORRY TO HAVE KEPT YOU WAITING.
SHALL WE GO, THEN?
SALUTE!
YES, MA'AM!
WAIT JUST A MINUTE! TESSA!
SOSUKE HERE JUST GOT BACK TO JAPAN, AND HIS WAY OF LOOKING AT THINGS IS PRETTY **OFF**. THIS IS AN INTERNATIONAL INCIDENT WAITING TO HAPPEN!
HEAD OF SECURITY, SOSUKE SAGARA, REPORTING FOR DUTY!
I AM HONORED TO HAVE THIS OPPORTUNITY TO SERVE AS YOUR GUIDE, **MA'AM!**

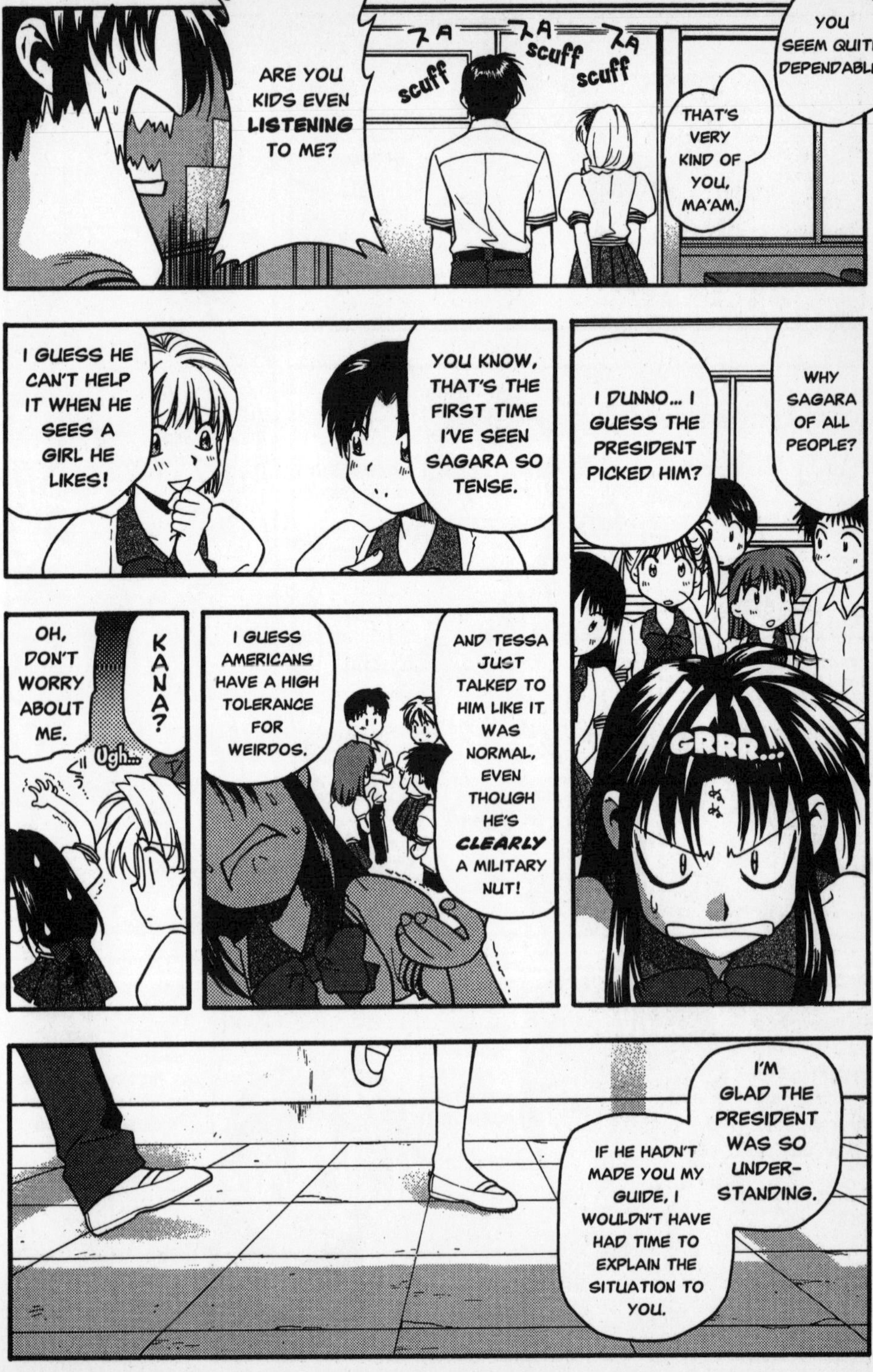
YOU SEEM QUITE DEPENDABLE.
THAT'S VERY KIND OF YOU, MA'AM.
scuff
scuff
scuff
ARE YOU KIDS EVEN **LISTENING** TO ME?
WHY SAGARA OF ALL PEOPLE?
I DUNNO... I GUESS THE PRESIDENT PICKED HIM?
GRRR...
YOU KNOW, THAT'S THE FIRST TIME I'VE SEEN SAGARA SO TENSE.
I GUESS HE CAN'T HELP IT WHEN HE SEES A GIRL HE LIKES!
AND TESSA JUST TALKED TO HIM LIKE IT WAS NORMAL, EVEN THOUGH HE'S ***CLEARLY*** A MILITARY NUT!
I GUESS AMERICANS HAVE A HIGH TOLERANCE FOR WEIRDOS.
KANA?
OH, DON'T WORRY ABOUT ME.
Ugh...
I'M GLAD THE PRESIDENT WAS SO UNDER-STANDING.
IF HE HADN'T MADE YOU MY GUIDE, I WOULDN'T HAVE HAD TIME TO EXPLAIN THE SITUATION TO YOU.

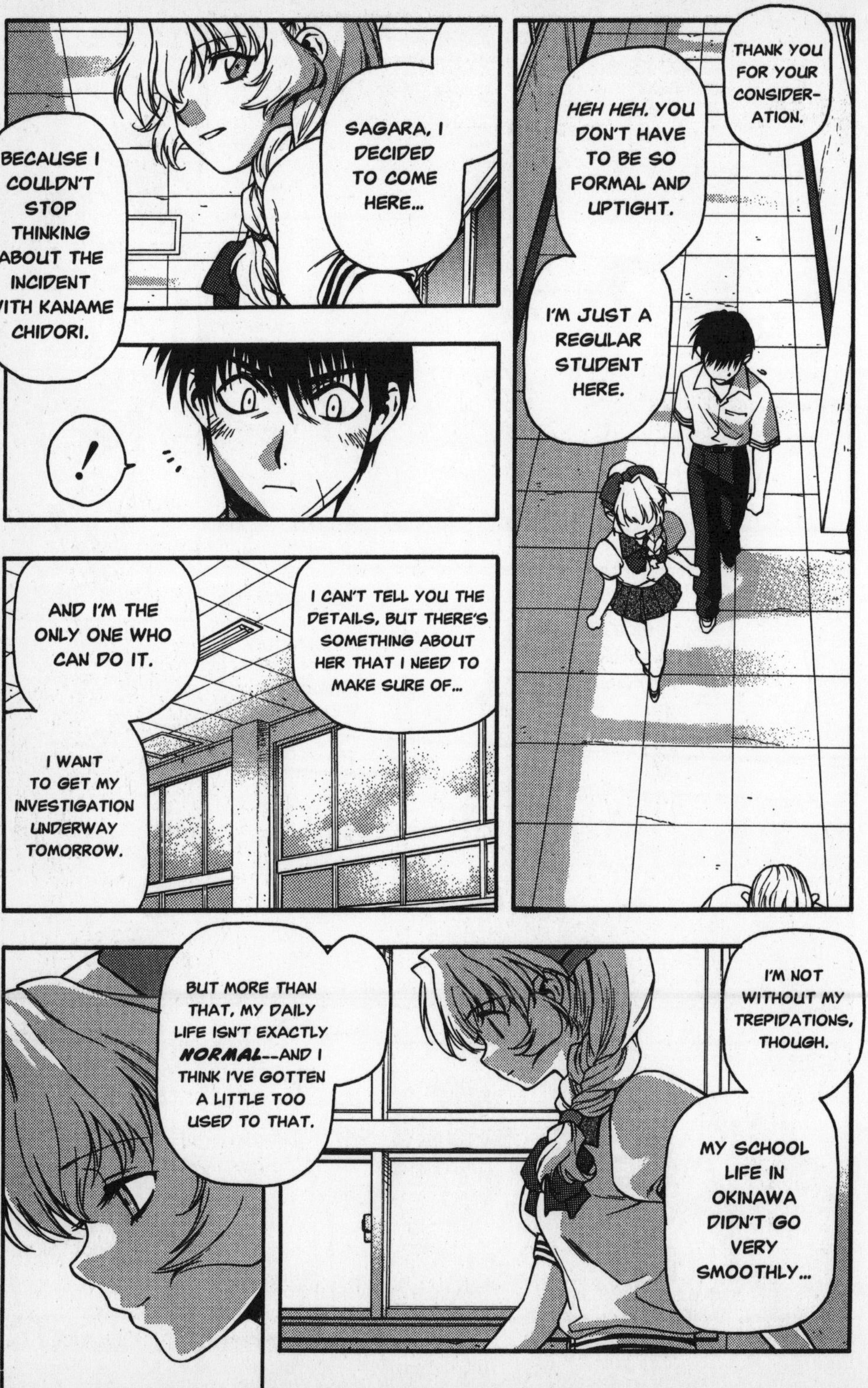
THANK YOU FOR YOUR CONSIDER-ATION.
HEH HEH. YOU DON'T HAVE TO BE SO FORMAL AND UPTIGHT.
I'M JUST A REGULAR STUDENT HERE.
SAGARA, I DECIDED TO COME HERE...
BECAUSE I COULDN'T STOP THINKING ABOUT THE INCIDENT WITH KANAME CHIDORI.
!
I CAN'T TELL YOU THE DETAILS, BUT THERE'S SOMETHING ABOUT HER THAT I NEED TO MAKE SURE OF...
AND I'M THE ONLY ONE WHO CAN DO IT.
I WANT TO GET MY INVESTIGATION UNDERWAY TOMORROW.
I'M NOT WITHOUT MY TREPIDATIONS, THOUGH.
MY SCHOOL LIFE IN OKINAWA DIDN'T GO VERY SMOOTHLY...
BUT MORE THAN THAT, MY DAILY LIFE ISN'T EXACTLY ***NORMAL***--AND I THINK I'VE GOTTEN A LITTLE TOO USED TO THAT.

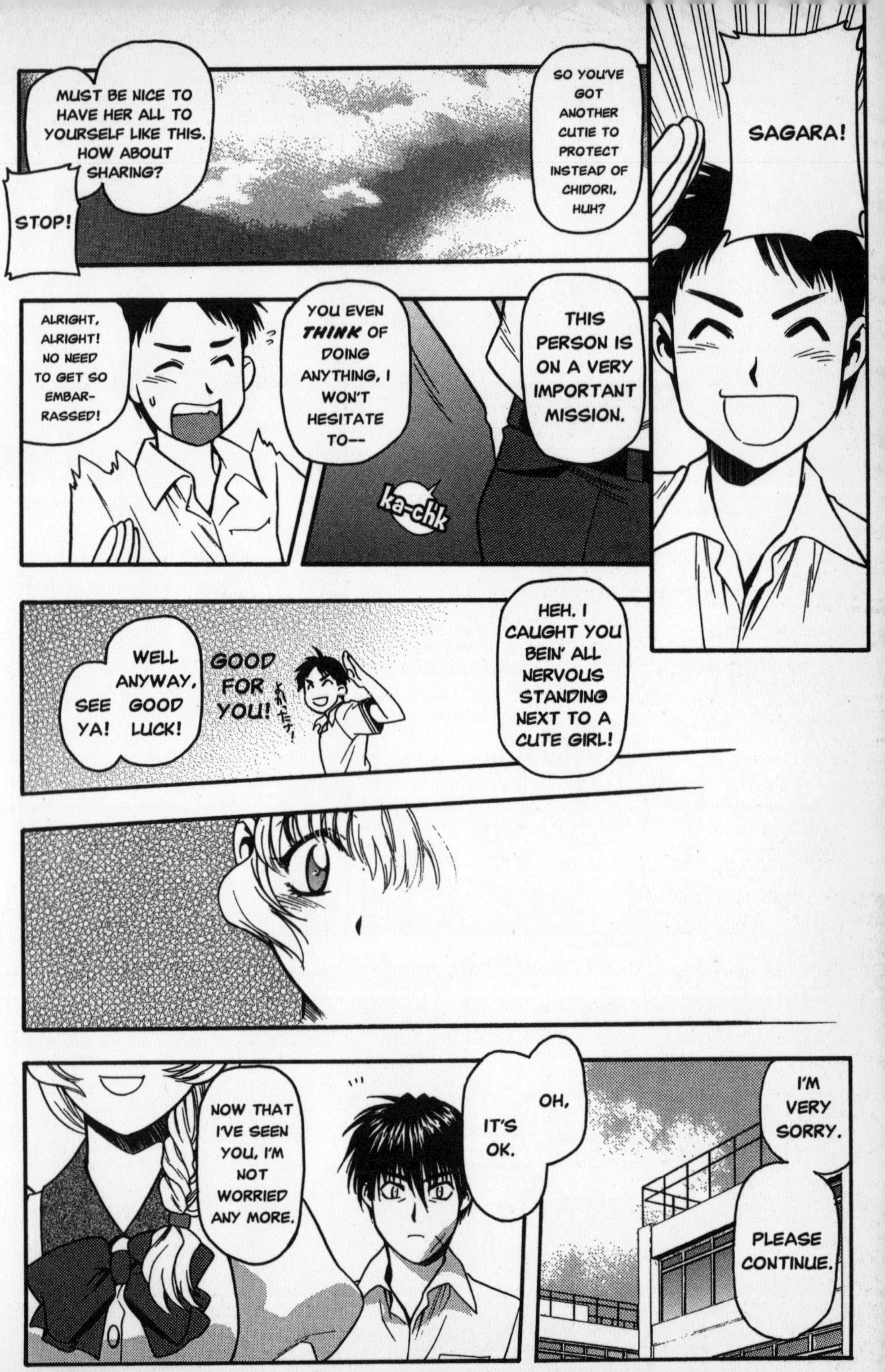
SAGARA!
SO YOU'VE GOT ANOTHER CUTIE TO PROTECT INSTEAD OF CHIDORI, HUH?
MUST BE NICE TO HAVE HER ALL TO YOURSELF LIKE THIS. HOW ABOUT SHARING?
STOP!
THIS PERSON IS ON A VERY IMPORTANT MISSION.
YOU EVEN *THINK* OF DOING ANYTHING, I WON'T HESITATE TO--
ka-ch'k
ALRIGHT, ALRIGHT! NO NEED TO GET SO EMBARRASSED!
HEH. I CAUGHT YOU BEIN' ALL NERVOUS STANDING NEXT TO A CUTE GIRL!
GOOD FOR YOU!
WELL ANYWAY, GOOD LUCK!
SEE YA!
I'M VERY SORRY.
PLEASE CONTINUE.
OH, IT'S OK.
NOW THAT I'VE SEEN YOU, I'M NOT WORRIED ANY MORE.

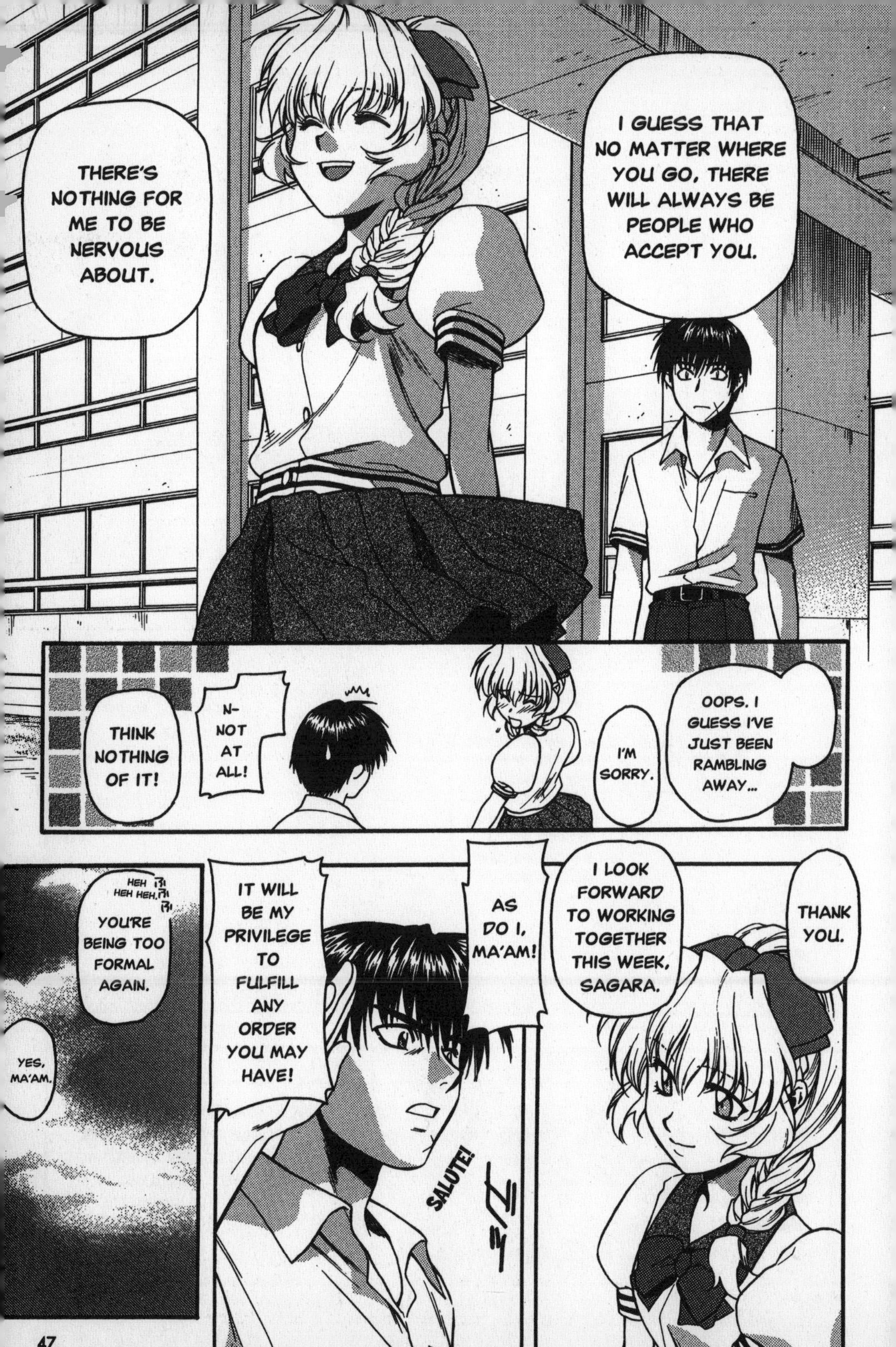
I GUESS THAT NO MATTER WHERE YOU GO, THERE WILL ALWAYS BE PEOPLE WHO ACCEPT YOU.
THERE'S NOTHING FOR ME TO BE NERVOUS ABOUT.
OOPS. I GUESS I'VE JUST BEEN RAMBLING AWAY...
I'M SORRY.
N-NOT AT ALL!
THINK NOTHING OF IT!
THANK YOU.
I LOOK FORWARD TO WORKING TOGETHER THIS WEEK, SAGARA.
AS DO I, MA'AM!
IT WILL BE MY PRIVILEGE TO FULFILL ANY ORDER YOU MAY HAVE!
SALUTE!
HEH HEH HEH.
YOU'RE BEING TOO FORMAL AGAIN.
YES, MA'AM.

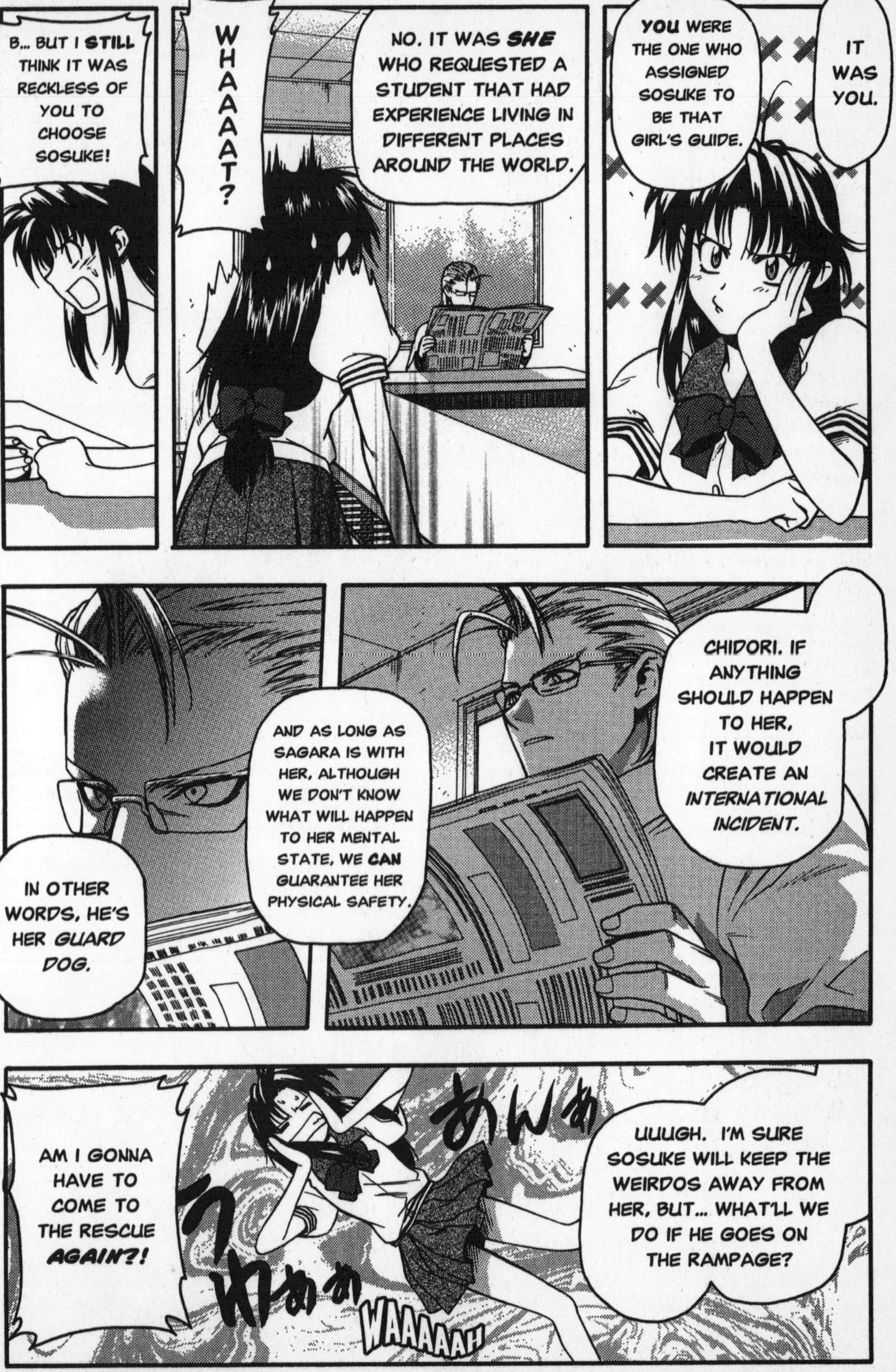

IT WAS YOU.
YOU WERE THE ONE WHO ASSIGNED SOSUKE TO BE THAT GIRL'S GUIDE.
NO. IT WAS SHE WHO REQUESTED A STUDENT THAT HAD EXPERIENCE LIVING IN DIFFERENT PLACES AROUND THE WORLD.
WHAAAAT?
B... BUT I STILL THINK IT WAS RECKLESS OF YOU TO CHOOSE SOSUKE!
CHIDORI. IF ANYTHING SHOULD HAPPEN TO HER, IT WOULD CREATE AN INTERNATIONAL INCIDENT.
AND AS LONG AS SAGARA IS WITH HER, ALTHOUGH WE DON'T KNOW WHAT WILL HAPPEN TO HER MENTAL STATE, WE CAN GUARANTEE HER PHYSICAL SAFETY.
IN OTHER WORDS, HE'S HER GUARD DOG.
UUUGH. I'M SURE SOSUKE WILL KEEP THE WEIRDOS AWAY FROM HER, BUT... WHAT'LL WE DO IF HE GOES ON THE RAMPAGE?
WAAAAAH
AM I GONNA HAVE TO COME TO THE RESCUE AGAIN?!

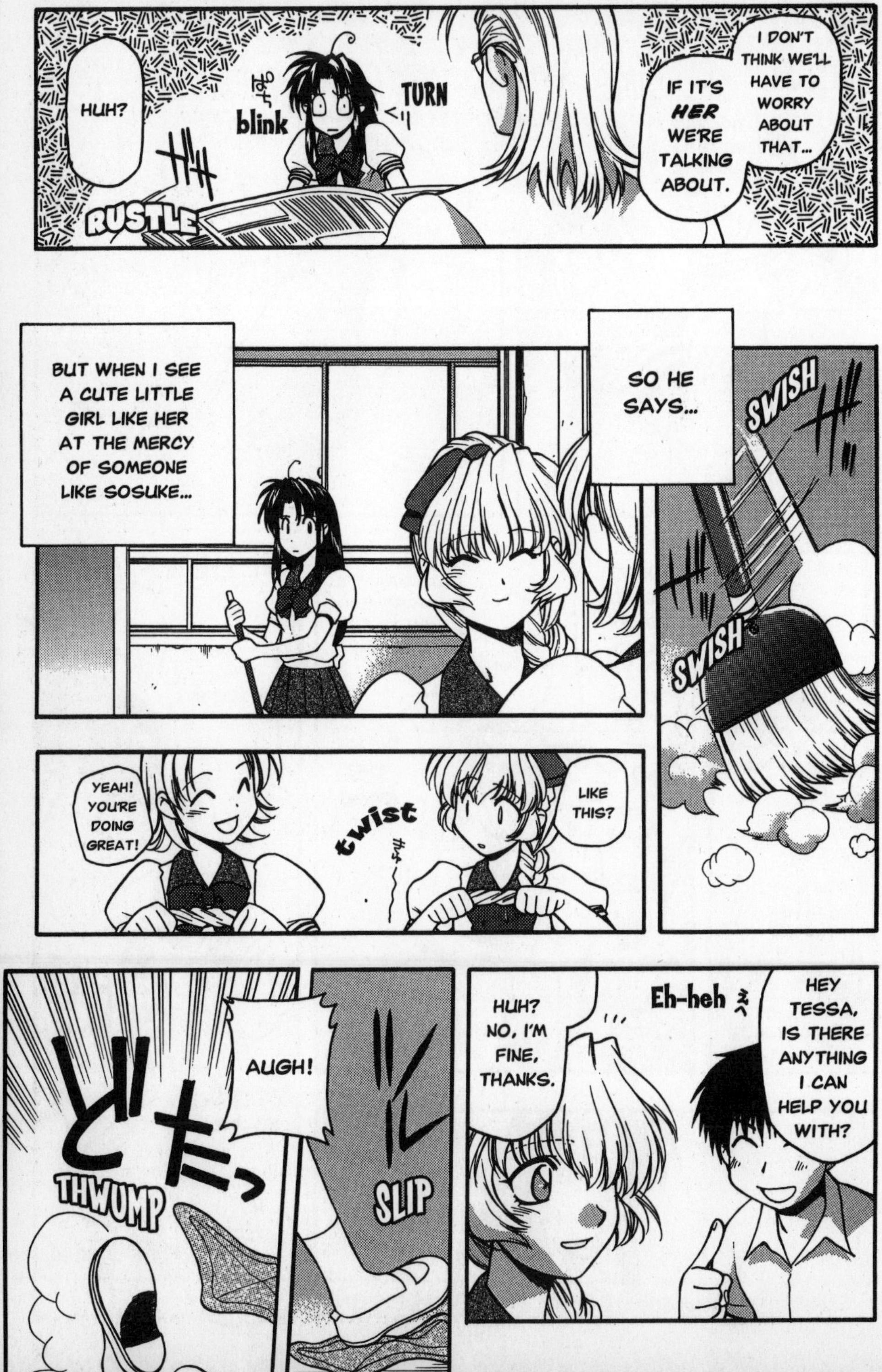

I DON'T THINK WE'LL HAVE TO WORRY ABOUT THAT...
IF IT'S HER WE'RE TALKING ABOUT.
TURN
blink
HUH?
RUSTLE
SWISH
SWISH
SO HE SAYS...
BUT WHEN I SEE A CUTE LITTLE GIRL LIKE HER AT THE MERCY OF SOMEONE LIKE SOSUKE...
LIKE THIS?
twist
YEAH! YOU'RE DOING GREAT!
HEY TESSA, IS THERE ANYTHING I CAN HELP YOU WITH?
Eh-heh
HUH? NO, I'M FINE, THANKS.
AUGH!
SLIP
THWUMP

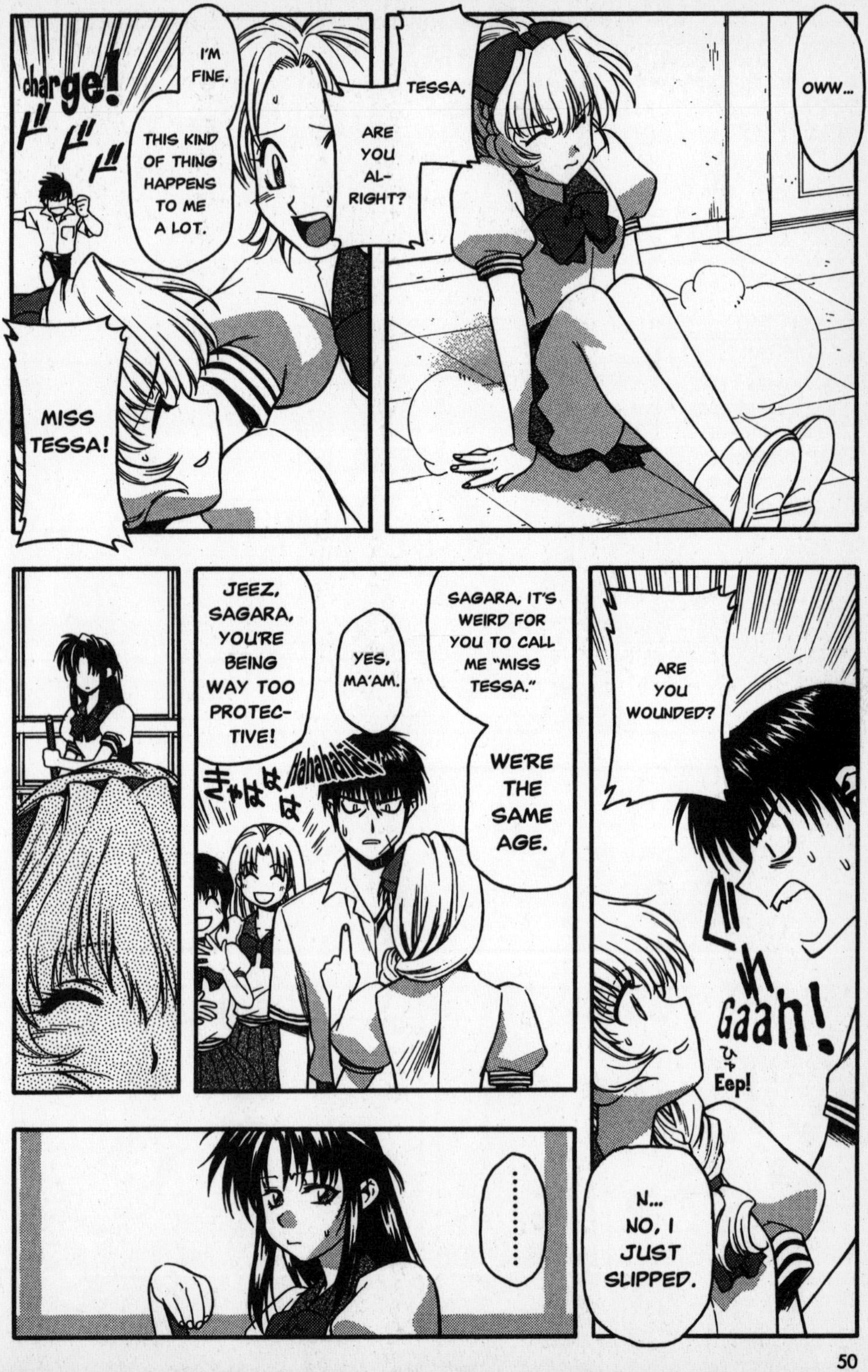
OWW...
TESSA,
ARE YOU AL-RIGHT?
I'M FINE.
THIS KIND OF THING HAPPENS TO ME A LOT.
charge!
ドドド
MISS TESSA!
ARE YOU WOUNDED?
Gaah!
ひゃ
Eep!
N... NO, I JUST SLIPPED.
SAGARA, IT'S WEIRD FOR YOU TO CALL ME "MISS TESSA."
WE'RE THE SAME AGE.
YES, MA'AM.
JEEZ, SAGARA, YOU'RE BEING WAY TOO PROTEC-TIVE!
きゃははは
Hahahaha
......

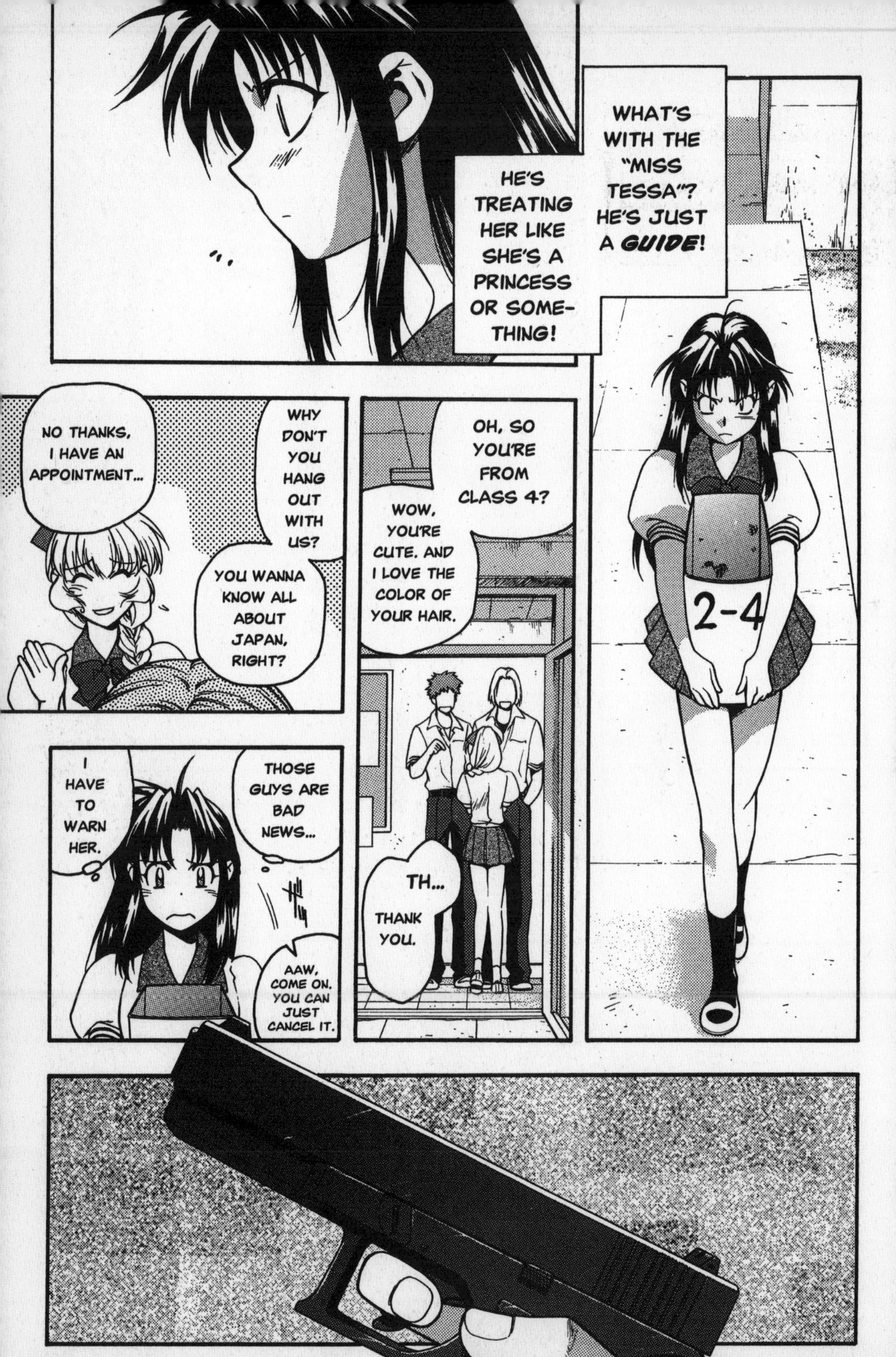

WHAT'S WITH THE "MISS TESSA"? HE'S JUST A GUIDE!
HE'S TREATING HER LIKE SHE'S A PRINCESS OR SOME-THING!
OH, SO YOU'RE FROM CLASS 4?
WOW, YOU'RE CUTE. AND I LOVE THE COLOR OF YOUR HAIR.
TH...
THANK YOU.
WHY DON'T YOU HANG OUT WITH US?
YOU WANNA KNOW ALL ABOUT JAPAN, RIGHT?
NO THANKS, I HAVE AN APPOINTMENT...
THOSE GUYS ARE BAD NEWS...
I HAVE TO WARN HER.
AAW, COME ON. YOU CAN JUST CANCEL IT.
2-4

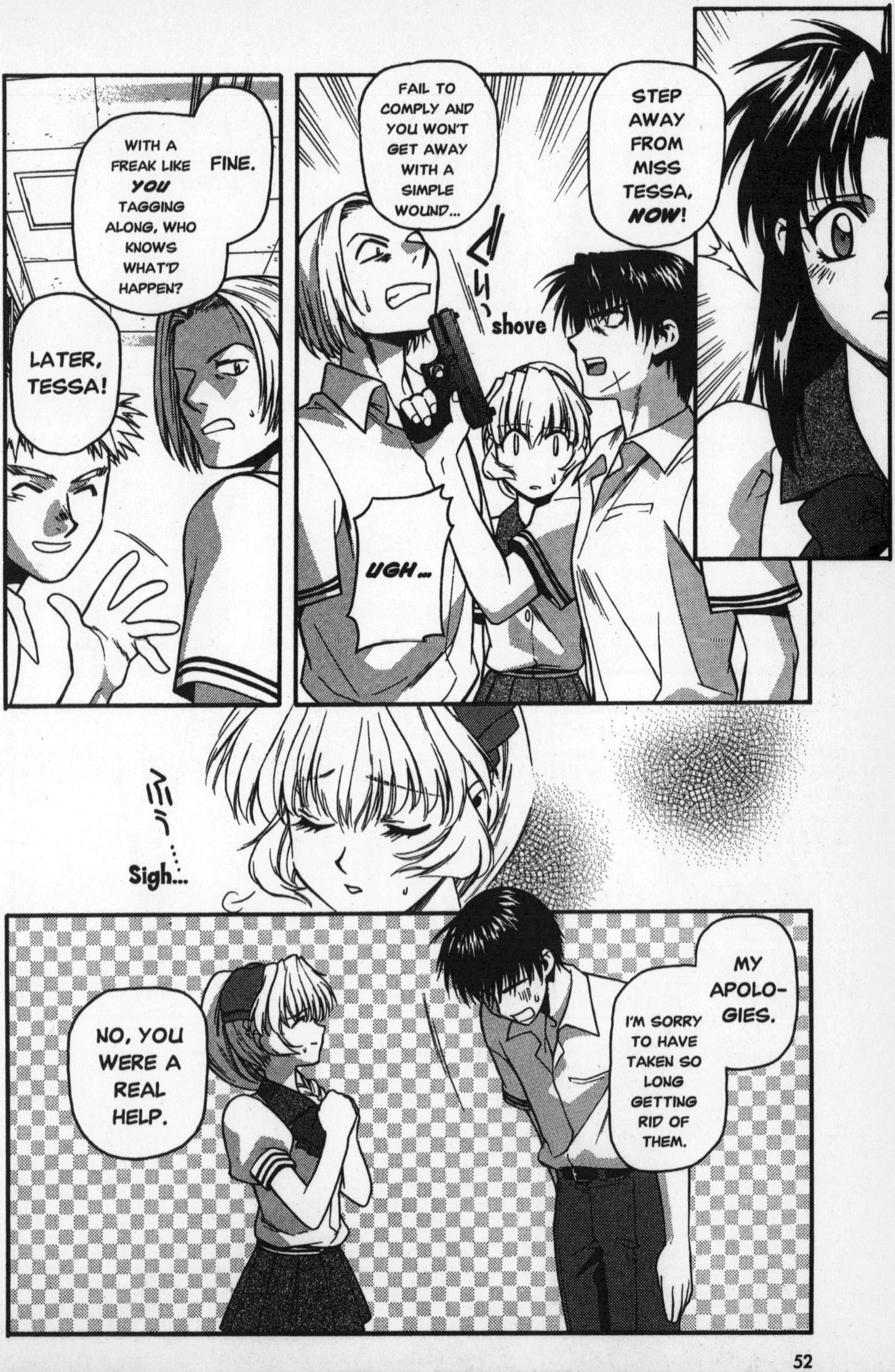
STEP AWAY FROM MISS TESSA, NOW!
FAIL TO COMPLY AND YOU WON'T GET AWAY WITH A SIMPLE WOUND...
shove
UGH...
FINE.
WITH A FREAK LIKE YOU TAGGING ALONG, WHO KNOWS WHAT'D HAPPEN?
LATER, TESSA!
Sigh...
MY APOLOGIES.
I'M SORRY TO HAVE TAKEN SO LONG GETTING RID OF THEM.
NO, YOU WERE A REAL HELP.

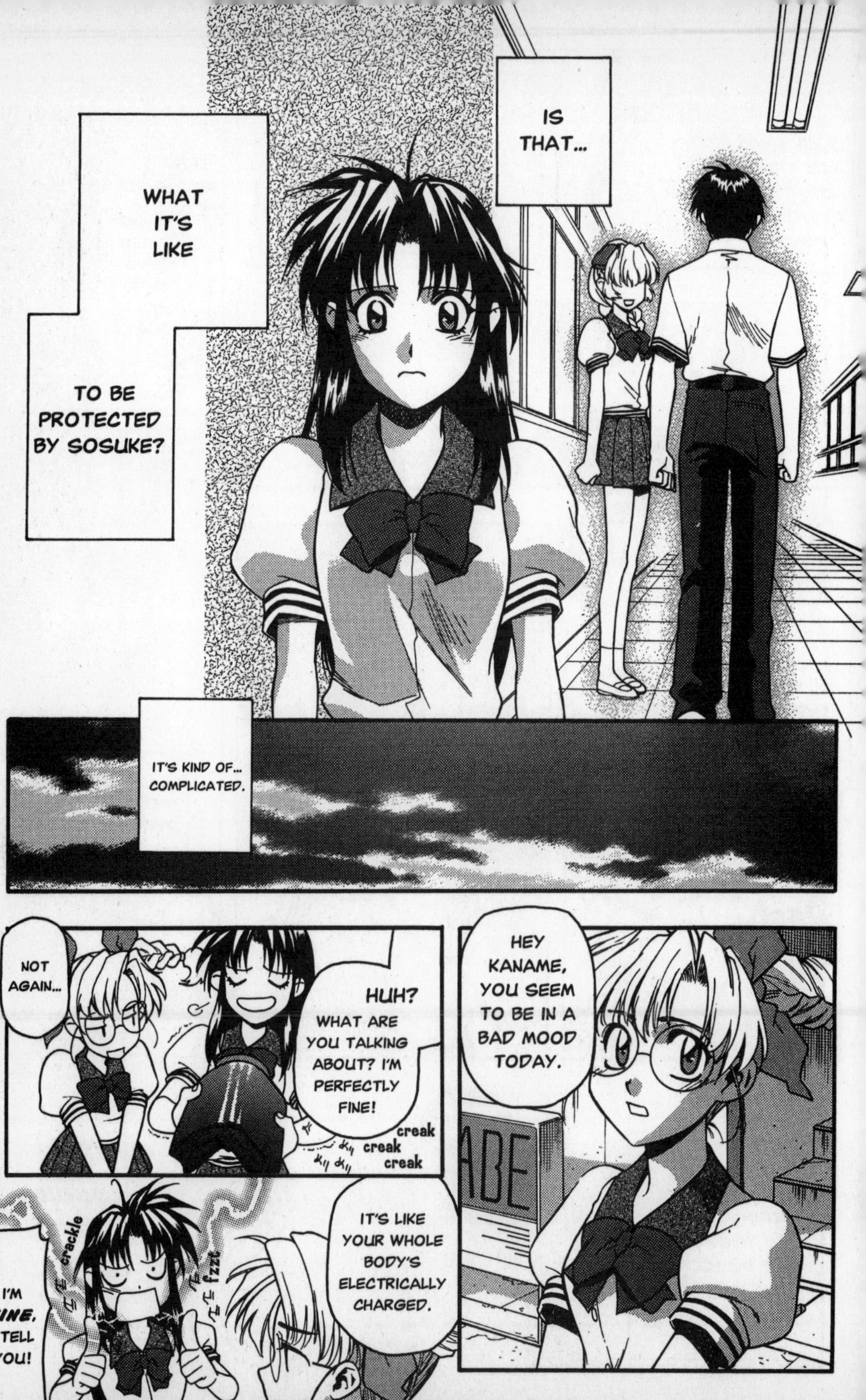
IS THAT...
WHAT IT'S LIKE
TO BE PROTECTED BY SOSUKE?
IT'S KIND OF... COMPLICATED.
HEY KANAME, YOU SEEM TO BE IN A BAD MOOD TODAY.
HUH? WHAT ARE YOU TALKING ABOUT? I'M PERFECTLY FINE!
creak creak creak
NOT AGAIN...
IT'S LIKE YOUR WHOLE BODY'S ELECTRICALLY CHARGED.
fzzt
crackle
I'M FINE, I TELL YOU!

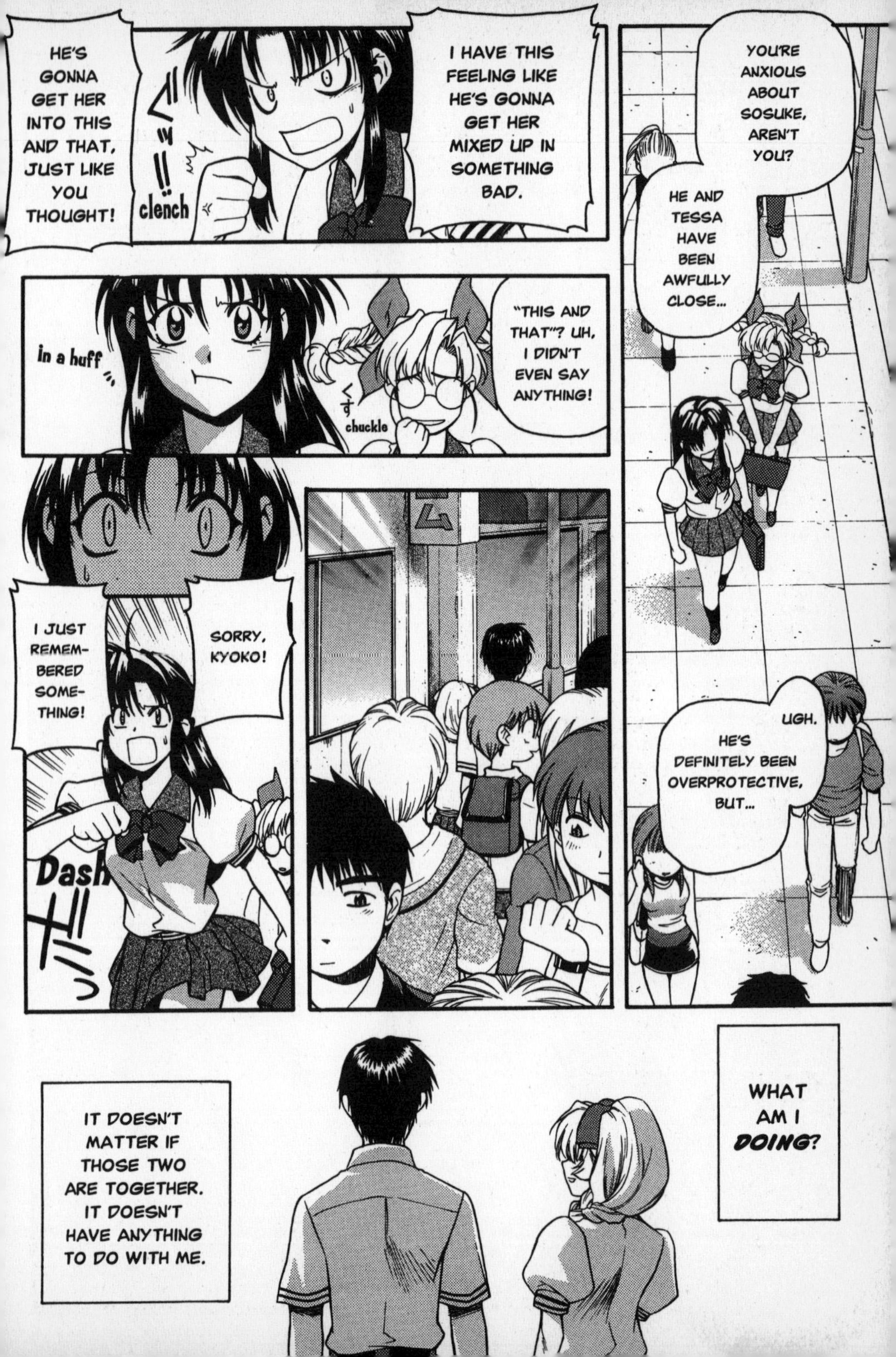
YOU'RE ANXIOUS ABOUT SOSUKE, AREN'T YOU?
HE AND TESSA HAVE BEEN AWFULLY CLOSE...
UGH. HE'S DEFINITELY BEEN OVERPROTECTIVE, BUT...
I HAVE THIS FEELING LIKE HE'S GONNA GET HER MIXED UP IN SOMETHING BAD.
clench
HE'S GONNA GET HER INTO THIS AND THAT, JUST LIKE YOU THOUGHT!
"THIS AND THAT"? UH, I DIDN'T EVEN SAY ANYTHING!
chuckle
in a huff
SORRY, KYOKO!
I JUST REMEMBERED SOMETHING!
Dash
WHAT AM I DOING?
IT DOESN'T MATTER IF THOSE TWO ARE TOGETHER. IT DOESN'T HAVE ANYTHING TO DO WITH ME.

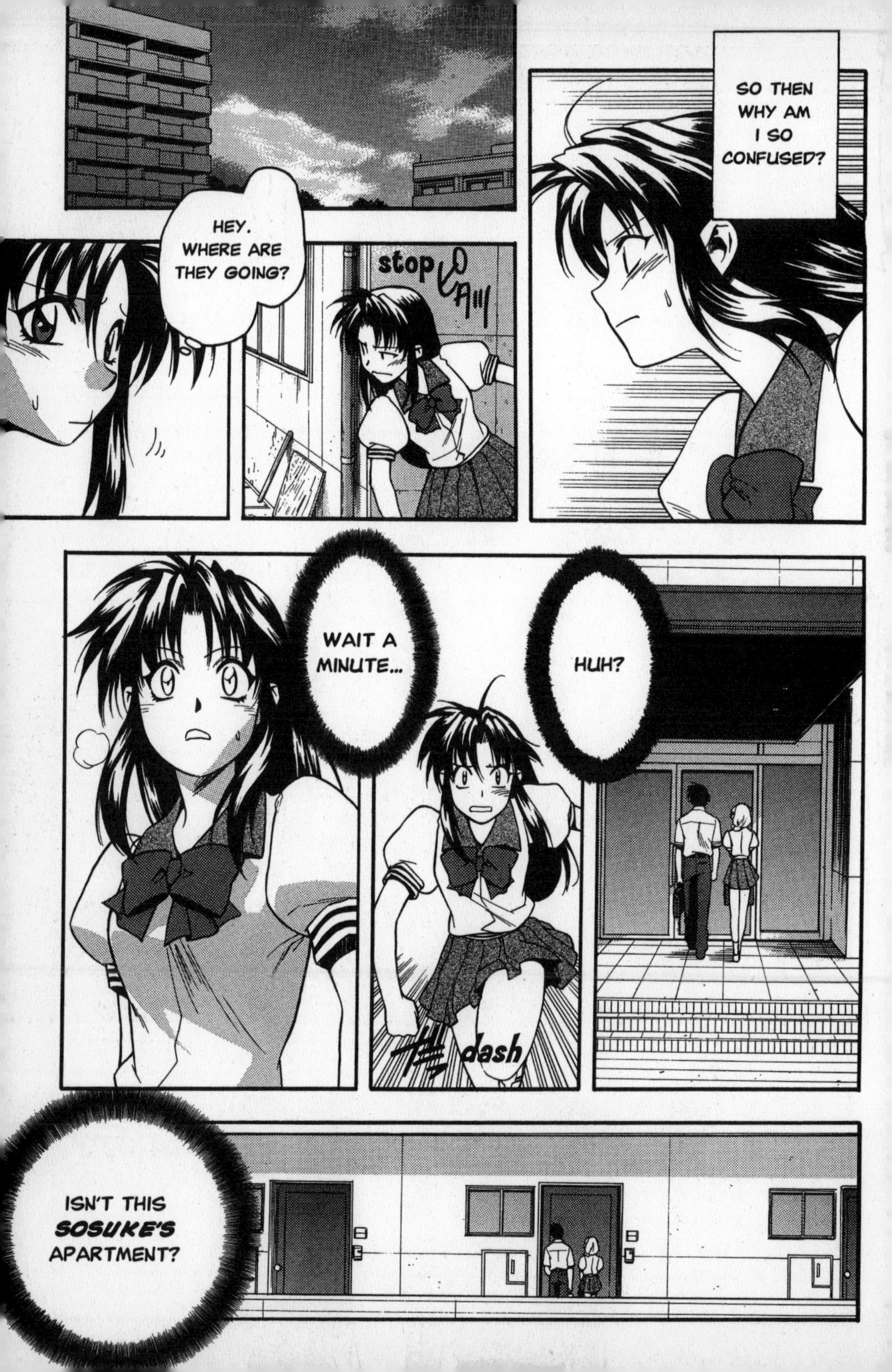
SO THEN WHY AM I SO CONFUSED?
stop
HEY. WHERE ARE THEY GOING?
HUH?
WAIT A MINUTE...
dash
ISN'T THIS **SOSUKE'S** APARTMENT?

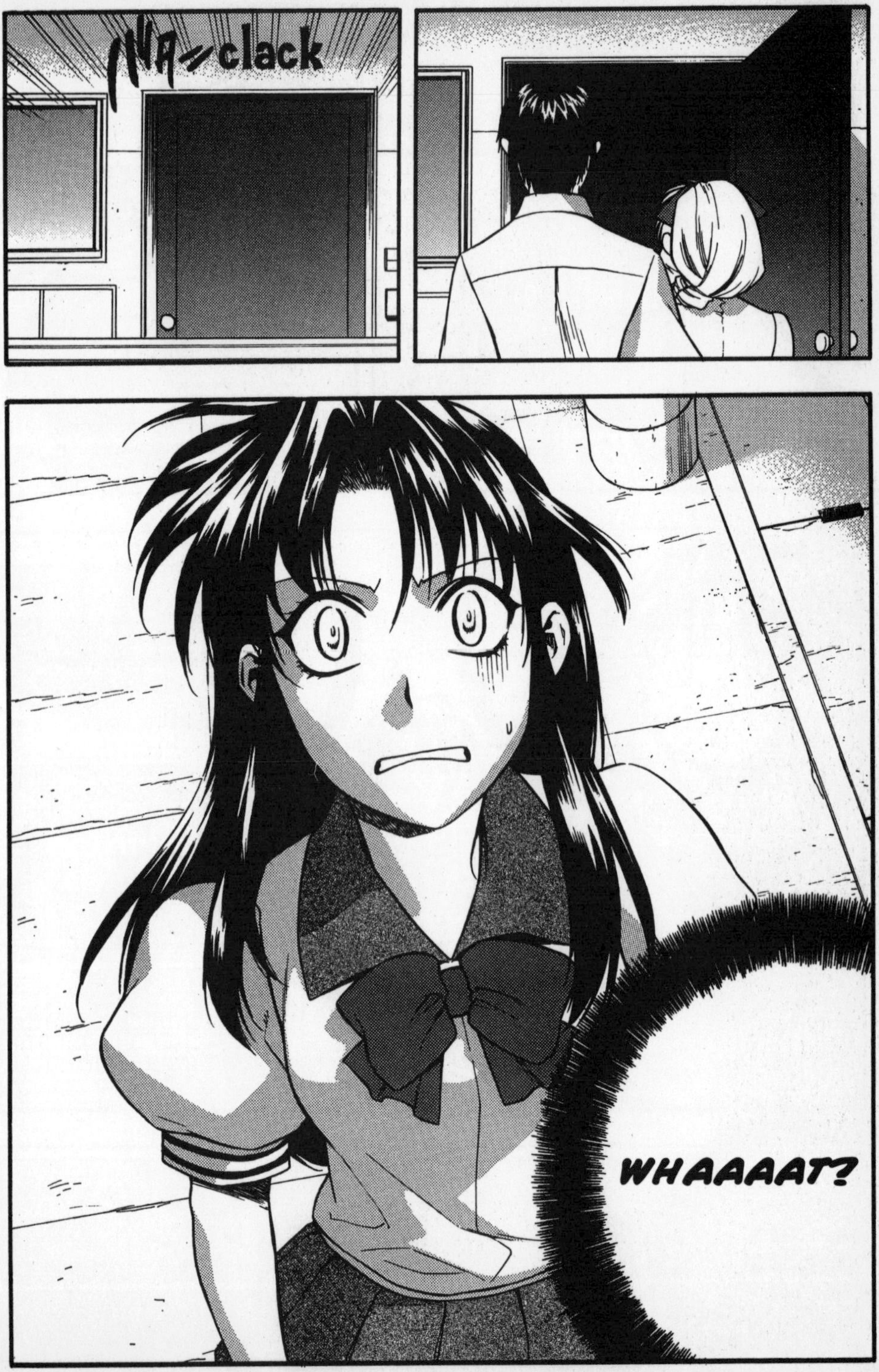
clack
WHAAAAT?

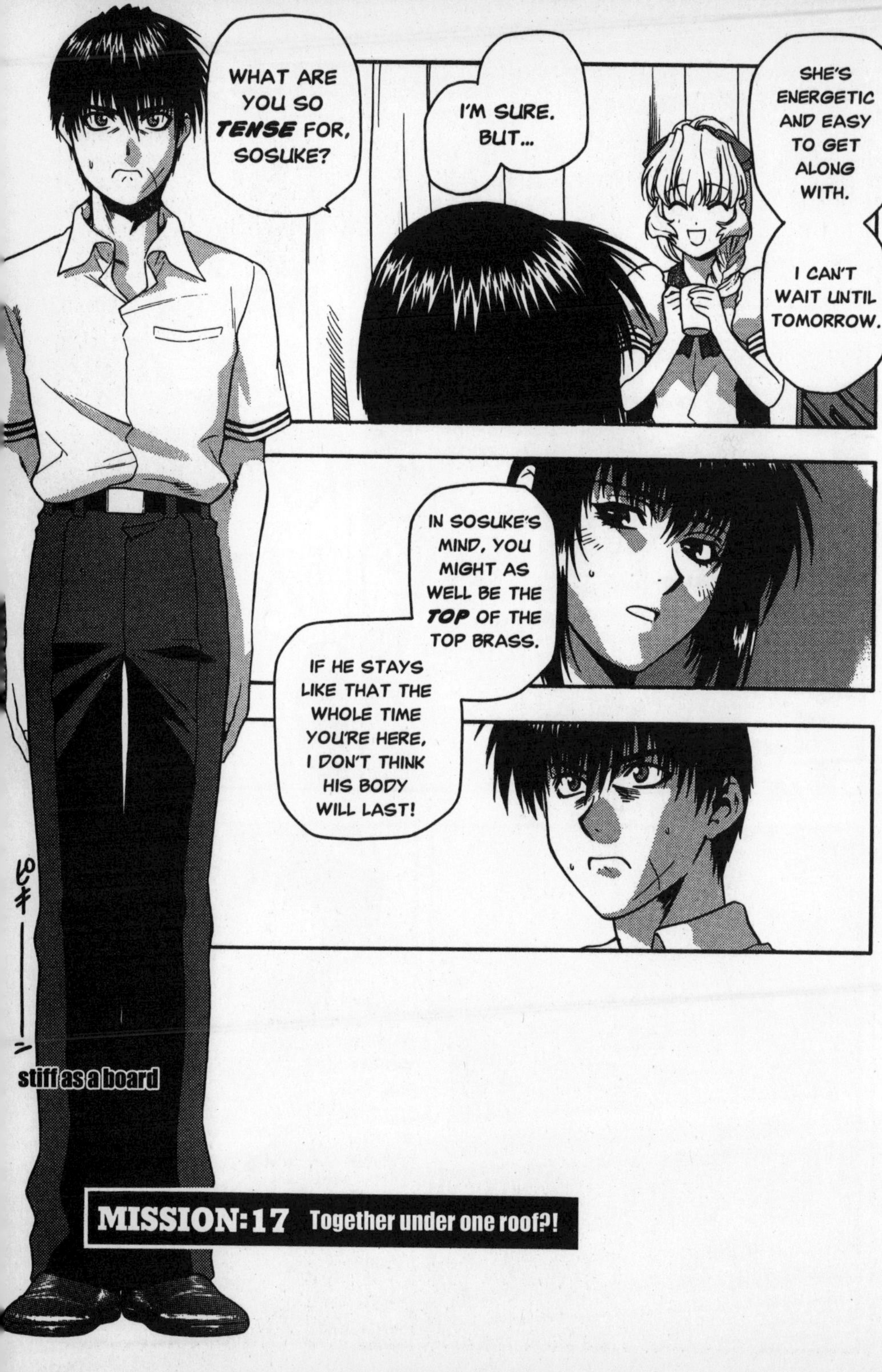
SHE'S ENERGETIC AND EASY TO GET ALONG WITH.
I CAN'T WAIT UNTIL TOMORROW.
I'M SURE. BUT...
WHAT ARE YOU SO *TENSE* FOR, SOSUKE?
IN SOSUKE'S MIND, YOU MIGHT AS WELL BE THE *TOP* OF THE TOP BRASS.
IF HE STAYS LIKE THAT THE WHOLE TIME YOU'RE HERE, I DON'T THINK HIS BODY WILL LAST!
ピキーーン
stiff as a board
MISSION:17 Together under one roof?!

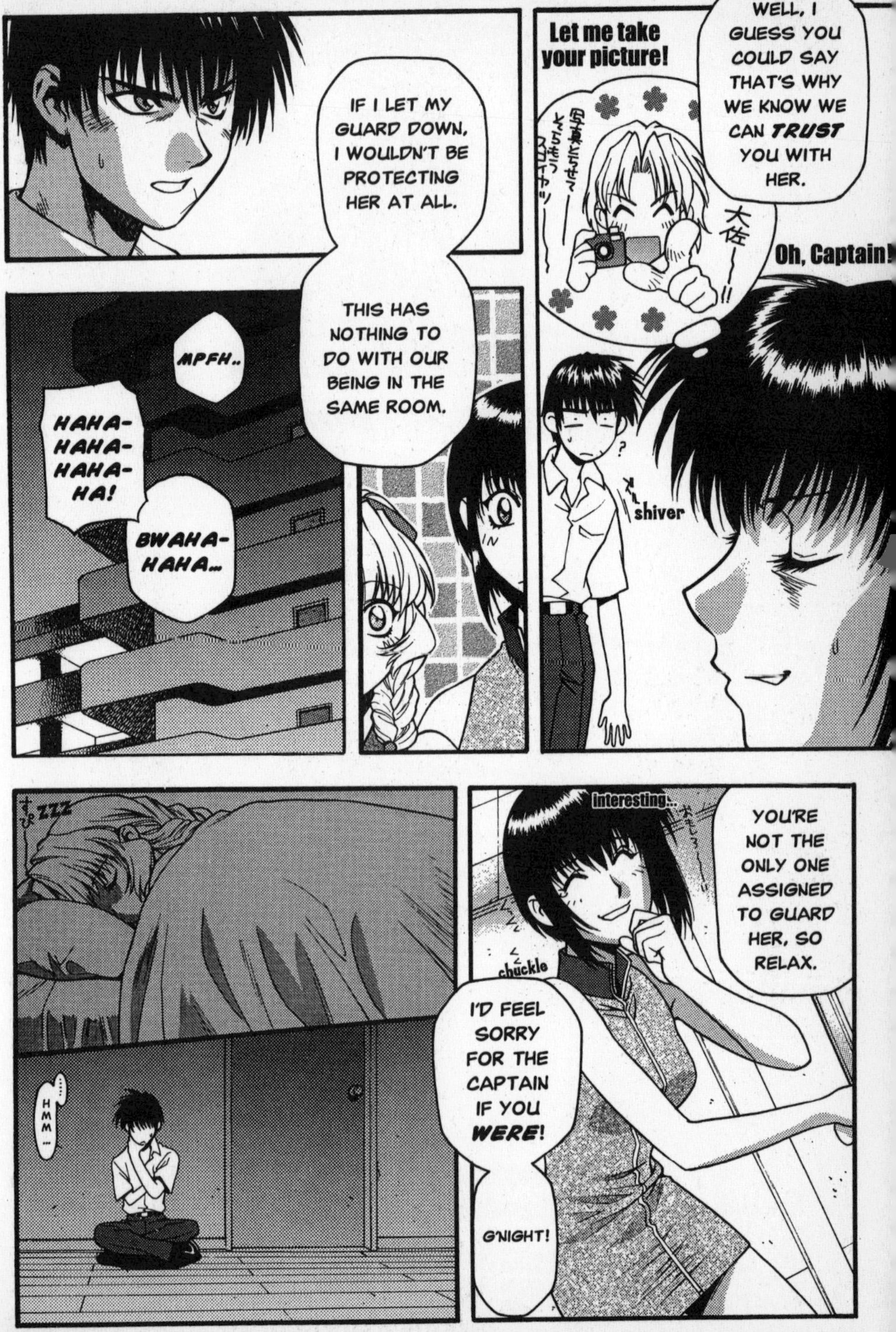
Let me take your picture!
WELL, I GUESS YOU COULD SAY THAT'S WHY WE KNOW WE CAN TRUST YOU WITH HER.
大佐～～!!
Oh, Captain!
shiver
IF I LET MY GUARD DOWN, I WOULDN'T BE PROTECTING HER AT ALL.
THIS HAS NOTHING TO DO WITH OUR BEING IN THE SAME ROOM.
MPFH..
HAHA-HAHA-HAHA-HA!
BWAHA-HAHA...
interesting..
YOU'RE NOT THE ONLY ONE ASSIGNED TO GUARD HER, SO RELAX.
chuckle
I'D FEEL SORRY FOR THE CAPTAIN IF YOU WERE!
G'NIGHT!
ZZZ
...... HMM...

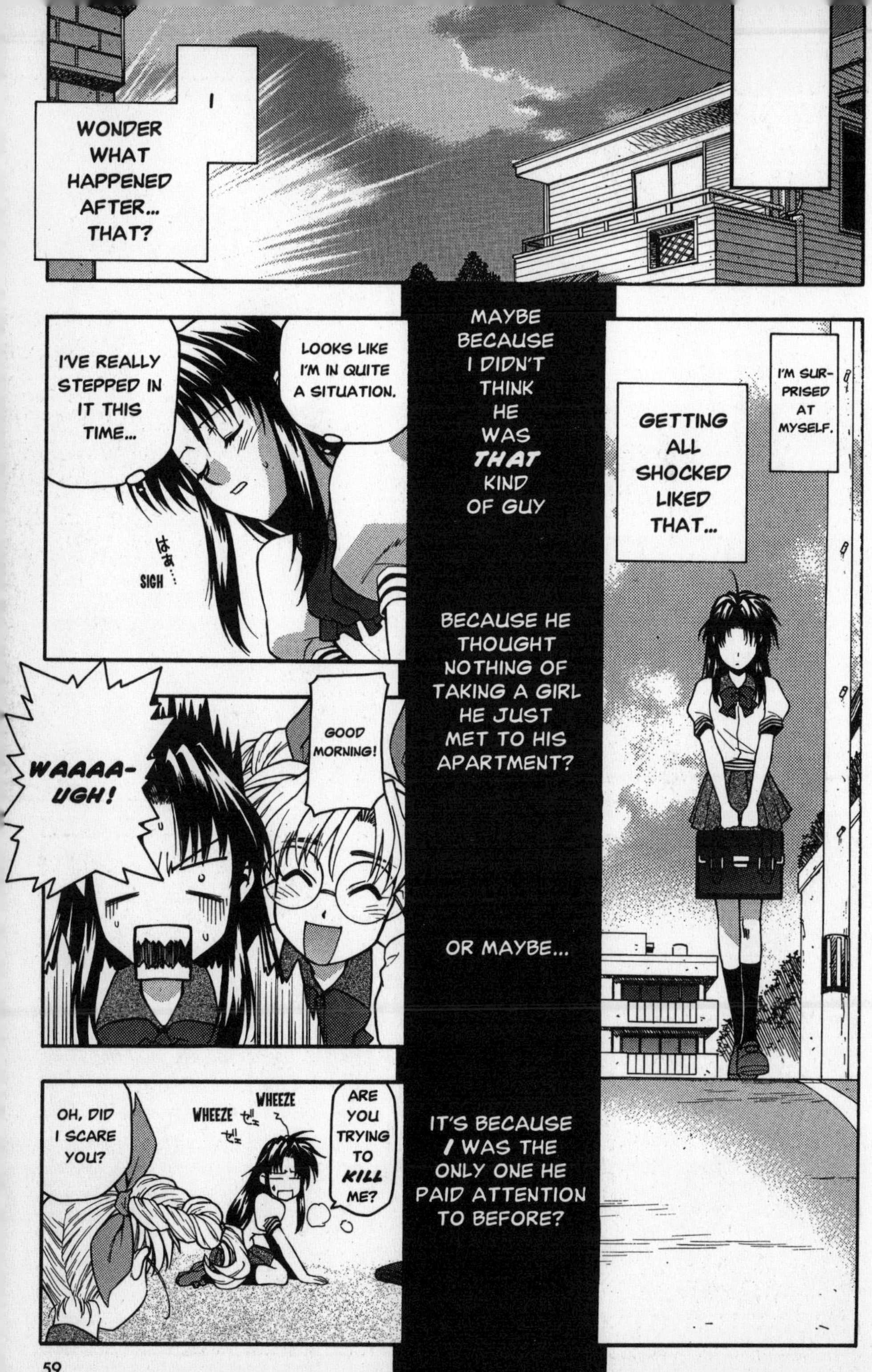
I
WONDER WHAT HAPPENED AFTER... THAT?
I'M SURPRISED AT MYSELF.
GETTING ALL SHOCKED LIKED THAT...
MAYBE BECAUSE I DIDN'T THINK HE WAS THAT KIND OF GUY
BECAUSE HE THOUGHT NOTHING OF TAKING A GIRL HE JUST MET TO HIS APARTMENT?
OR MAYBE...
IT'S BECAUSE I WAS THE ONLY ONE HE PAID ATTENTION TO BEFORE?
LOOKS LIKE I'M IN QUITE A SITUATION.
I'VE REALLY STEPPED IN IT THIS TIME...
はぁ…
SIGH
GOOD MORNING!
WAAAA-UGH!
ARE YOU TRYING TO KILL ME?
WHEEZE ぜぇ
WHEEZE ぜぇ
OH, DID I SCARE YOU?

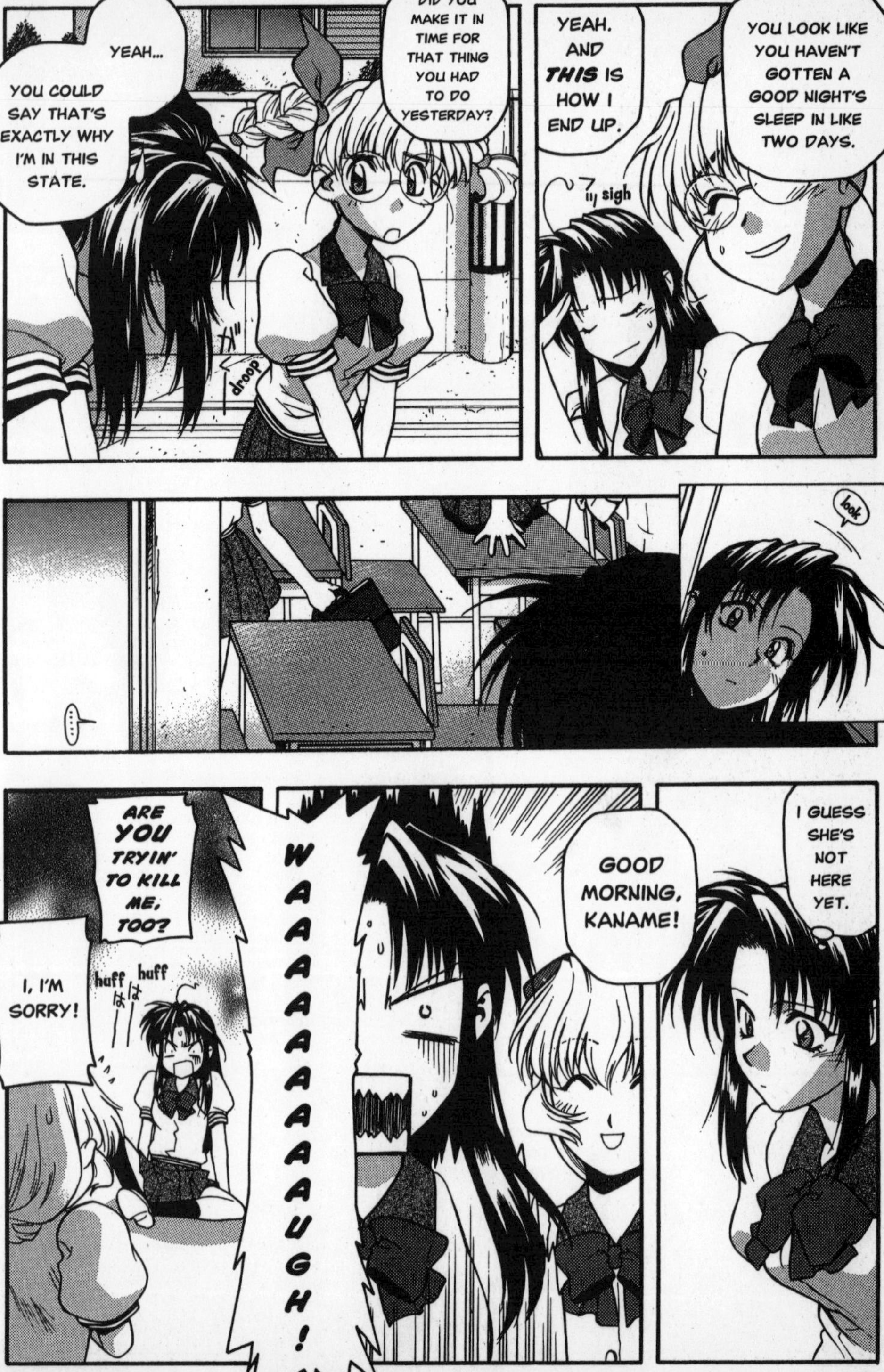
YOU LOOK LIKE YOU HAVEN'T GOTTEN A GOOD NIGHT'S SLEEP IN LIKE TWO DAYS.
YEAH. AND THIS IS HOW I END UP.
sigh
DID YOU MAKE IT IN TIME FOR THAT THING YOU HAD TO DO YESTERDAY?
YEAH... YOU COULD SAY THAT'S EXACTLY WHY I'M IN THIS STATE.
droop
look
......
I GUESS SHE'S NOT HERE YET.
GOOD MORNING, KANAME!
WAAAAAAAAAUGH!
ARE YOU TRYIN' TO KILL ME, TOO?
huff huff
I, I'M SORRY!

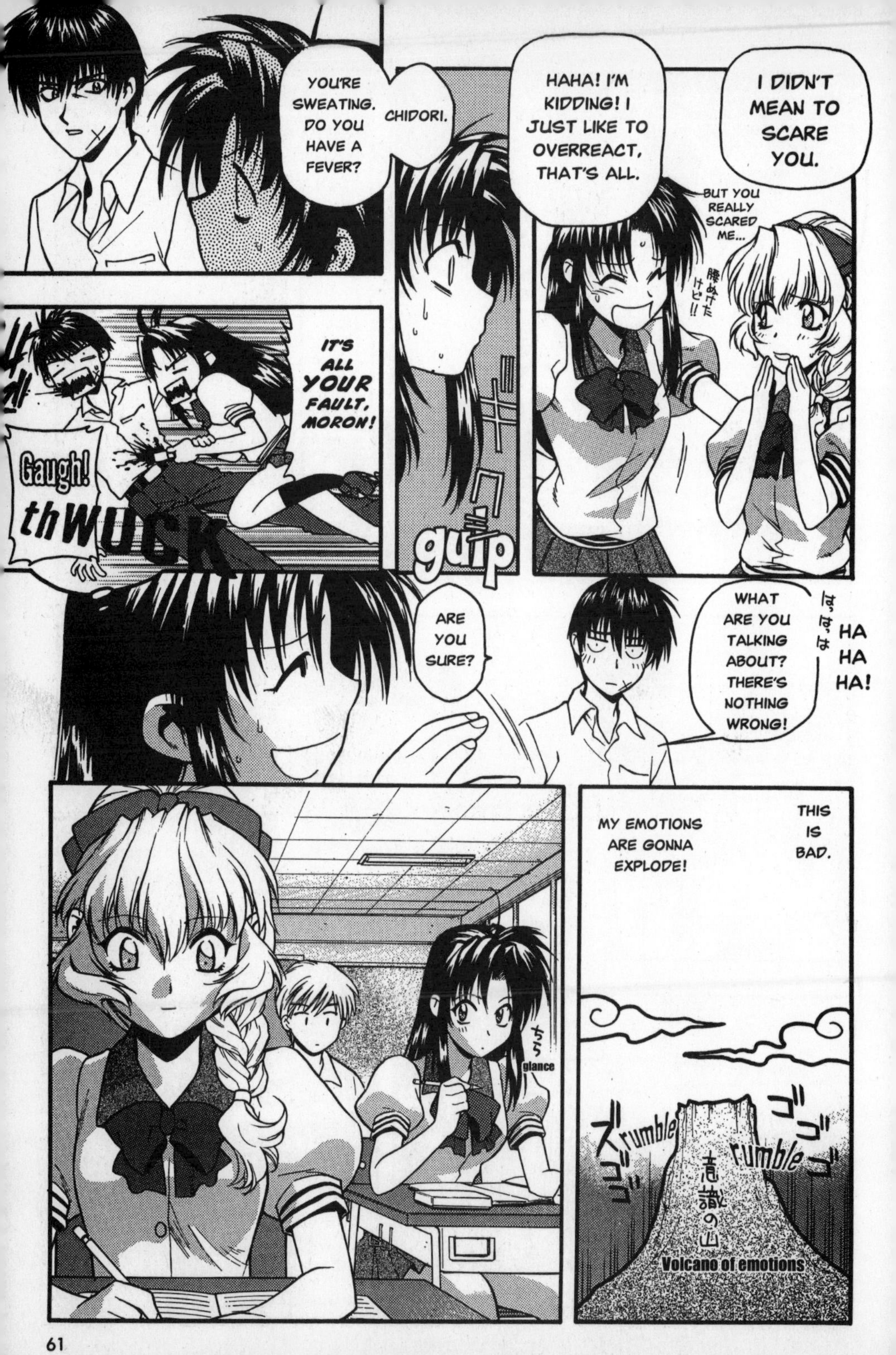
I DIDN'T MEAN TO SCARE YOU.
BUT YOU REALLY SCARED ME...
腰ぬけたけど!!
HAHA! I'M KIDDING! I JUST LIKE TO OVERREACT, THAT'S ALL.
gulp
CHIDORI.
YOU'RE SWEATING. DO YOU HAVE A FEVER?
IT'S ALL YOUR FAULT, MORON!
Gaugh!
thWUCK
ははは
HA HA HA!
WHAT ARE YOU TALKING ABOUT? THERE'S NOTHING WRONG!
ARE YOU SURE?
THIS IS BAD.
MY EMOTIONS ARE GONNA EXPLODE!
ゴゴ
rumble
ズゴゴ
rumble
意識の山
Volcano of emotions
ちら
glance

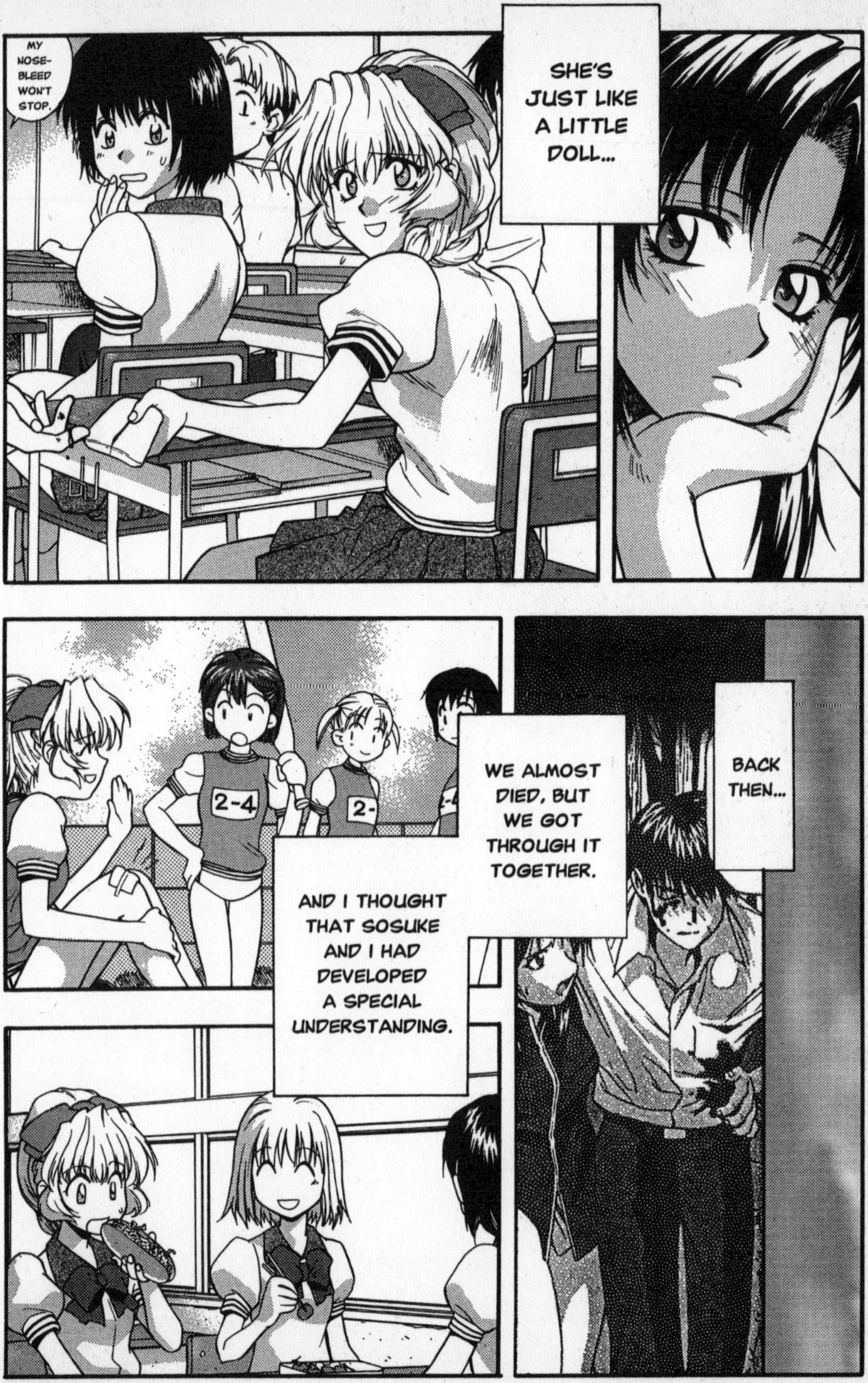
SHE'S JUST LIKE A LITTLE DOLL...
MY NOSE-BLEED WON'T STOP.
BACK THEN...
WE ALMOST DIED, BUT WE GOT THROUGH IT TOGETHER.
AND I THOUGHT THAT SOSUKE AND I HAD DEVELOPED A SPECIAL UNDERSTANDING.

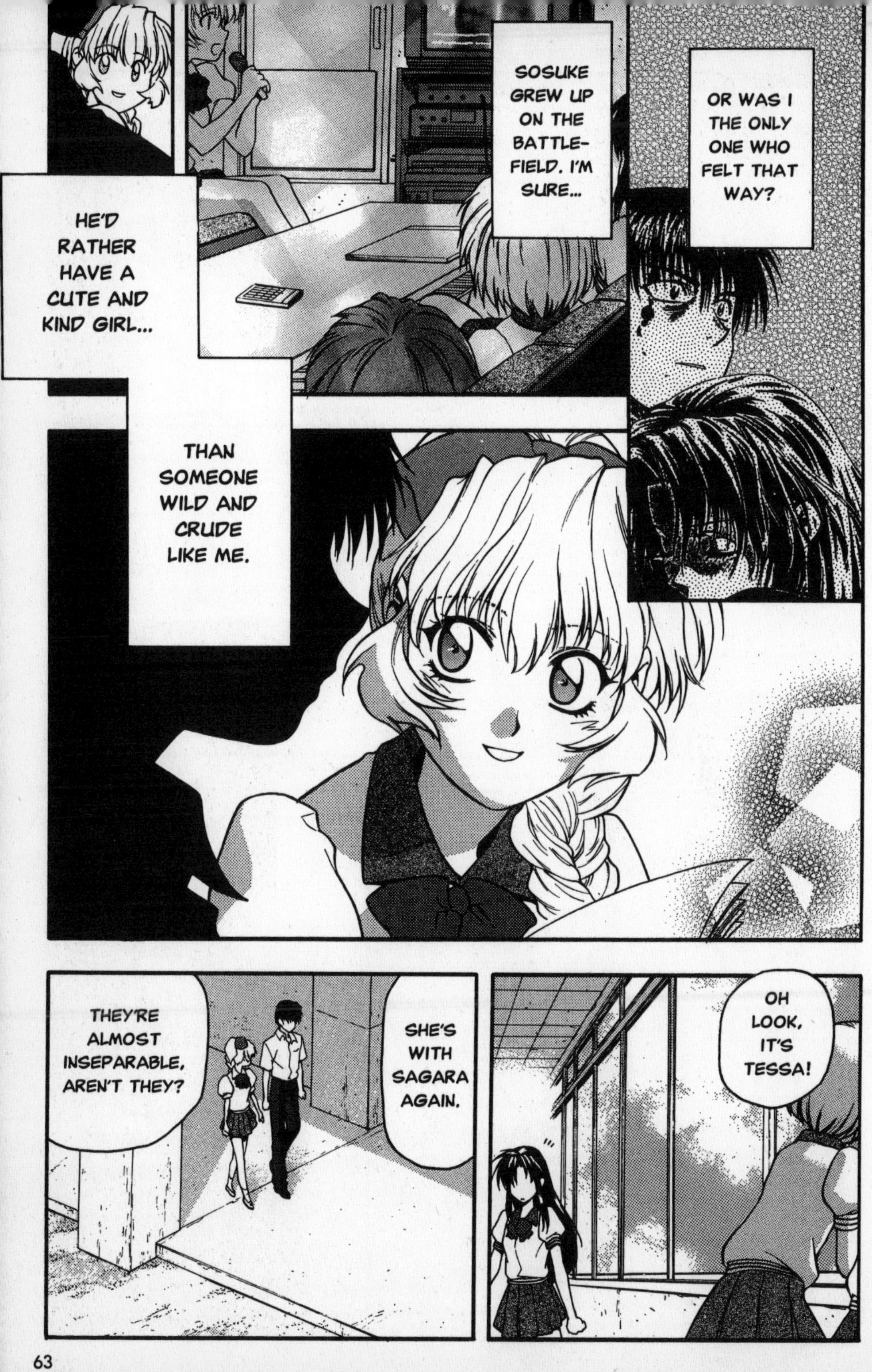
OR WAS I THE ONLY ONE WHO FELT THAT WAY?
SOSUKE GREW UP ON THE BATTLE-FIELD. I'M SURE...
HE'D RATHER HAVE A CUTE AND KIND GIRL...
THAN SOMEONE WILD AND CRUDE LIKE ME.
OH LOOK, IT'S TESSA!
SHE'S WITH SAGARA AGAIN.
THEY'RE ALMOST INSEPARABLE, AREN'T THEY?

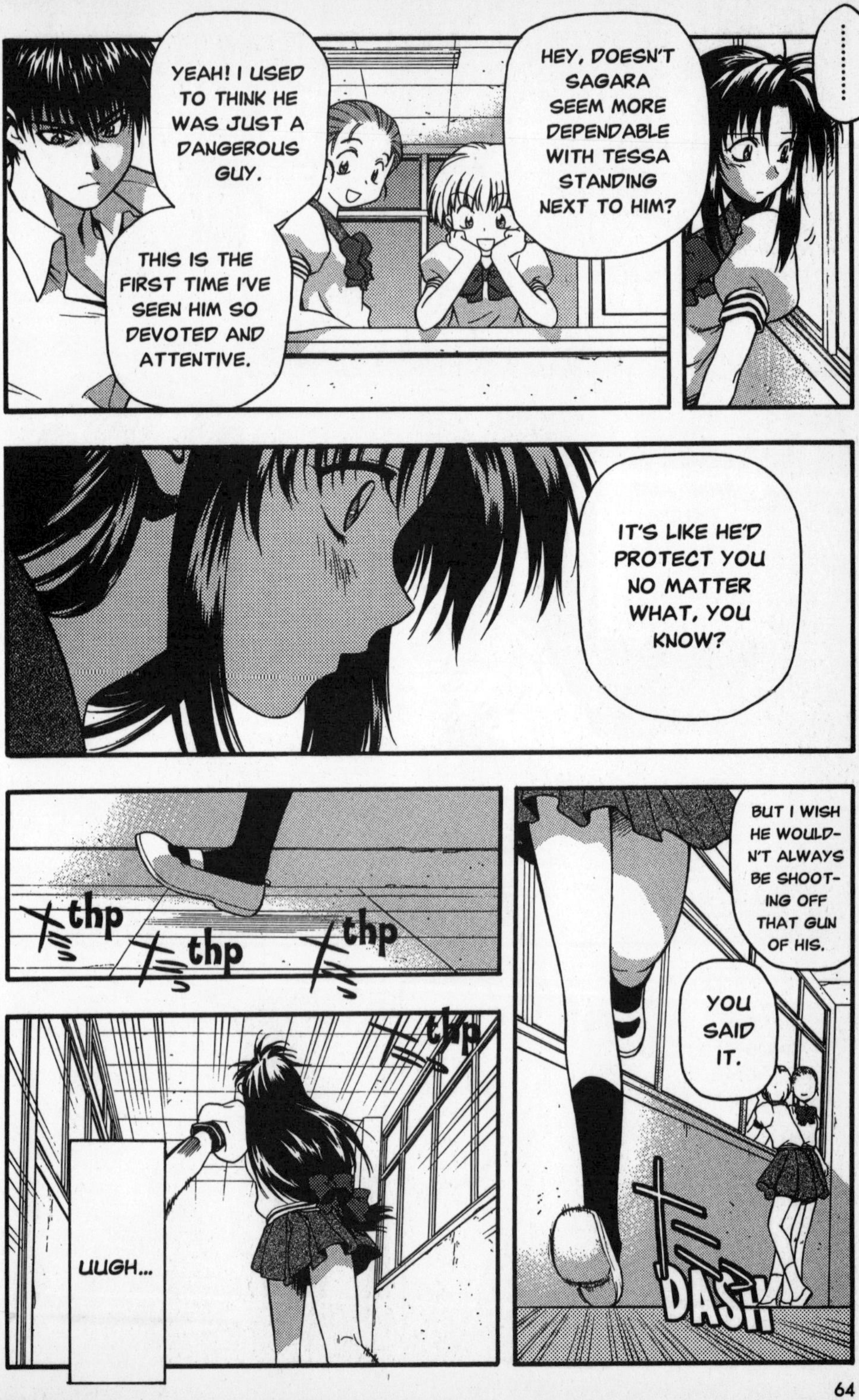
....
HEY, DOESN'T SAGARA SEEM MORE DEPENDABLE WITH TESSA STANDING NEXT TO HIM?
YEAH! I USED TO THINK HE WAS JUST A DANGEROUS GUY.
THIS IS THE FIRST TIME I'VE SEEN HIM SO DEVOTED AND ATTENTIVE.
IT'S LIKE HE'D PROTECT YOU NO MATTER WHAT, YOU KNOW?
BUT I WISH HE WOULD-N'T ALWAYS BE SHOOT-ING OFF THAT GUN OF HIS.
YOU SAID IT.
DASH!!
thp
thp
thp
thp
UUGH...

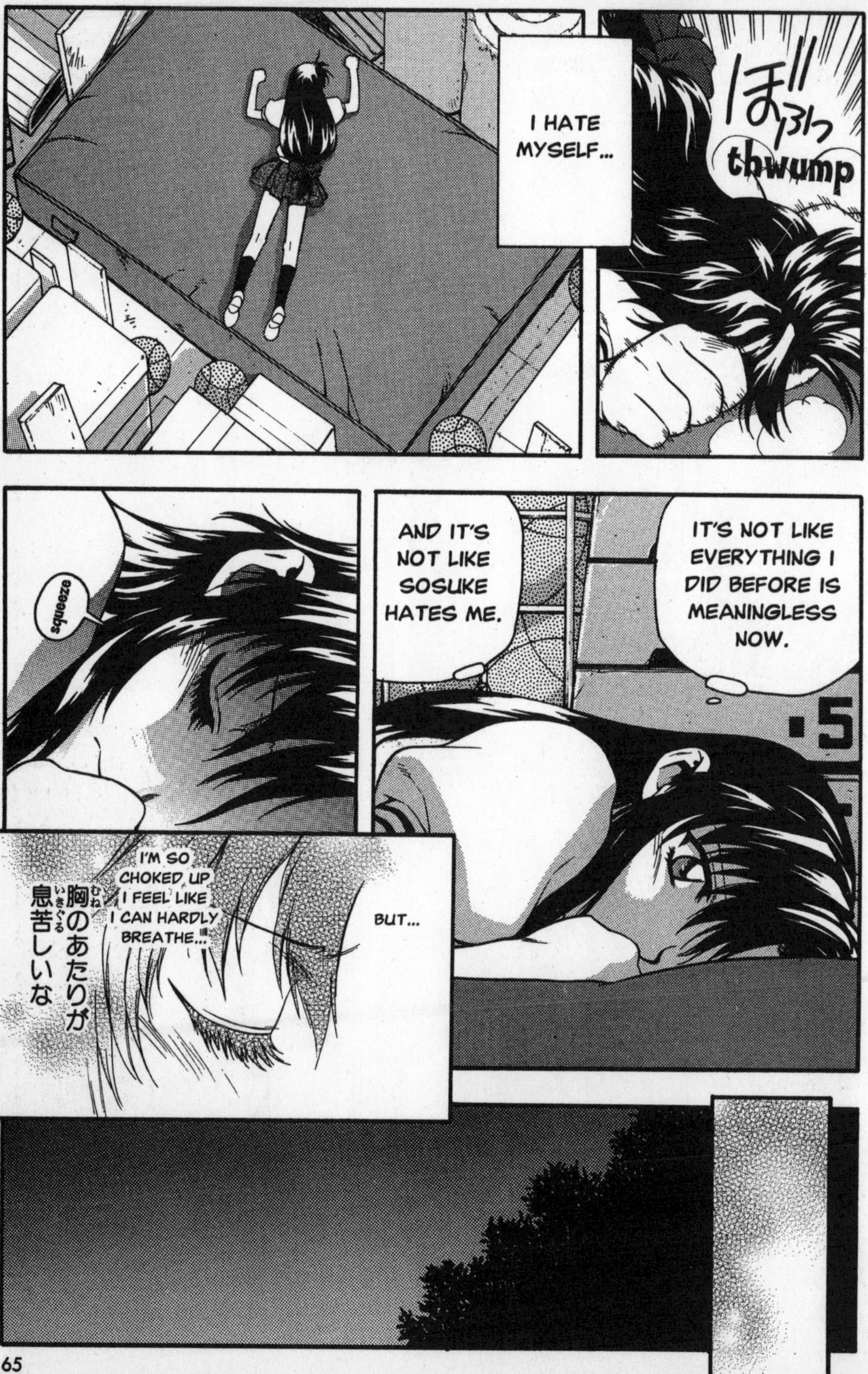
ぼふっ
thwump
I HATE MYSELF...
IT'S NOT LIKE EVERYTHING I DID BEFORE IS MEANINGLESS NOW.
AND IT'S NOT LIKE SOSUKE HATES ME.
BUT...
squeeze
胸のあたりが息苦しいな
I'M SO CHOKED UP I FEEL LIKE I CAN HARDLY BREATHE...

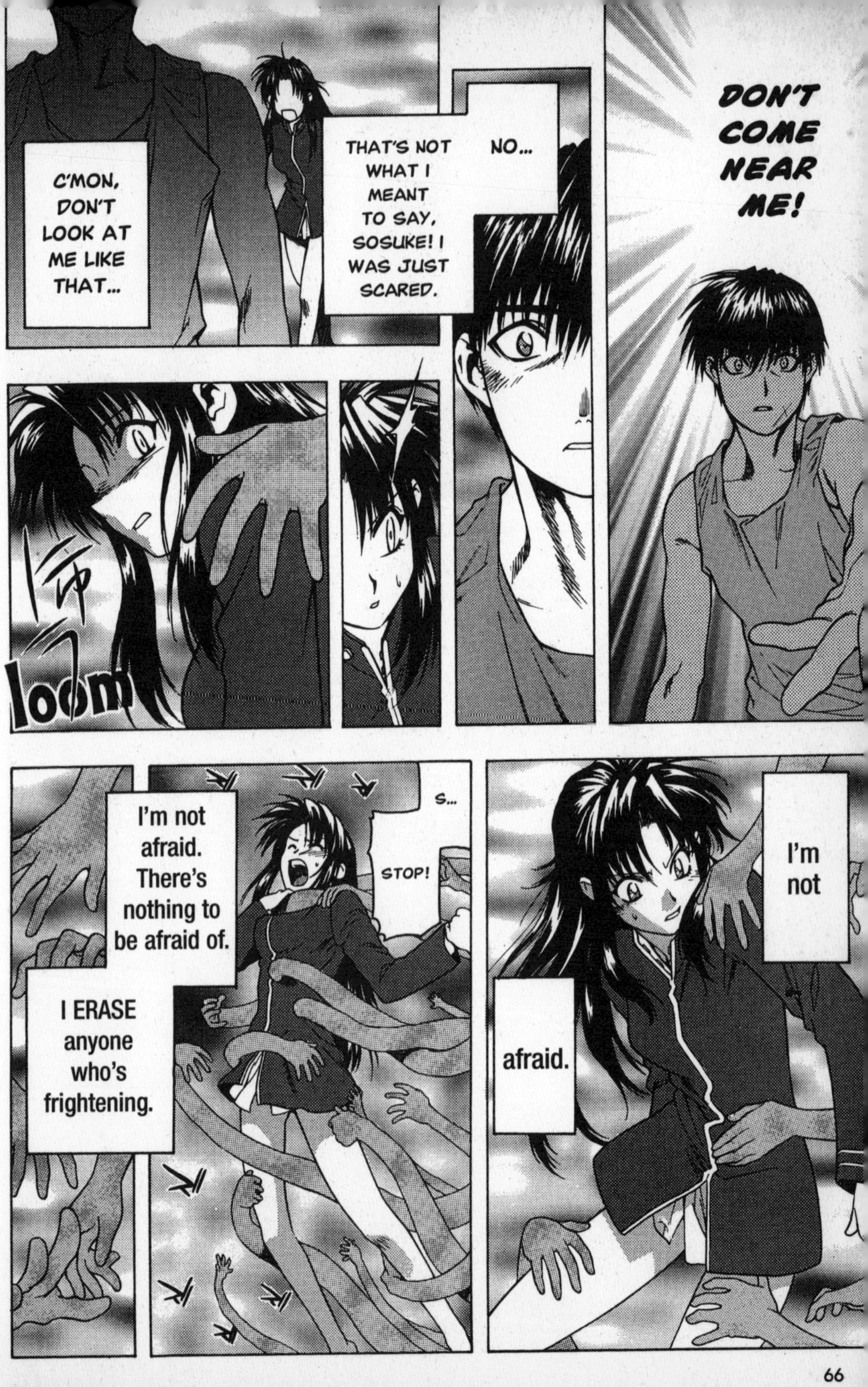
DON'T COME NEAR ME!
NO...
THAT'S NOT WHAT I MEANT TO SAY, SOSUKE! I WAS JUST SCARED.
C'MON, DON'T LOOK AT ME LIKE THAT...
loom
I'm not
afraid.
S...
STOP!
I'm not afraid. There's nothing to be afraid of.
I ERASE anyone who's frightening.

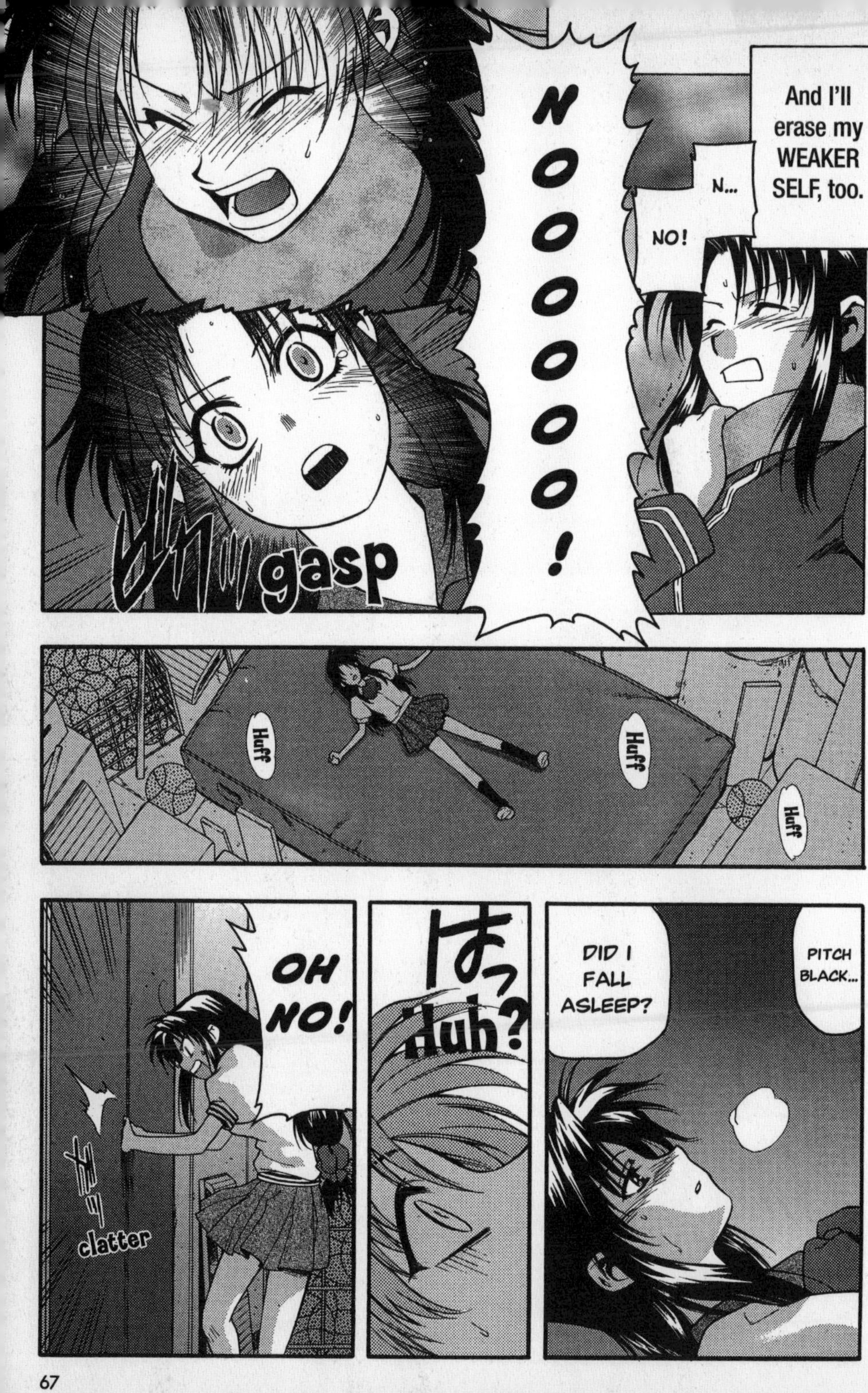
And I'll erase my WEAKER SELF, too.
N...
NO!
NOOOOOOO!
gasp
Huff
Huff
Huff
PITCH BLACK...
DID I FALL ASLEEP?
はっ
Huh?
OH NO!
clatter

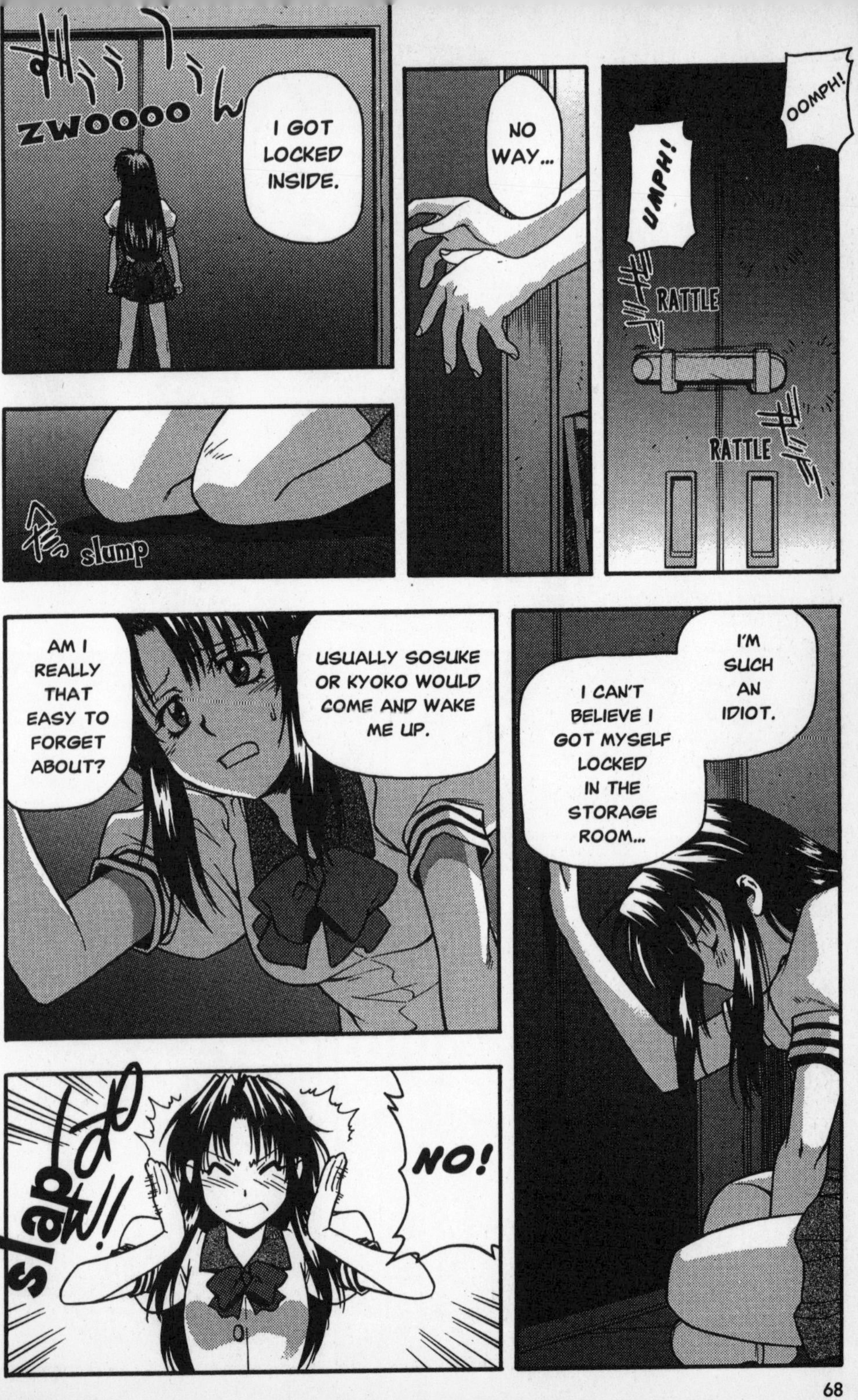
OOMPH!
UMPH!
RATTLE
RATTLE
NO WAY...
ZWOOOO
I GOT LOCKED INSIDE.
slump
I'M SUCH AN IDIOT.
I CAN'T BELIEVE I GOT MYSELF LOCKED IN THE STORAGE ROOM...
USUALLY SOSUKE OR KYOKO WOULD COME AND WAKE ME UP.
AM I REALLY THAT EASY TO FORGET ABOUT?
NO!
slap!!

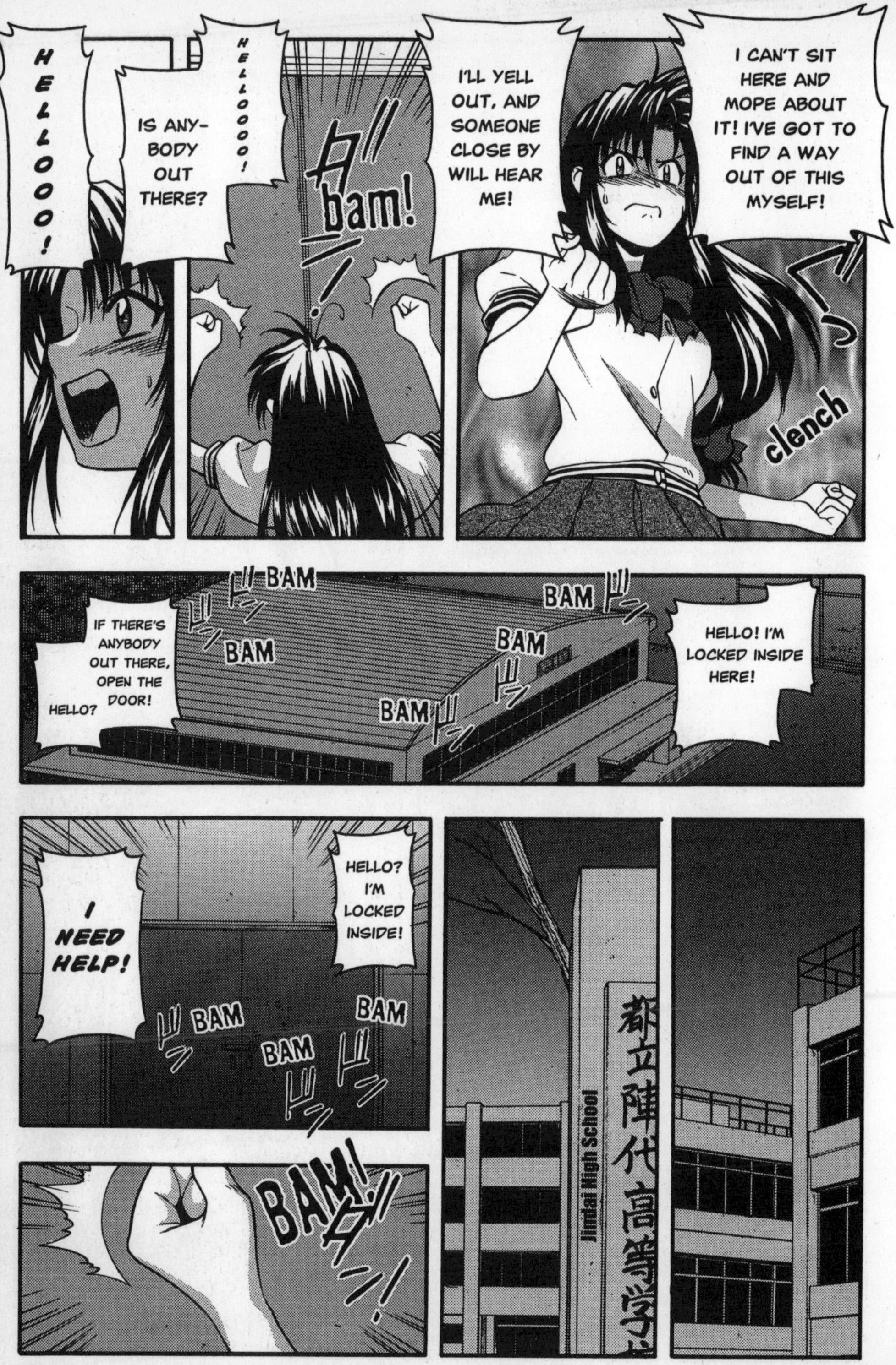
I CAN'T SIT HERE AND MOPE ABOUT IT! I'VE GOT TO FIND A WAY OUT OF THIS MYSELF!
clench
I'LL YELL OUT, AND SOMEONE CLOSE BY WILL HEAR ME!
bam!
HELLOOOO!
IS ANY-BODY OUT THERE?
HELLOOOO!
HELLO! I'M LOCKED INSIDE HERE!
BAM
BAM
BAM
BAM
BAM
IF THERE'S ANYBODY OUT THERE, OPEN THE DOOR!
HELLO?
都立陣代高等学
Jindai High School
HELLO? I'M LOCKED INSIDE!
I NEED HELP!
BAM
BAM
BAM
BAM!

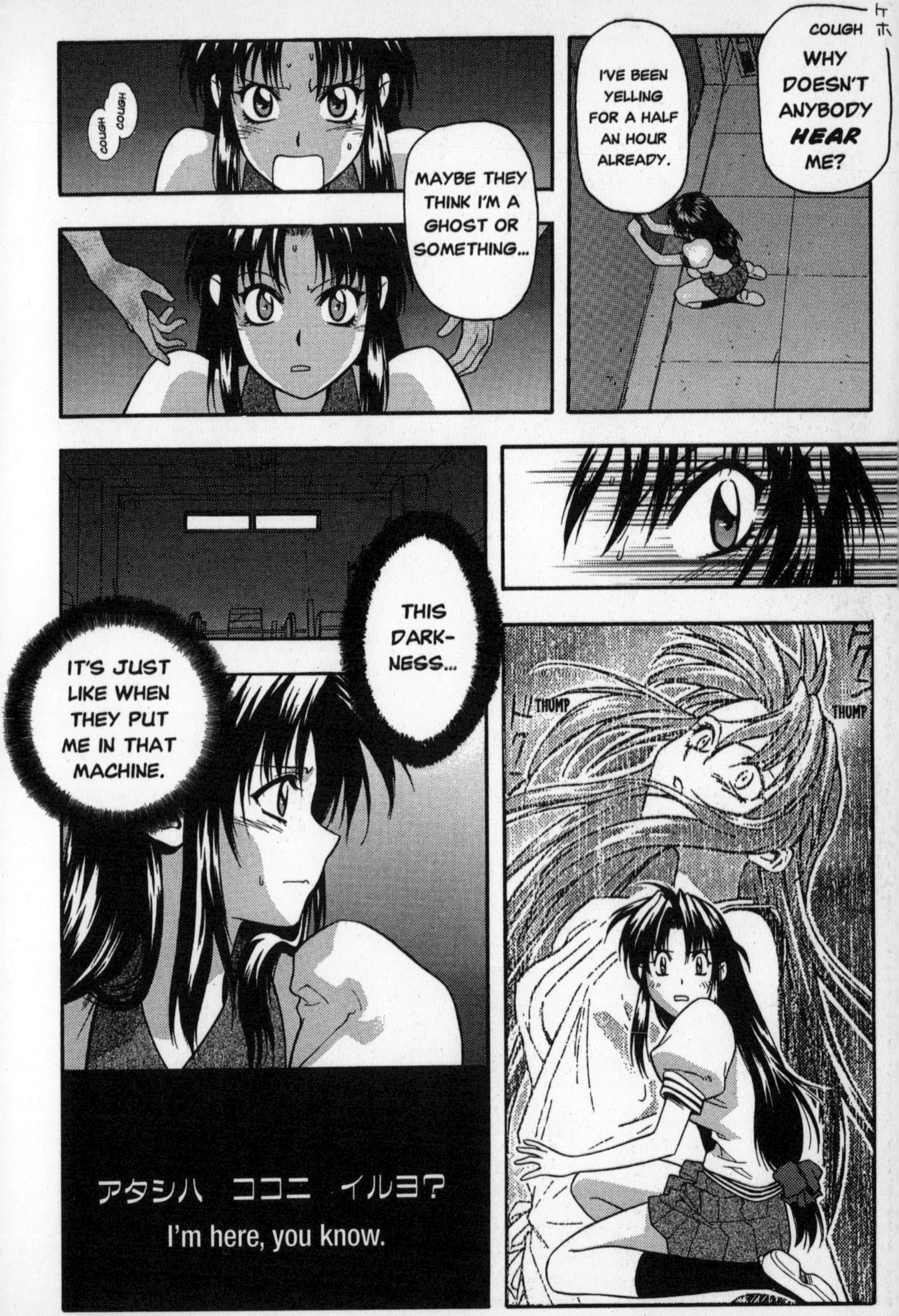
ケホ
COUGH
WHY DOESN'T ANYBODY HEAR ME?
I'VE BEEN YELLING FOR A HALF AN HOUR ALREADY.
COUGH COUGH
MAYBE THEY THINK I'M A GHOST OR SOMETHING...
THUMP
THUMP
THIS DARK-NESS...
IT'S JUST LIKE WHEN THEY PUT ME IN THAT MACHINE.
アタシハ　ココニ　イルヨ?
I'm here, you know.

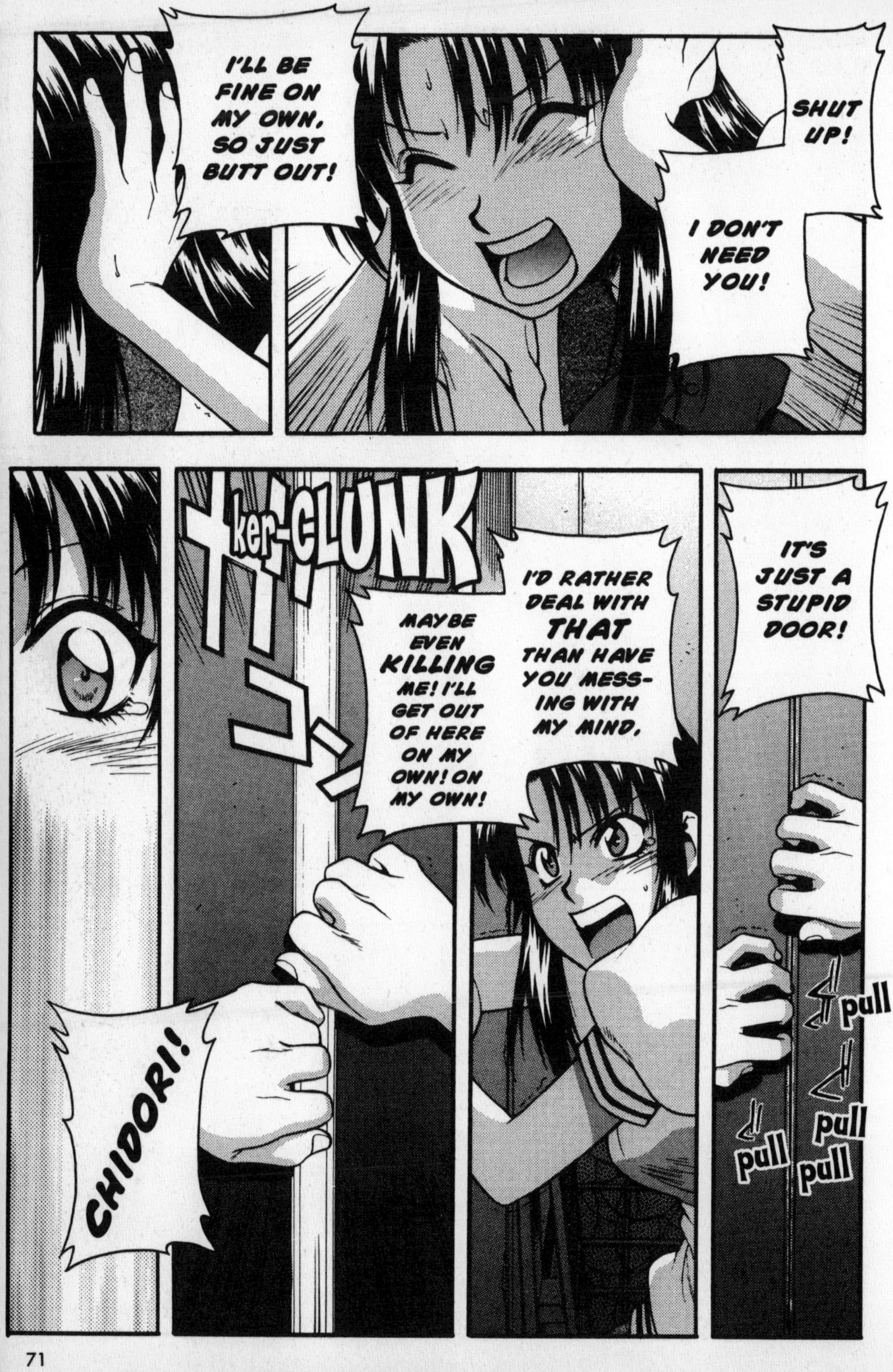
SHUT UP!
I DON'T NEED YOU!
I'LL BE FINE ON MY OWN, SO JUST BUTT OUT!
IT'S JUST A STUPID DOOR!
pull
pull
pull
pull
ker-CLUNK
I'D RATHER DEAL WITH THAT THAN HAVE YOU MESSING WITH MY MIND,
MAYBE EVEN KILLING ME! I'LL GET OUT OF HERE ON MY OWN! ON MY OWN!
CHIDORI!

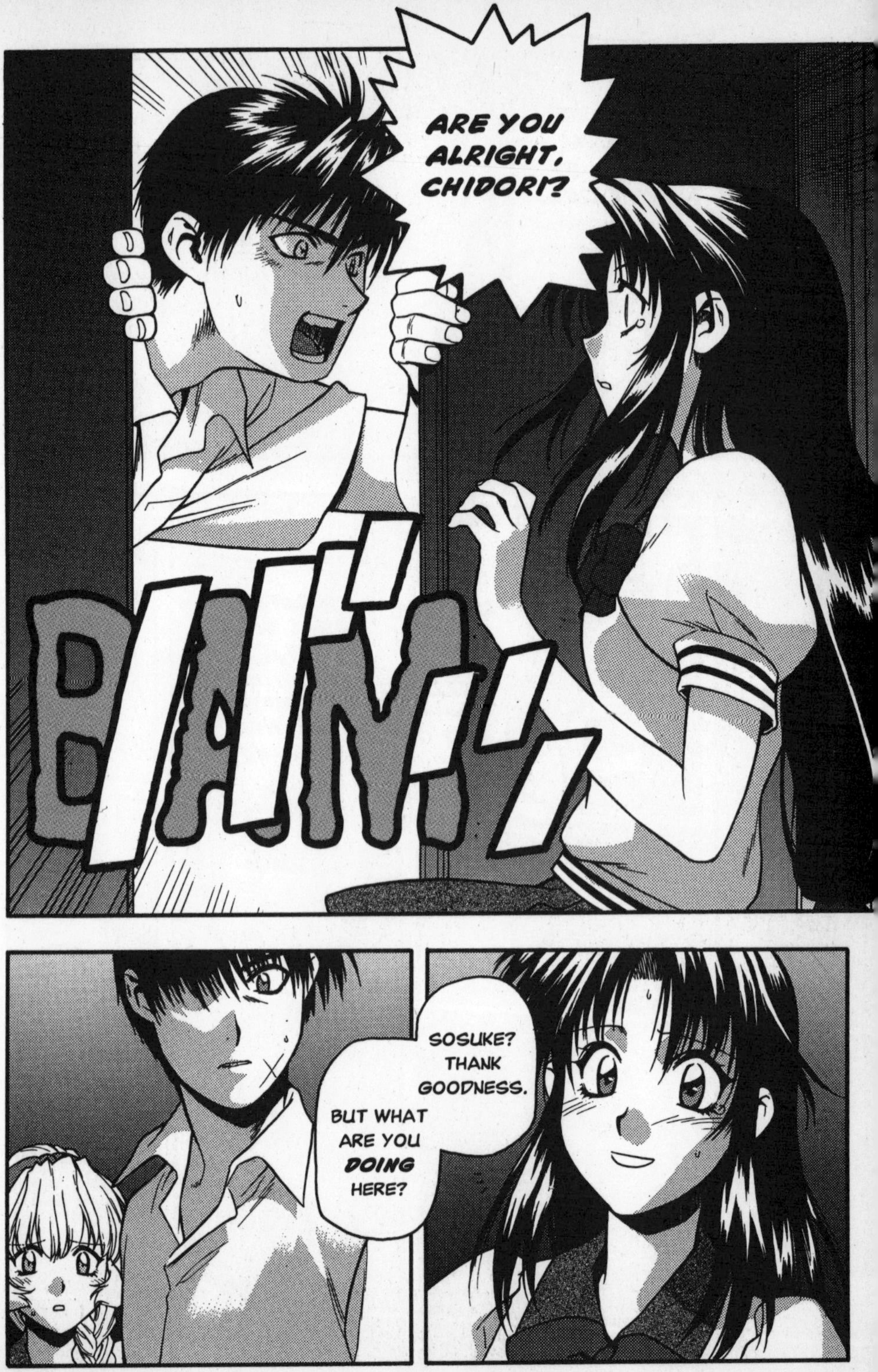
ARE YOU ALRIGHT, CHIDORI!?
BAM!!
SOSUKE? THANK GOODNESS.
BUT WHAT ARE YOU **DOING** HERE?

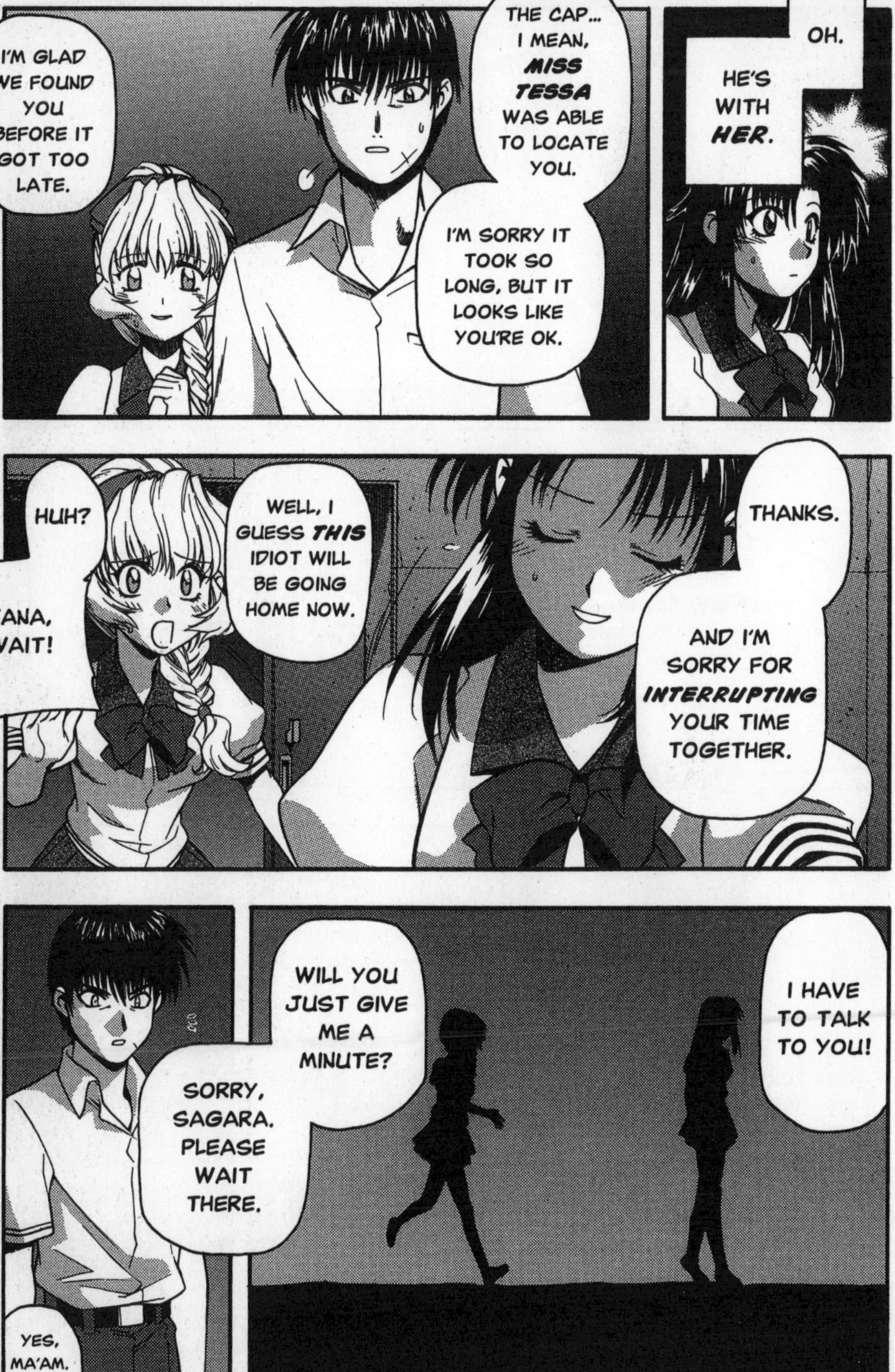
OH.
HE'S WITH HER.
THE CAP... I MEAN, MISS TESSA WAS ABLE TO LOCATE YOU.
I'M SORRY IT TOOK SO LONG, BUT IT LOOKS LIKE YOU'RE OK.
I'M GLAD WE FOUND YOU BEFORE IT GOT TOO LATE.
THANKS.
AND I'M SORRY FOR INTERRUPTING YOUR TIME TOGETHER.
WELL, I GUESS THIS IDIOT WILL BE GOING HOME NOW.
HUH?
KANA, WAIT!
I HAVE TO TALK TO YOU!
WILL YOU JUST GIVE ME A MINUTE?
SORRY, SAGARA. PLEASE WAIT THERE.
YES, MA'AM.

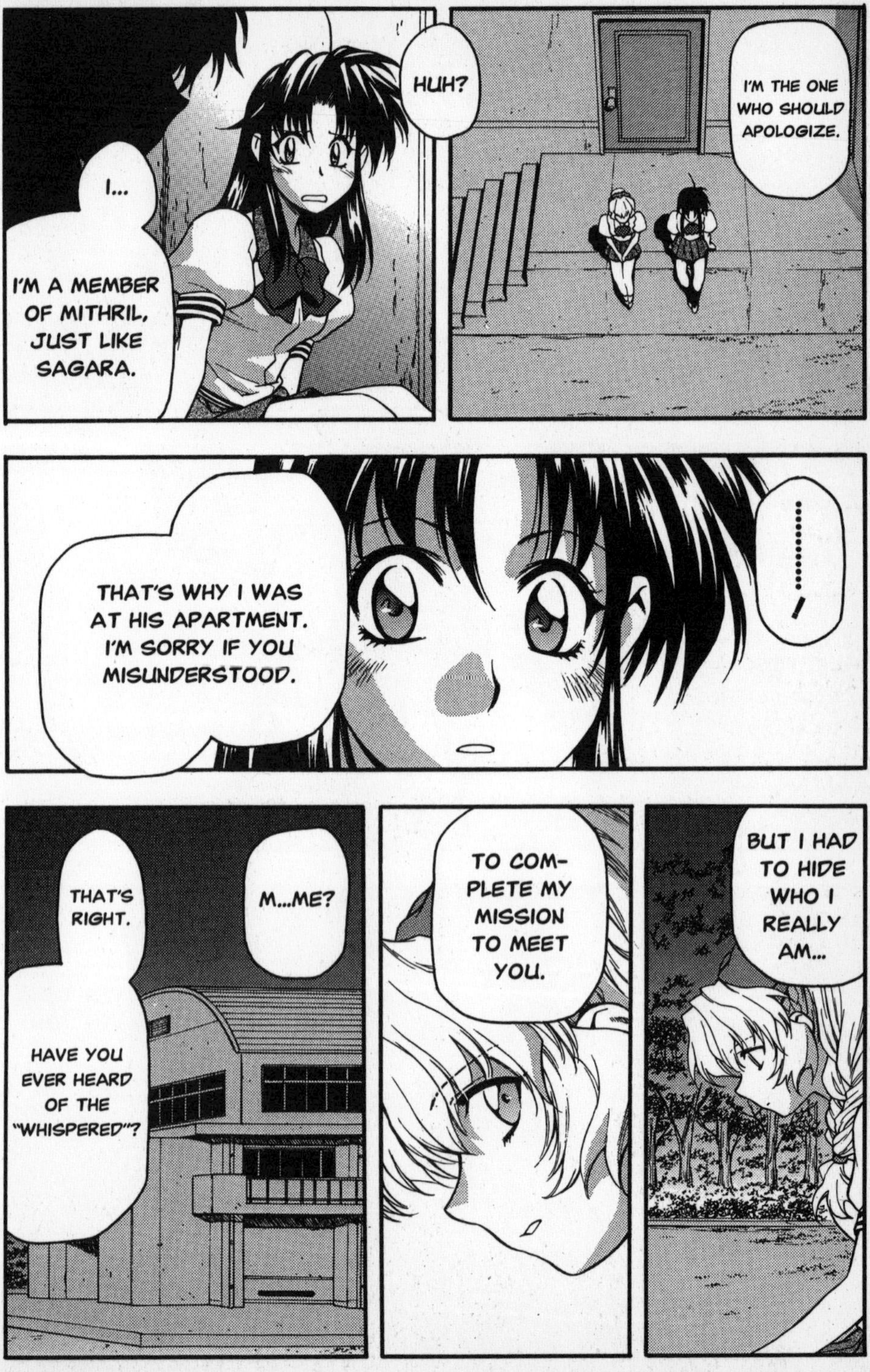
I'M THE ONE WHO SHOULD APOLOGIZE.
HUH?
I...
I'M A MEMBER OF MITHRIL, JUST LIKE SAGARA.
......!
THAT'S WHY I WAS AT HIS APARTMENT. I'M SORRY IF YOU MISUNDERSTOOD.
BUT I HAD TO HIDE WHO I REALLY AM...
TO COM-PLETE MY MISSION TO MEET YOU.
M...ME?
THAT'S RIGHT.
HAVE YOU EVER HEARD OF THE "WHISPERED"?

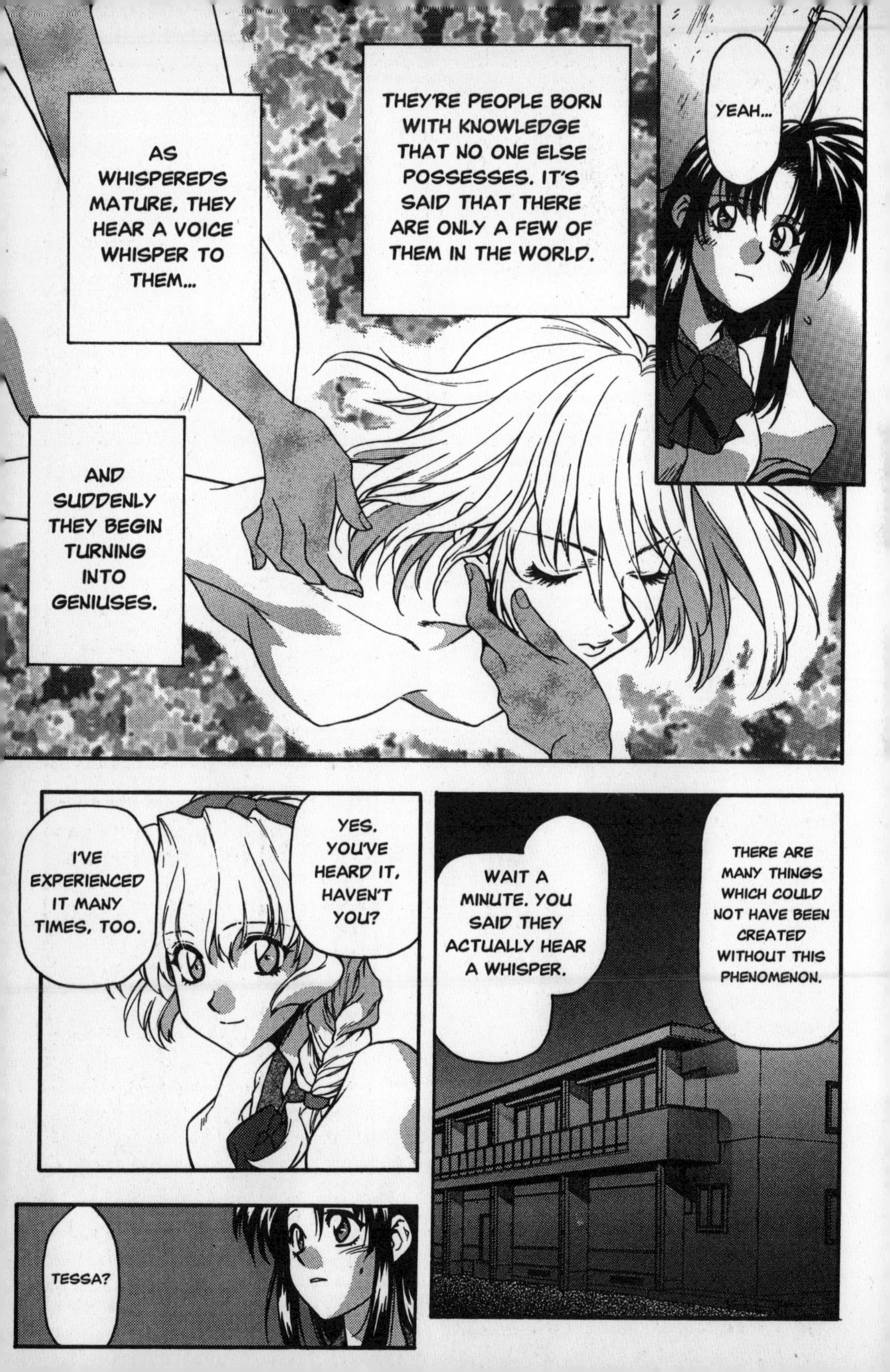
YEAH...
THEY'RE PEOPLE BORN WITH KNOWLEDGE THAT NO ONE ELSE POSSESSES. IT'S SAID THAT THERE ARE ONLY A FEW OF THEM IN THE WORLD.
AS WHISPEREDS MATURE, THEY HEAR A VOICE WHISPER TO THEM...
AND SUDDENLY THEY BEGIN TURNING INTO GENIUSES.
THERE ARE MANY THINGS WHICH COULD NOT HAVE BEEN CREATED WITHOUT THIS PHENOMENON.
WAIT A MINUTE. YOU SAID THEY ACTUALLY HEAR A WHISPER.
YES. YOU'VE HEARD IT, HAVEN'T YOU?
I'VE EXPERIENCED IT MANY TIMES, TOO.
TESSA?

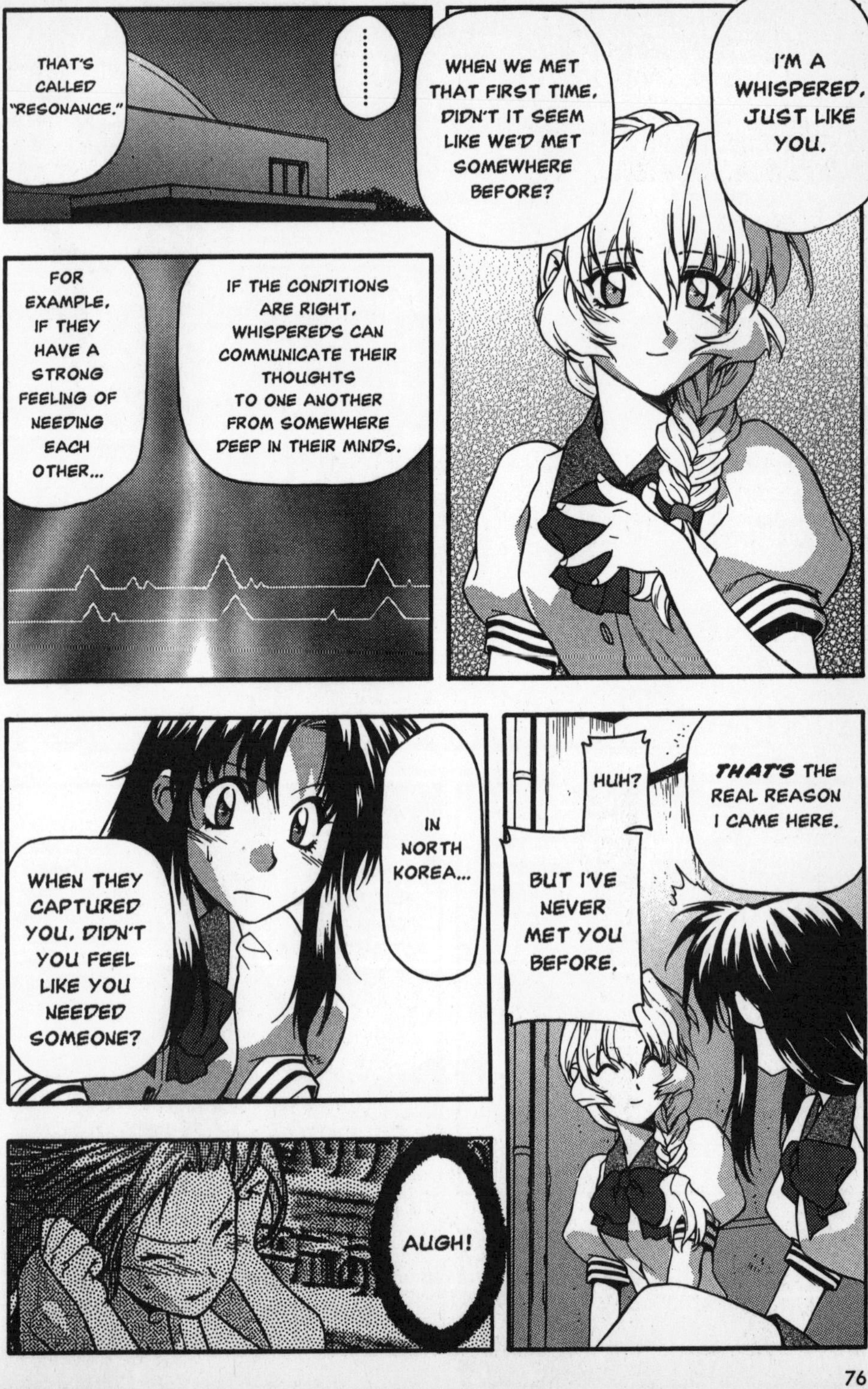

I'M A WHISPERED, JUST LIKE YOU.
WHEN WE MET THAT FIRST TIME, DIDN'T IT SEEM LIKE WE'D MET SOMEWHERE BEFORE?
......
THAT'S CALLED "RESONANCE."
IF THE CONDITIONS ARE RIGHT, WHISPEREDS CAN COMMUNICATE THEIR THOUGHTS TO ONE ANOTHER FROM SOMEWHERE DEEP IN THEIR MINDS.
FOR EXAMPLE, IF THEY HAVE A STRONG FEELING OF NEEDING EACH OTHER...
THAT'S THE REAL REASON I CAME HERE.
HUH?
BUT I'VE NEVER MET YOU BEFORE.
IN NORTH KOREA...
WHEN THEY CAPTURED YOU, DIDN'T YOU FEEL LIKE YOU NEEDED SOMEONE?
AUGH!

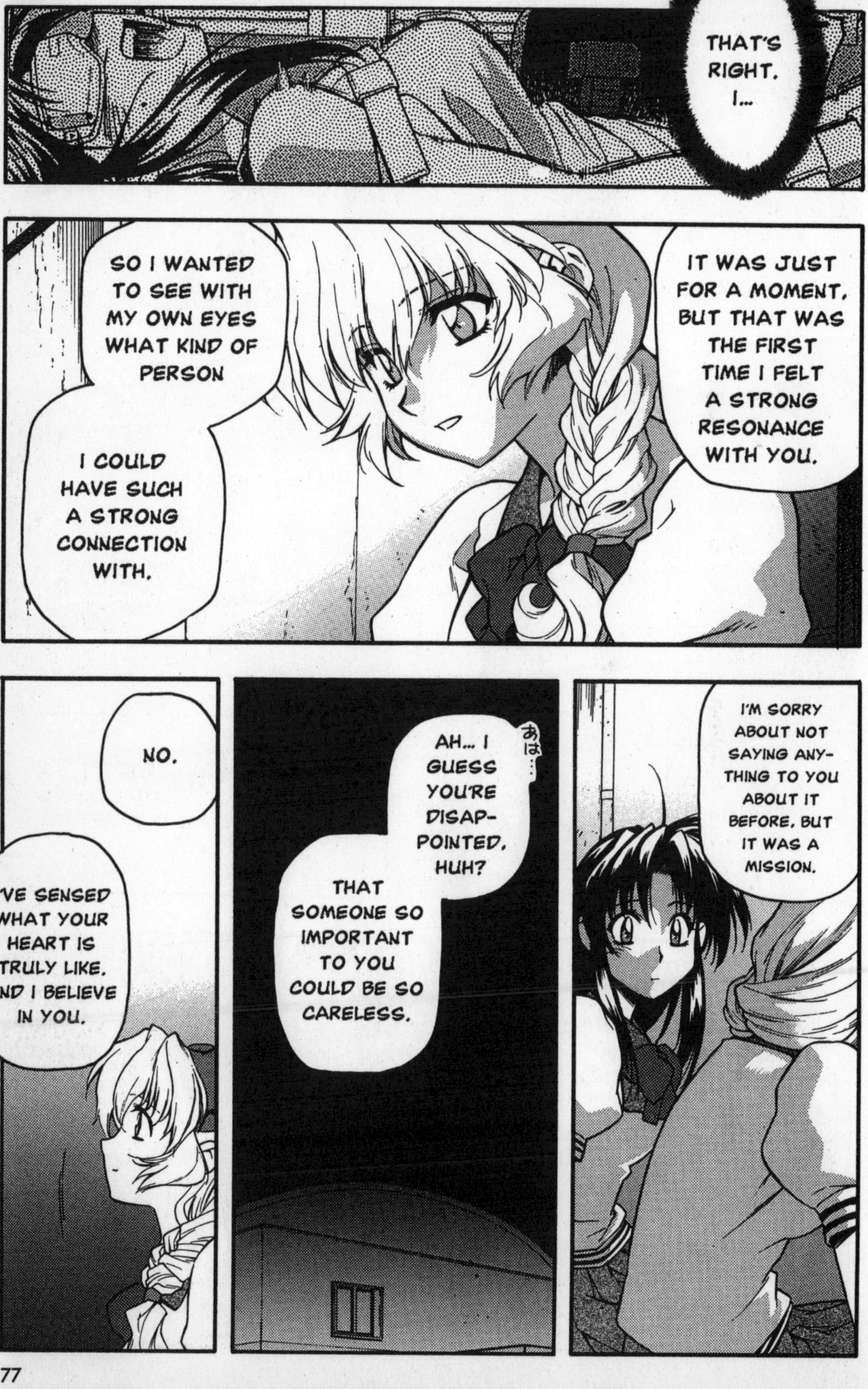
THAT'S RIGHT. I...
IT WAS JUST FOR A MOMENT, BUT THAT WAS THE FIRST TIME I FELT A STRONG RESONANCE WITH YOU.
SO I WANTED TO SEE WITH MY OWN EYES WHAT KIND OF PERSON
I COULD HAVE SUCH A STRONG CONNECTION WITH.
I'M SORRY ABOUT NOT SAYING ANY-THING TO YOU ABOUT IT BEFORE, BUT IT WAS A MISSION.
あは…
AH... I GUESS YOU'RE DISAP-POINTED, HUH?
THAT SOMEONE SO IMPORTANT TO YOU COULD BE SO CARELESS.
NO.
I'VE SENSED WHAT YOUR HEART IS TRULY LIKE. AND I BELIEVE IN YOU.

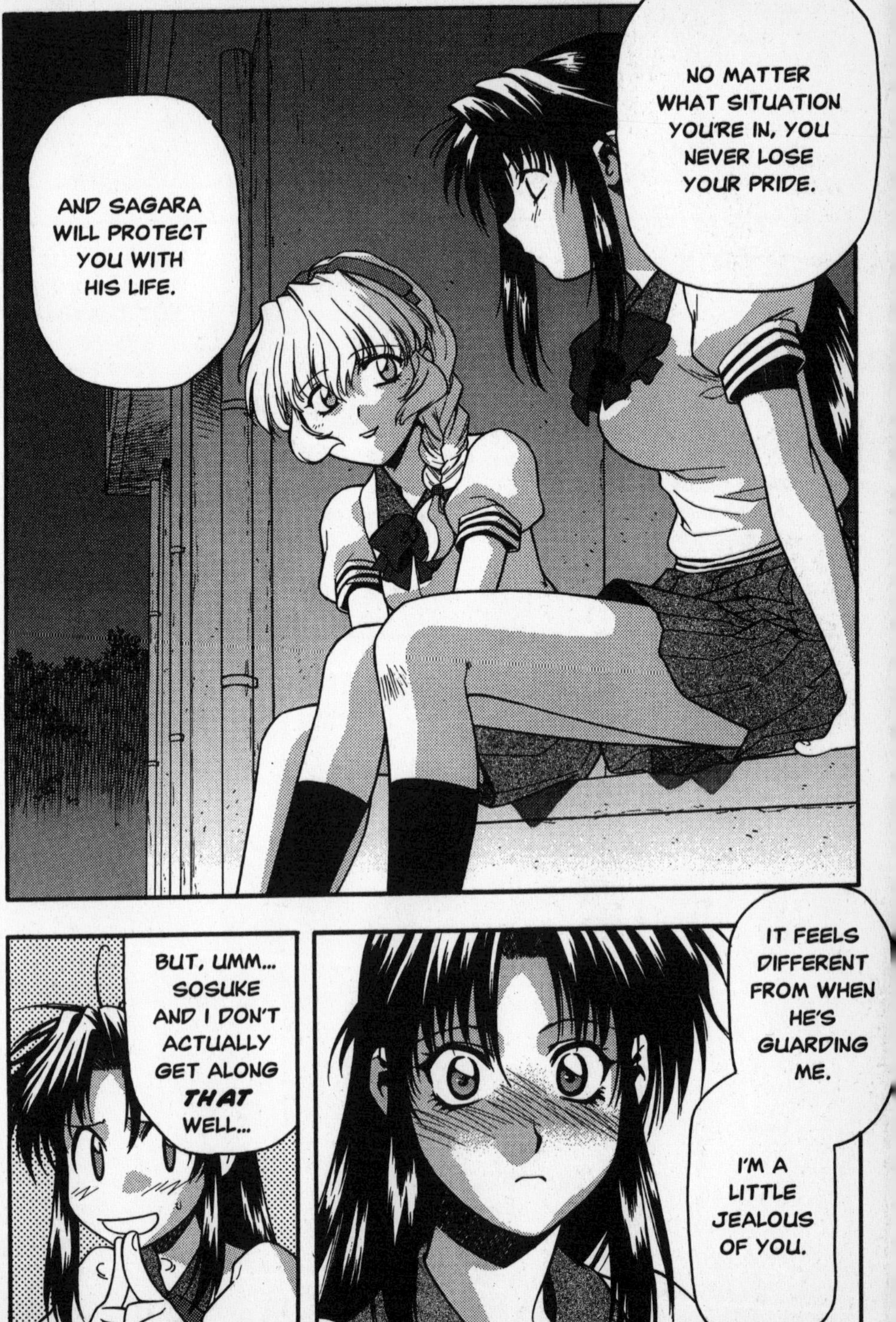
NO MATTER WHAT SITUATION YOU'RE IN, YOU NEVER LOSE YOUR PRIDE.
AND SAGARA WILL PROTECT YOU WITH HIS LIFE.
IT FEELS DIFFERENT FROM WHEN HE'S GUARDING ME.
I'M A LITTLE JEALOUS OF YOU.
BUT, UMM... SOSUKE AND I DON'T ACTUALLY GET ALONG *THAT* WELL...

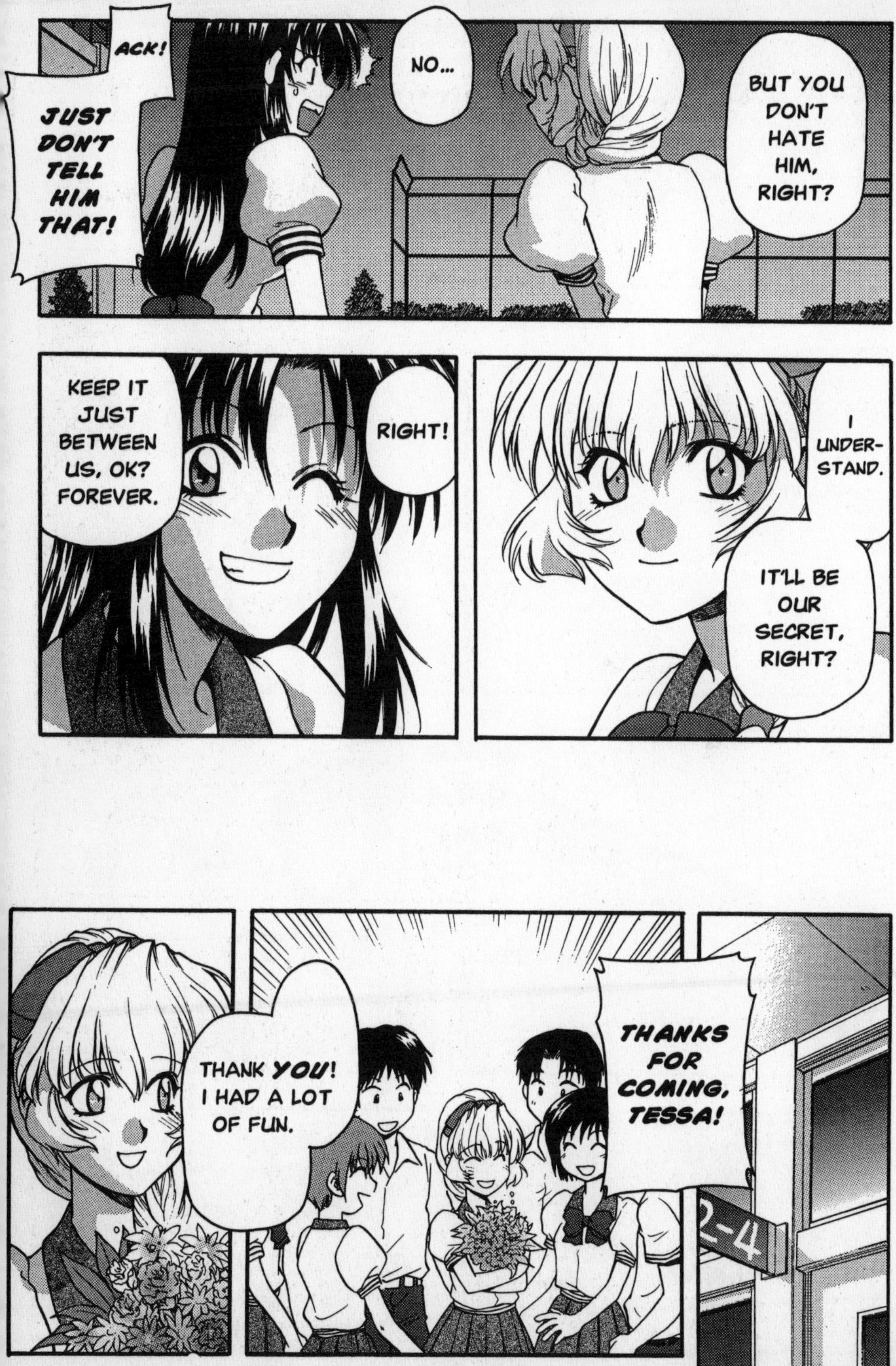

BUT YOU DON'T HATE HIM, RIGHT?
NO...
ACK!
JUST DON'T TELL HIM THAT!
I UNDERSTAND.
IT'LL BE OUR SECRET, RIGHT?
RIGHT!
KEEP IT JUST BETWEEN US, OK? FOREVER.
THANKS FOR COMING, TESSA!
THANK YOU! I HAD A LOT OF FUN.

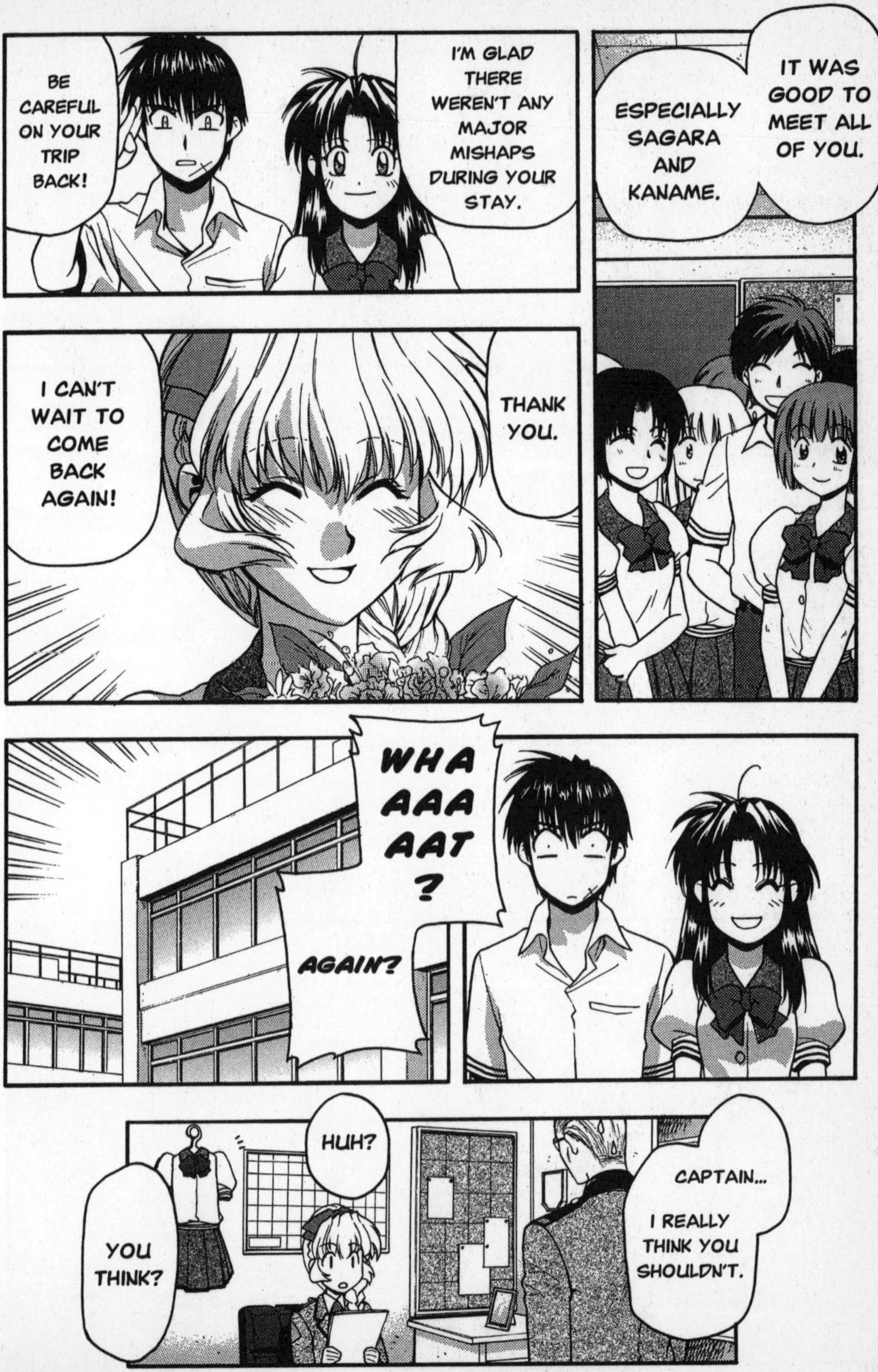
IT WAS GOOD TO MEET ALL OF YOU.
ESPECIALLY SAGARA AND KANAME.
I'M GLAD THERE WEREN'T ANY MAJOR MISHAPS DURING YOUR STAY.
BE CAREFUL ON YOUR TRIP BACK!
THANK YOU.
I CAN'T WAIT TO COME BACK AGAIN!
WHA AAA AAT ?
AGAIN?
CAPTAIN...
I REALLY THINK YOU SHOULDN'T.
HUH?
YOU THINK?

MISSION:18 The Miracle Animal Mission!!

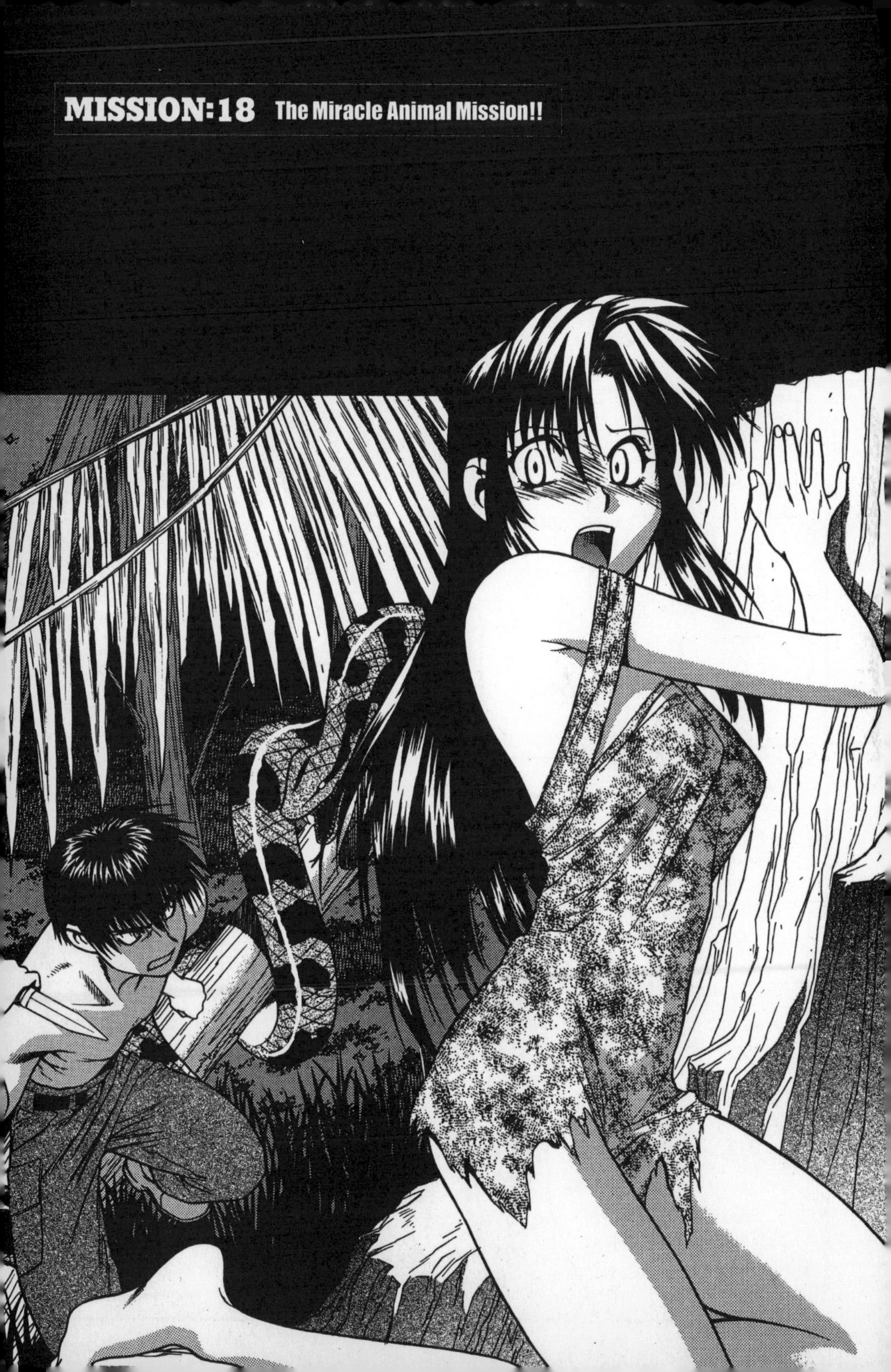

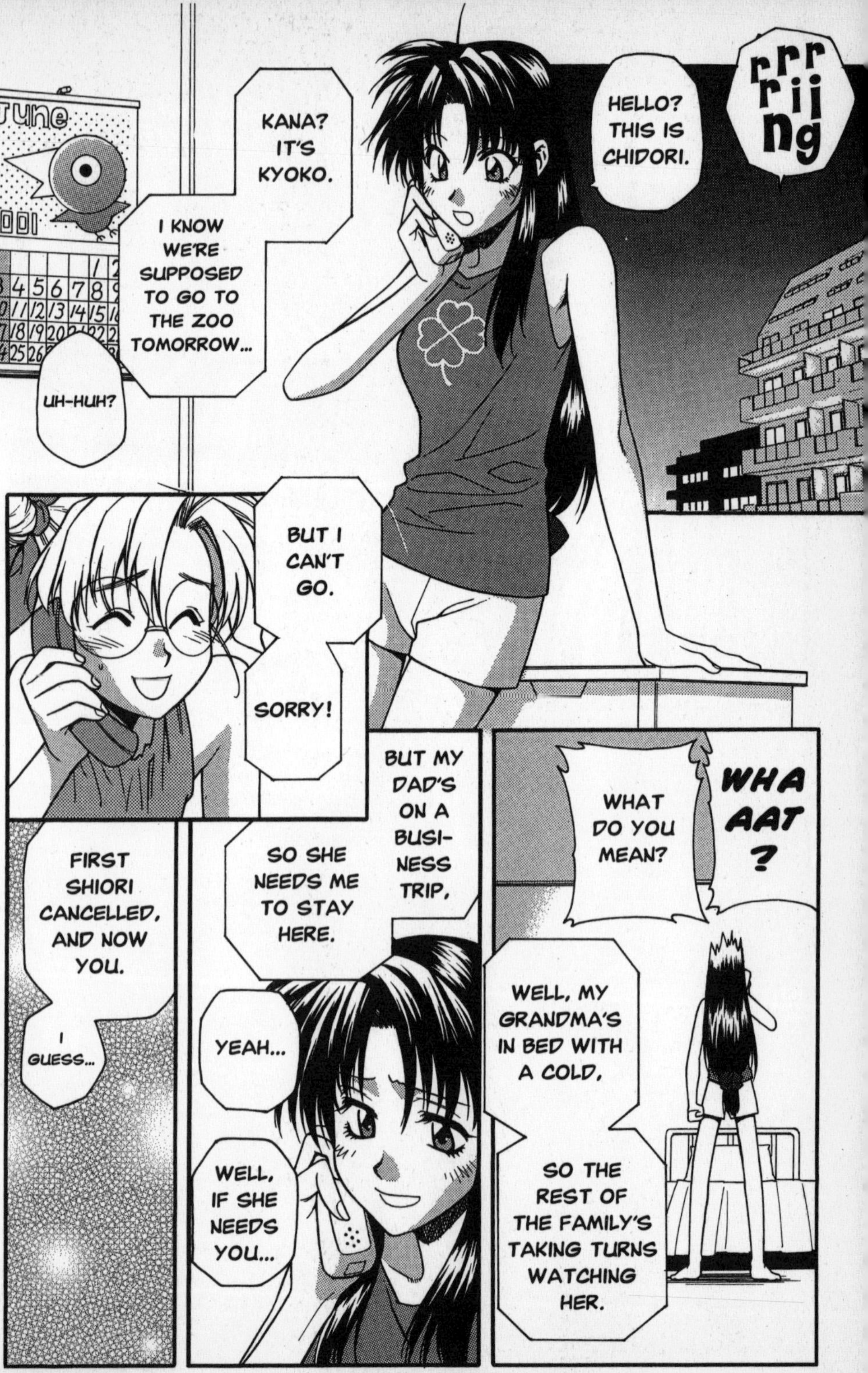
rrrrijng
HELLO? THIS IS CHIDORI.
KANA? IT'S KYOKO.
I KNOW WE'RE SUPPOSED TO GO TO THE ZOO TOMORROW...
UH-HUH?
BUT I CAN'T GO.
SORRY!
WHAAAT?
WHAT DO YOU MEAN?
WELL, MY GRANDMA'S IN BED WITH A COLD,
SO THE REST OF THE FAMILY'S TAKING TURNS WATCHING HER.
BUT MY DAD'S ON A BUSINESS TRIP,
SO SHE NEEDS ME TO STAY HERE.
YEAH...
WELL, IF SHE NEEDS YOU...
FIRST SHIORI CANCELLED, AND NOW YOU.
I GUESS...

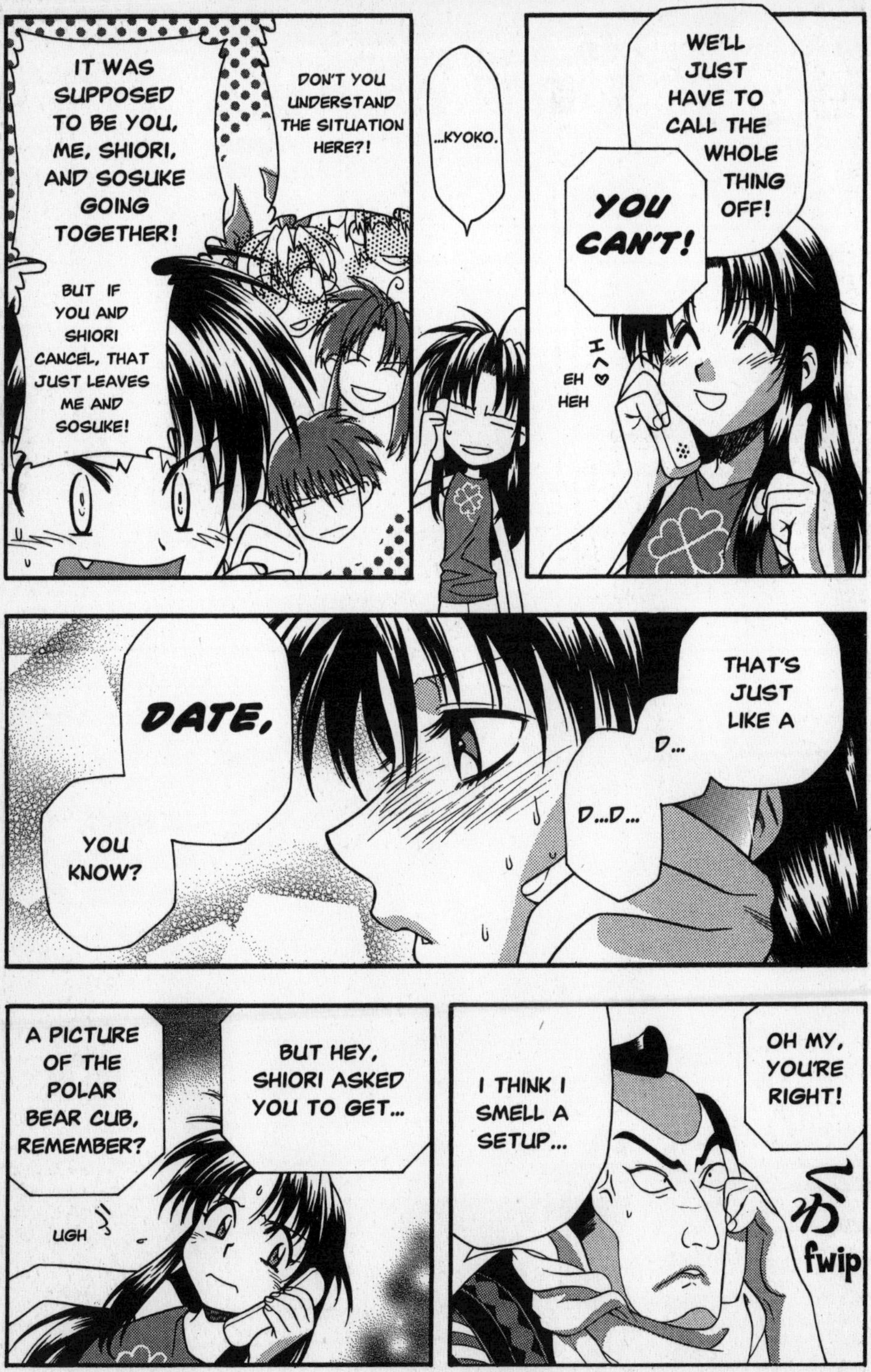

WE'LL JUST HAVE TO CALL THE WHOLE THING OFF!
YOU CAN'T!
EH HEH
...KYOKO.
DON'T YOU UNDERSTAND THE SITUATION HERE?!
IT WAS SUPPOSED TO BE YOU, ME, SHIORI, AND SOSUKE GOING TOGETHER!
BUT IF YOU AND SHIORI CANCEL, THAT JUST LEAVES ME AND SOSUKE!
THAT'S JUST LIKE A
D...
D...D...
DATE,
YOU KNOW?
OH MY, YOU'RE RIGHT!
fwip
I THINK I SMELL A SETUP...
BUT HEY, SHIORI ASKED YOU TO GET...
A PICTURE OF THE POLAR BEAR CUB, REMEMBER?
UGH

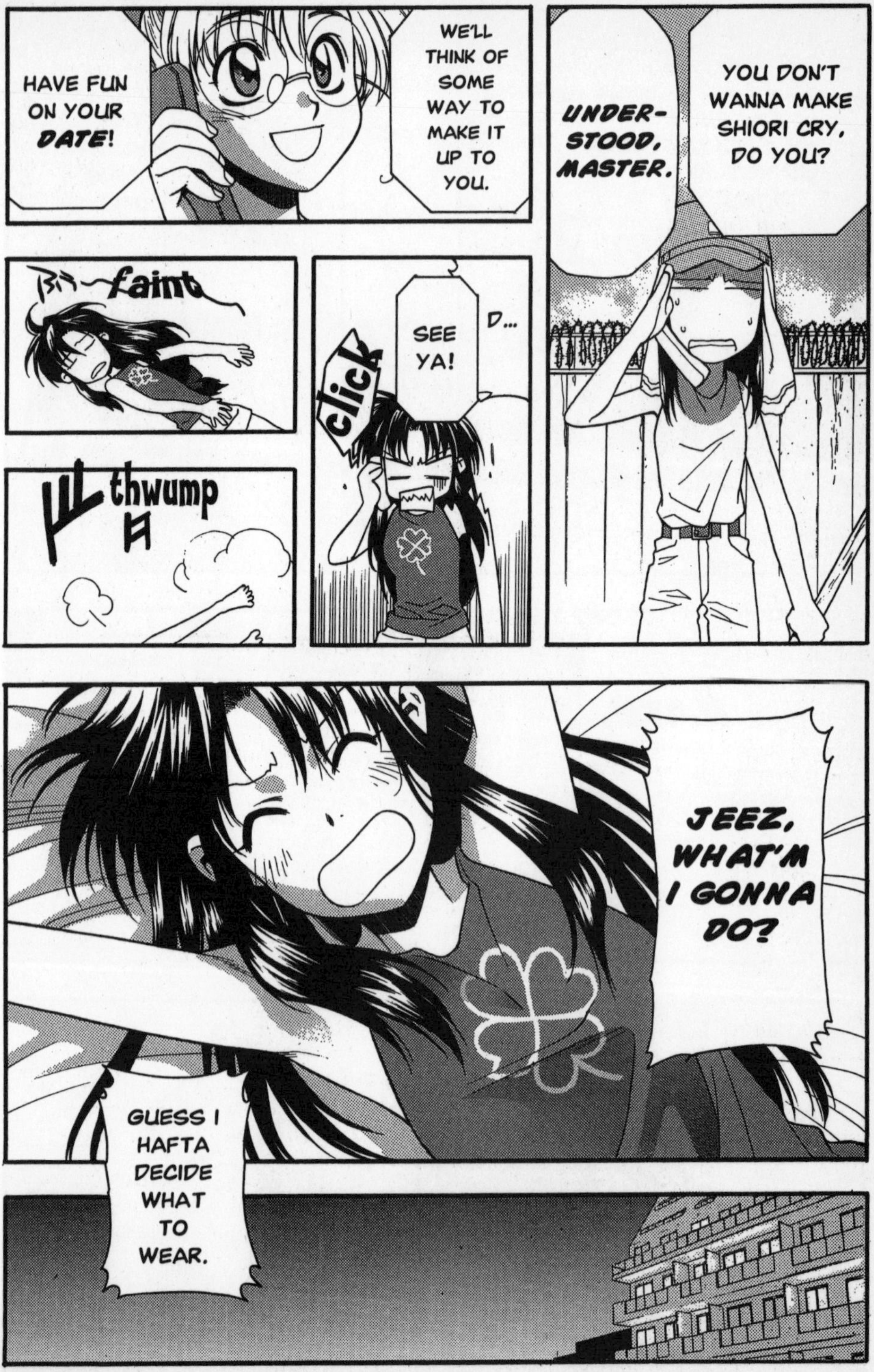
YOU DON'T WANNA MAKE SHIORI CRY, DO YOU?
UNDER-STOOD, MASTER.
WE'LL THINK OF SOME WAY TO MAKE IT UP TO YOU.
HAVE FUN ON YOUR DATE!
D...
SEE YA!
click
faint
thwump
JEEZ, WHAT'M I GONNA DO?
GUESS I HAFTA DECIDE WHAT TO WEAR.

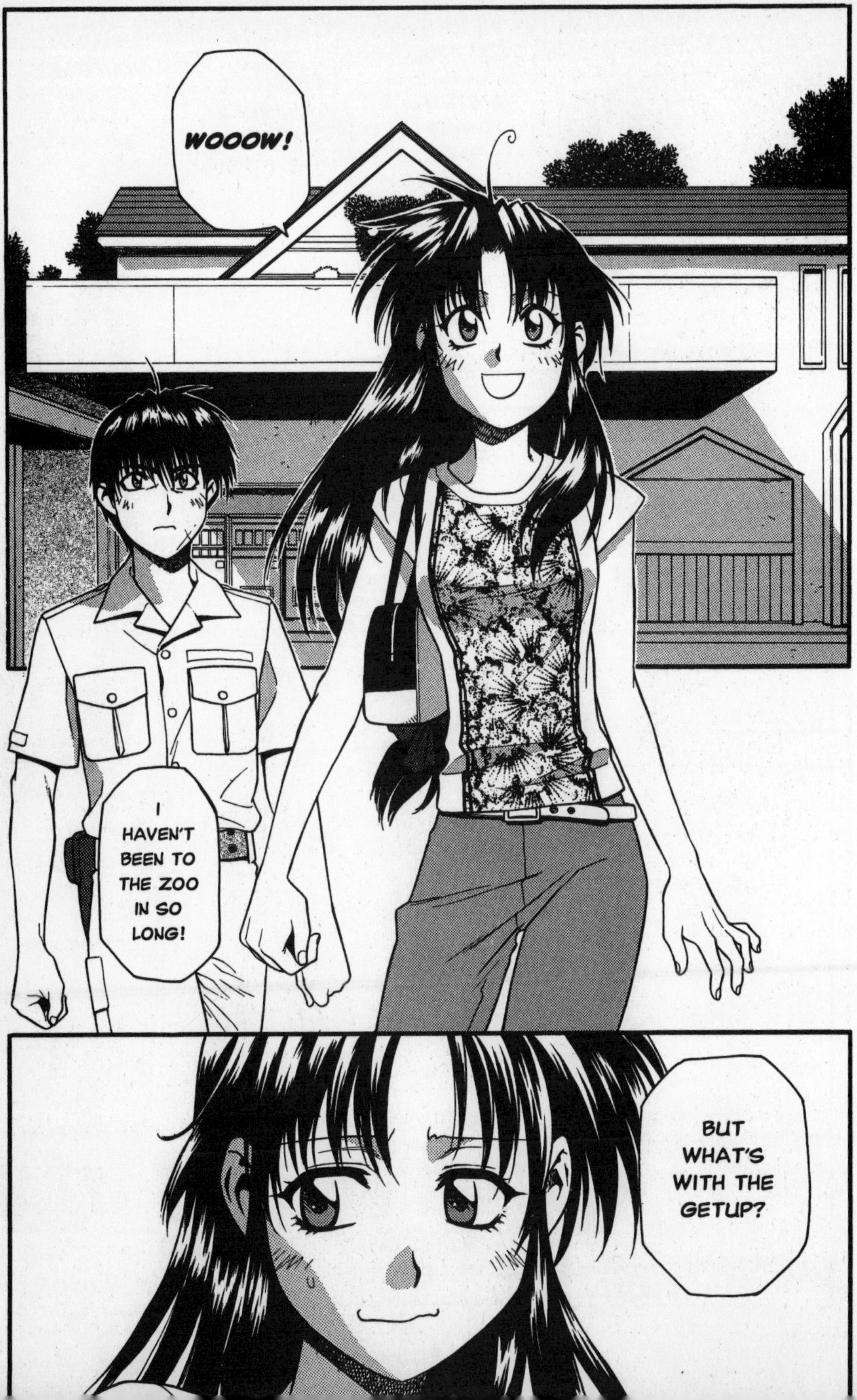
WOOOW!
I HAVEN'T BEEN TO THE ZOO IN SO LONG!
BUT WHAT'S WITH THE GETUP?

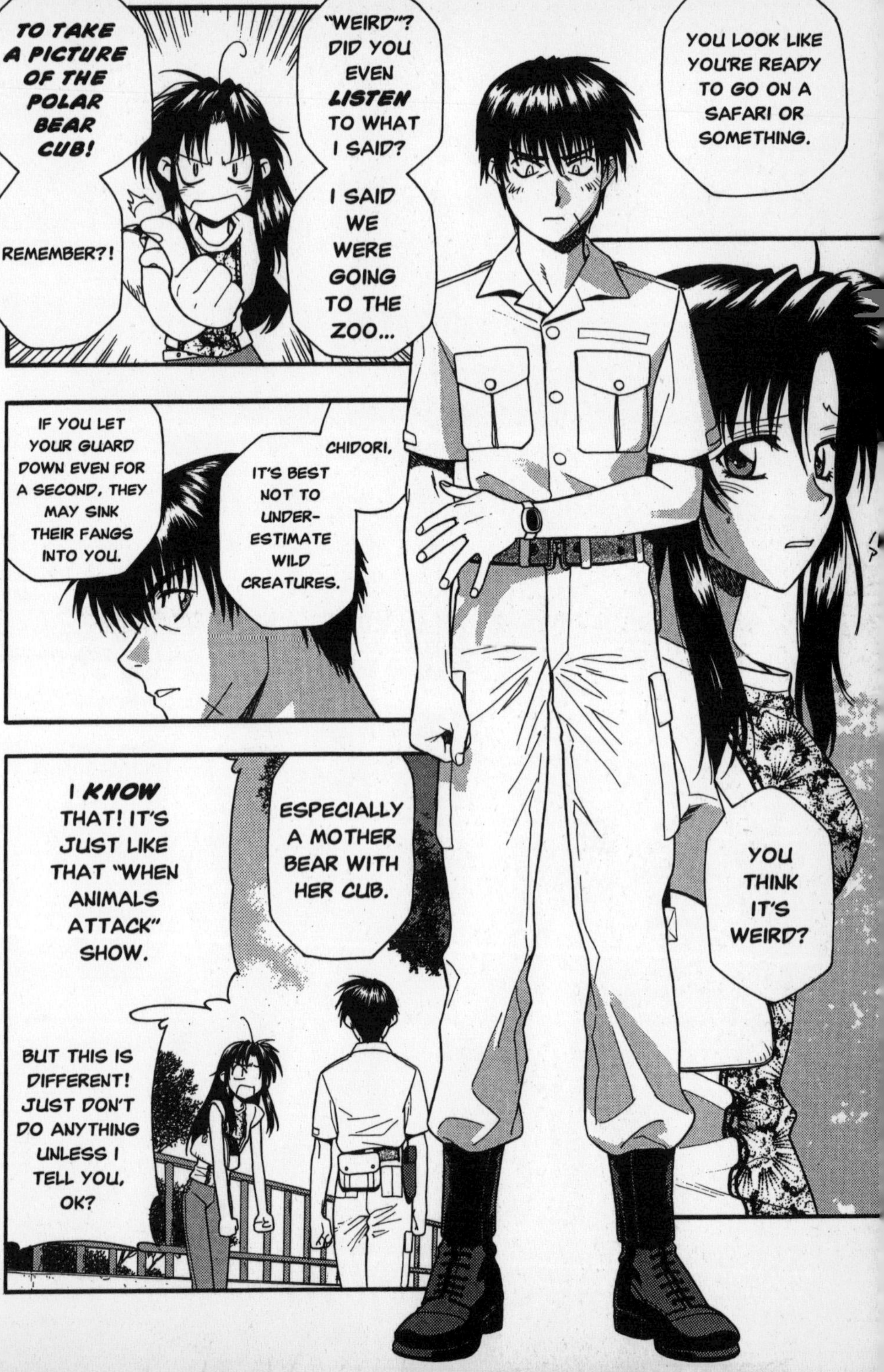
YOU LOOK LIKE YOU'RE READY TO GO ON A SAFARI OR SOMETHING.
YOU THINK IT'S WEIRD?
"WEIRD"? DID YOU EVEN LISTEN TO WHAT I SAID?
I SAID WE WERE GOING TO THE ZOO...
TO TAKE A PICTURE OF THE POLAR BEAR CUB!
REMEMBER?!
CHIDORI, IT'S BEST NOT TO UNDER-ESTIMATE WILD CREATURES.
IF YOU LET YOUR GUARD DOWN EVEN FOR A SECOND, THEY MAY SINK THEIR FANGS INTO YOU.
ESPECIALLY A MOTHER BEAR WITH HER CUB.
I KNOW THAT! IT'S JUST LIKE THAT "WHEN ANIMALS ATTACK" SHOW.
BUT THIS IS DIFFERENT! JUST DON'T DO ANYTHING UNLESS I TELL YOU, OK?

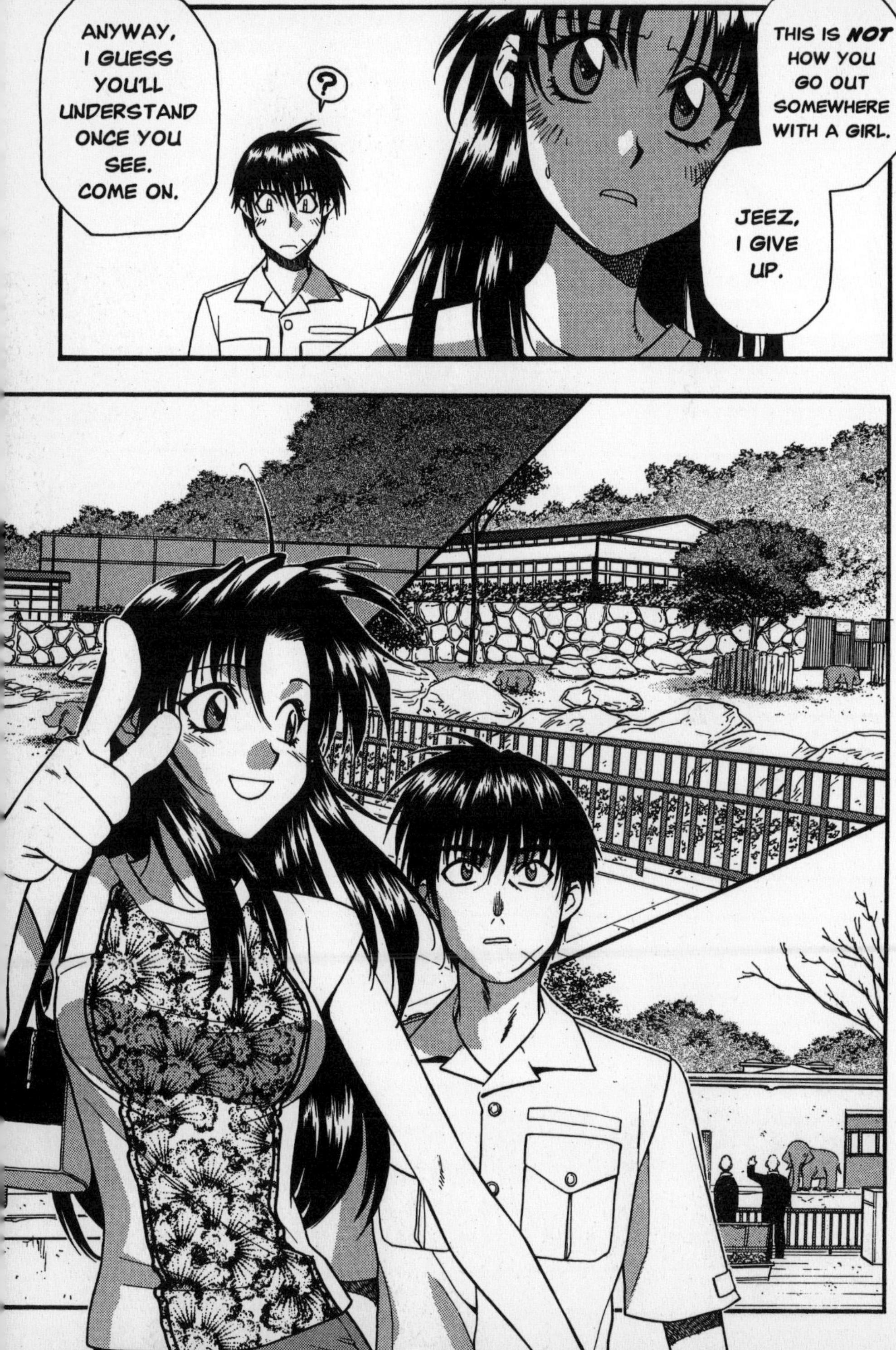
THIS IS NOT HOW YOU GO OUT SOMEWHERE WITH A GIRL.
JEEZ, I GIVE UP.
?
ANYWAY, I GUESS YOU'LL UNDERSTAND ONCE YOU SEE. COME ON.

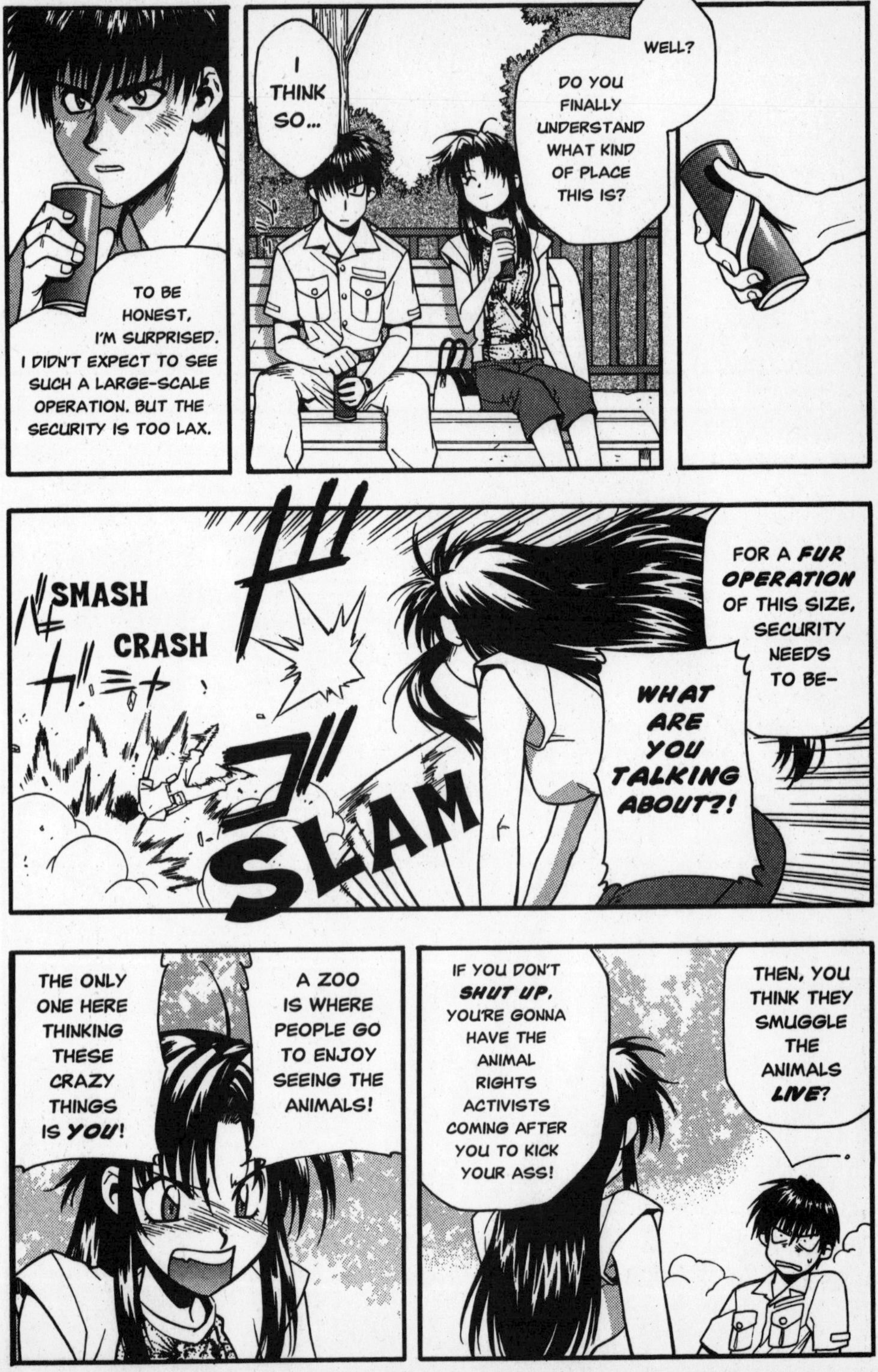
WELL?
DO YOU FINALLY UNDERSTAND WHAT KIND OF PLACE THIS IS?
I THINK SO...
TO BE HONEST, I'M SURPRISED. I DIDN'T EXPECT TO SEE SUCH A LARGE-SCALE OPERATION. BUT THE SECURITY IS TOO LAX.
FOR A *FUR OPERATION* OF THIS SIZE, SECURITY NEEDS TO BE-
WHAT ARE YOU TALKING ABOUT?!
SLAM
SMASH
CRASH
THEN, YOU THINK THEY SMUGGLE THE ANIMALS *LIVE*?
IF YOU DON'T *SHUT UP*, YOU'RE GONNA HAVE THE ANIMAL RIGHTS ACTIVISTS COMING AFTER YOU TO KICK YOUR ASS!
A ZOO IS WHERE PEOPLE GO TO ENJOY SEEING THE ANIMALS!
THE ONLY ONE HERE THINKING THESE CRAZY THINGS IS *YOU*!

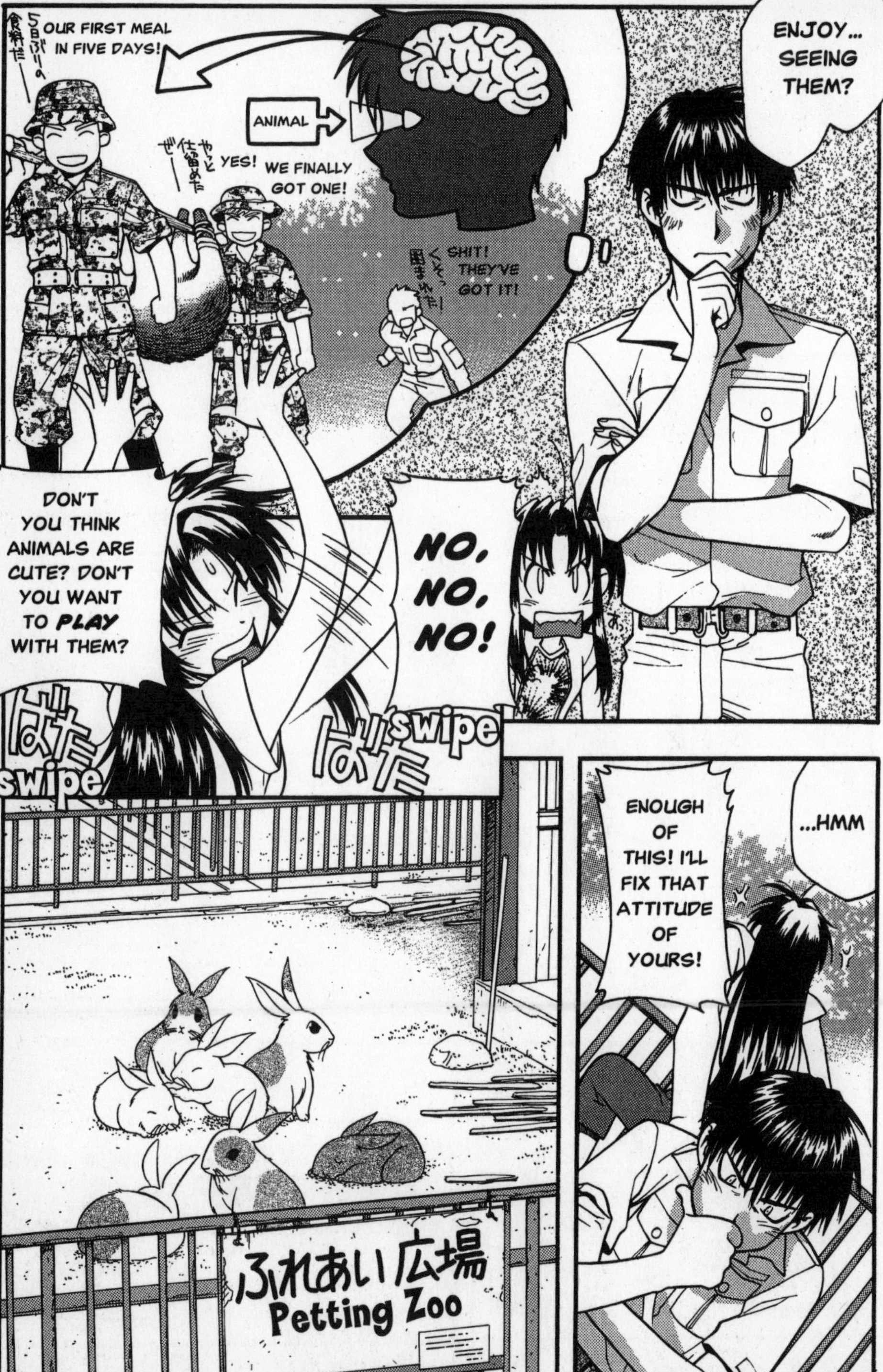
ENJOY... SEEING THEM?
5日ぶりの食料だー
OUR FIRST MEAL IN FIVE DAYS!
ANIMAL
やっと仕留めたぜー
YES! WE FINALLY GOT ONE!
くそっ 囲まれた!
SHIT! THEY'VE GOT IT!
NO, NO, NO!
DON'T YOU THINK ANIMALS ARE CUTE? DON'T YOU WANT TO PLAY WITH THEM?
ばた swipe
ばた swipe
...HMM
ENOUGH OF THIS! I'LL FIX THAT ATTITUDE OF YOURS!
ふれあい広場
Petting Zoo

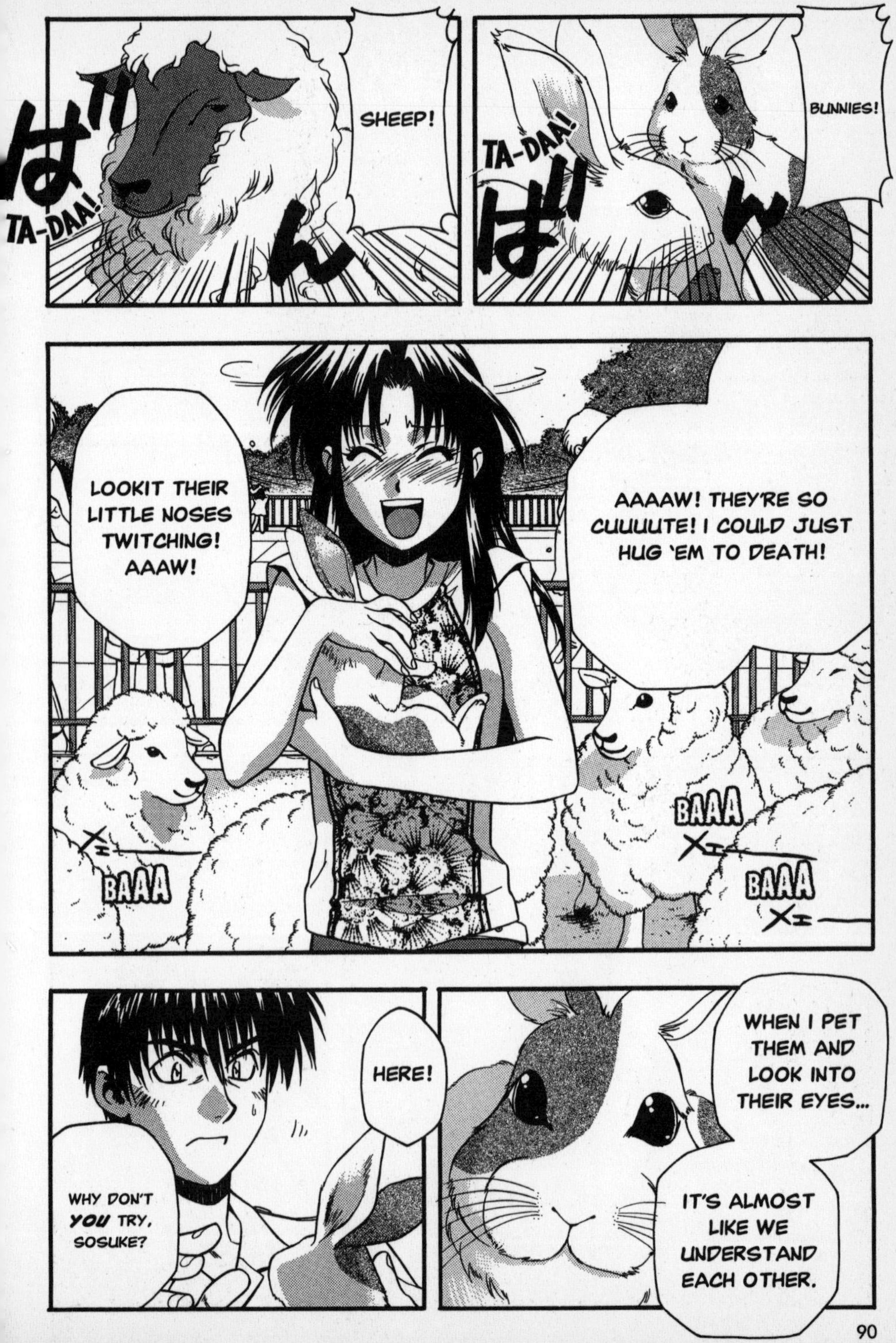
BUNNIES!
TA-DAA!
SHEEP!
TA-DAA!
AAAAW! THEY'RE SO CUUUUTE! I COULD JUST HUG 'EM TO DEATH!
LOOKIT THEIR LITTLE NOSES TWITCHING! AAAW!
BAAA
BAAA
BAAA
WHEN I PET THEM AND LOOK INTO THEIR EYES...
IT'S ALMOST LIKE WE UNDERSTAND EACH OTHER.
HERE!
WHY DON'T *YOU* TRY, SOSUKE?

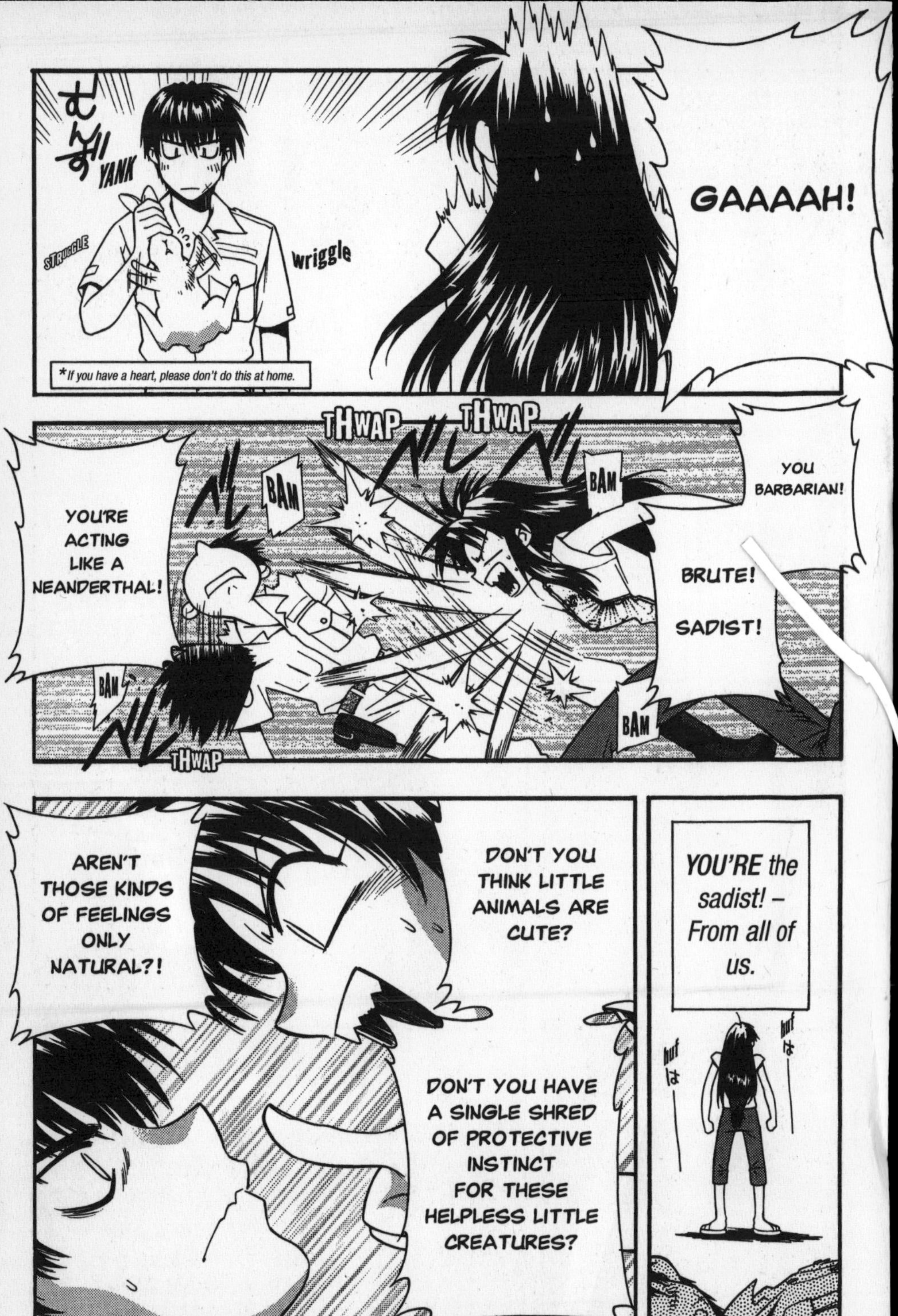
GAAAAH!
むんず YANK
STRUGGLE
wriggle
*If you have a heart, please don't do this at home.
YOU BARBARIAN!
BRUTE!
SADIST!
tHWAP tHWAP
BAM
BAM
YOU'RE ACTING LIKE A NEANDERTHAL!
BAM
BAM
tHWAP
YOU'RE the sadist! – From all of us.
huf は
huf は
DON'T YOU THINK LITTLE ANIMALS ARE CUTE?
AREN'T THOSE KINDS OF FEELINGS ONLY NATURAL?!
DON'T YOU HAVE A SINGLE SHRED OF PROTECTIVE INSTINCT FOR THESE HELPLESS LITTLE CREATURES?

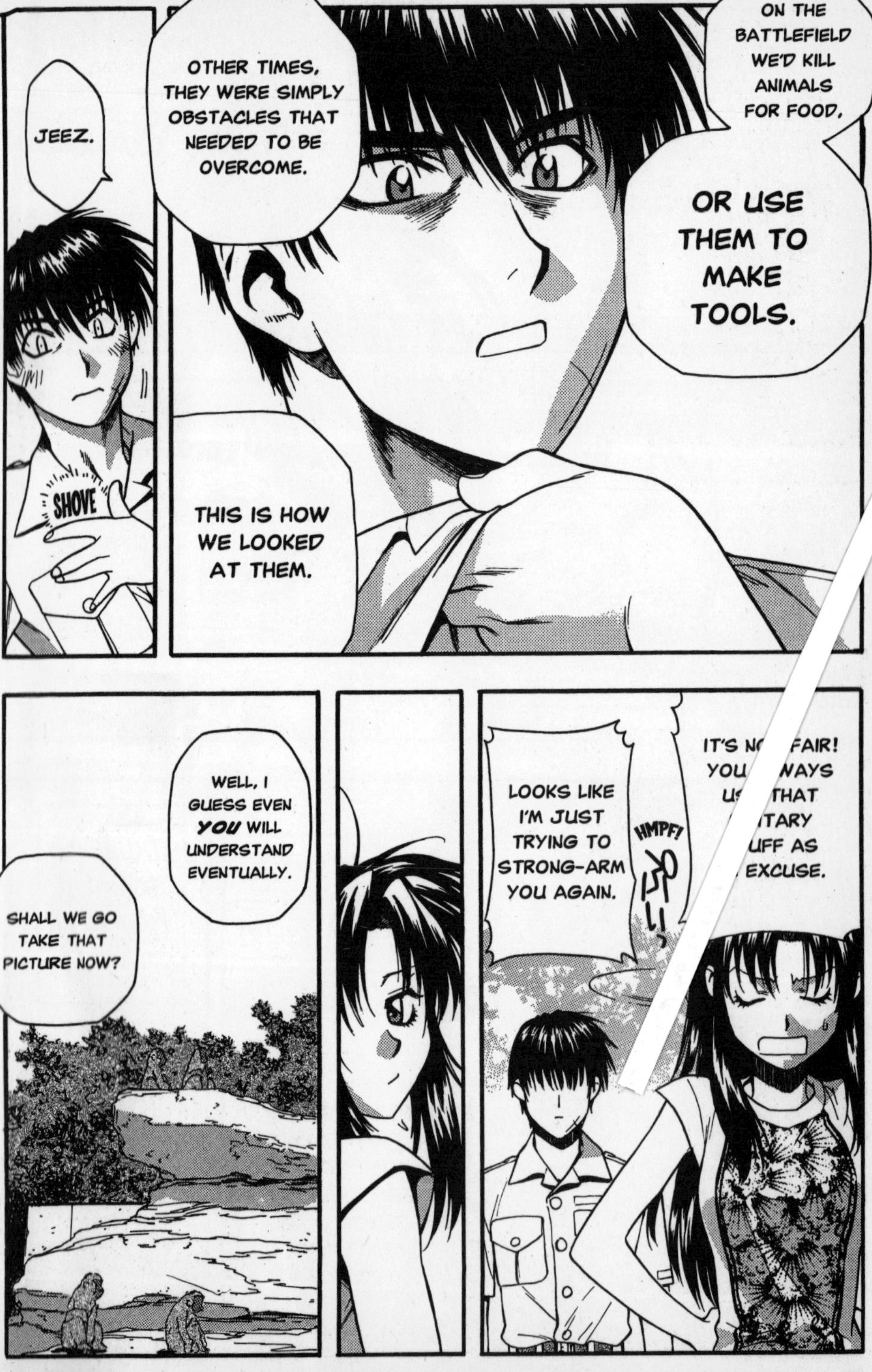
ON THE BATTLEFIELD WE'D KILL ANIMALS FOR FOOD,
OR USE THEM TO MAKE TOOLS.
OTHER TIMES, THEY WERE SIMPLY OBSTACLES THAT NEEDED TO BE OVERCOME.
THIS IS HOW WE LOOKED AT THEM.
JEEZ.
SHOVE
IT'S N FAIR! YOU WAYS US THAT ITARY UFF AS EXCUSE.
HMPF!
LOOKS LIKE I'M JUST TRYING TO STRONG-ARM YOU AGAIN.
WELL, I GUESS EVEN *YOU* WILL UNDERSTAND EVENTUALLY.
SHALL WE GO TAKE THAT PICTURE NOW?

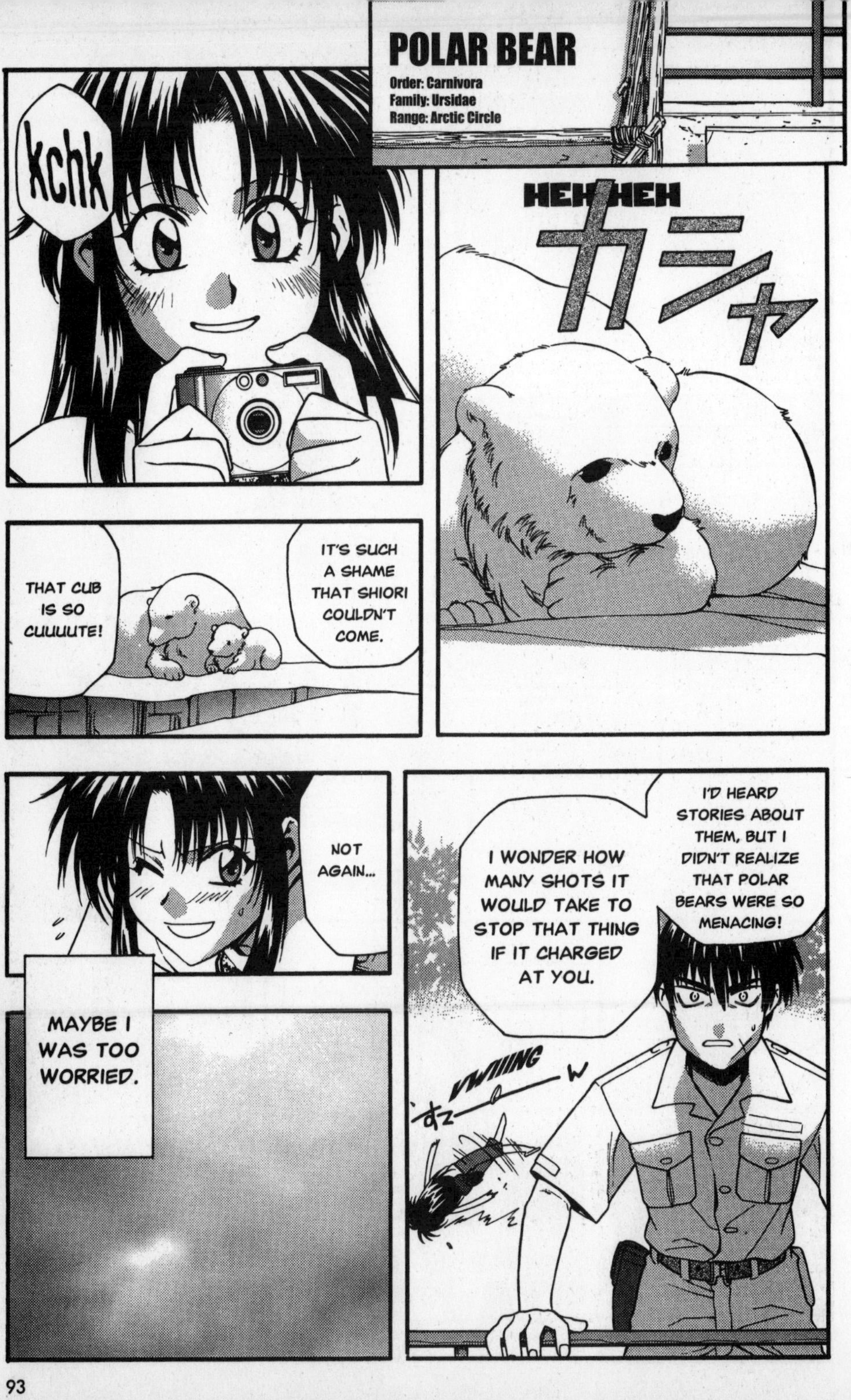
POLAR BEAR
Order: Carnivora
Family: Ursidae
Range: Arctic Circle
kchk
HEH HEH
カシャ
IT'S SUCH A SHAME THAT SHIORI COULDN'T COME.
THAT CUB IS SO CUUUUTE!
I'D HEARD STORIES ABOUT THEM, BUT I DIDN'T REALIZE THAT POLAR BEARS WERE SO MENACING!
I WONDER HOW MANY SHOTS IT WOULD TAKE TO STOP THAT THING IF IT CHARGED AT YOU.
VWIIING
W
NOT AGAIN...
MAYBE I WAS TOO WORRIED.

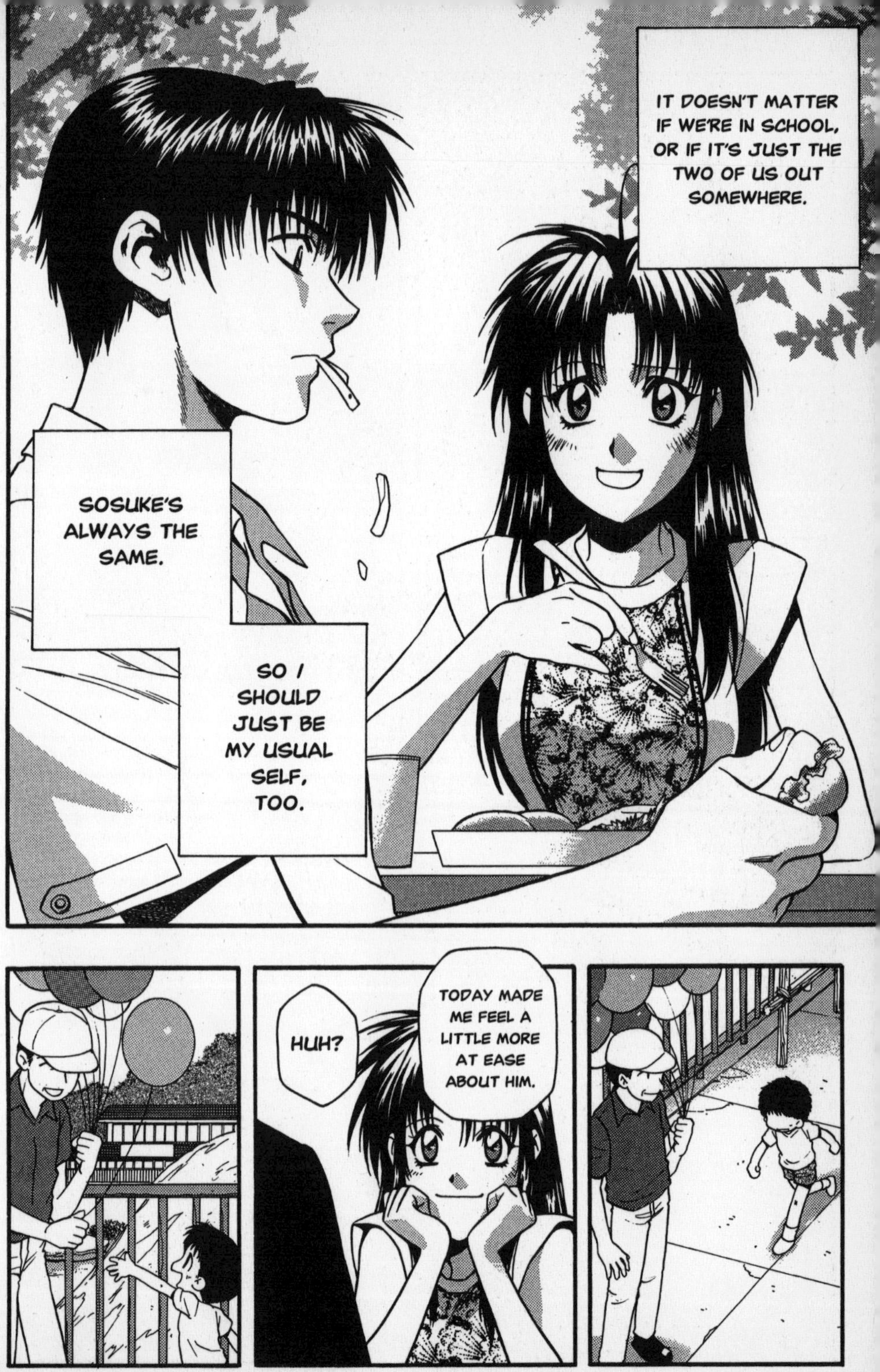
IT DOESN'T MATTER IF WE'RE IN SCHOOL, OR IF IT'S JUST THE TWO OF US OUT SOMEWHERE.
SOSUKE'S ALWAYS THE SAME.
SO I SHOULD JUST BE MY USUAL SELF, TOO.
TODAY MADE ME FEEL A LITTLE MORE AT EASE ABOUT HIM.
HUH?

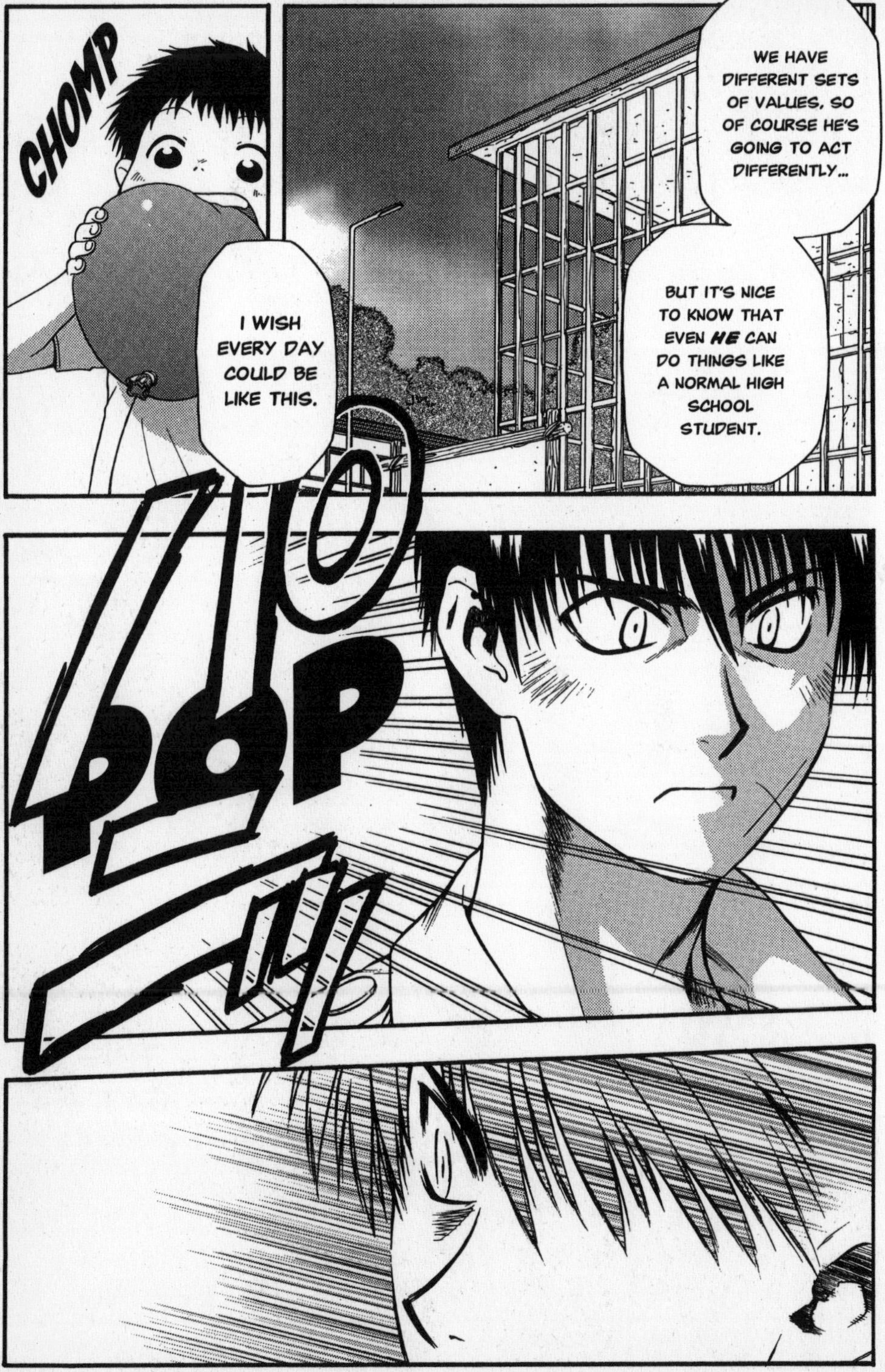
WE HAVE DIFFERENT SETS OF VALUES, SO OF COURSE HE'S GOING TO ACT DIFFERENTLY...
BUT IT'S NICE TO KNOW THAT EVEN HE CAN DO THINGS LIKE A NORMAL HIGH SCHOOL STUDENT.
CHOMP
I WISH EVERY DAY COULD BE LIKE THIS.
POP

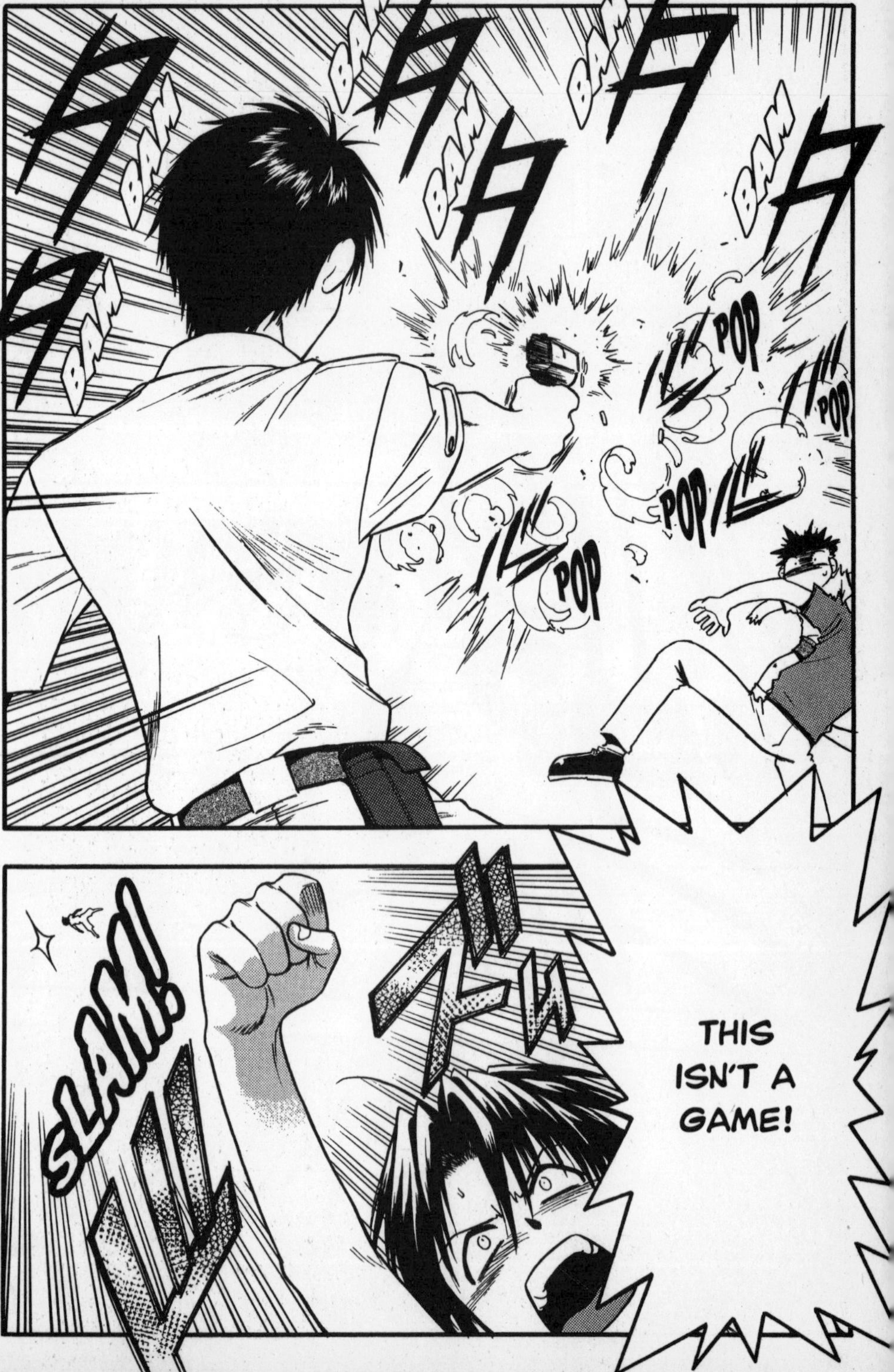
BAM
BAM
BAM
BAM
BAM
BAM
POP
POP
POP
POP
THIS ISN'T A GAME!
SLAM!

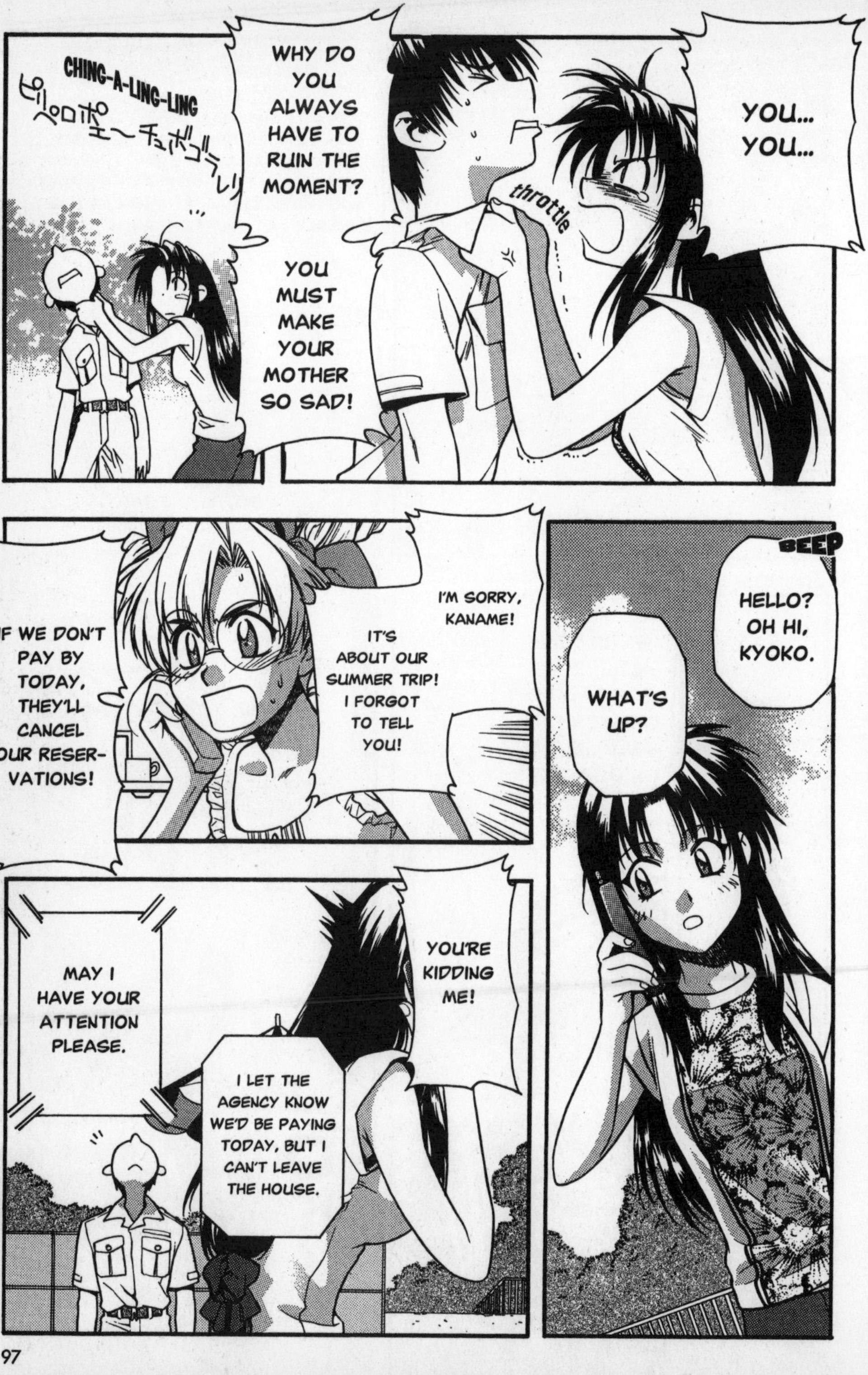
YOU... YOU...
WHY DO YOU ALWAYS HAVE TO RUIN THE MOMENT?
throttle
YOU MUST MAKE YOUR MOTHER SO SAD!
CHING-A-LING-LING
BEEP
HELLO? OH HI, KYOKO.
WHAT'S UP?
I'M SORRY, KANAME!
IT'S ABOUT OUR SUMMER TRIP! I FORGOT TO TELL YOU!
IF WE DON'T PAY BY TODAY, THEY'LL CANCEL OUR RESER-VATIONS!
YOU'RE KIDDING ME!
I LET THE AGENCY KNOW WE'D BE PAYING TODAY, BUT I CAN'T LEAVE THE HOUSE.
MAY I HAVE YOUR ATTENTION PLEASE.

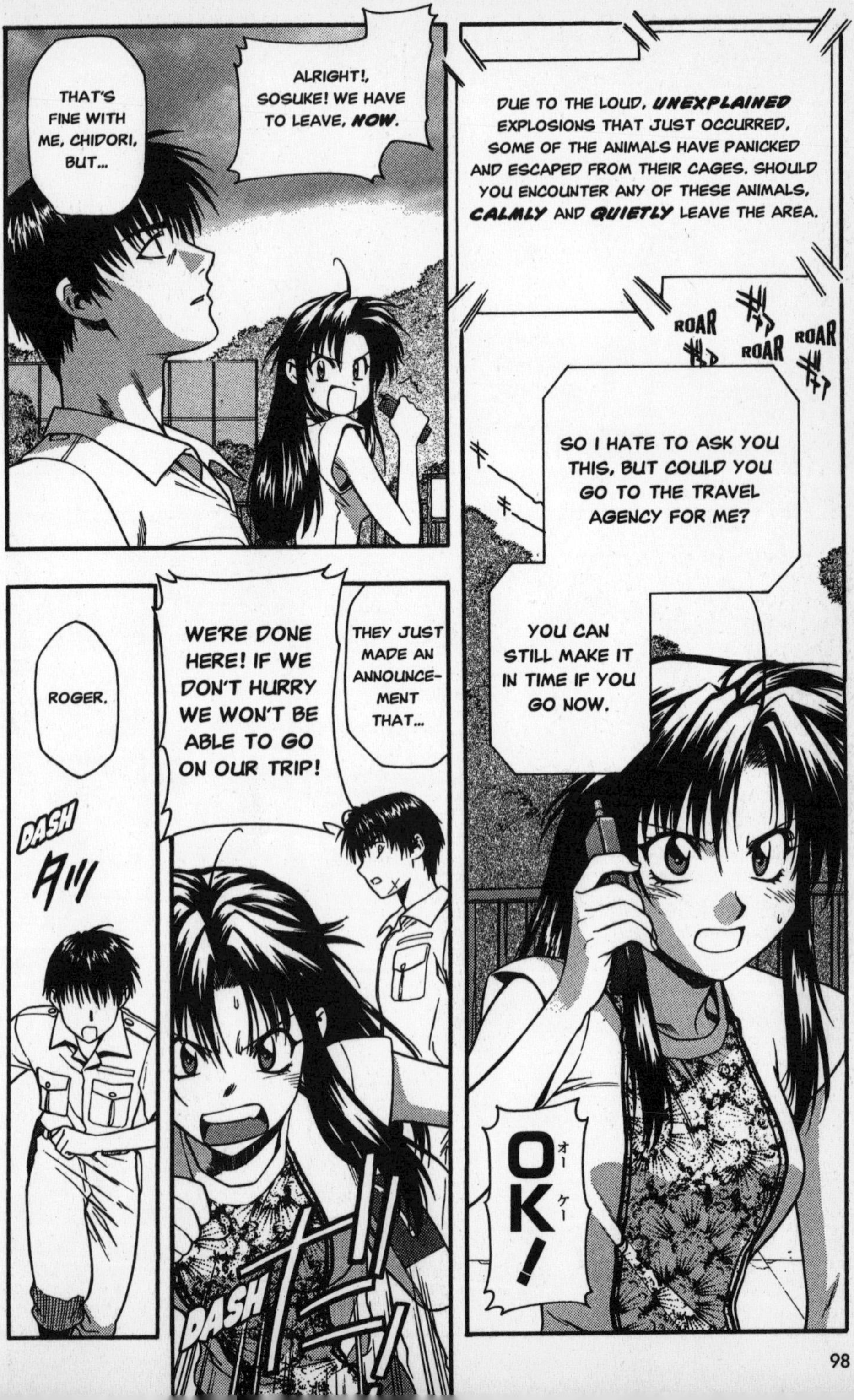

DUE TO THE LOUD, UNEXPLAINED EXPLOSIONS THAT JUST OCCURRED, SOME OF THE ANIMALS HAVE PANICKED AND ESCAPED FROM THEIR CAGES. SHOULD YOU ENCOUNTER ANY OF THESE ANIMALS, CALMLY AND QUIETLY LEAVE THE AREA.
ROAR
ROAR
ROAR
SO I HATE TO ASK YOU THIS, BUT COULD YOU GO TO THE TRAVEL AGENCY FOR ME?
YOU CAN STILL MAKE IT IN TIME IF YOU GO NOW.
OK!
オー ケー
ALRIGHT!, SOSUKE! WE HAVE TO LEAVE, NOW.
THAT'S FINE WITH ME, CHIDORI, BUT...
THEY JUST MADE AN ANNOUNCE-MENT THAT...
WE'RE DONE HERE! IF WE DON'T HURRY WE WON'T BE ABLE TO GO ON OUR TRIP!
ROGER.
DASH
DASH

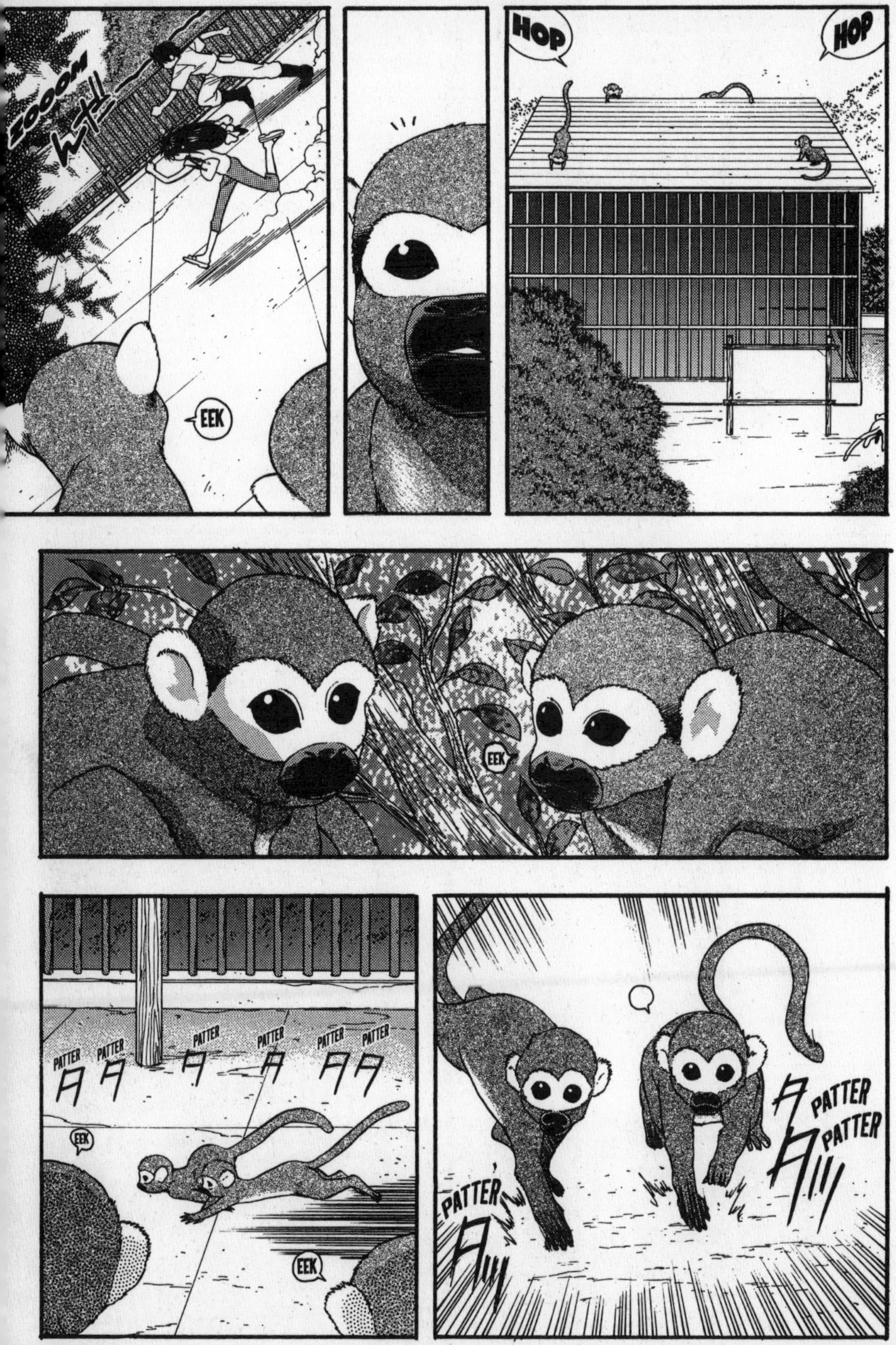
HOP
HOP
ZOOOOM
EEK
EEK
PATTER PATTER
PATTER
PATTER PATTER PATTER PATTER PATTER PATTER
EEK
EEK

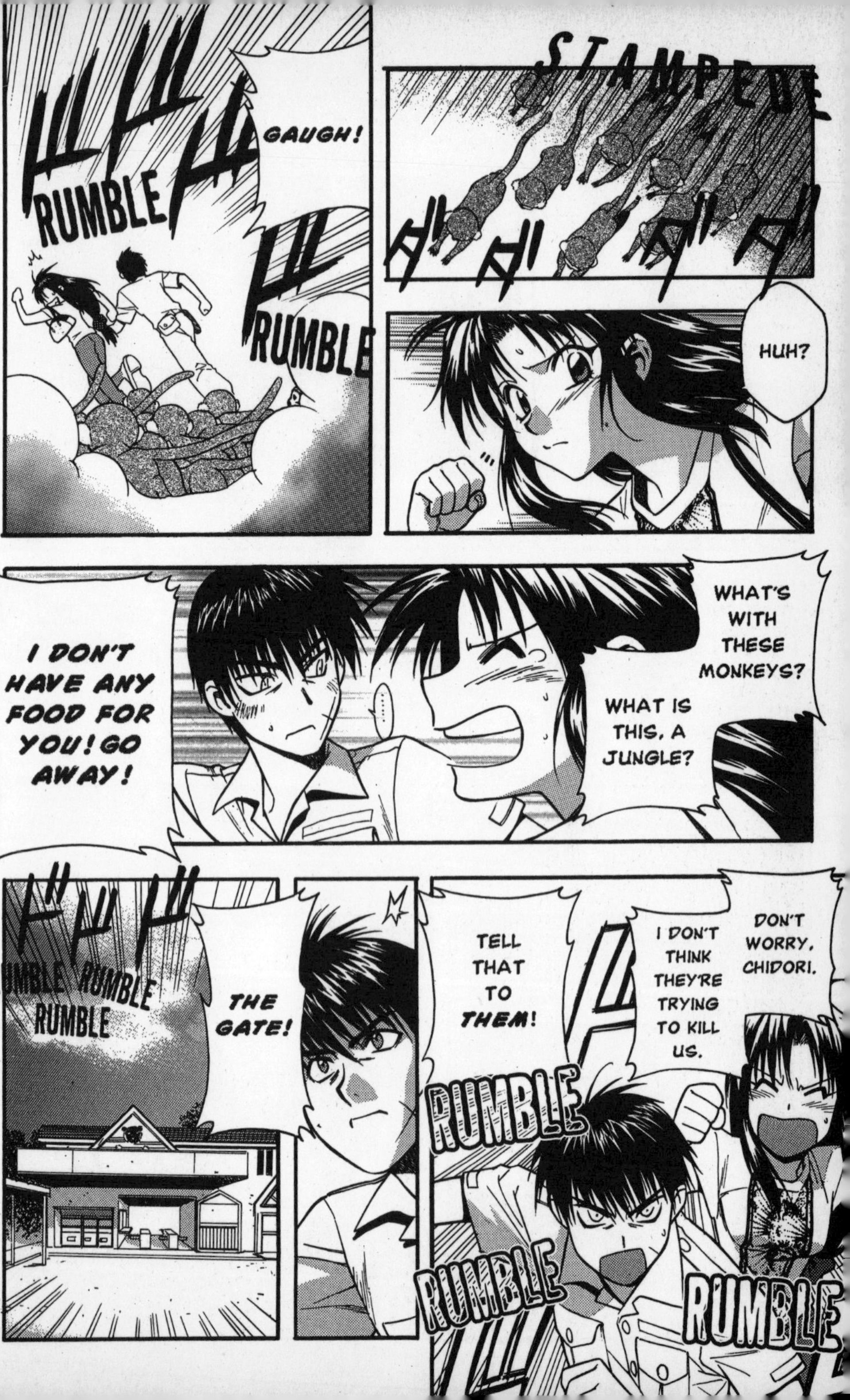

STAMPEDE
HUH?
GAUGH!
RUMBLE
RUMBLE
WHAT'S WITH THESE MONKEYS?
WHAT IS THIS, A JUNGLE?
I DON'T HAVE ANY FOOD FOR YOU! GO AWAY!
DON'T WORRY, CHIDORI.
I DON'T THINK THEY'RE TRYING TO KILL US.
TELL THAT TO THEM!
RUMBLE
RUMBLE
RUMBLE
THE GATE!
RUMBLE RUMBLE RUMBLE

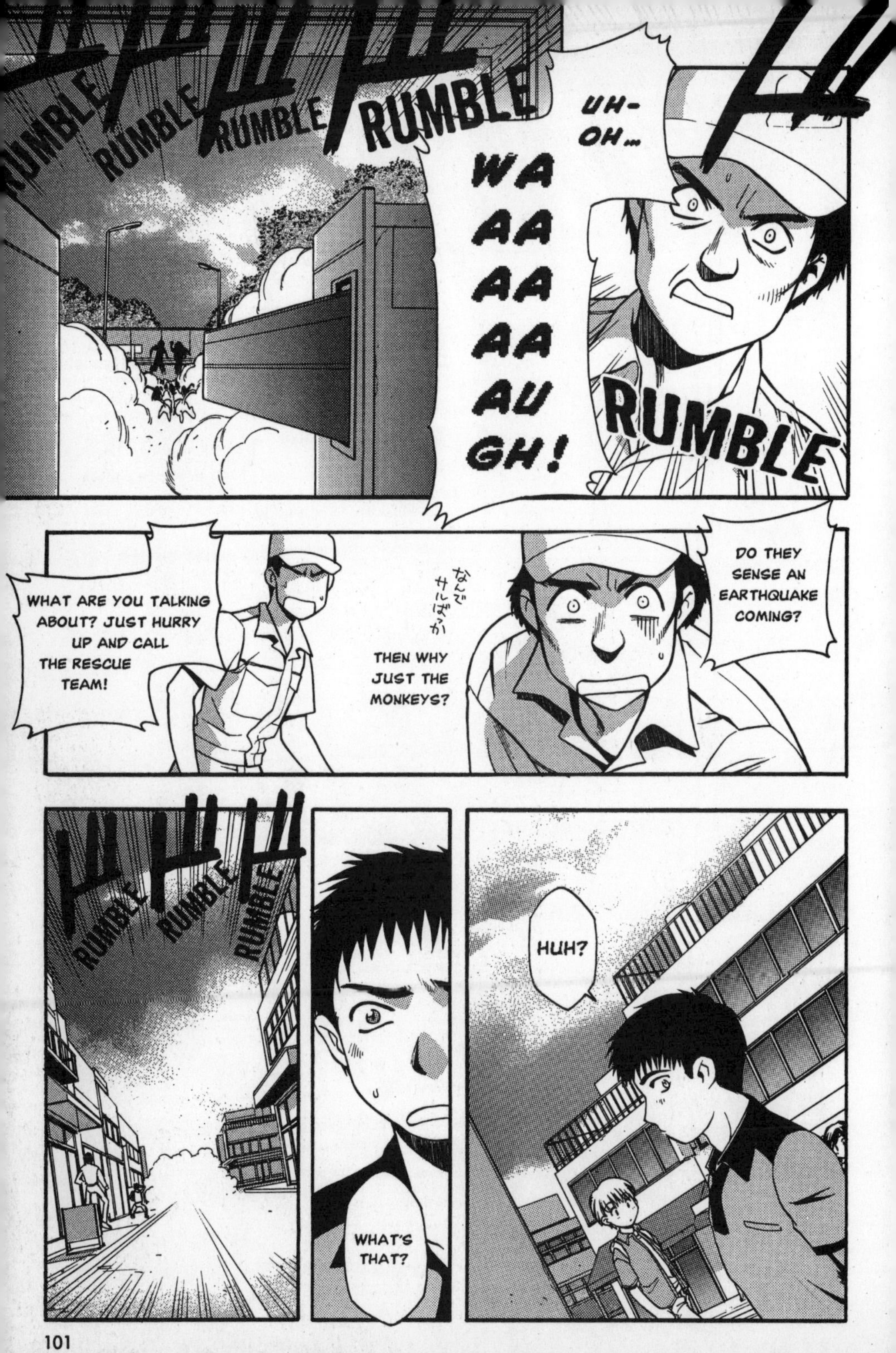
UH-OH...
WAAAAAAAAAUGH!
RUMBLE
RUMBLE RUMBLE RUMBLE RUMBLE
DO THEY SENSE AN EARTHQUAKE COMING?
なんでサルばっか
THEN WHY JUST THE MONKEYS?
WHAT ARE YOU TALKING ABOUT? JUST HURRY UP AND CALL THE RESCUE TEAM!
HUH?
WHAT'S THAT?
RUMBLE RUMBLE RUMBLE

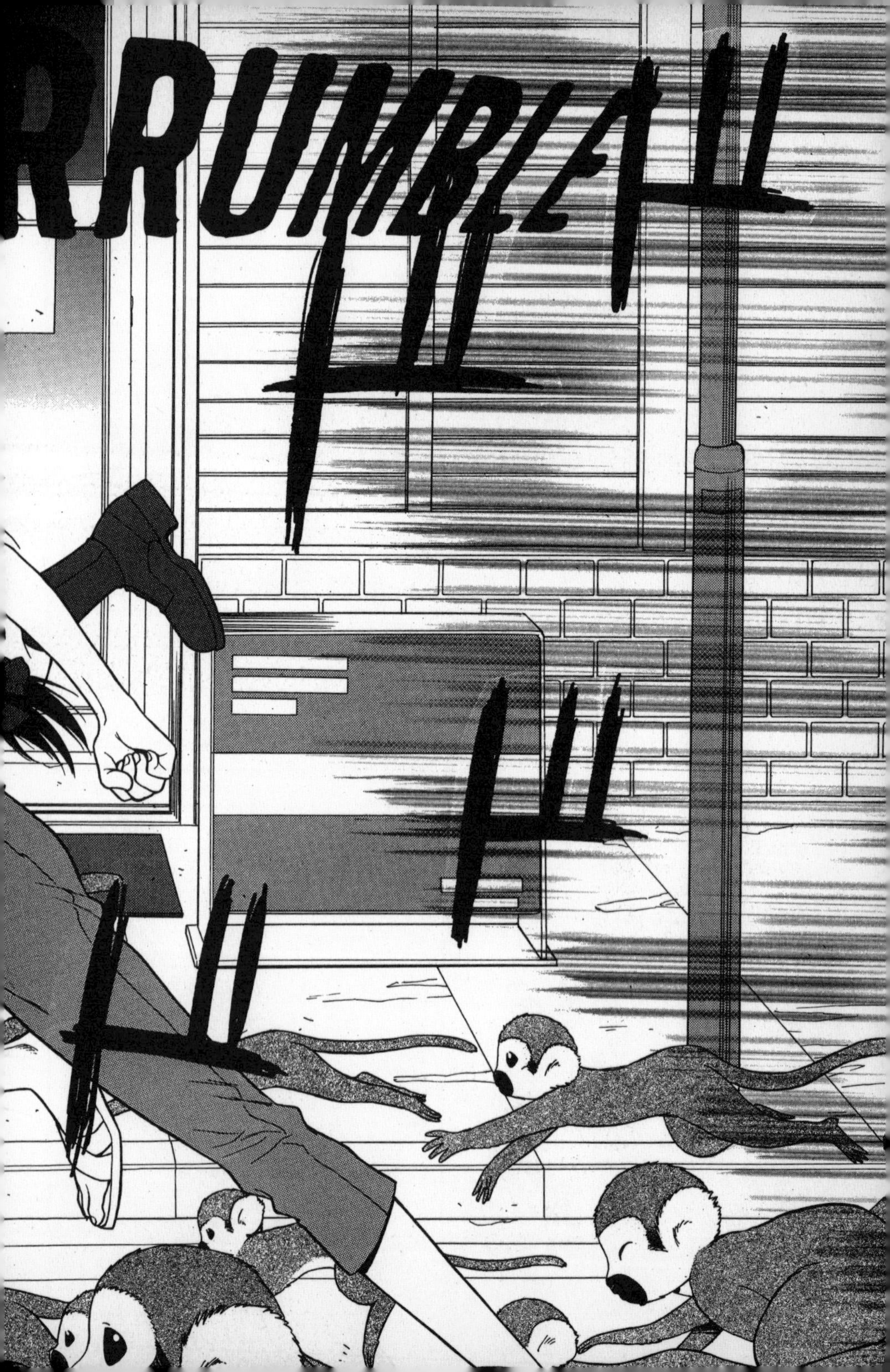
RRUMBLE

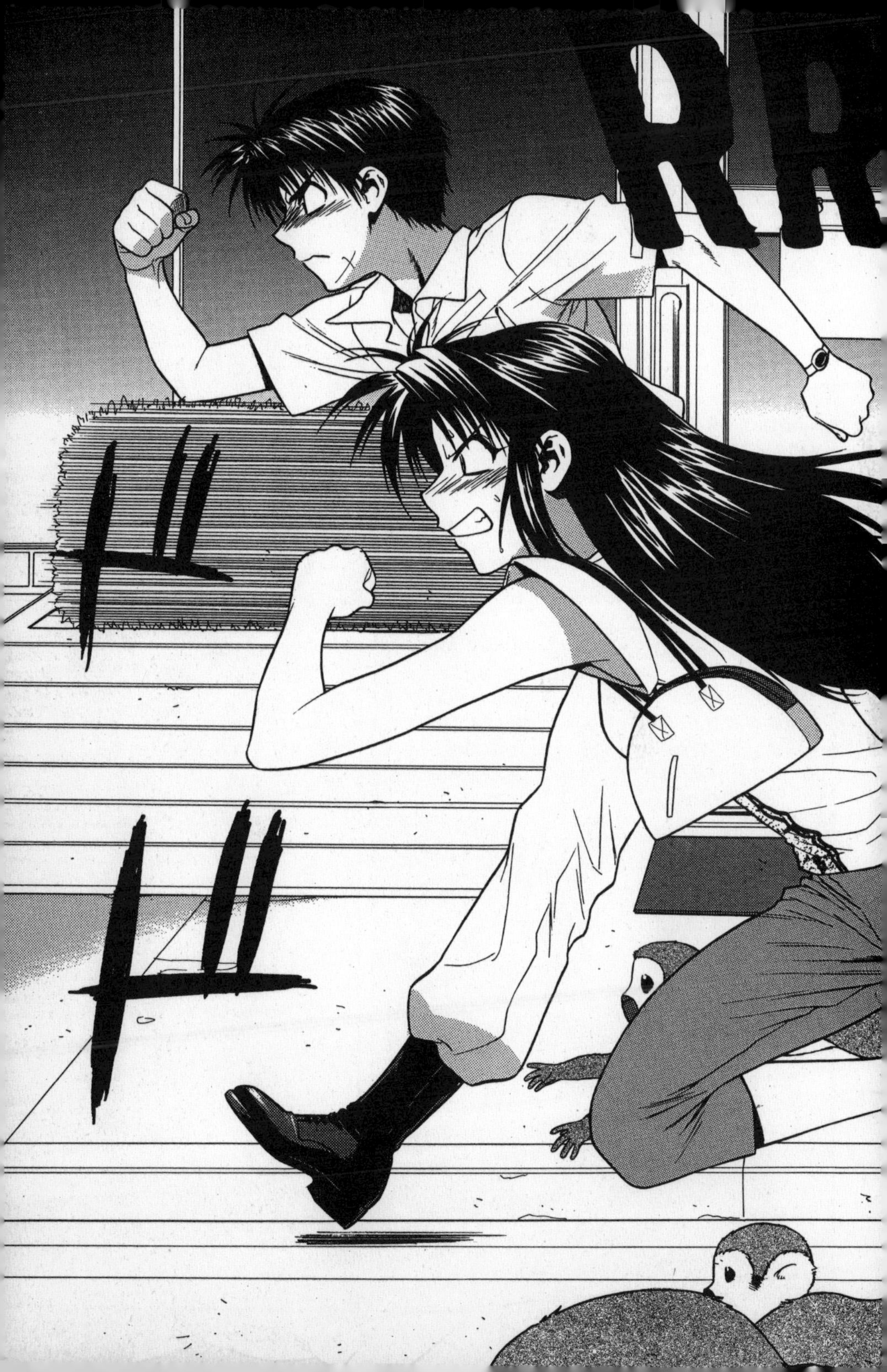

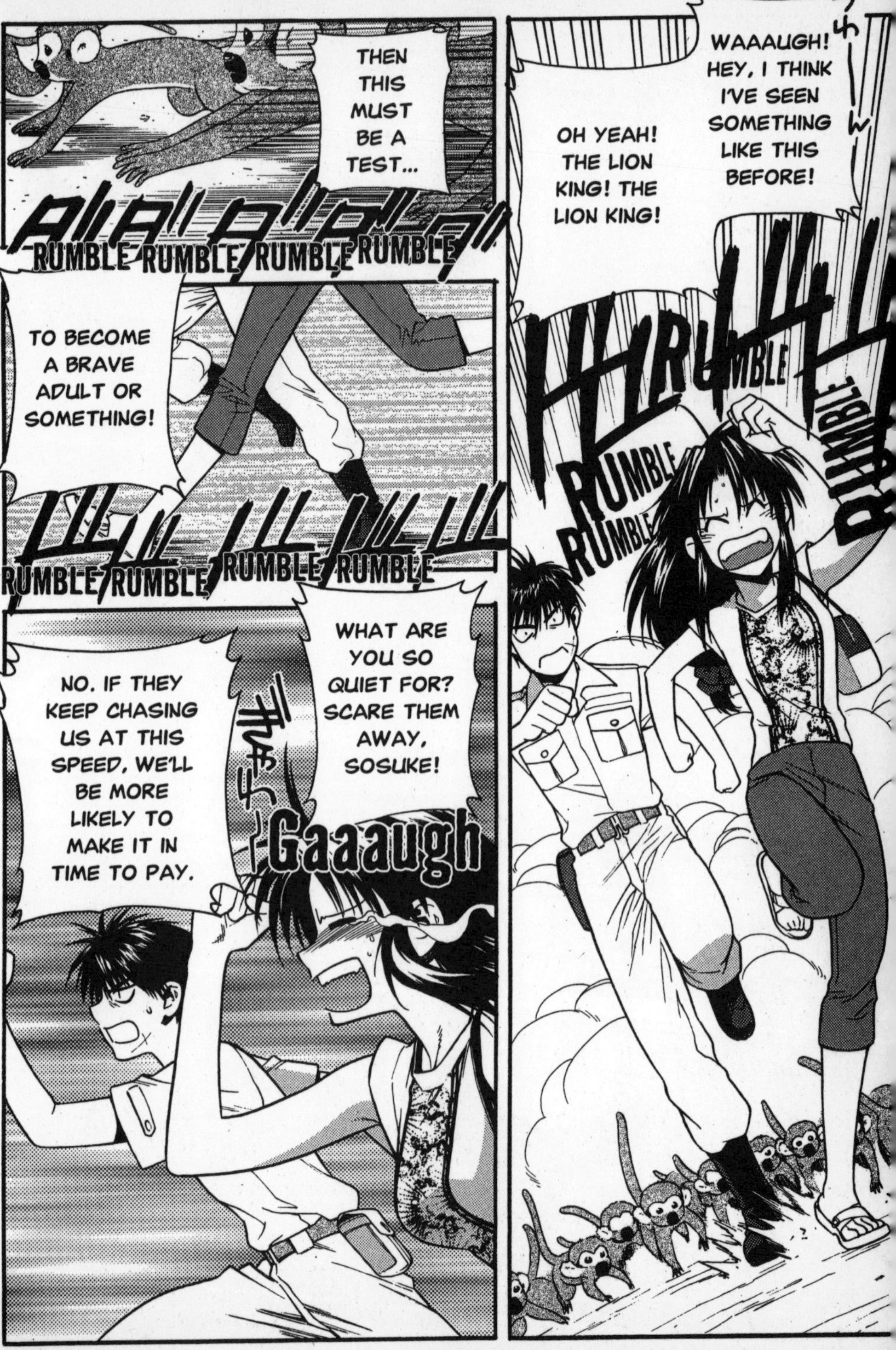
WAAAUGH! HEY, I THINK I'VE SEEN SOMETHING LIKE THIS BEFORE!
OH YEAH! THE LION KING! THE LION KING!
RUMBLE
RUMBLE
RUMBLE
RUMBLE
THEN THIS MUST BE A TEST...
RUMBLE RUMBLE RUMBLE RUMBLE
TO BECOME A BRAVE ADULT OR SOMETHING!
RUMBLE RUMBLE RUMBLE RUMBLE
WHAT ARE YOU SO QUIET FOR? SCARE THEM AWAY, SOSUKE!
Gaaaugh
NO. IF THEY KEEP CHASING US AT THIS SPEED, WE'LL BE MORE LIKELY TO MAKE IT IN TIME TO PAY.

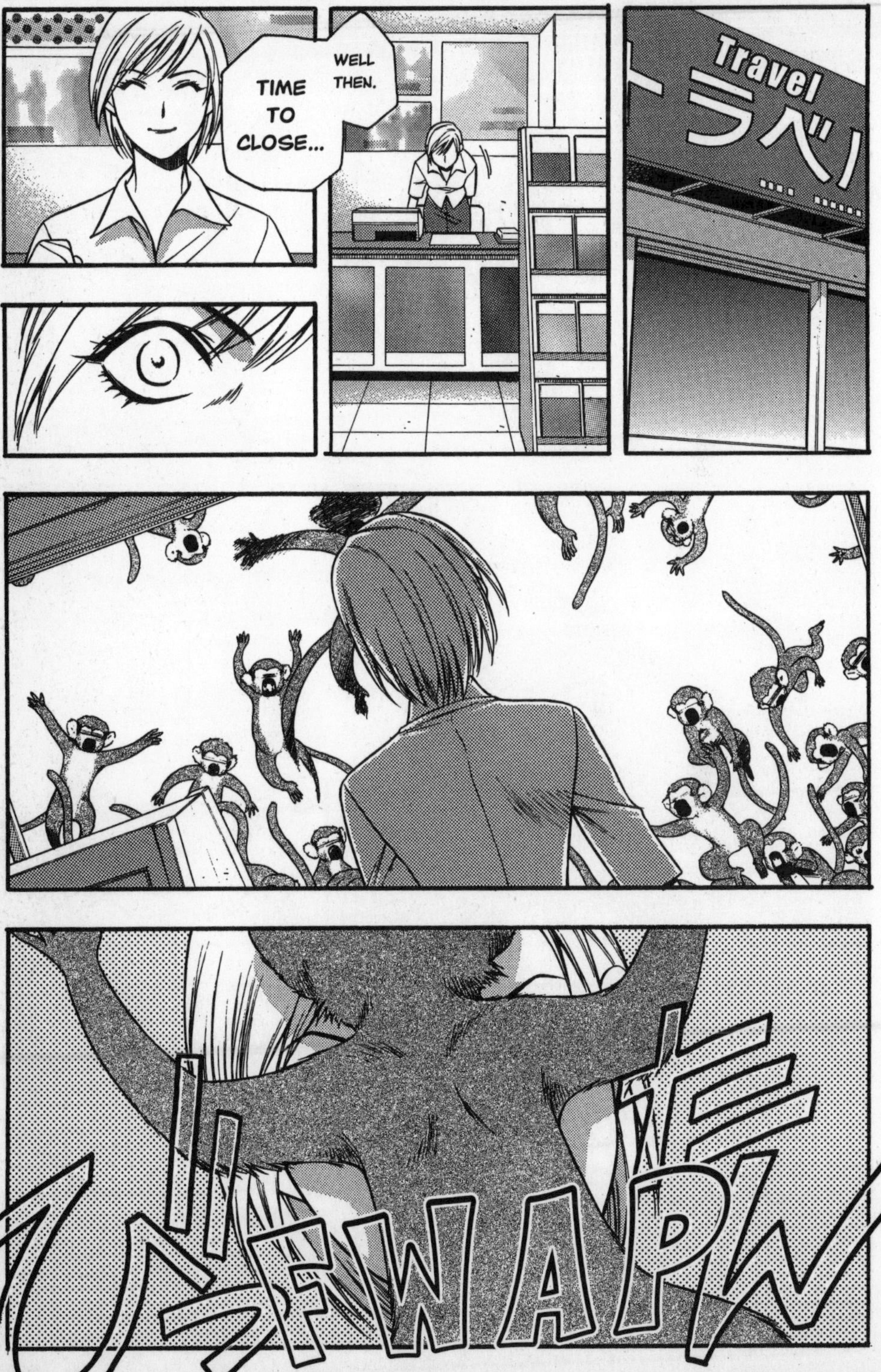
Travel
トラベ
WELL THEN.
TIME TO CLOSE...
FWAP

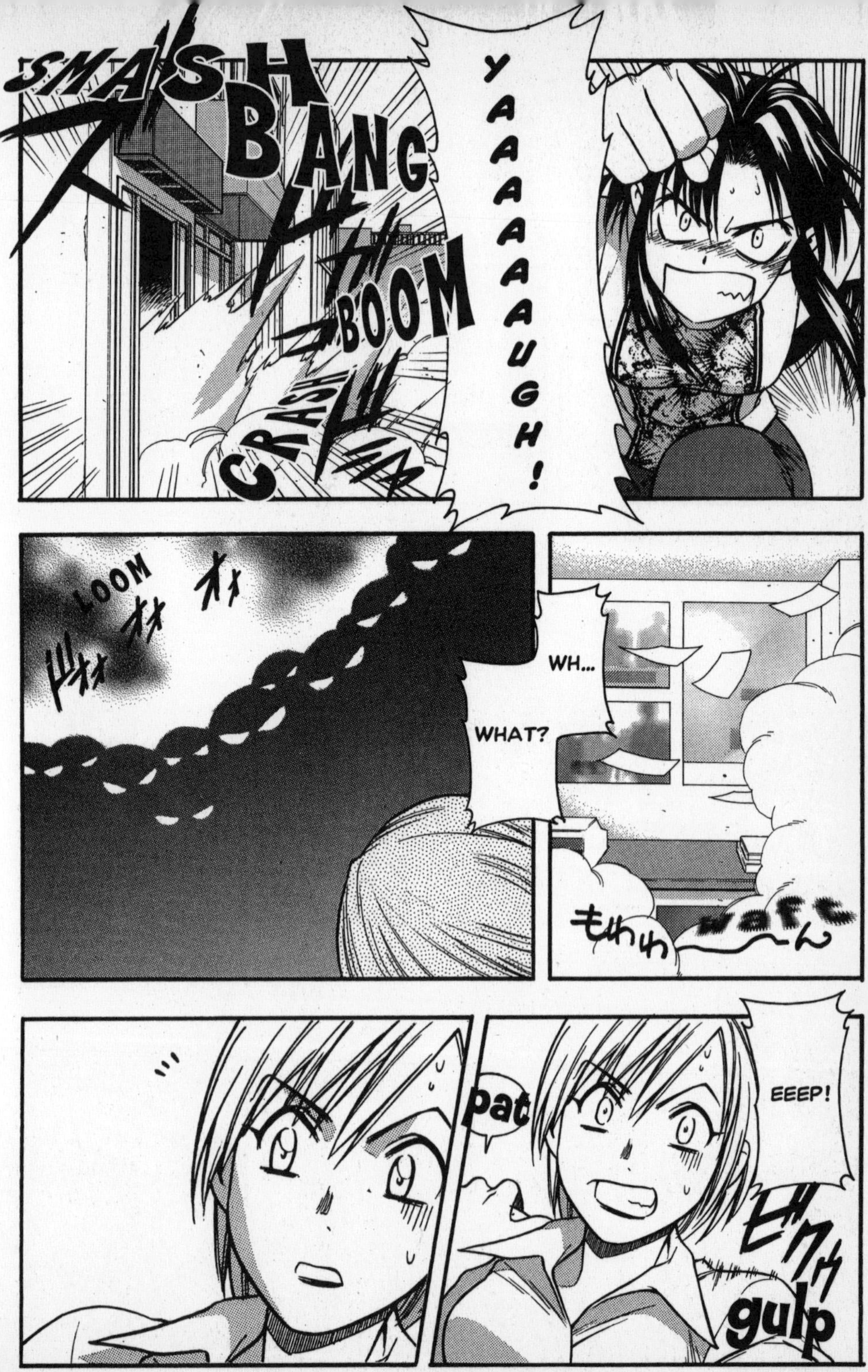
YAAAAAAUGH!
SMASH
BANG
BOOM
CRASH
WH...
WHAT?
wafc
LOOM
EEEP!
pat
gulp
...

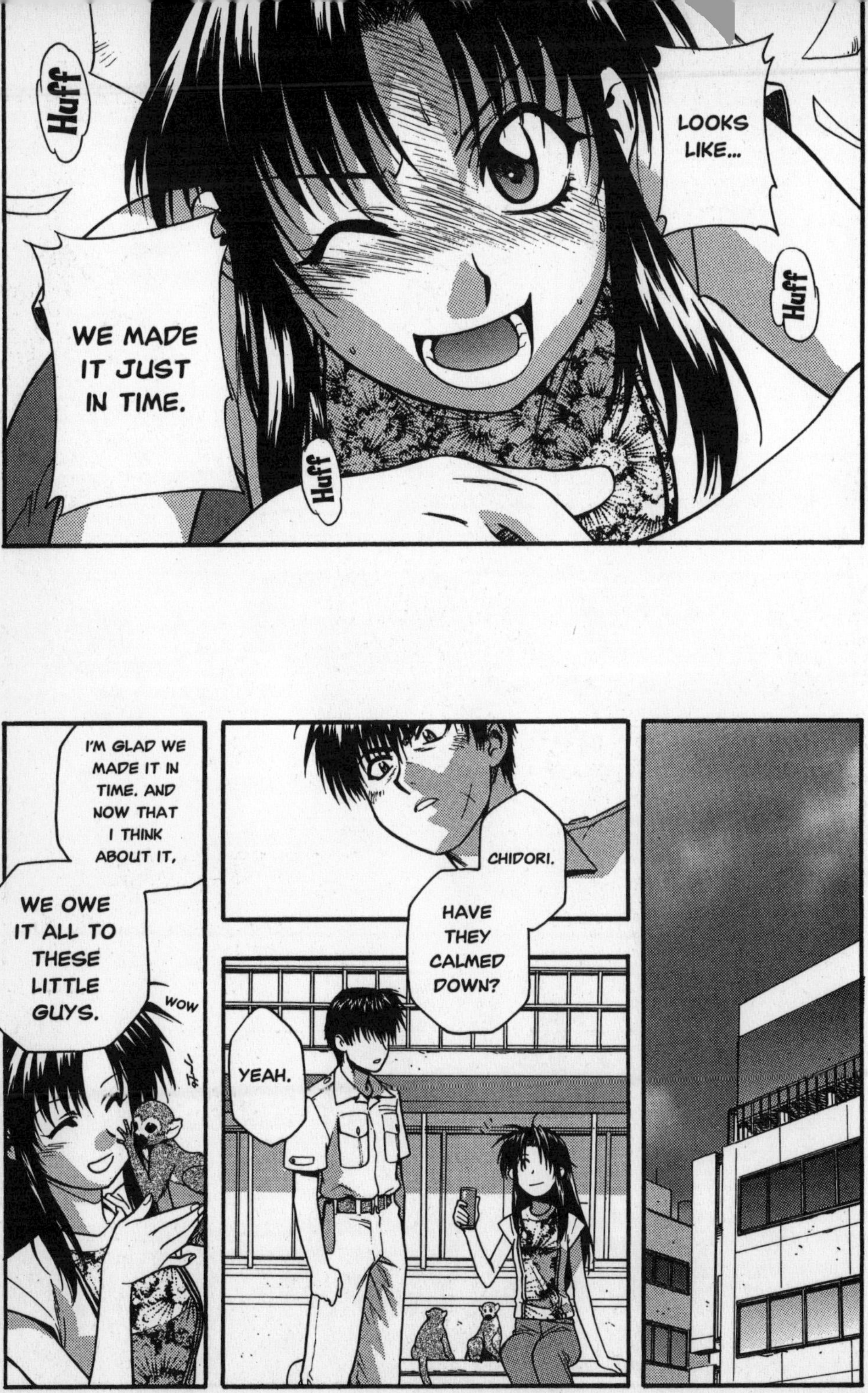
LOOKS LIKE...
Huff
Huff
WE MADE IT JUST IN TIME.
Huff
CHIDORI.
HAVE THEY CALMED DOWN?
YEAH.
I'M GLAD WE MADE IT IN TIME. AND NOW THAT I THINK ABOUT IT,
WE OWE IT ALL TO THESE LITTLE GUYS.
WOW

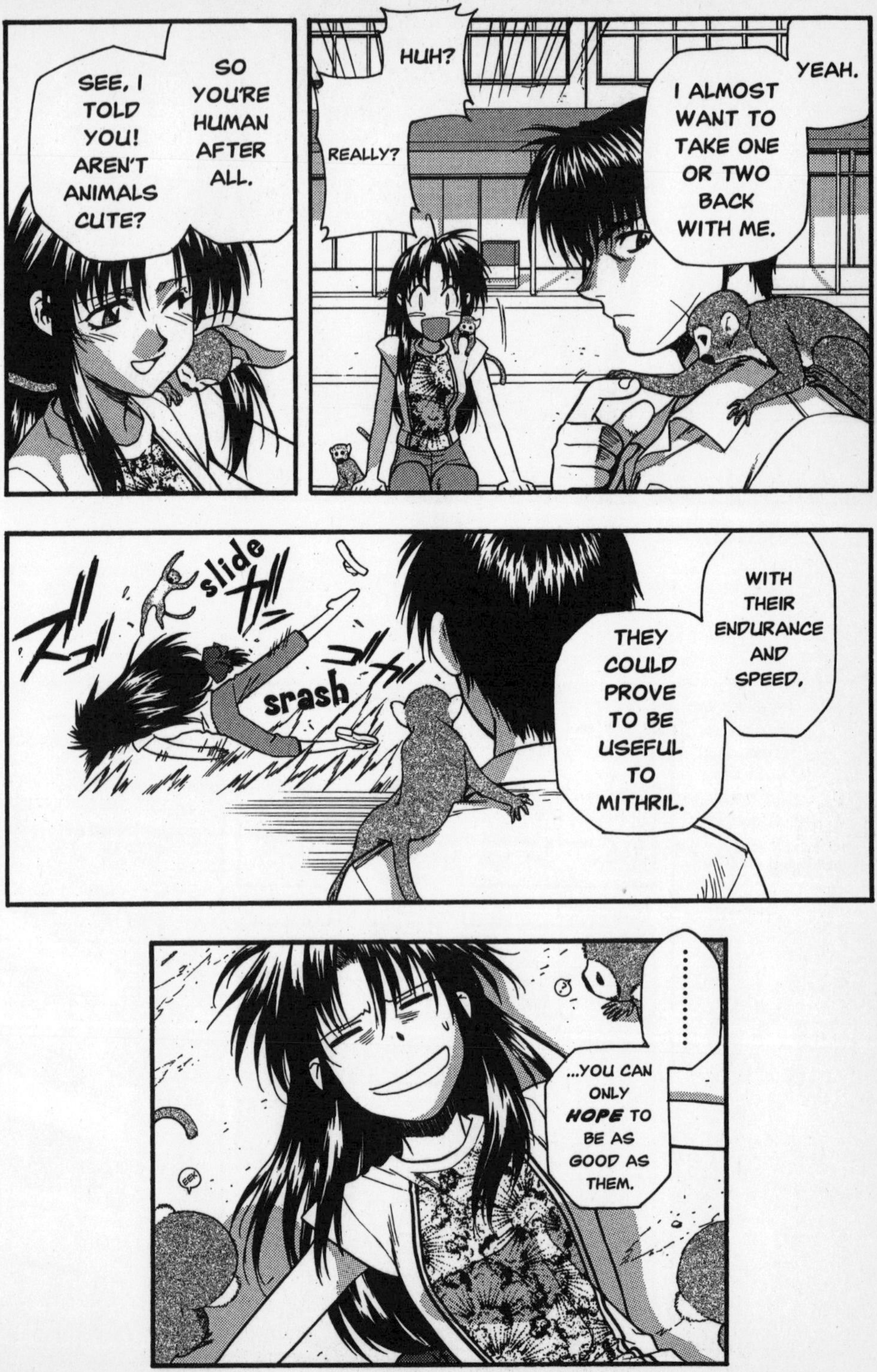
YEAH.
I ALMOST WANT TO TAKE ONE OR TWO BACK WITH ME.
HUH?
REALLY?
SO YOU'RE HUMAN AFTER ALL.
SEE, I TOLD YOU! AREN'T ANIMALS CUTE?
WITH THEIR ENDURANCE AND SPEED,
THEY COULD PROVE TO BE USEFUL TO MITHRIL.
slide
srash
....
...YOU CAN ONLY **HOPE** TO BE AS GOOD AS THEM.
EEK

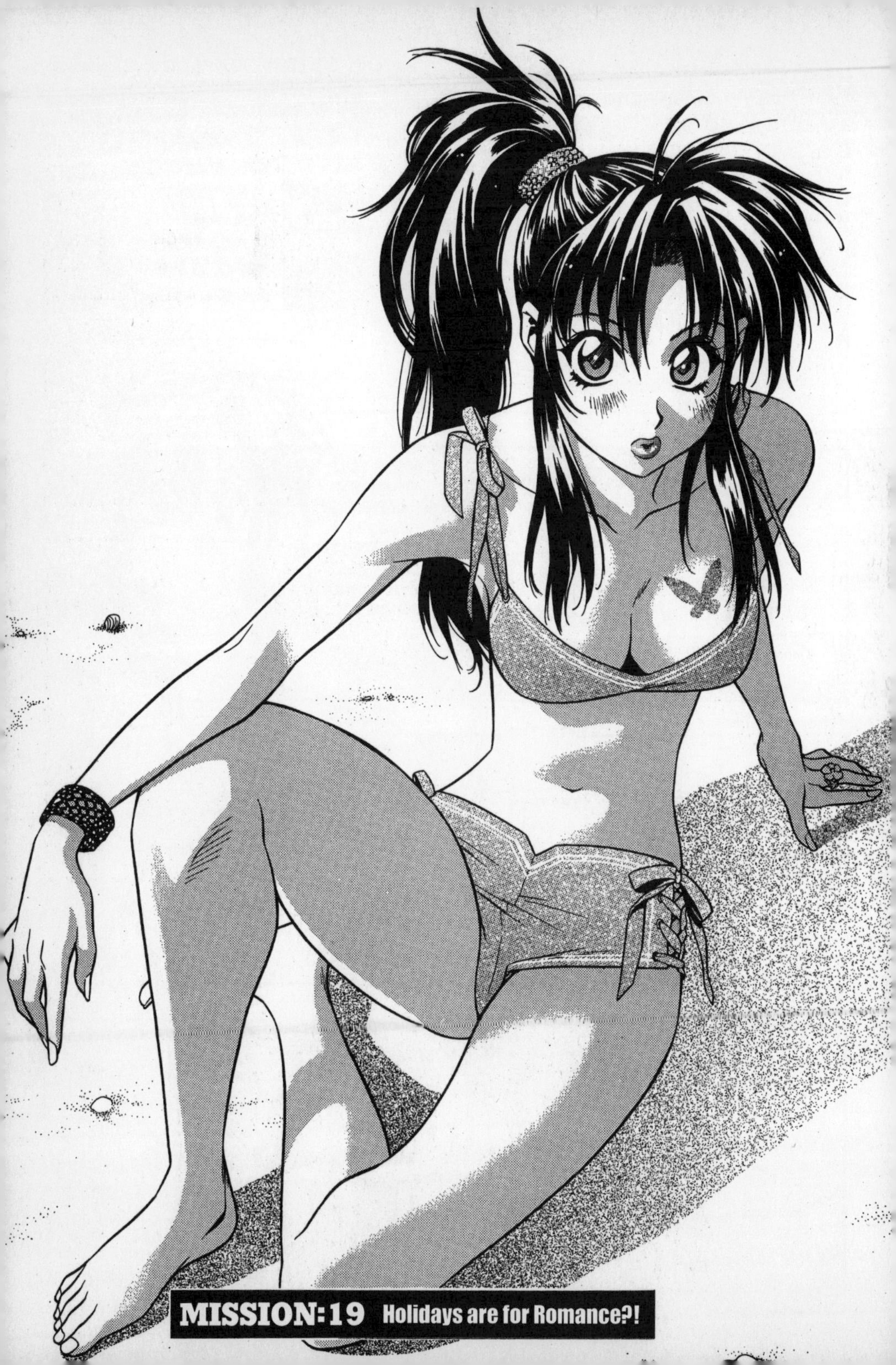

MISSION:19 Holidays are for Romance?!

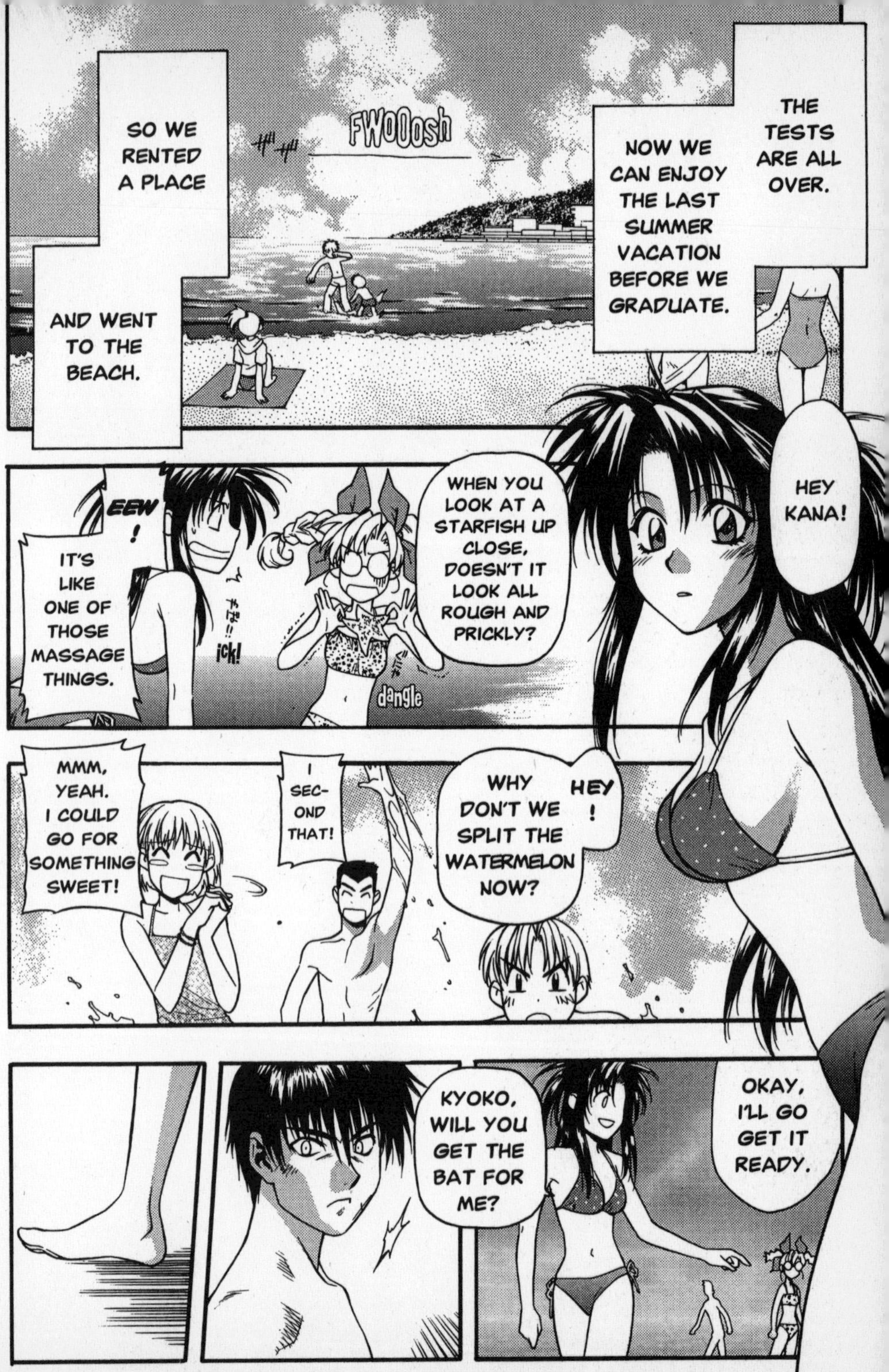
THE TESTS ARE ALL OVER.
NOW WE CAN ENJOY THE LAST SUMMER VACATION BEFORE WE GRADUATE.
FWOOosh
SO WE RENTED A PLACE
AND WENT TO THE BEACH.
HEY KANA!
WHEN YOU LOOK AT A STARFISH UP CLOSE, DOESN'T IT LOOK ALL ROUGH AND PRICKLY?
dangle
ick!
EEW!
IT'S LIKE ONE OF THOSE MASSAGE THINGS.
HEY!
WHY DON'T WE SPLIT THE WATERMELON NOW?
I SEC-OND THAT!
MMM, YEAH. I COULD GO FOR SOMETHING SWEET!
OKAY, I'LL GO GET IT READY.
KYOKO, WILL YOU GET THE BAT FOR ME?

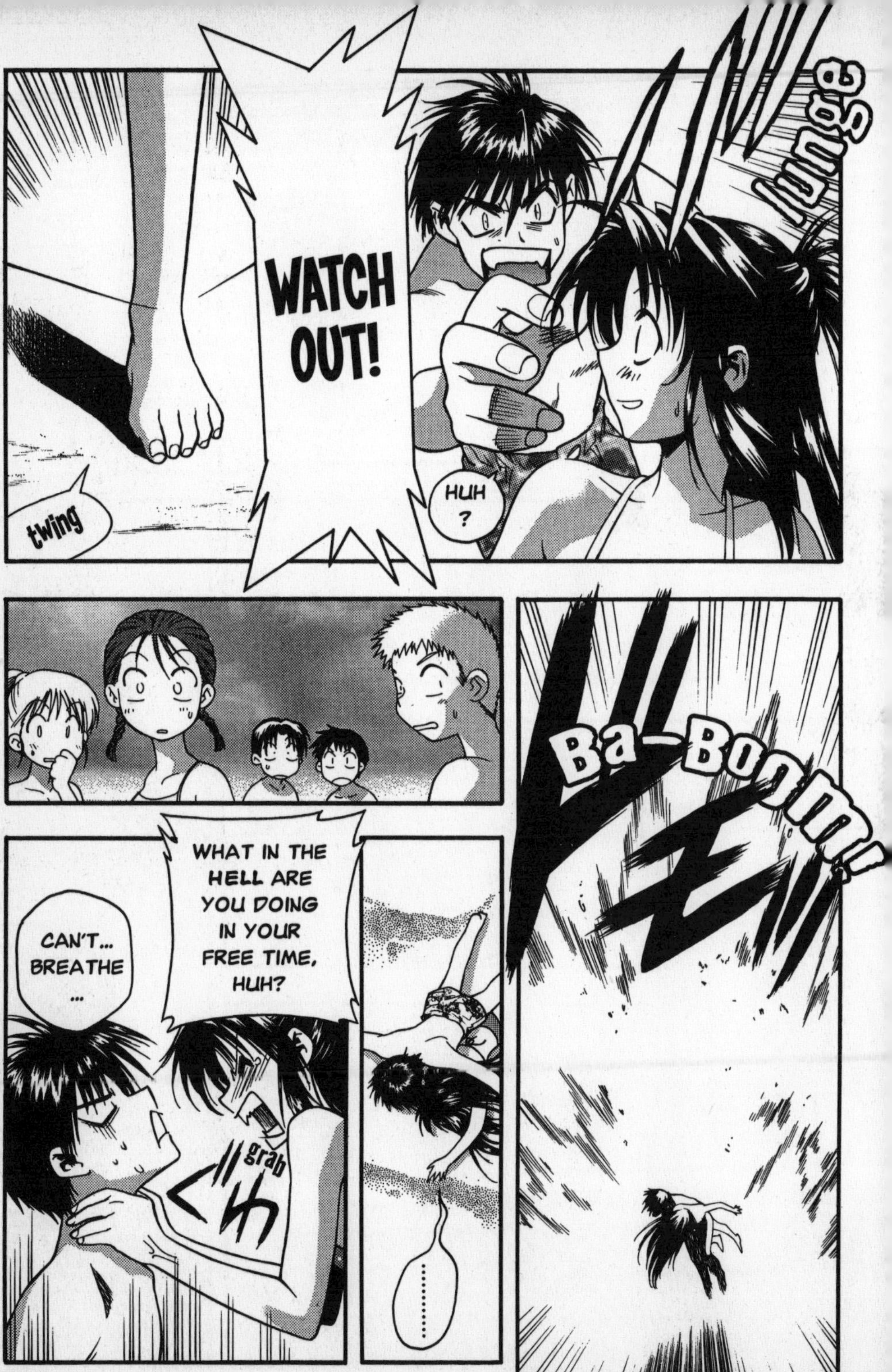
lunge
WATCH OUT!
HUH ?
twing
Ba-Boom!!
......
WHAT IN THE HELL ARE YOU DOING IN YOUR FREE TIME, HUH?
CAN'T... BREATHE ...
grab

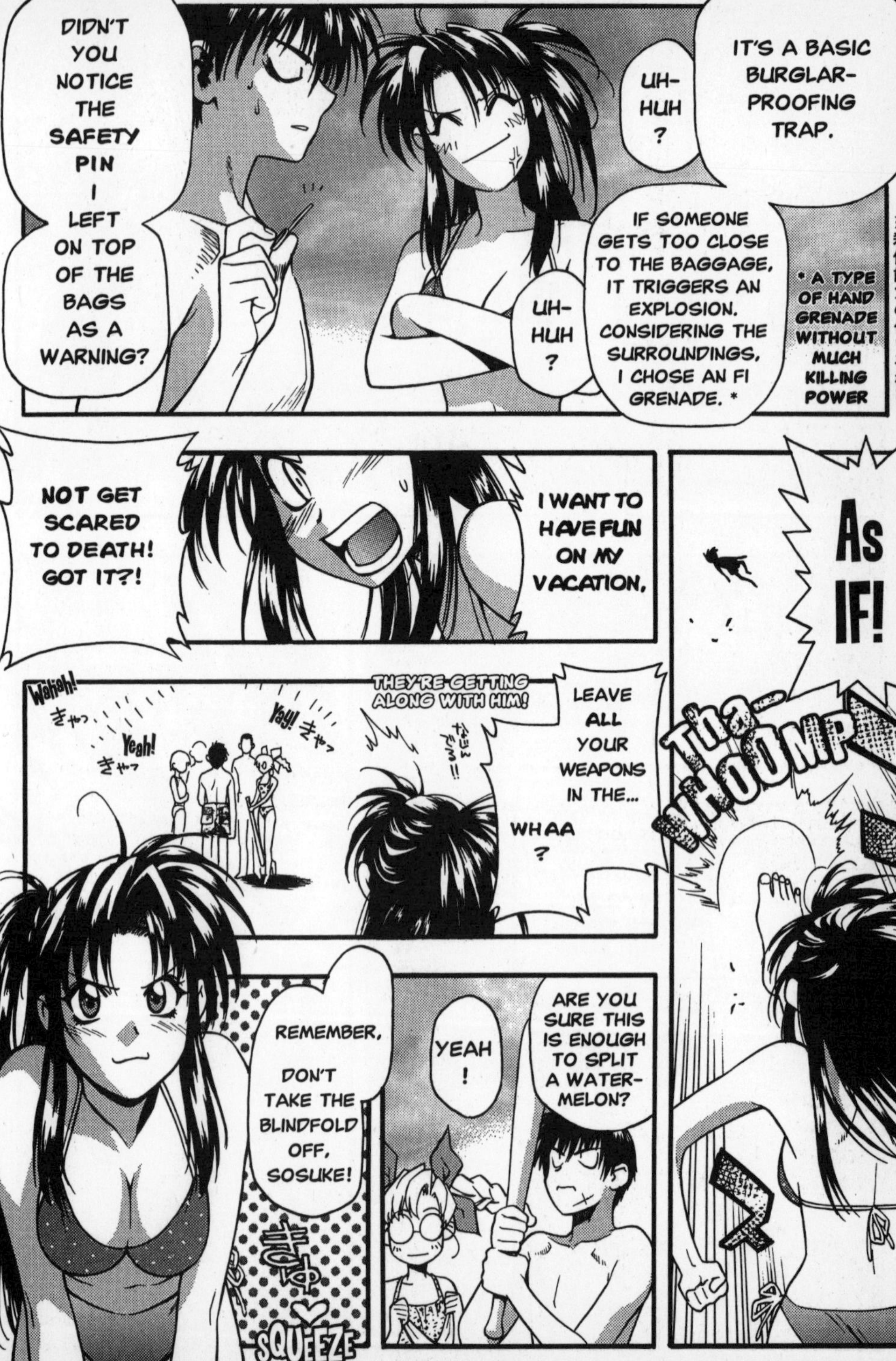
IT'S A BASIC BURGLAR-PROOFING TRAP.
UH-HUH?
IF SOMEONE GETS TOO CLOSE TO THE BAGGAGE, IT TRIGGERS AN EXPLOSION. CONSIDERING THE SURROUNDINGS, I CHOSE AN FI GRENADE. *
UH-HUH?
DIDN'T YOU NOTICE THE SAFETY PIN I LEFT ON TOP OF THE BAGS AS A WARNING?
As IF!
Tha-WHOOMP
I WANT TO HAVE FUN ON MY VACATION,
NOT GET SCARED TO DEATH! GOT IT?!
LEAVE ALL YOUR WEAPONS IN THE...
WHAA?
THEY'RE GETTING ALONG WITH HIM!
なじんでる!!
Yay! きゃっ
Wahah! きゃっ
Yeah! きゃっ
ARE YOU SURE THIS IS ENOUGH TO SPLIT A WATER-MELON?
YEAH!
REMEMBER, DON'T TAKE THE BLINDFOLD OFF, SOSUKE!
ぎゅ
SQUEEZE

* A TYPE OF HAND GRENADE WITHOUT MUCH KILLING POWER

※殺傷能力の低い手榴弾。

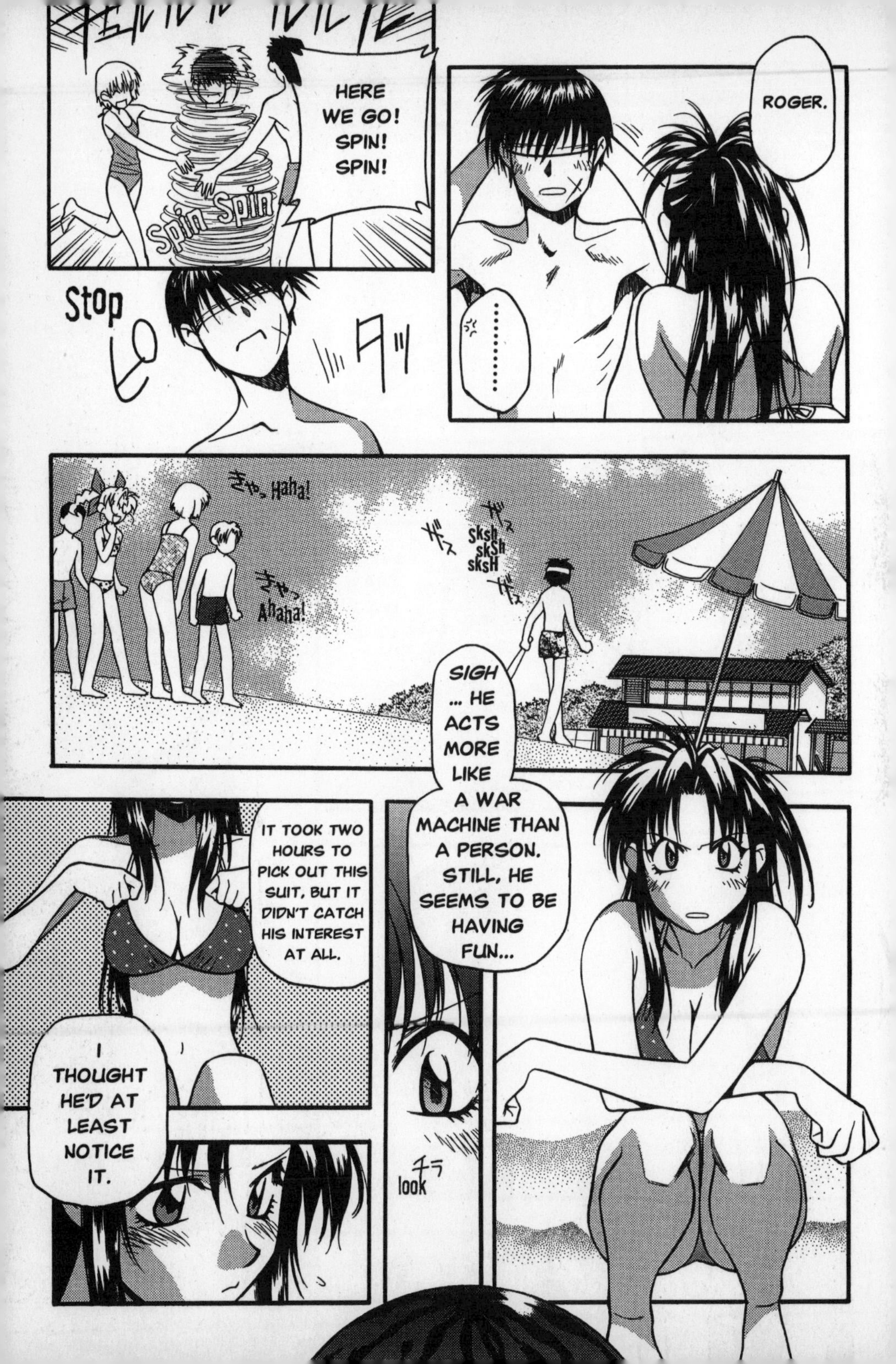
ROGER.
......
HERE WE GO! SPIN! SPIN!
Spin Spin
Stop
sksh sksh sksh
きゃ、Haha!
きゃっ Ahaha!
SIGH ... HE ACTS MORE LIKE A WAR MACHINE THAN A PERSON. STILL, HE SEEMS TO BE HAVING FUN...
チラ look
IT TOOK TWO HOURS TO PICK OUT THIS SUIT, BUT IT DIDN'T CATCH HIS INTEREST AT ALL.
I THOUGHT HE'D AT LEAST NOTICE IT.

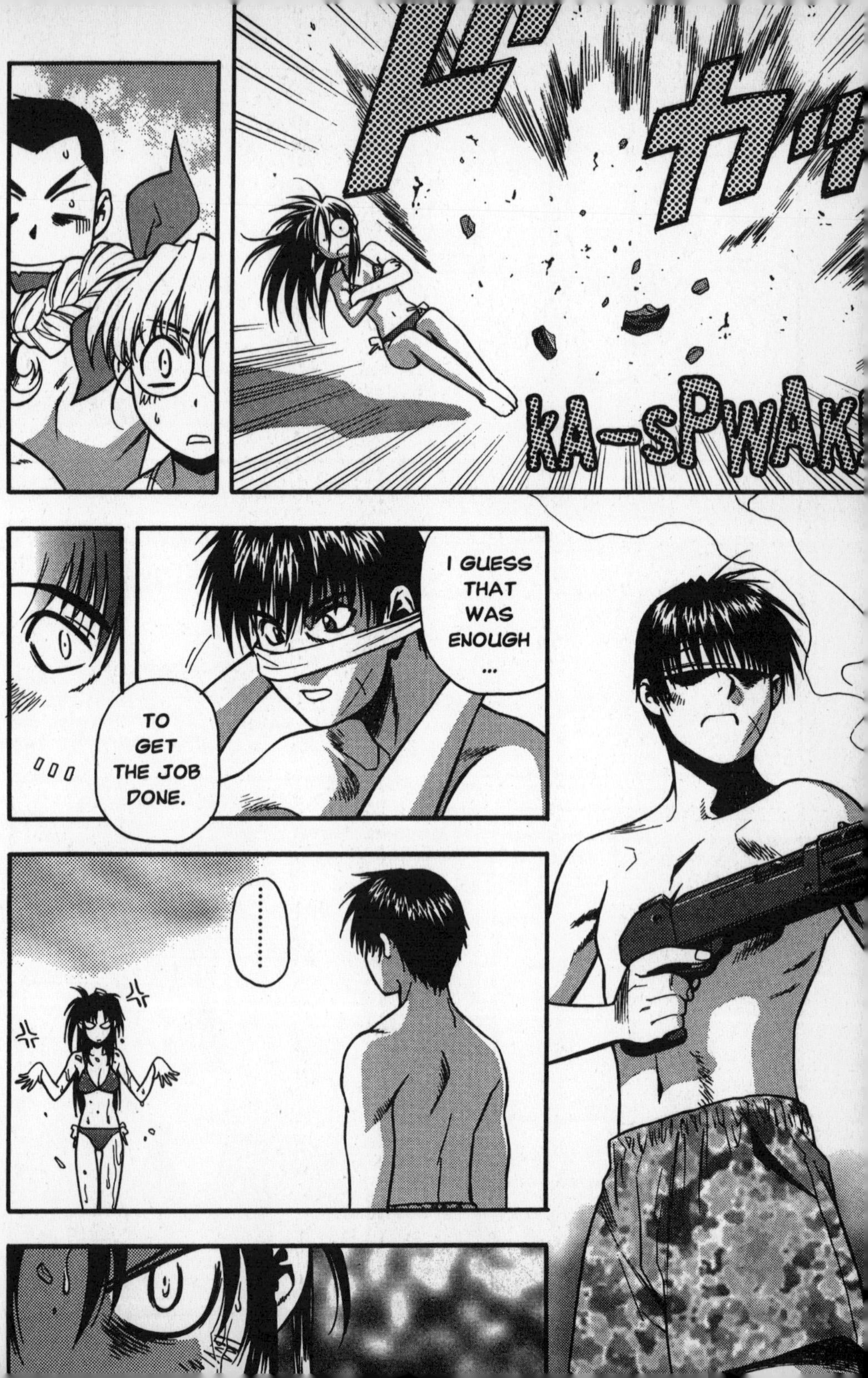
ドカッ
KA-SPWAK!
I GUESS THAT WAS ENOUGH ...
TO GET THE JOB DONE.
...
....

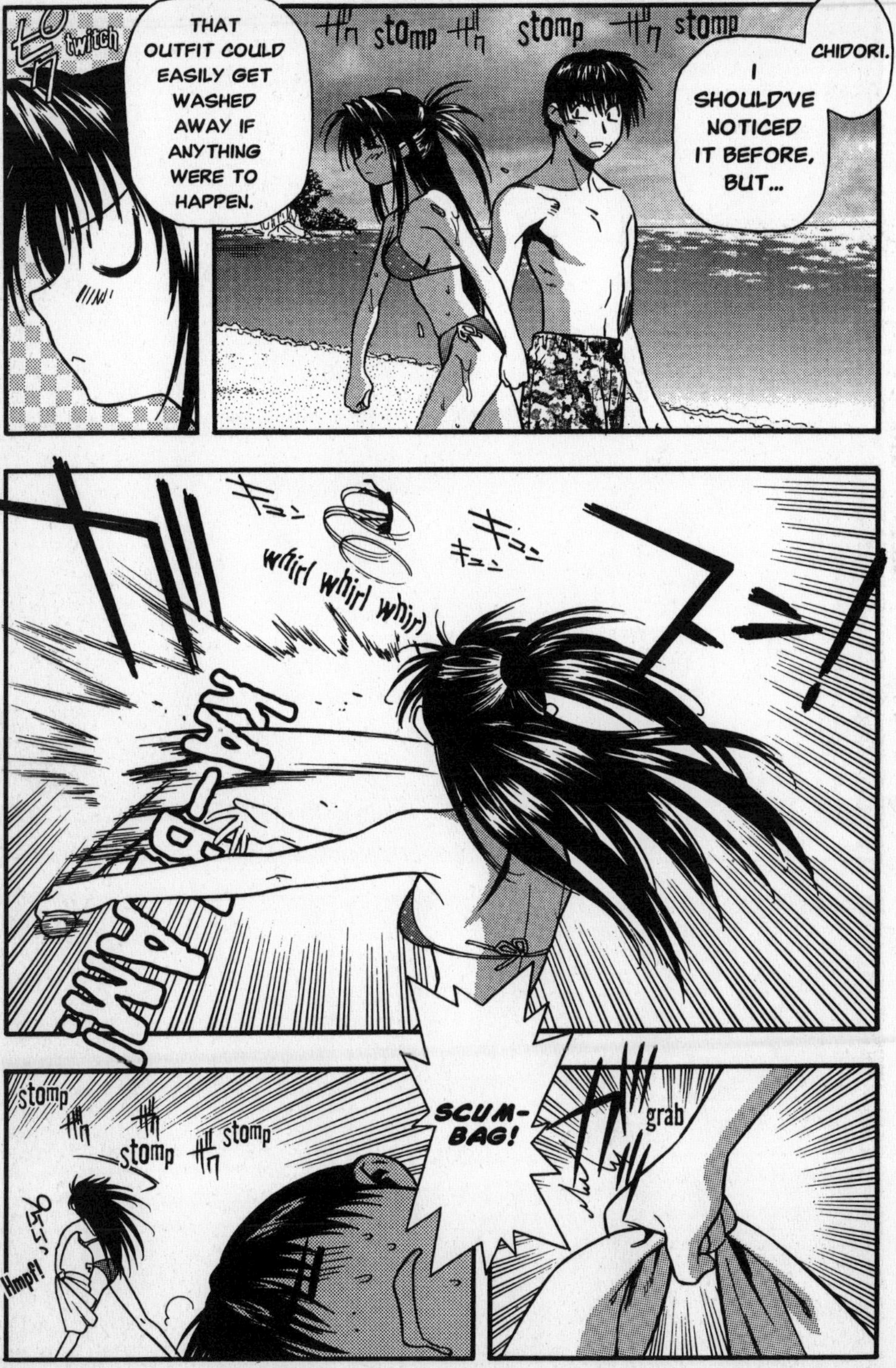
stomp stomp stomp
CHIDORI.
I SHOULD'VE NOTICED IT BEFORE, BUT...
twitch
THAT OUTFIT COULD EASILY GET WASHED AWAY IF ANYTHING WERE TO HAPPEN.
whirl whirl whirl
KA-BAM!!
SCUM-BAG!
grab
stomp
stomp
stomp
Hmpf!

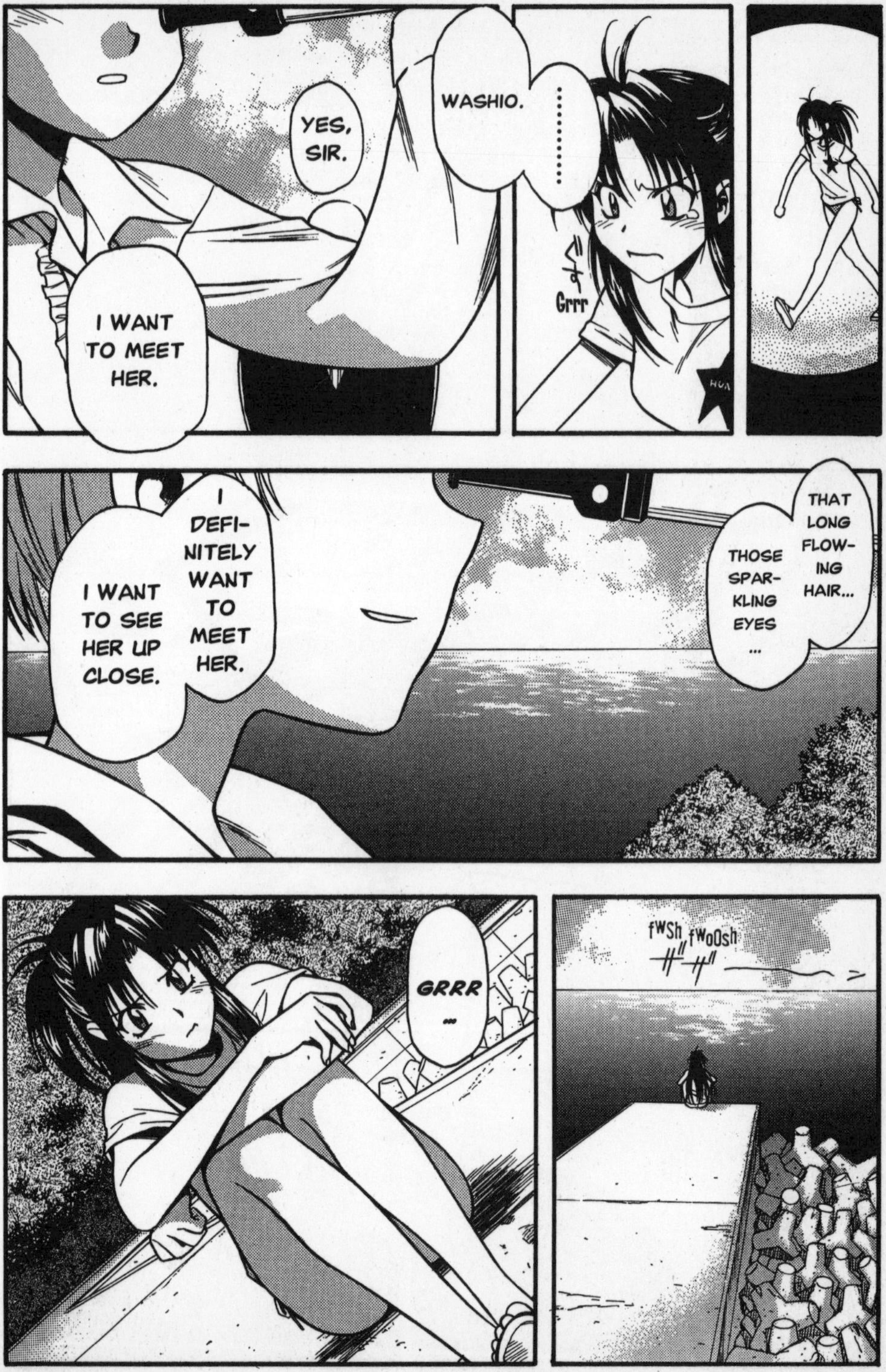
......
Grrr
WASHIO.
YES, SIR.
I WANT TO MEET HER.
THAT LONG FLOWING HAIR...
THOSE SPARKLING EYES...
I DEFINITELY WANT TO MEET HER.
I WANT TO SEE HER UP CLOSE.
fWSh fWoOsh
GRRR...

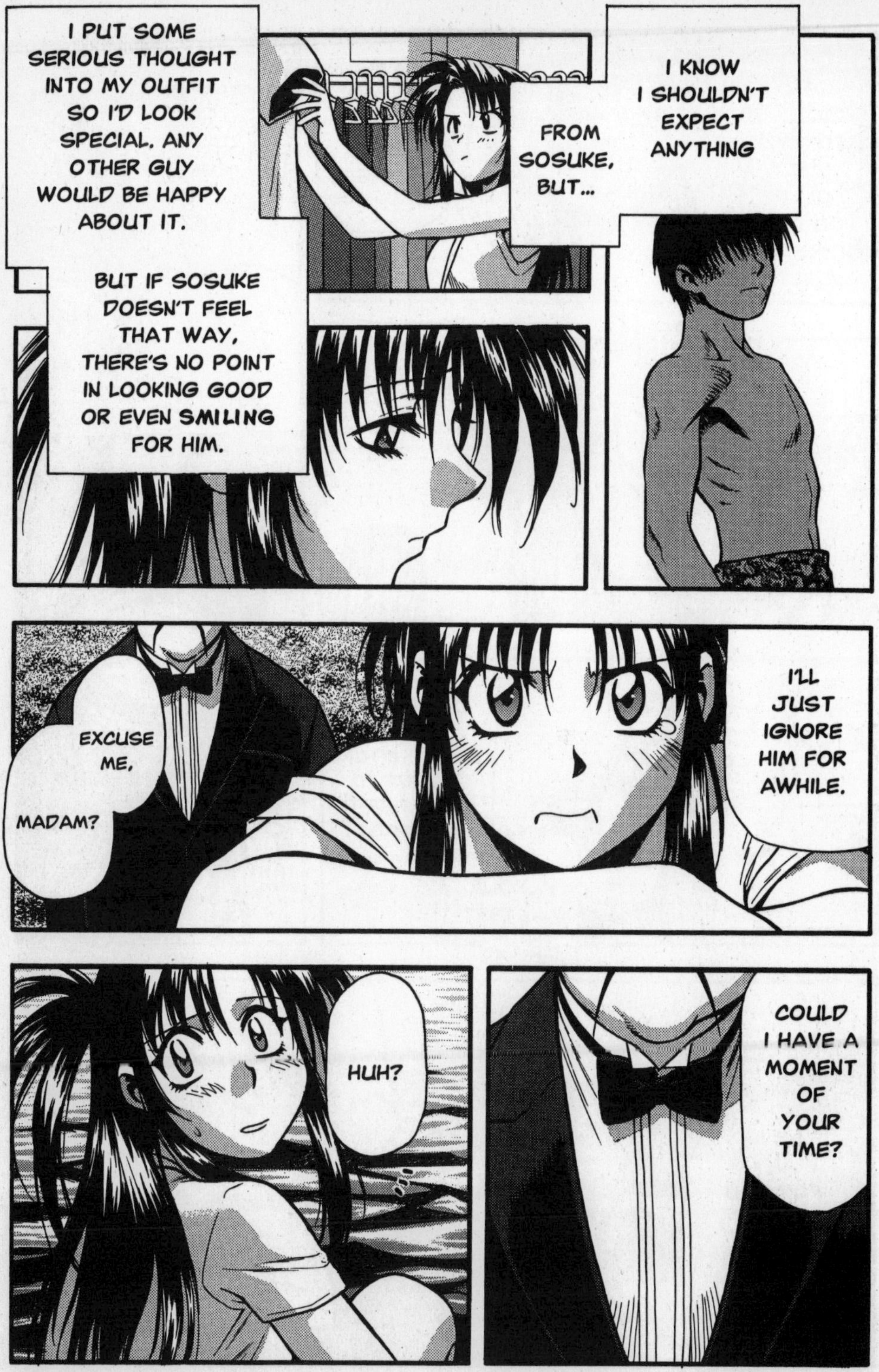
I KNOW I SHOULDN'T EXPECT ANYTHING
FROM SOSUKE, BUT...
I PUT SOME SERIOUS THOUGHT INTO MY OUTFIT SO I'D LOOK SPECIAL. ANY OTHER GUY WOULD BE HAPPY ABOUT IT.
BUT IF SOSUKE DOESN'T FEEL THAT WAY, THERE'S NO POINT IN LOOKING GOOD OR EVEN SMILING FOR HIM.
I'LL JUST IGNORE HIM FOR AWHILE.
EXCUSE ME,
MADAM?
COULD I HAVE A MOMENT OF YOUR TIME?
HUH?

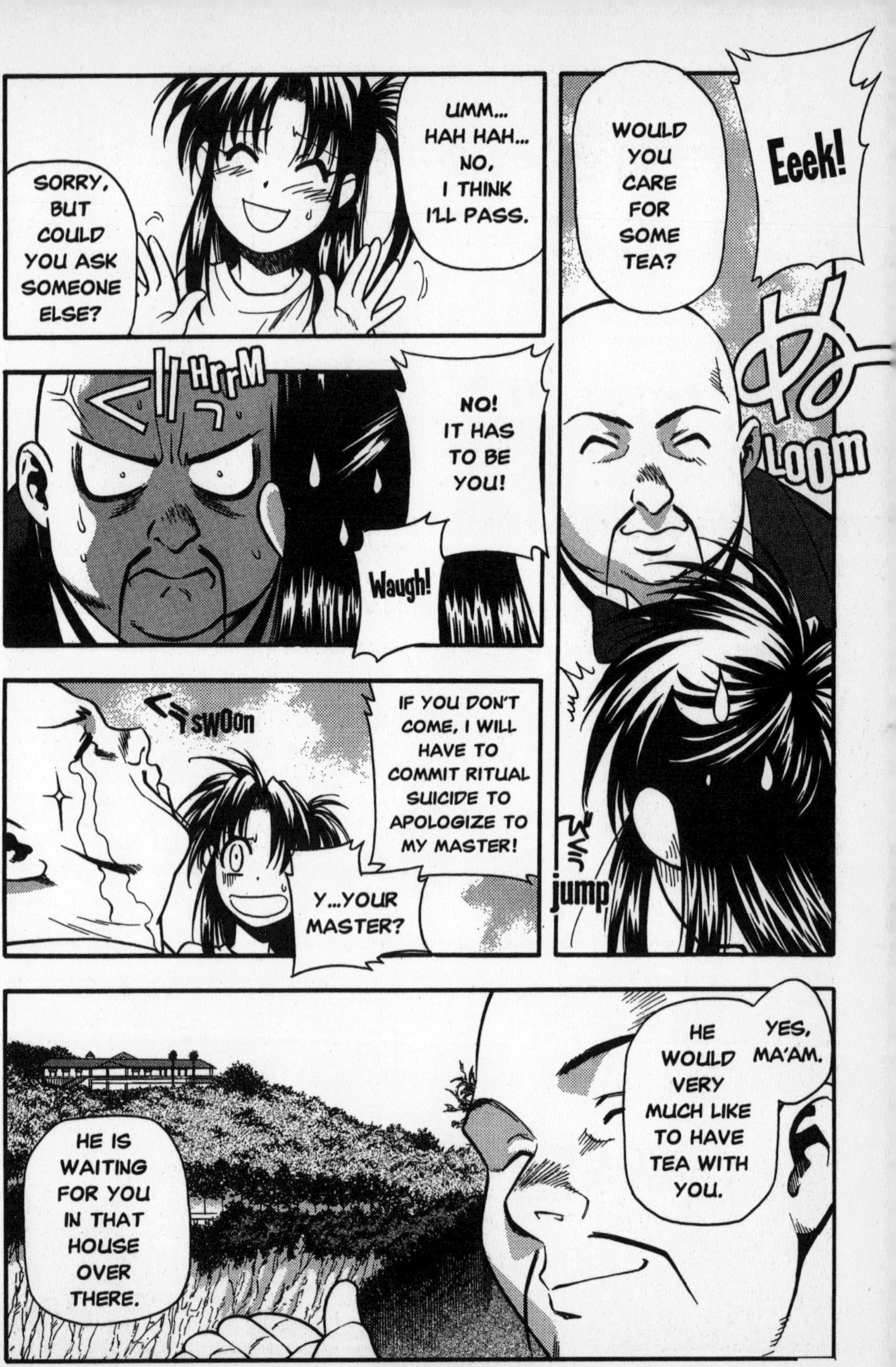
WOULD YOU CARE FOR SOME TEA?
Eeek!
LOOM
jump
UMM... HAH HAH... NO, I THINK I'LL PASS.
SORRY, BUT COULD YOU ASK SOMEONE ELSE?
HrrM
NO! IT HAS TO BE YOU!
Waugh!
sWOon
IF YOU DON'T COME, I WILL HAVE TO COMMIT RITUAL SUICIDE TO APOLOGIZE TO MY MASTER!
Y...YOUR MASTER?
YES, MA'AM.
HE WOULD VERY MUCH LIKE TO HAVE TEA WITH YOU.
HE IS WAITING FOR YOU IN THAT HOUSE OVER THERE.

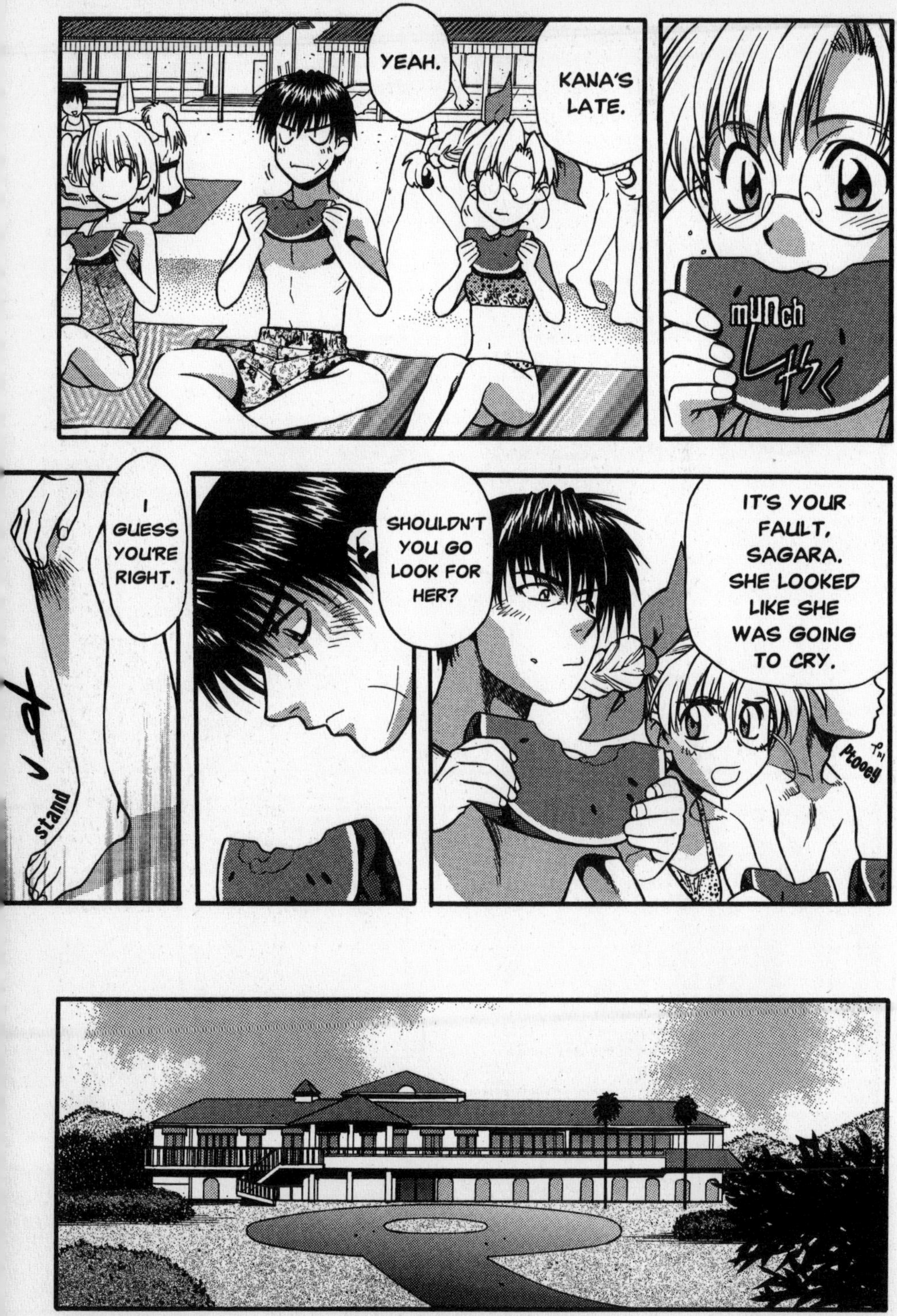
munch
KANA'S LATE.
YEAH.
IT'S YOUR FAULT, SAGARA. SHE LOOKED LIKE SHE WAS GOING TO CRY.
Ptooey
SHOULDN'T YOU GO LOOK FOR HER?
I GUESS YOU'RE RIGHT.
stand

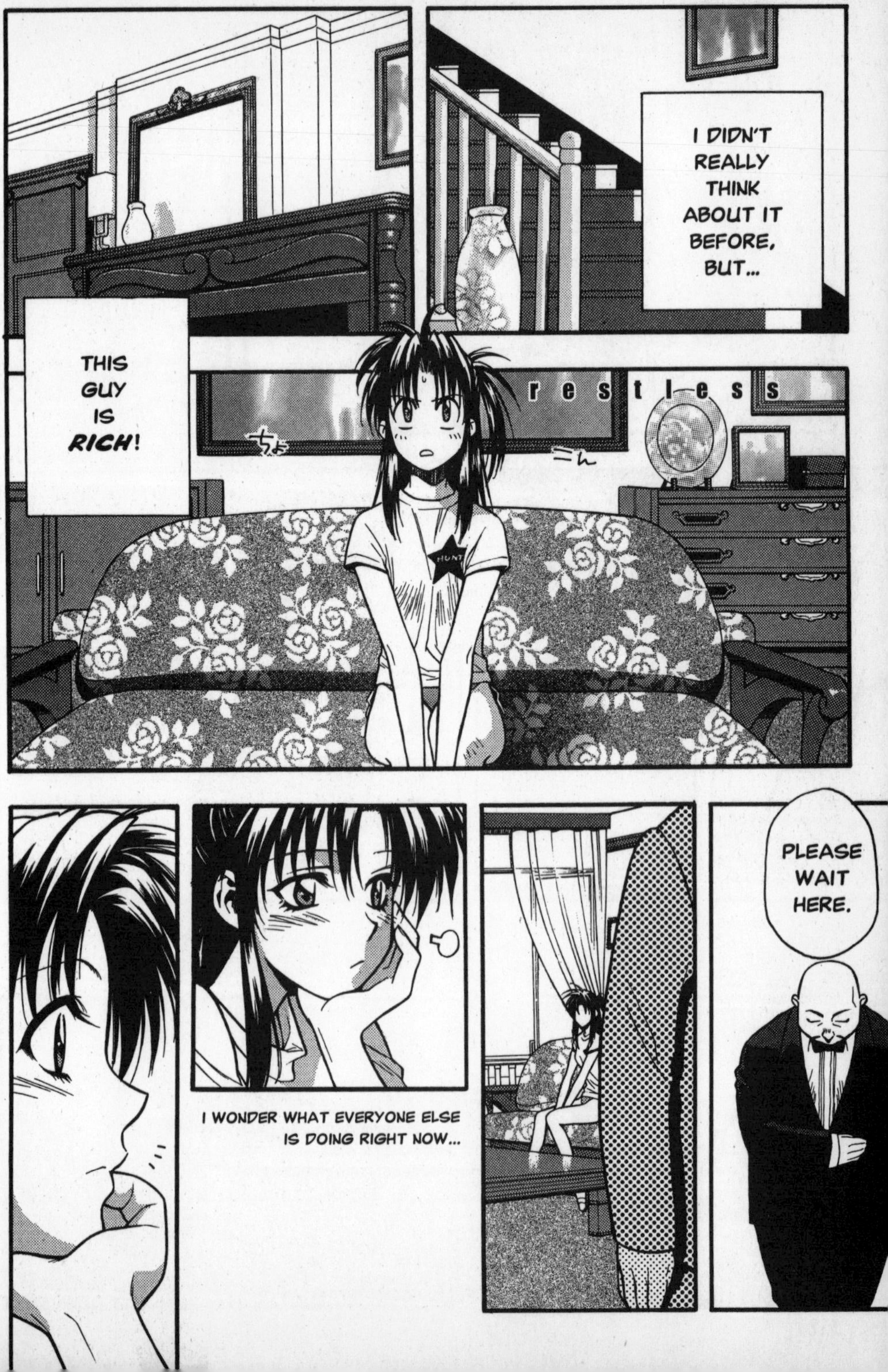
I DIDN'T REALLY THINK ABOUT IT BEFORE, BUT...
THIS GUY IS *RICH*!
restless
PLEASE WAIT HERE.
I WONDER WHAT EVERYONE ELSE IS DOING RIGHT NOW...

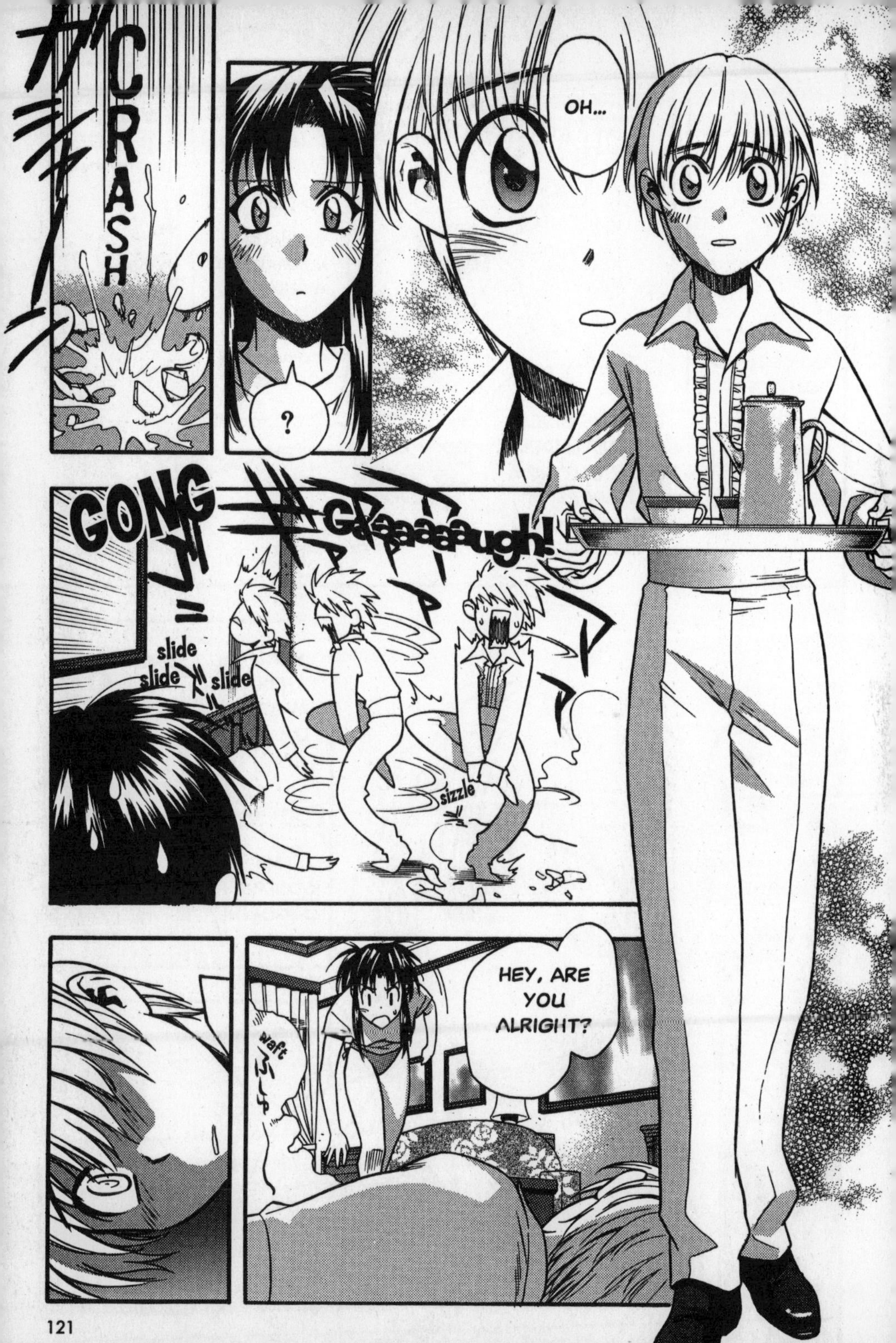
OH...
?
CRASH
Gaaaaaaaugh!
GONG
slide
slide
slide
sizzle
HEY, ARE YOU ALRIGHT?
waft

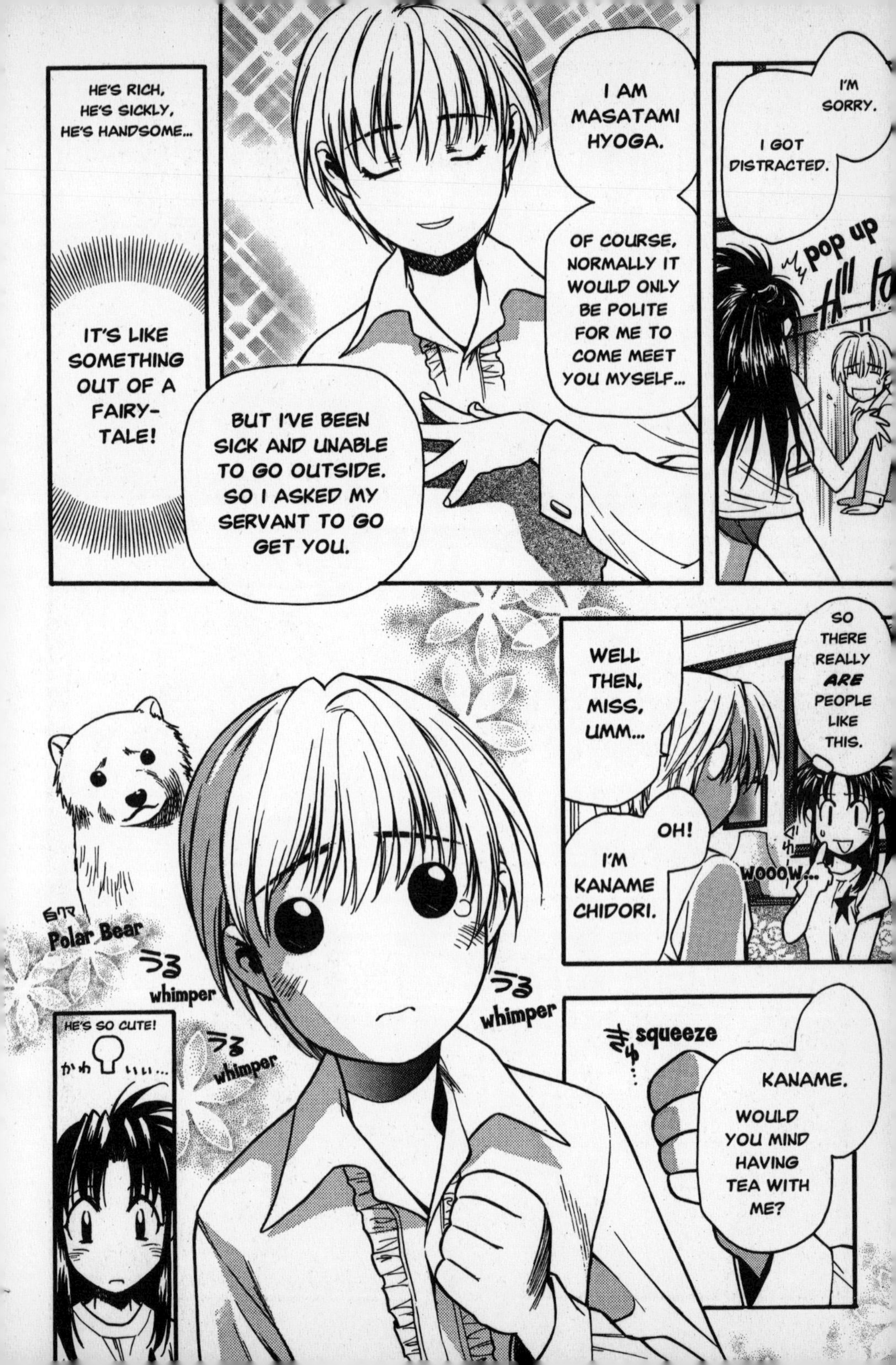

I'M SORRY.
I GOT DISTRACTED.
pop up
I AM MASATAMI HYOGA.
OF COURSE, NORMALLY IT WOULD ONLY BE POLITE FOR ME TO COME MEET YOU MYSELF...
BUT I'VE BEEN SICK AND UNABLE TO GO OUTSIDE. SO I ASKED MY SERVANT TO GO GET YOU.
HE'S RICH, HE'S SICKLY, HE'S HANDSOME...
IT'S LIKE SOMETHING OUT OF A FAIRY-TALE!
SO THERE REALLY ARE PEOPLE LIKE THIS.
WELL THEN, MISS, UMM...
OH!
I'M KANAME CHIDORI.
WOOOW...
squeeze
KANAME.
WOULD YOU MIND HAVING TEA WITH ME?
うる
whimper
うる
whimper
Polar Bear
うる
whimper
HE'S SO CUTE!

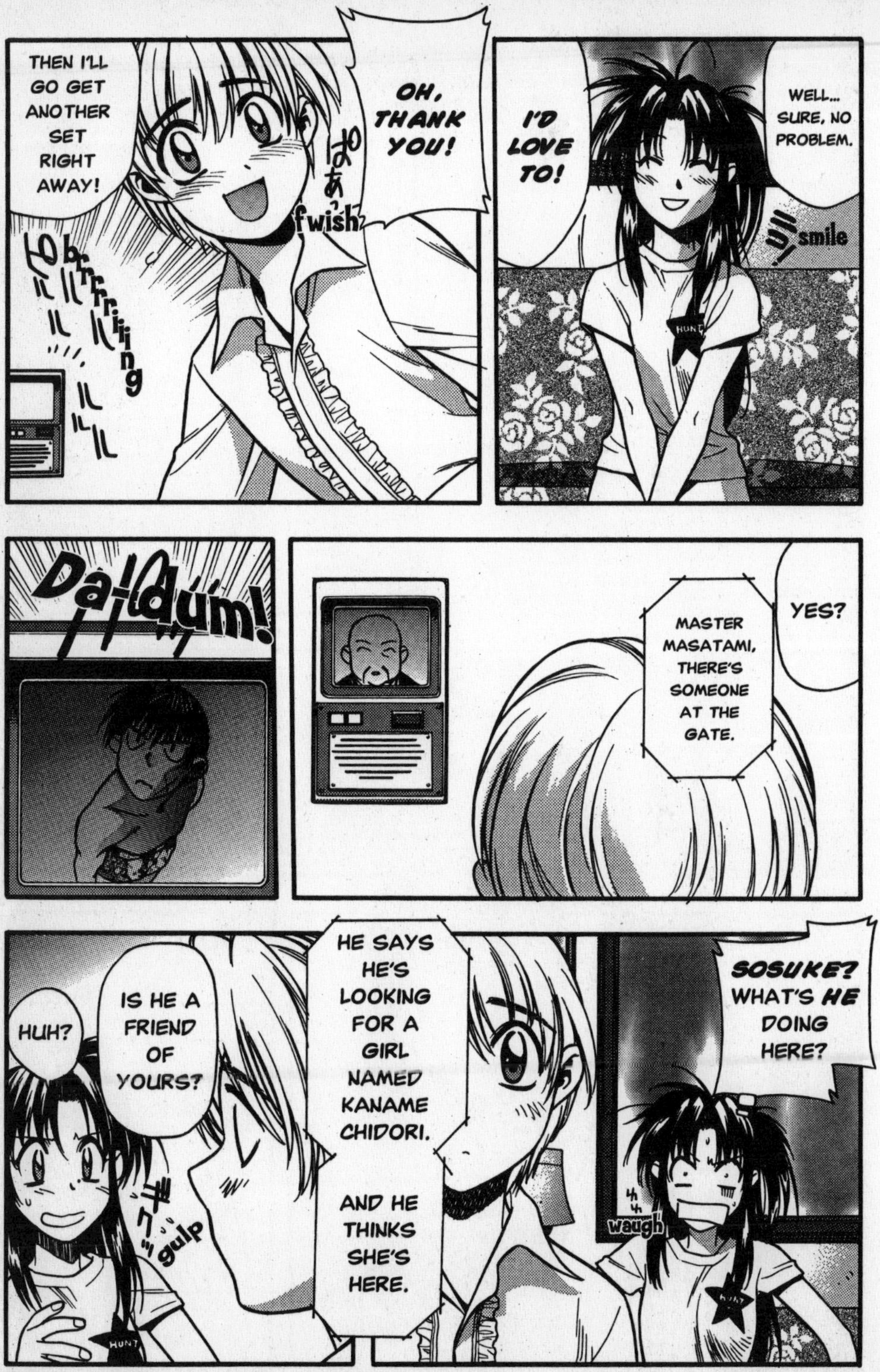
WELL... SURE, NO PROBLEM.
I'D LOVE TO!
smile
OH, THANK YOU!
fwish
THEN I'LL GO GET ANOTHER SET RIGHT AWAY!
brrrrriiing
YES?
MASTER MASATAMI, THERE'S SOMEONE AT THE GATE.
Dadum!
SOSUKE? WHAT'S HE DOING HERE?
waugh
HE SAYS HE'S LOOKING FOR A GIRL NAMED KANAME CHIDORI.
IS HE A FRIEND OF YOURS?
HUH?
AND HE THINKS SHE'S HERE.
gulp

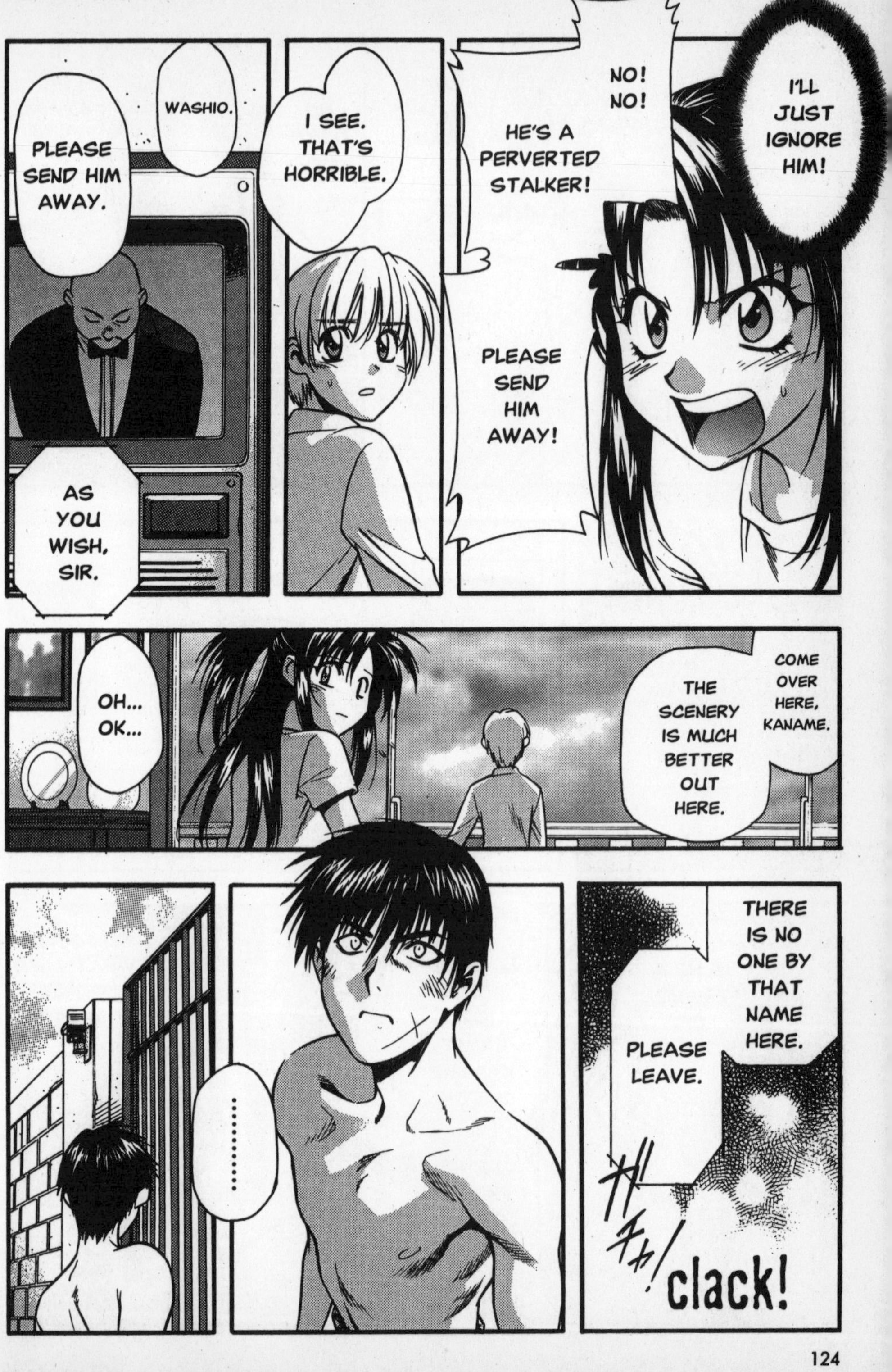
I'LL JUST IGNORE HIM!
NO! NO!
HE'S A PERVERTED STALKER!
PLEASE SEND HIM AWAY!
I SEE. THAT'S HORRIBLE.
WASHIO.
PLEASE SEND HIM AWAY.
AS YOU WISH, SIR.
COME OVER HERE, KANAME.
THE SCENERY IS MUCH BETTER OUT HERE.
OH... OK...
THERE IS NO ONE BY THAT NAME HERE.
PLEASE LEAVE.
clack!
....

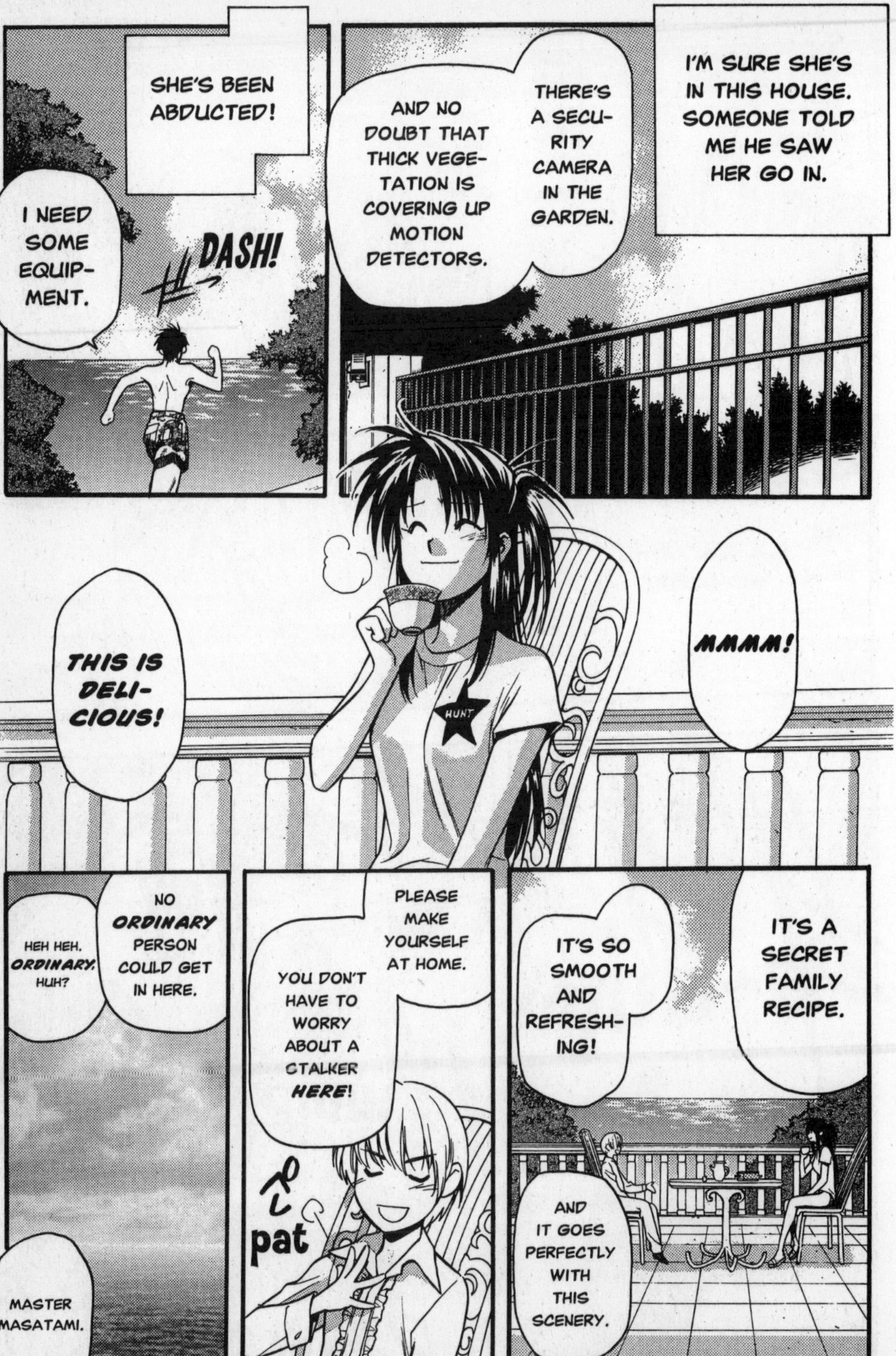
I'M SURE SHE'S IN THIS HOUSE. SOMEONE TOLD ME HE SAW HER GO IN.
THERE'S A SECURITY CAMERA IN THE GARDEN.
AND NO DOUBT THAT THICK VEGETATION IS COVERING UP MOTION DETECTORS.
SHE'S BEEN ABDUCTED!
I NEED SOME EQUIPMENT.
DASH!
MMMM!
THIS IS DELICIOUS!
IT'S A SECRET FAMILY RECIPE.
IT'S SO SMOOTH AND REFRESHING!
AND IT GOES PERFECTLY WITH THIS SCENERY.
PLEASE MAKE YOURSELF AT HOME.
YOU DON'T HAVE TO WORRY ABOUT A STALKER *HERE*!
pat
NO *ORDINARY* PERSON COULD GET IN HERE.
HEH HEH. *ORDINARY*, HUH?
MASTER MASATAMI.

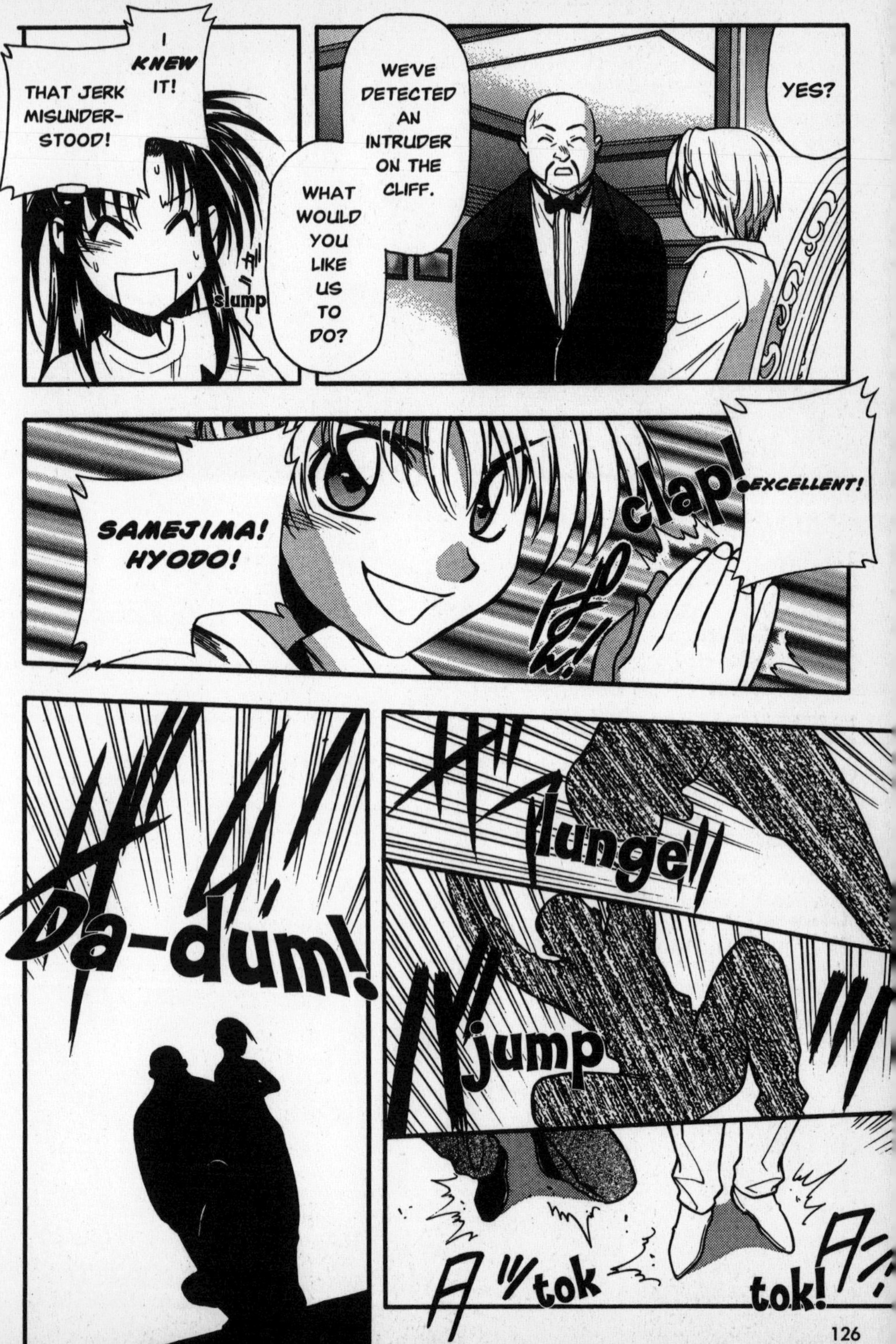
YES?
WE'VE DETECTED AN INTRUDER ON THE CLIFF.
WHAT WOULD YOU LIKE US TO DO?
I KNEW IT!
THAT JERK MISUNDERSTOOD!
slump
EXCELLENT!
clap!
SAMEJIMA! HYODO!
lunge!
jump
tok
tok!
Da-dum!

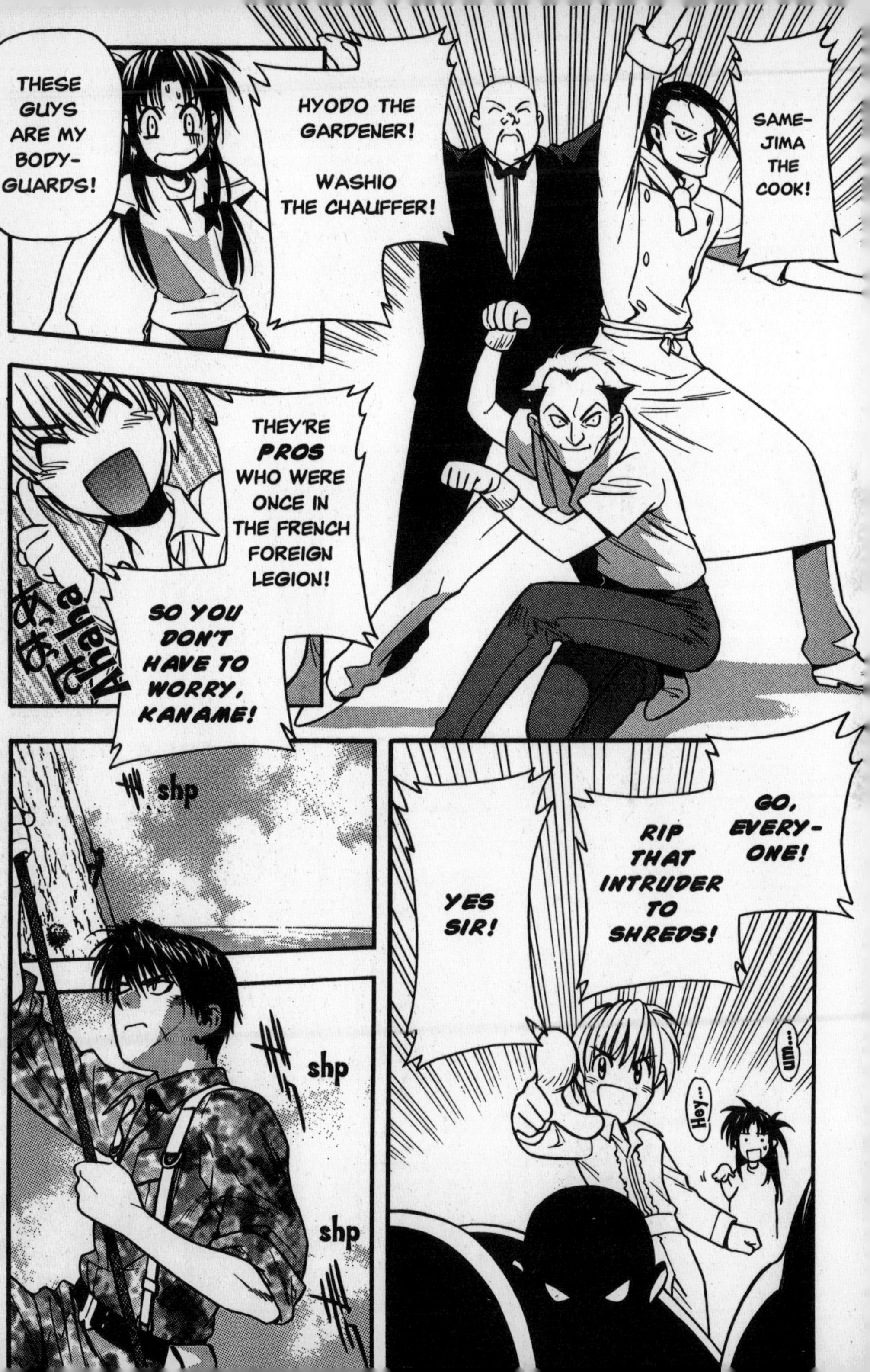
SAME-JIMA THE COOK!
HYODO THE GARDENER!
WASHIO THE CHAUFFER!
THESE GUYS ARE MY BODY-GUARDS!
THEY'RE PROS WHO WERE ONCE IN THE FRENCH FOREIGN LEGION!
SO YOU DON'T HAVE TO WORRY, KANAME!
あはは
Ahaha
GO, EVERY-ONE!
RIP THAT INTRUDER TO SHREDS!
YES SIR!
um...
Hey...
shp
shp
shp

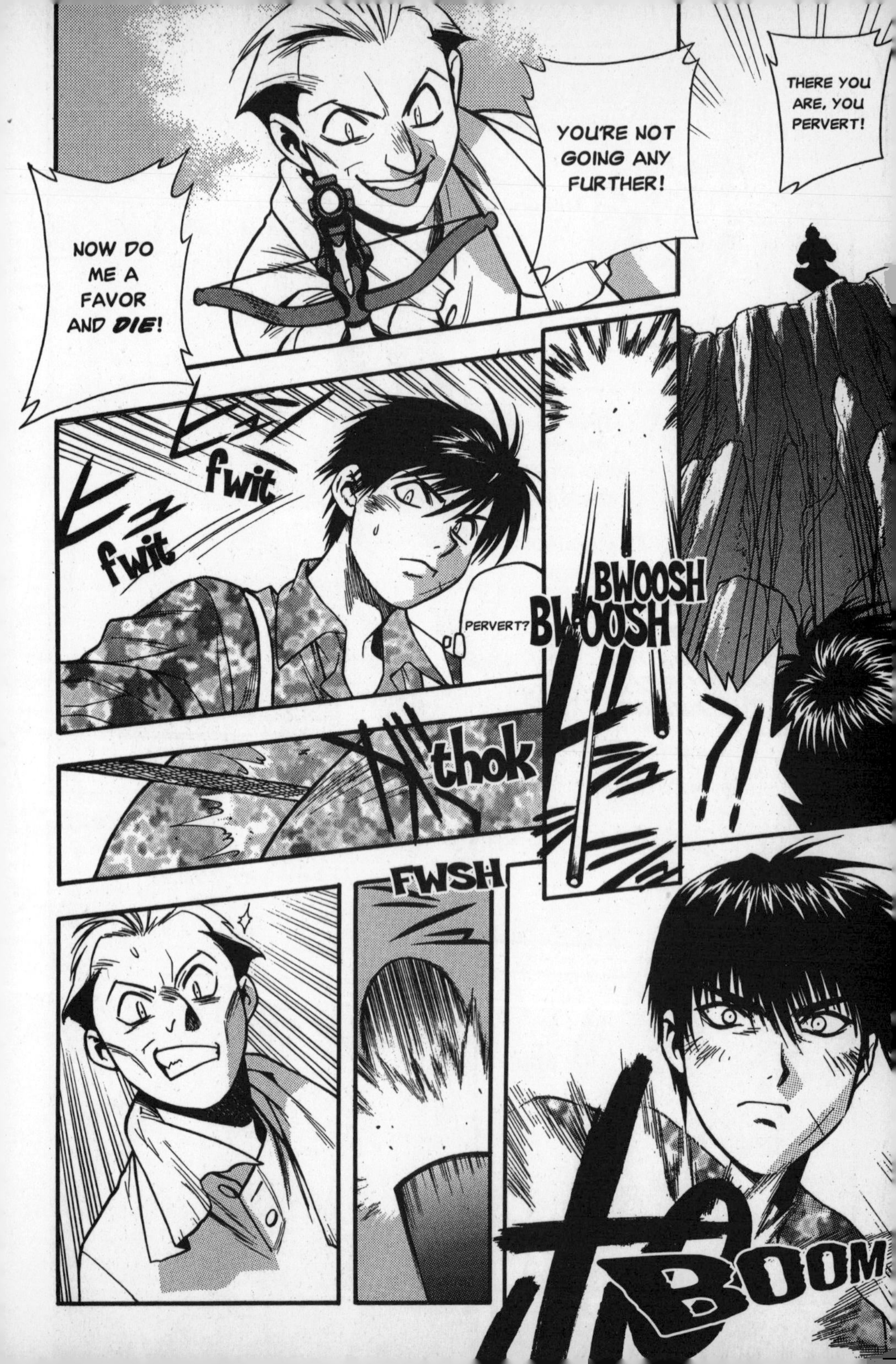

THERE YOU ARE, YOU PERVERT!
YOU'RE NOT GOING ANY FURTHER!
NOW DO ME A FAVOR AND DIE!
BWOOSH
BWOOSH
?!
fwit
fwit
PERVERT?
thok
BOOM
FWSH

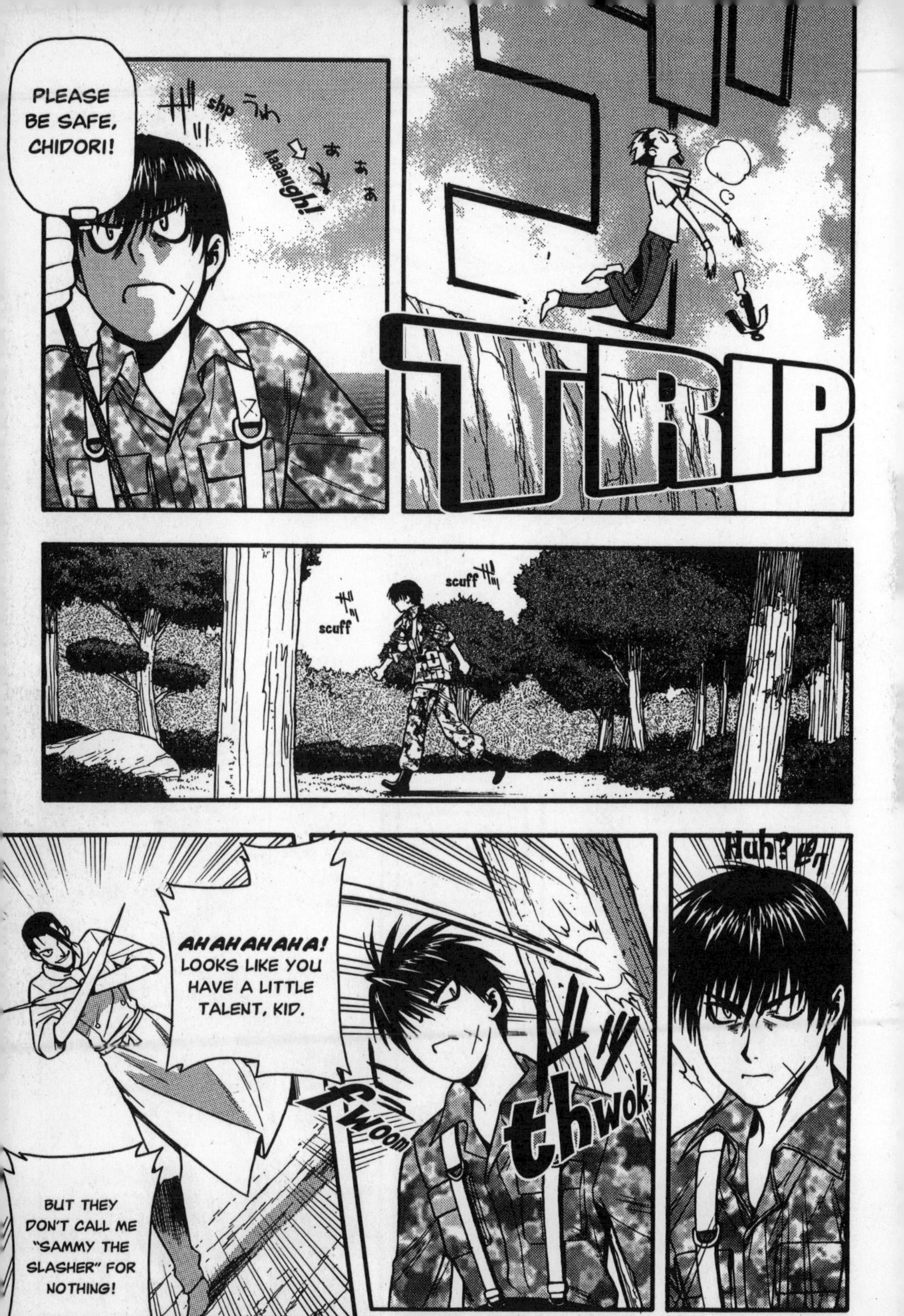
TRIP
PLEASE BE SAFE, CHIDORI!
shp
aaaaugh!
scuff
scuff
Huh?
thwok
fwoom
AHAHAHAHA! LOOKS LIKE YOU HAVE A LITTLE TALENT, KID.
BUT THEY DON'T CALL ME "SAMMY THE SLASHER" FOR NOTHING!

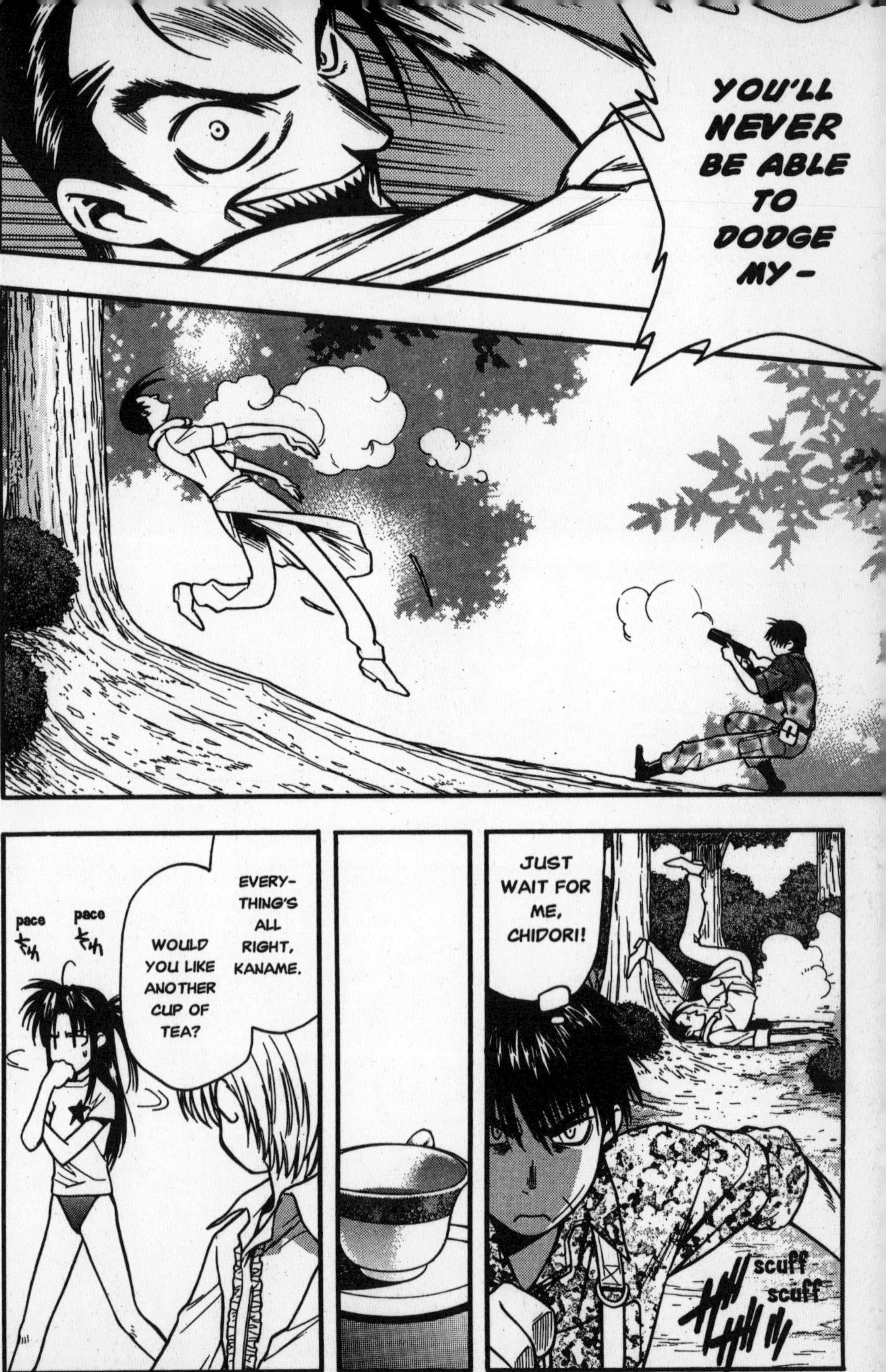
YOU'LL NEVER BE ABLE TO DODGE MY-
JUST WAIT FOR ME, CHIDORI!
scuff-scuff
EVERY-THING'S ALL RIGHT, KANAME.
WOULD YOU LIKE ANOTHER CUP OF TEA?
pace pace

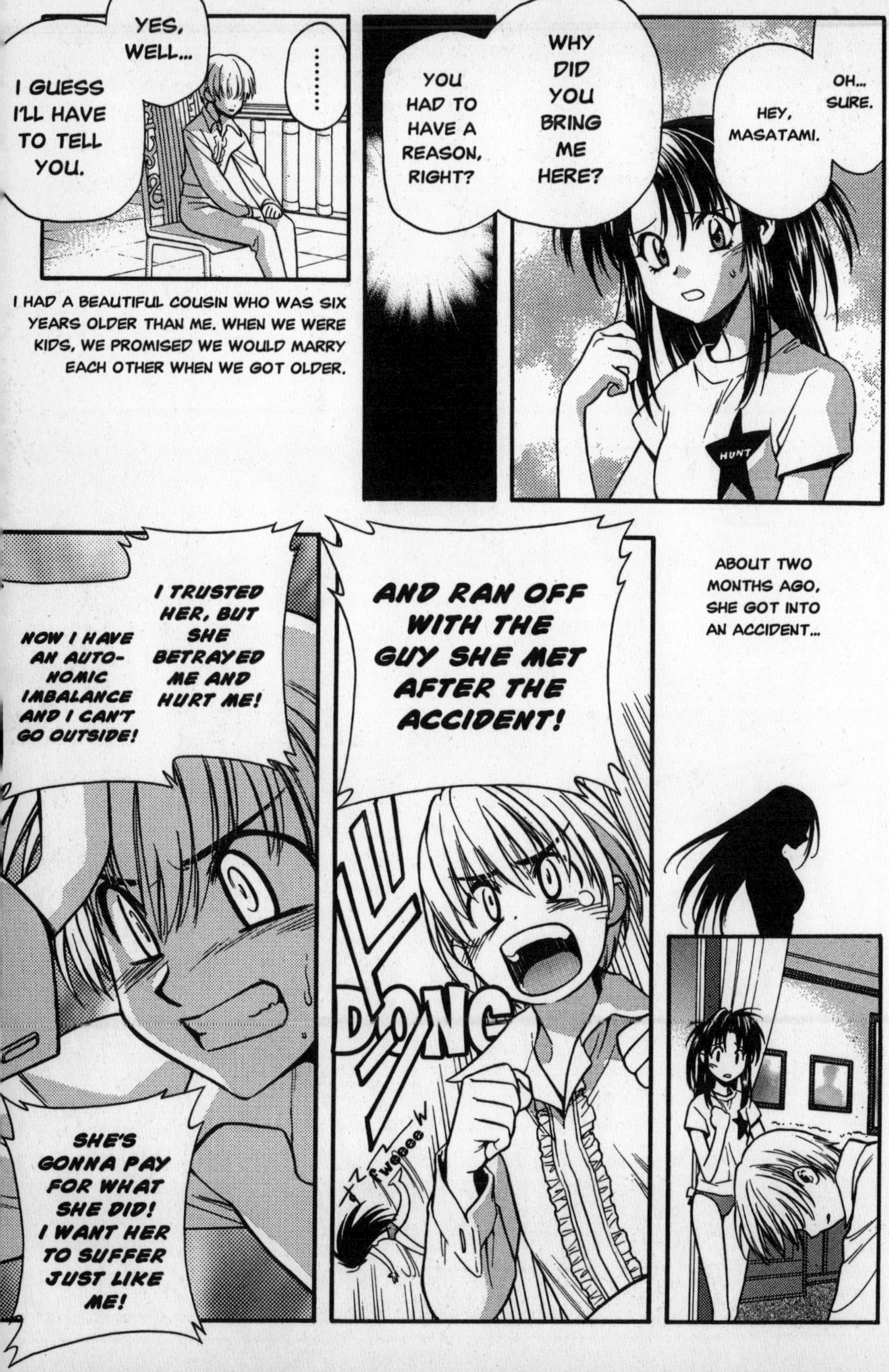
OH... SURE.
HEY, MASATAMI.
WHY DID YOU BRING ME HERE?
YOU HAD TO HAVE A REASON, RIGHT?
......
YES, WELL...
I GUESS I'LL HAVE TO TELL YOU.
I HAD A BEAUTIFUL COUSIN WHO WAS SIX YEARS OLDER THAN ME. WHEN WE WERE KIDS, WE PROMISED WE WOULD MARRY EACH OTHER WHEN WE GOT OLDER.
ABOUT TWO MONTHS AGO, SHE GOT INTO AN ACCIDENT...
AND RAN OFF WITH THE GUY SHE MET AFTER THE ACCIDENT!
DONG
fweeeew
I TRUSTED HER, BUT SHE BETRAYED ME AND HURT ME!
NOW I HAVE AN AUTO-NOMIC IMBALANCE AND I CAN'T GO OUTSIDE!
SHE'S GONNA PAY FOR WHAT SHE DID! I WANT HER TO SUFFER JUST LIKE ME!

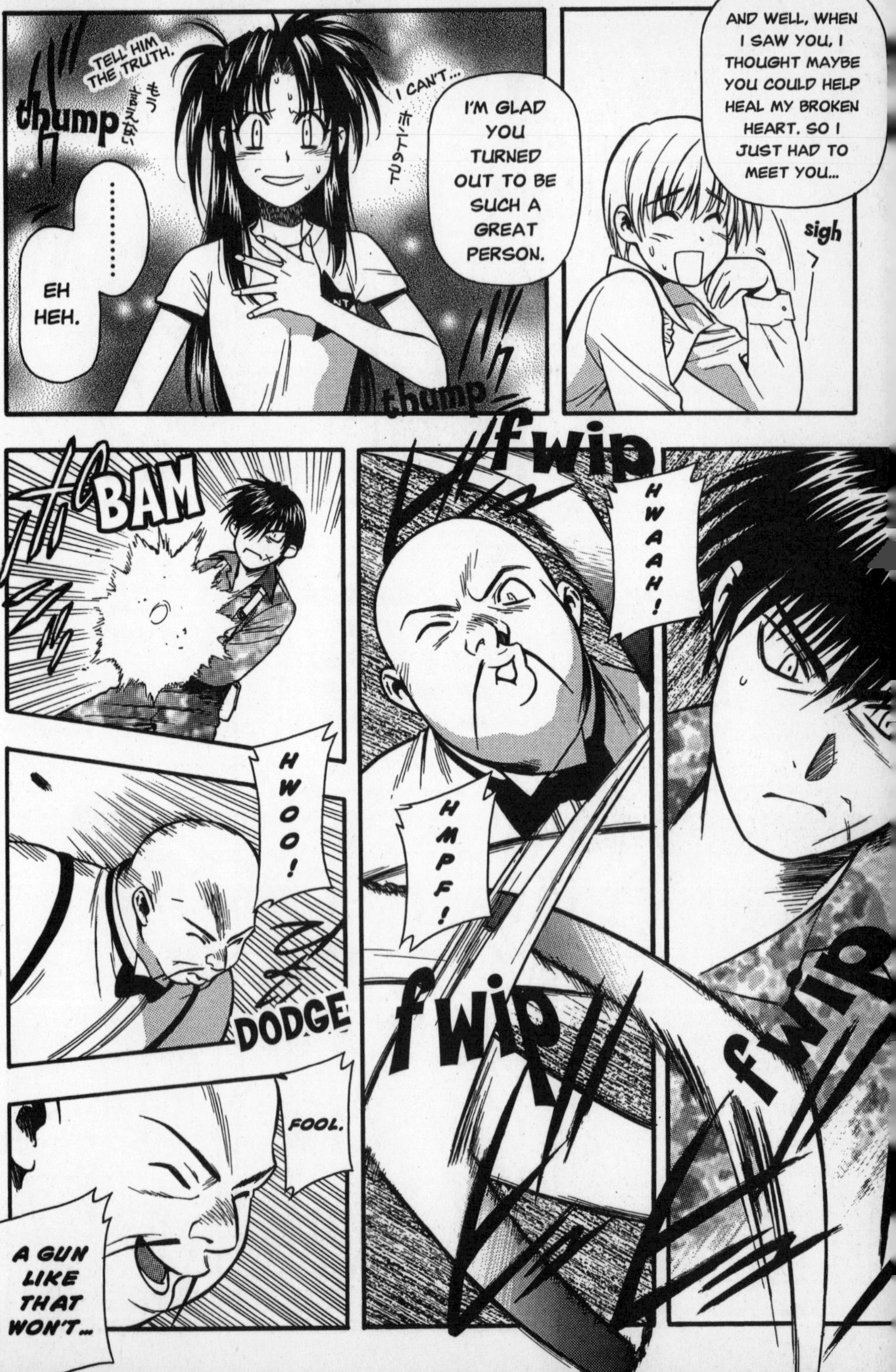
AND WELL, WHEN I SAW YOU, I THOUGHT MAYBE YOU COULD HELP HEAL MY BROKEN HEART. SO I JUST HAD TO MEET YOU...
sigh
I'M GLAD YOU TURNED OUT TO BE SUCH A GREAT PERSON.
I CAN'T...
TELL HIM THE TRUTH.
thump
.... EH HEH.
thump
fwip
fwip
fwip
HWAAAH!
HMPF!
fwip
BAM
HWOOO!
DODGE
FOOL.
A GUN LIKE THAT WON'T...

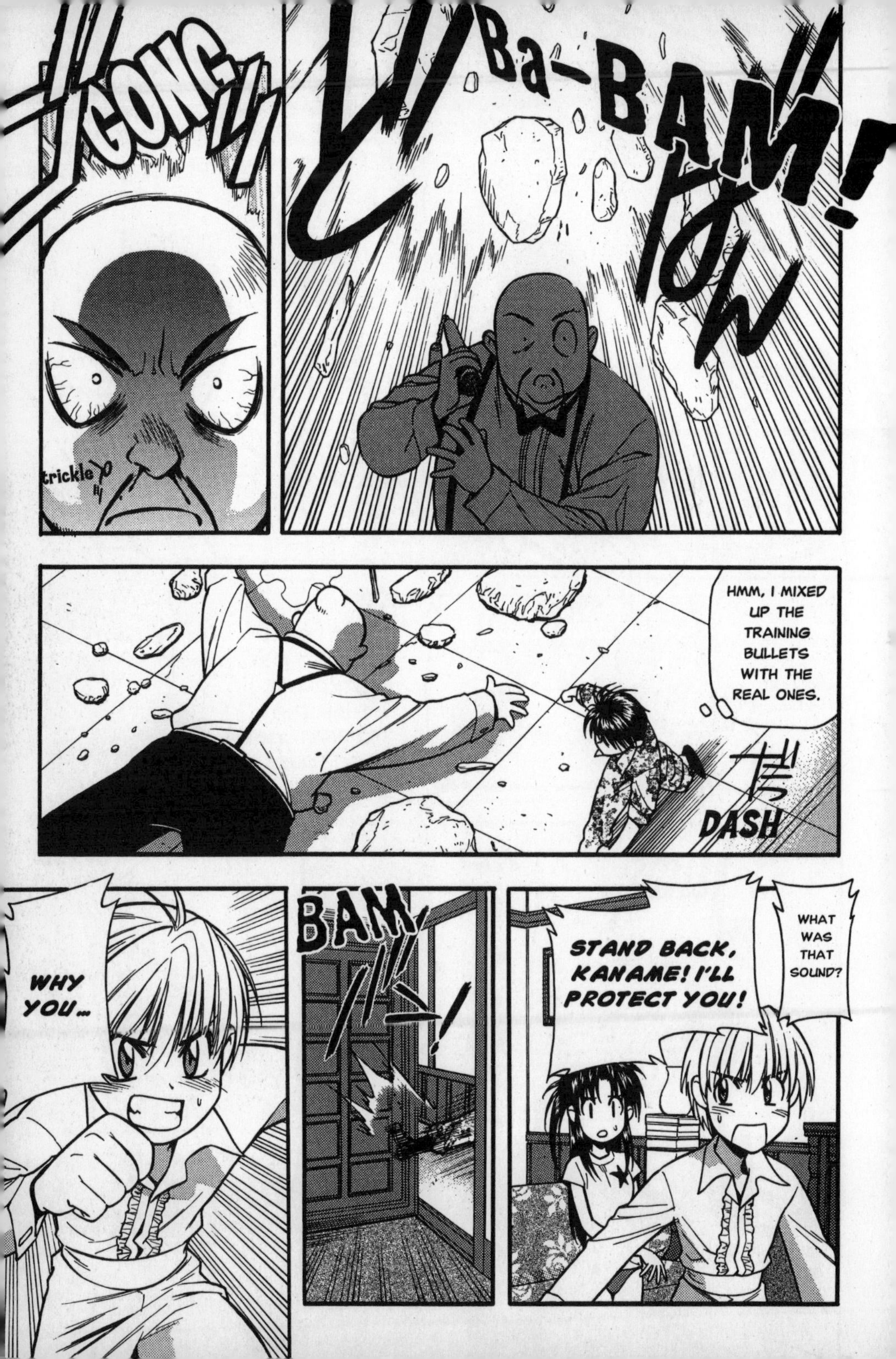
Ba-BAM!
POW
GONG!!
trickle
HMM, I MIXED UP THE TRAINING BULLETS WITH THE REAL ONES.
DASH
WHAT WAS THAT SOUND?
STAND BACK, KANAME! I'LL PROTECT YOU!
BAM
WHY YOU...

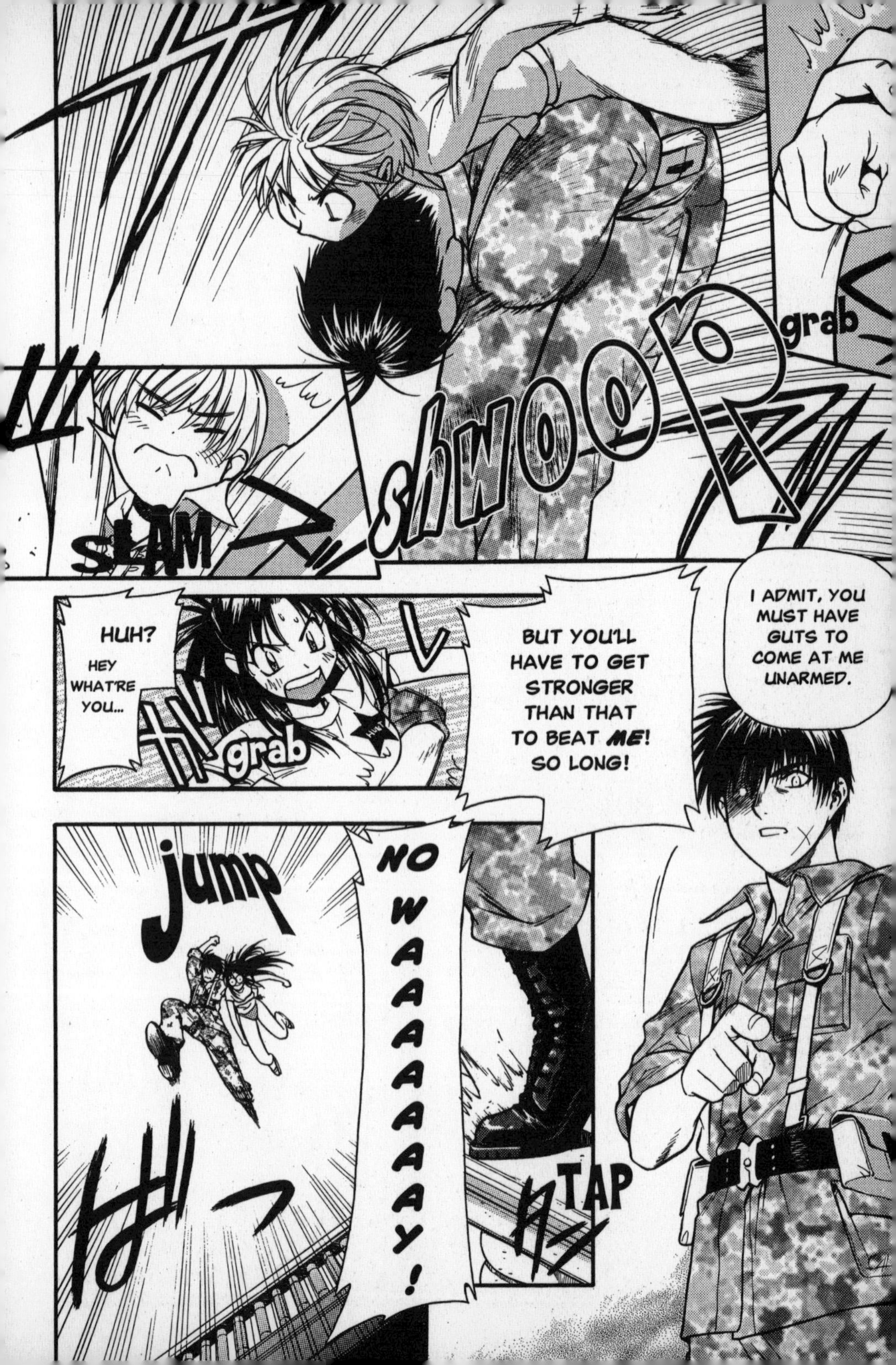
grab
shWOOP
SLAM
I ADMIT, YOU MUST HAVE GUTS TO COME AT ME UNARMED.
BUT YOU'LL HAVE TO GET STRONGER THAN THAT TO BEAT ME! SO LONG!
HUH?
HEY WHAT'RE YOU...
grab
TAP
NO WAAAAAAAY!
jump

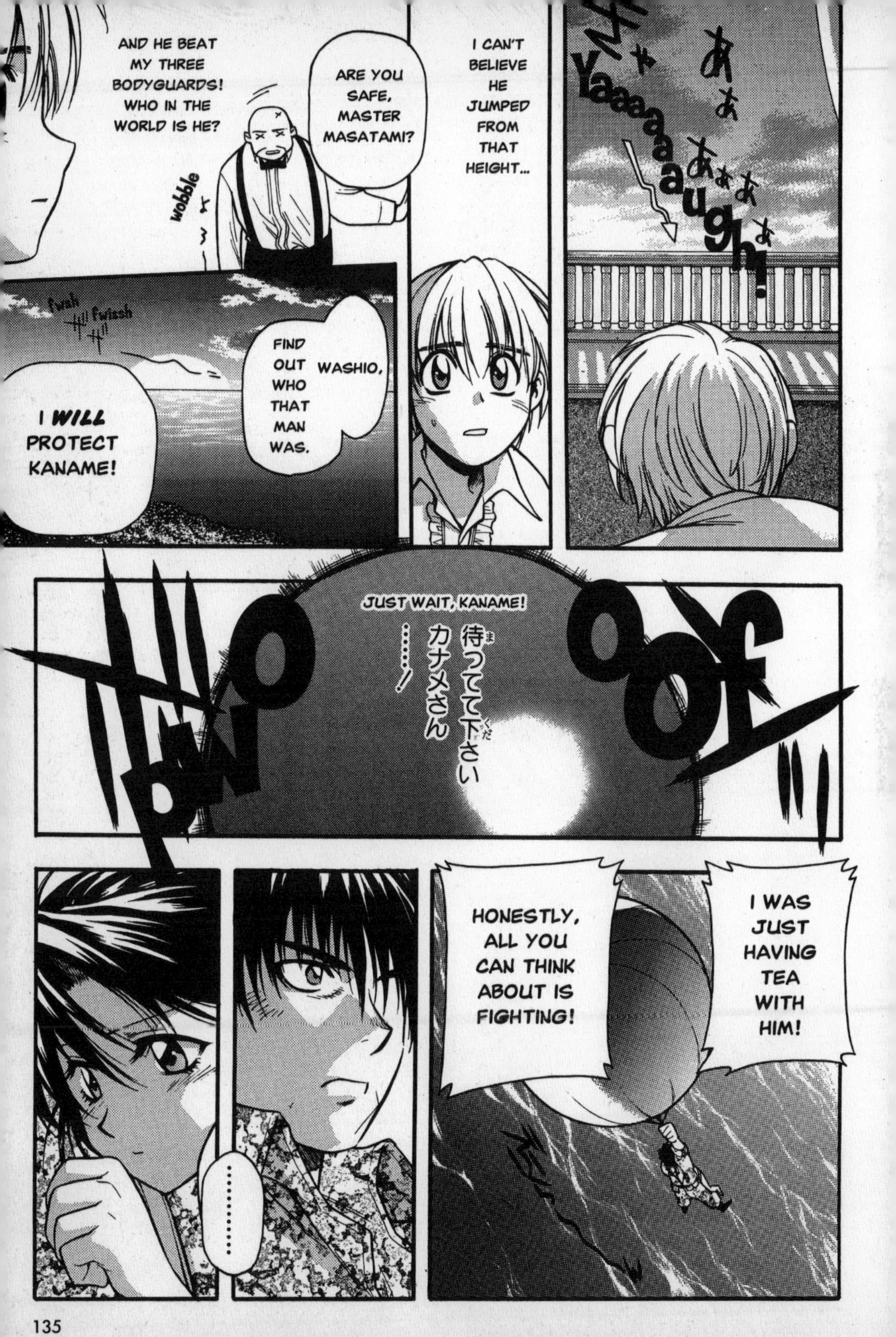

Yaaaaaaaugh!
I CAN'T BELIEVE HE JUMPED FROM THAT HEIGHT...
ARE YOU SAFE, MASTER MASATAMI?
wobble
AND HE BEAT MY THREE BODYGUARDS! WHO IN THE WORLD IS HE?
WASHIO, FIND OUT WHO THAT MAN WAS.
fwsh fwissh
I WILL PROTECT KANAME!
THWOOOF
JUST WAIT, KANAME!
待ってて下さいカナメさん……!
I WAS JUST HAVING TEA WITH HIM!
HONESTLY, ALL YOU CAN THINK ABOUT IS FIGHTING!
……

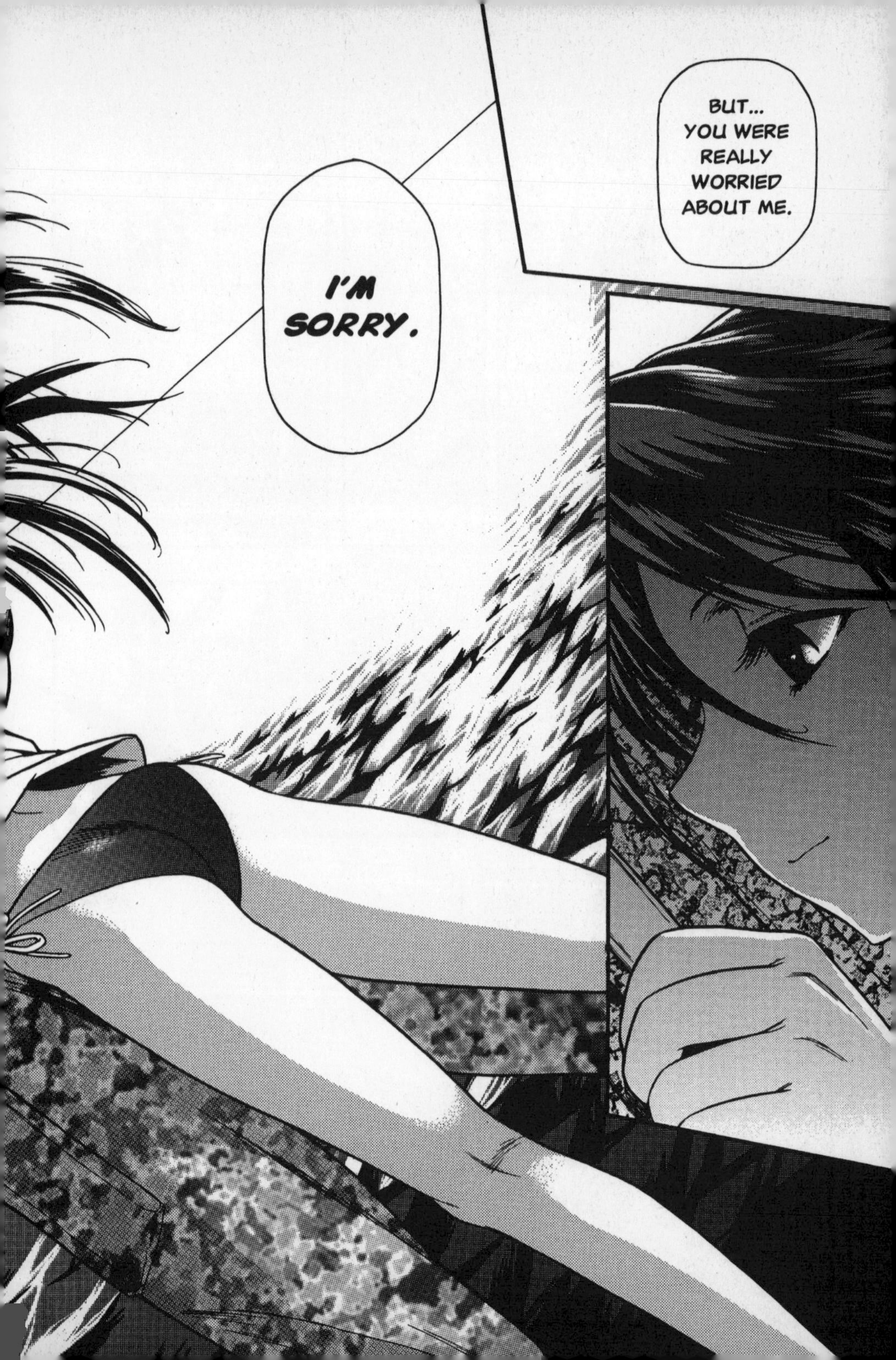
BUT... YOU WERE REALLY WORRIED ABOUT ME.
I'M SORRY.

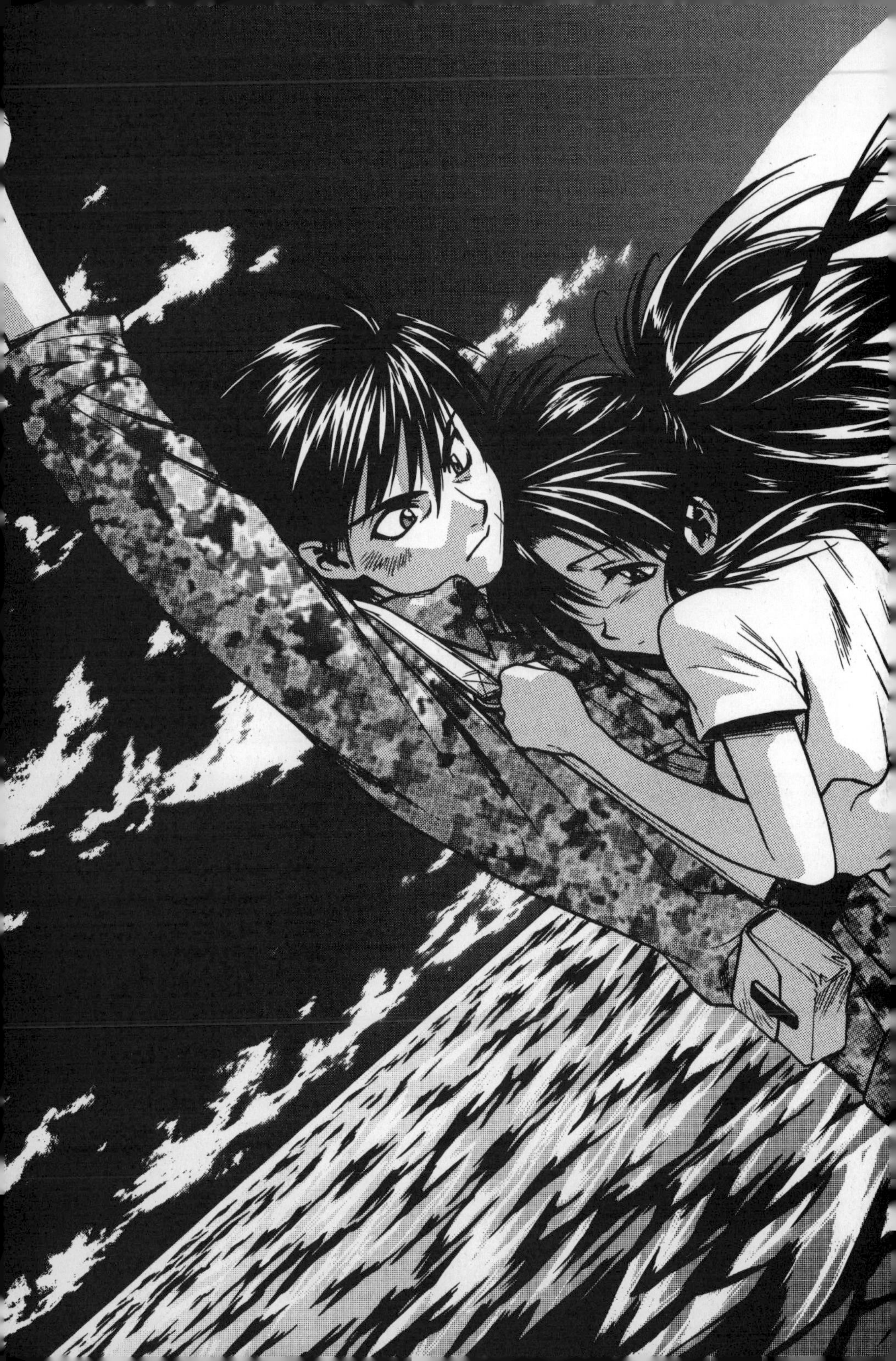

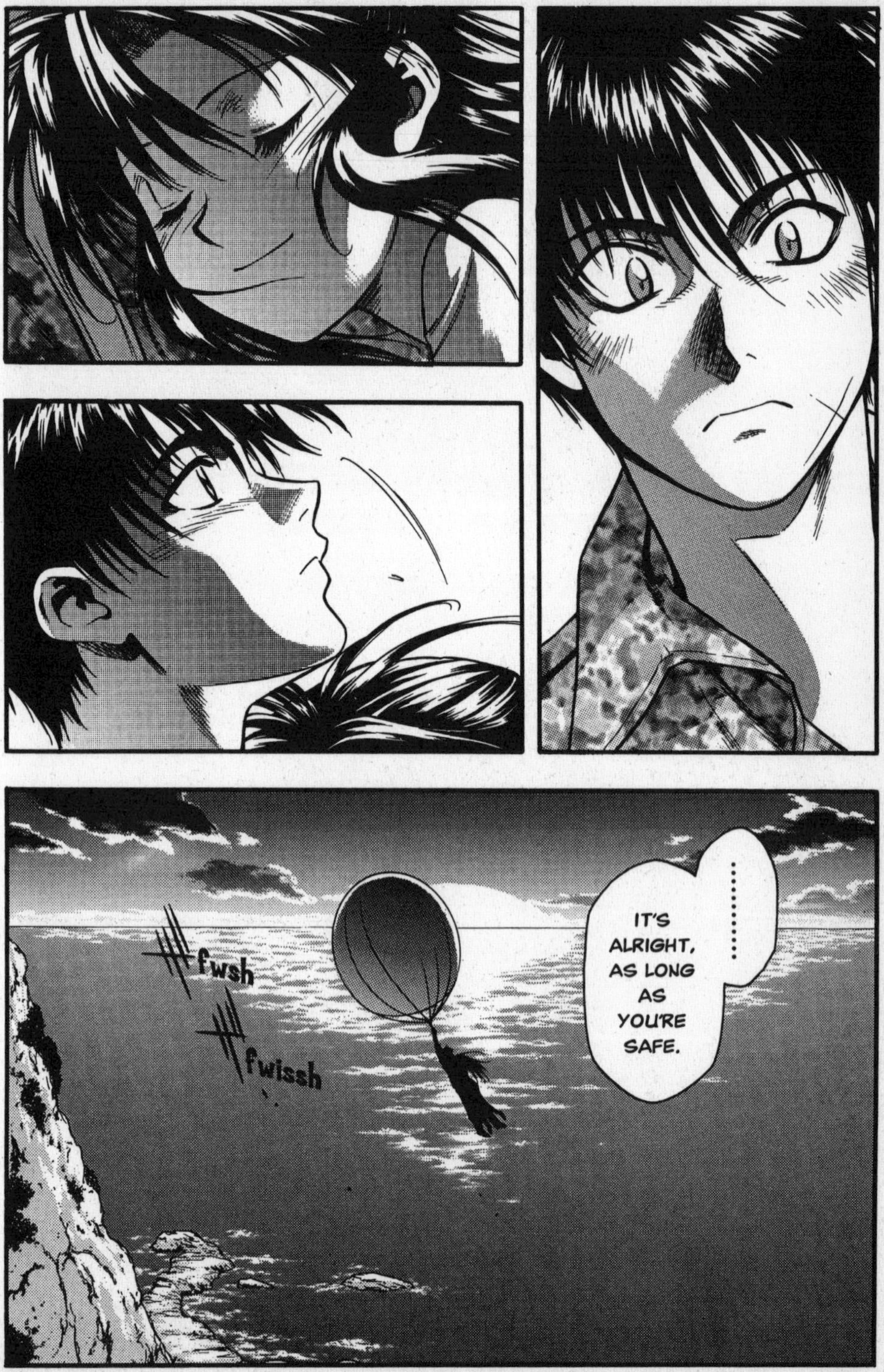
......
IT'S ALRIGHT, AS LONG AS YOU'RE SAFE.
fwsh
fwissh

MISSION:20 I ain't afraid of no ghost! Deserted island search team!!

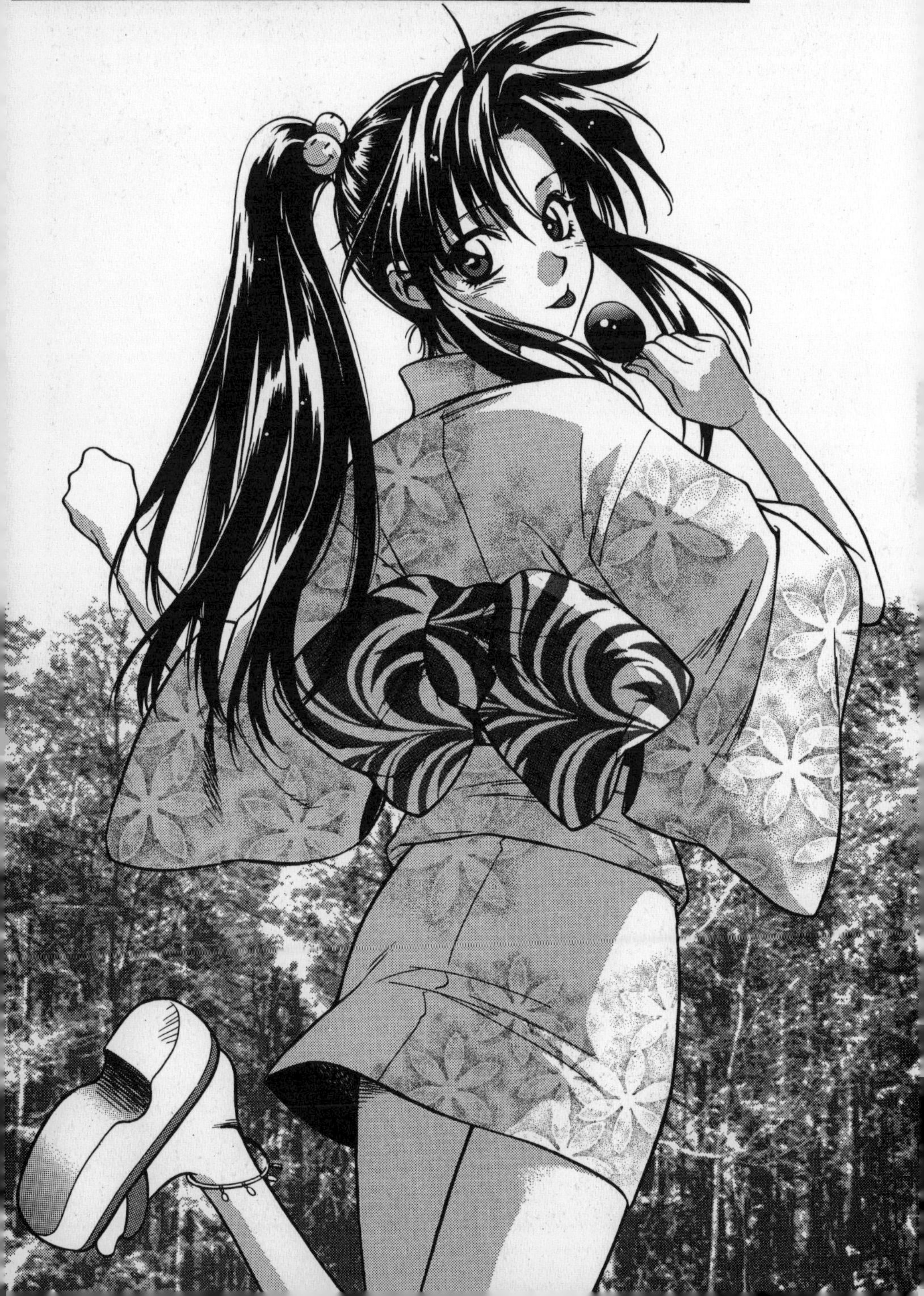

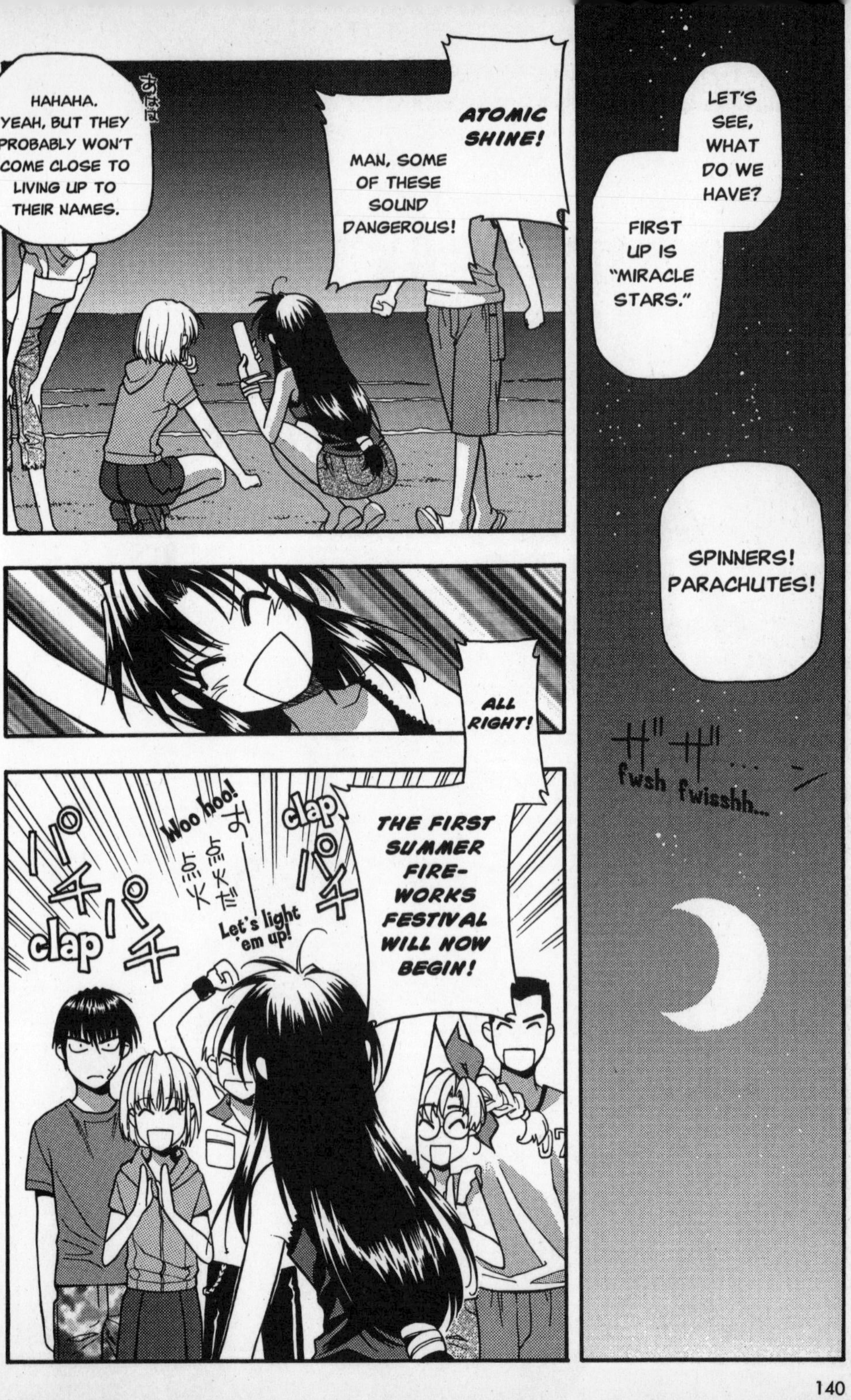
LET'S SEE, WHAT DO WE HAVE?
FIRST UP IS "MIRACLE STARS."
SPINNERS! PARACHUTES!
ザザ
fwsh fwisshh...
ATOMIC SHINE!
MAN, SOME OF THESE SOUND DANGEROUS!
あはは
HAHAHA. YEAH, BUT THEY PROBABLY WON'T COME CLOSE TO LIVING UP TO THEIR NAMES.
ALL RIGHT!
THE FIRST SUMMER FIRE-WORKS FESTIVAL WILL NOW BEGIN!
パチ
clap
おー
Woo hoo!
点火だ
点火
Let's light 'em up!
パチパチ
clap

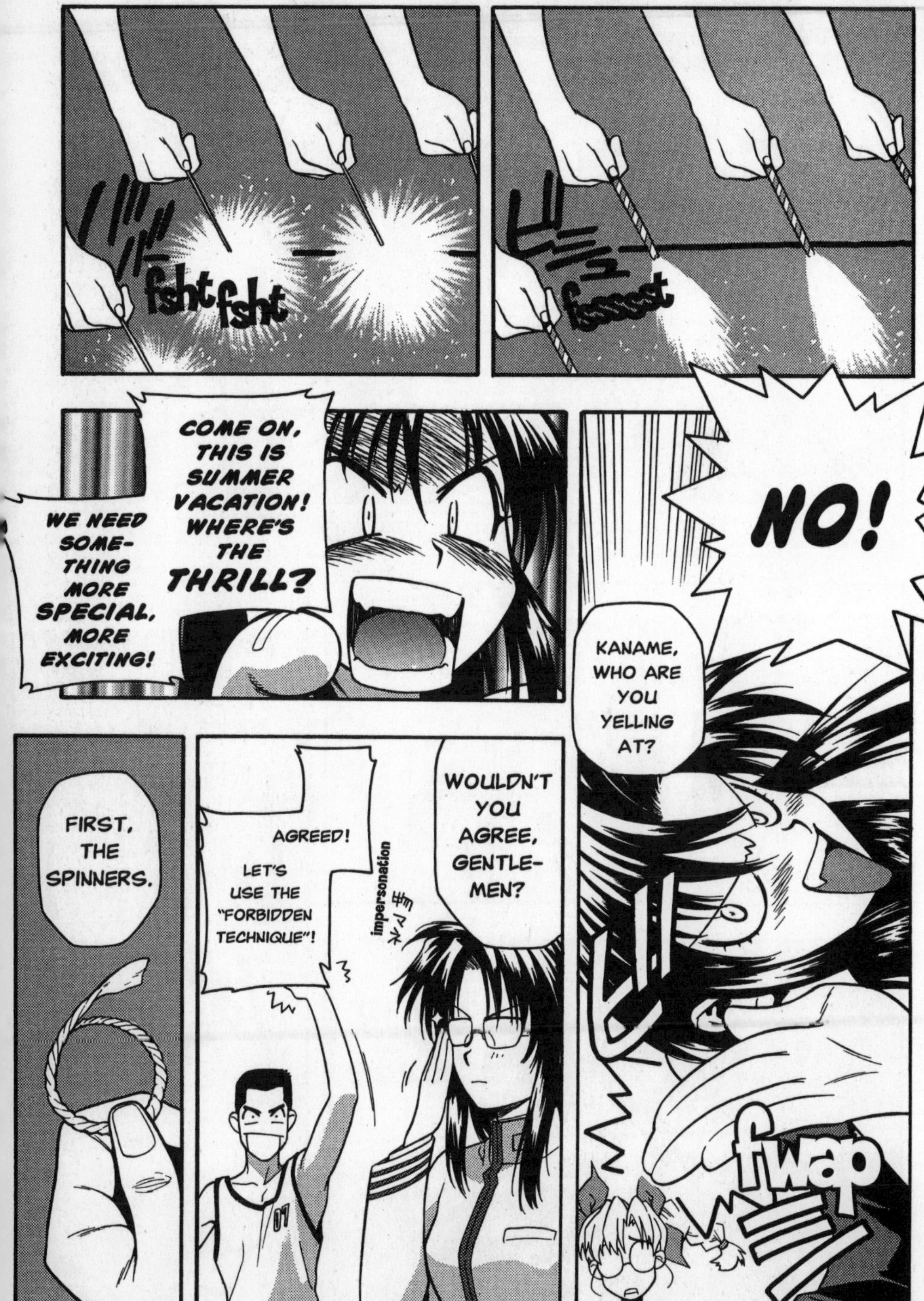
fsssst
fsht fsht
NO!
KANAME, WHO ARE YOU YELLING AT?
fwap
COME ON, THIS IS SUMMER VACATION! WHERE'S THE THRILL?
WE NEED SOME-THING MORE SPECIAL, MORE EXCITING!
WOULDN'T YOU AGREE, GENTLE-MEN?
AGREED!
LET'S USE THE "FORBIDDEN TECHNIQUE"!
impersonation
FIRST, THE SPINNERS.

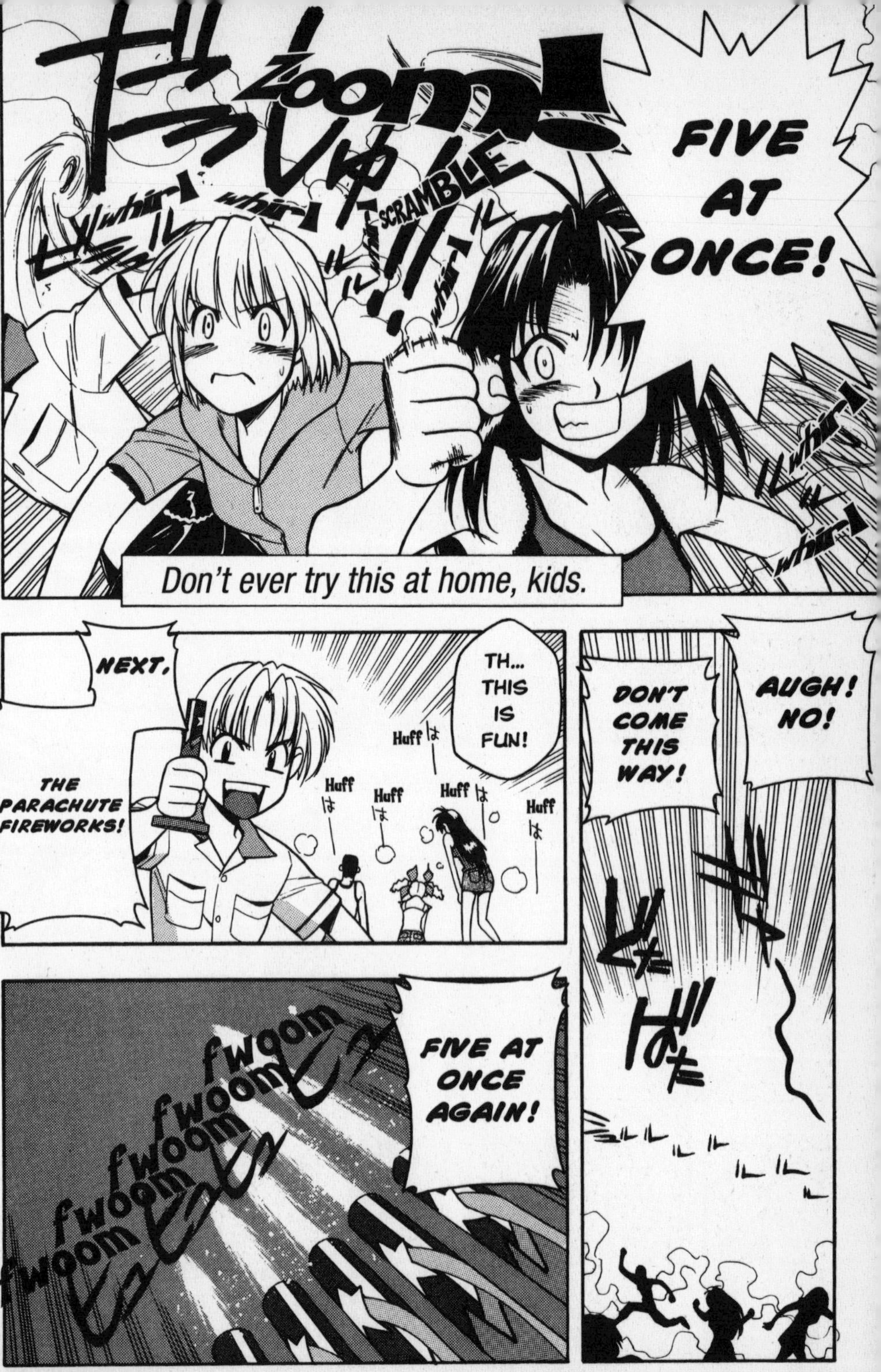
zoom!
whirl whirl whirl
SCRAMBLE
FIVE AT ONCE!
whirl whirl
Don't ever try this at home, kids.
AUGH! NO!
DON'T COME THIS WAY!
TH... THIS IS FUN!
Huff Huff Huff Huff Huff
NEXT,
THE PARACHUTE FIREWORKS!
FIVE AT ONCE AGAIN!
fwoom fwoom fwoom fwoom fwoom

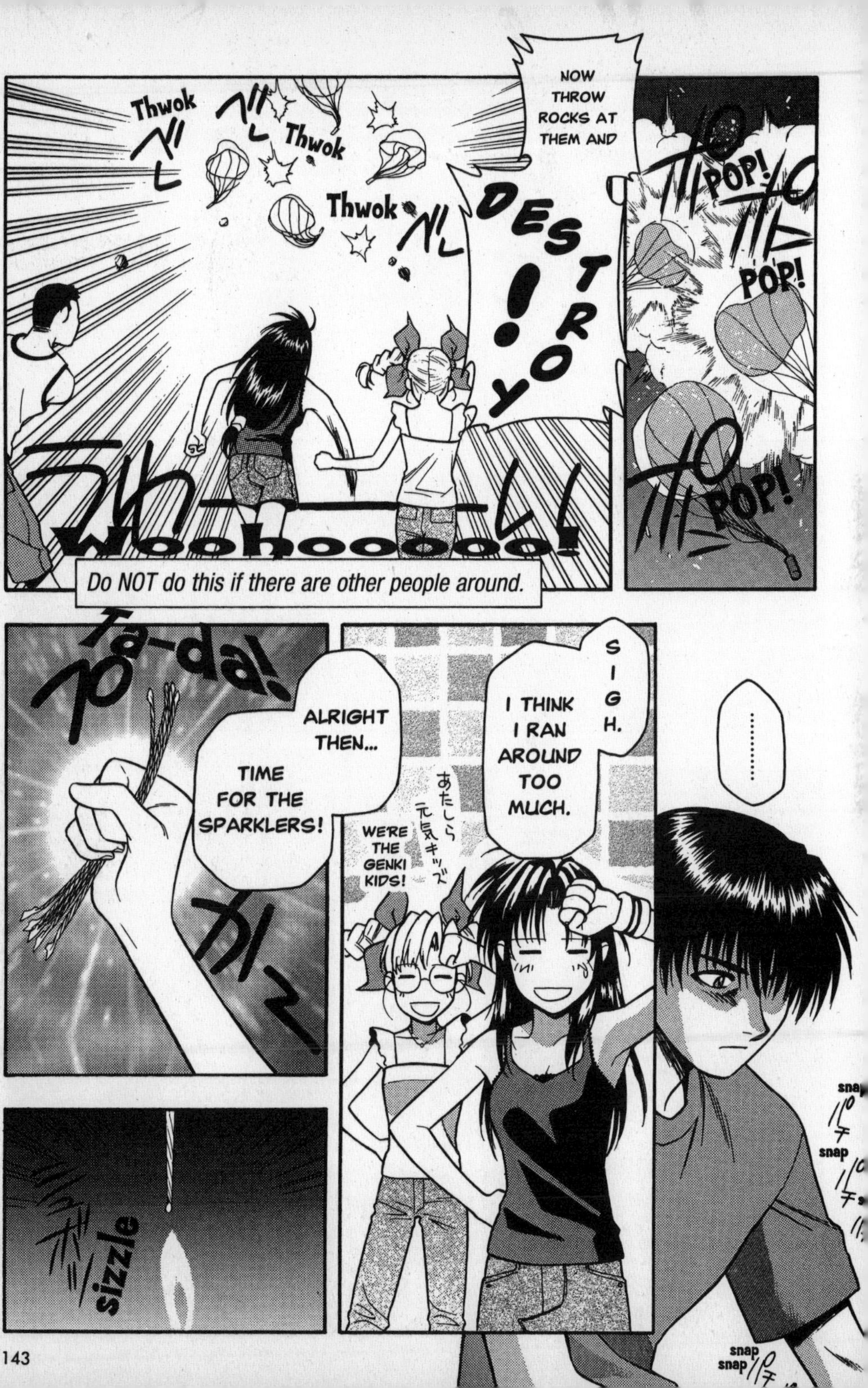
POP!
POP!
POP!
NOW THROW ROCKS AT THEM AND
DESTROY!!
Thwok
Thwok
Thwok
woohoooooo!
Do NOT do this if there are other people around.
....
SIGH.
I THINK I RAN AROUND TOO MUCH.
あたしら元気キッズ
WE'RE THE GENKI KIDS!
snap
snap
snap
snap
ALRIGHT THEN...
TIME FOR THE SPARKLERS!
Ta-da!
sizzle

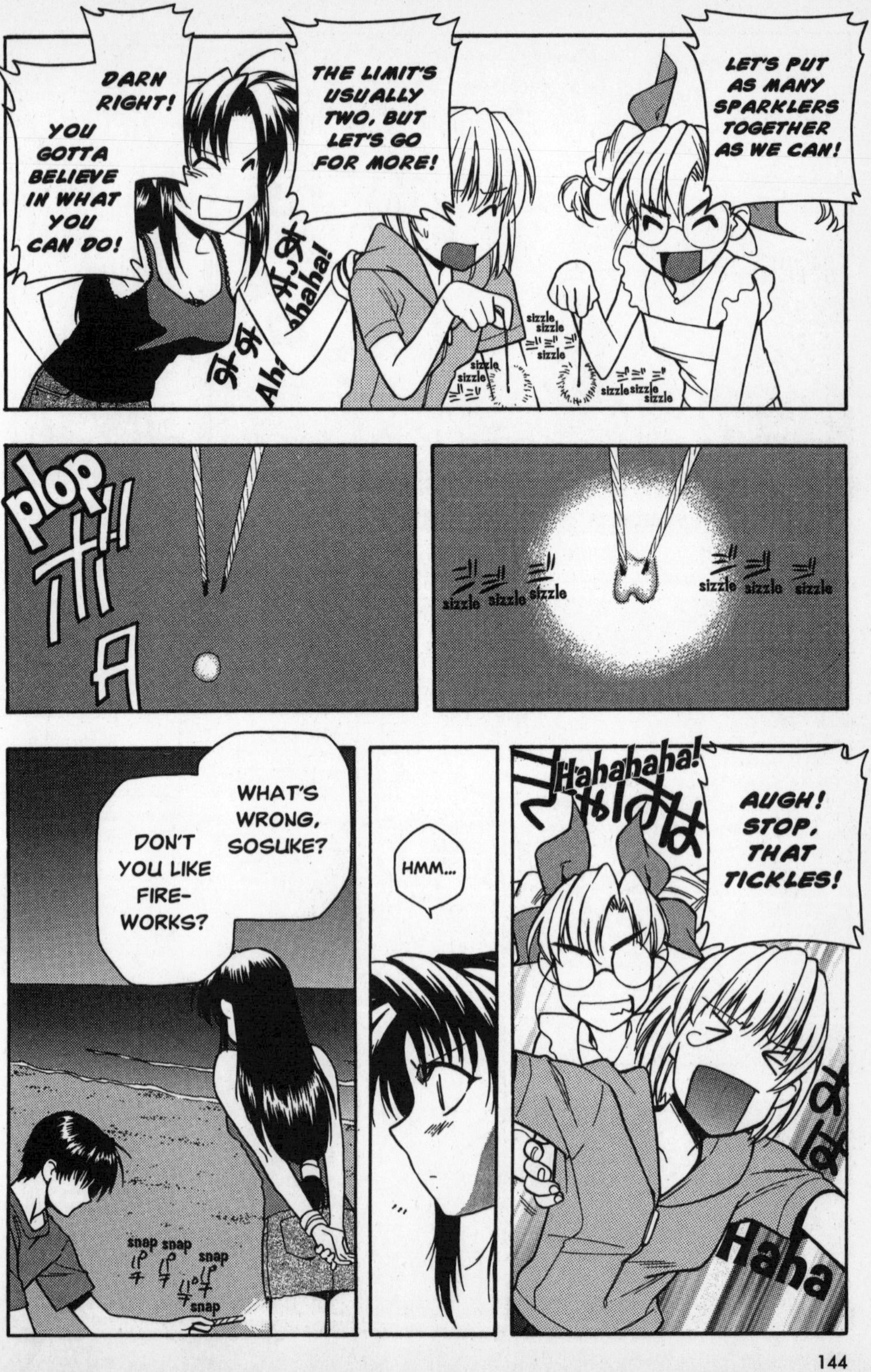
LET'S PUT AS MANY SPARKLERS TOGETHER AS WE CAN!
THE LIMIT'S USUALLY TWO, BUT LET'S GO FOR MORE!
DARN RIGHT! YOU GOTTA BELIEVE IN WHAT YOU CAN DO!
Ahahaha!
sizzle sizzle sizzle sizzle sizzle sizzle sizzle sizzle
sizzle sizzle sizzle sizzle sizzle sizzle
plop
Hahahaha!
AUGH! STOP, THAT TICKLES!
Haha
HMM...
...
WHAT'S WRONG, SOSUKE?
DON'T YOU LIKE FIRE-WORKS?
snap snap snap snap

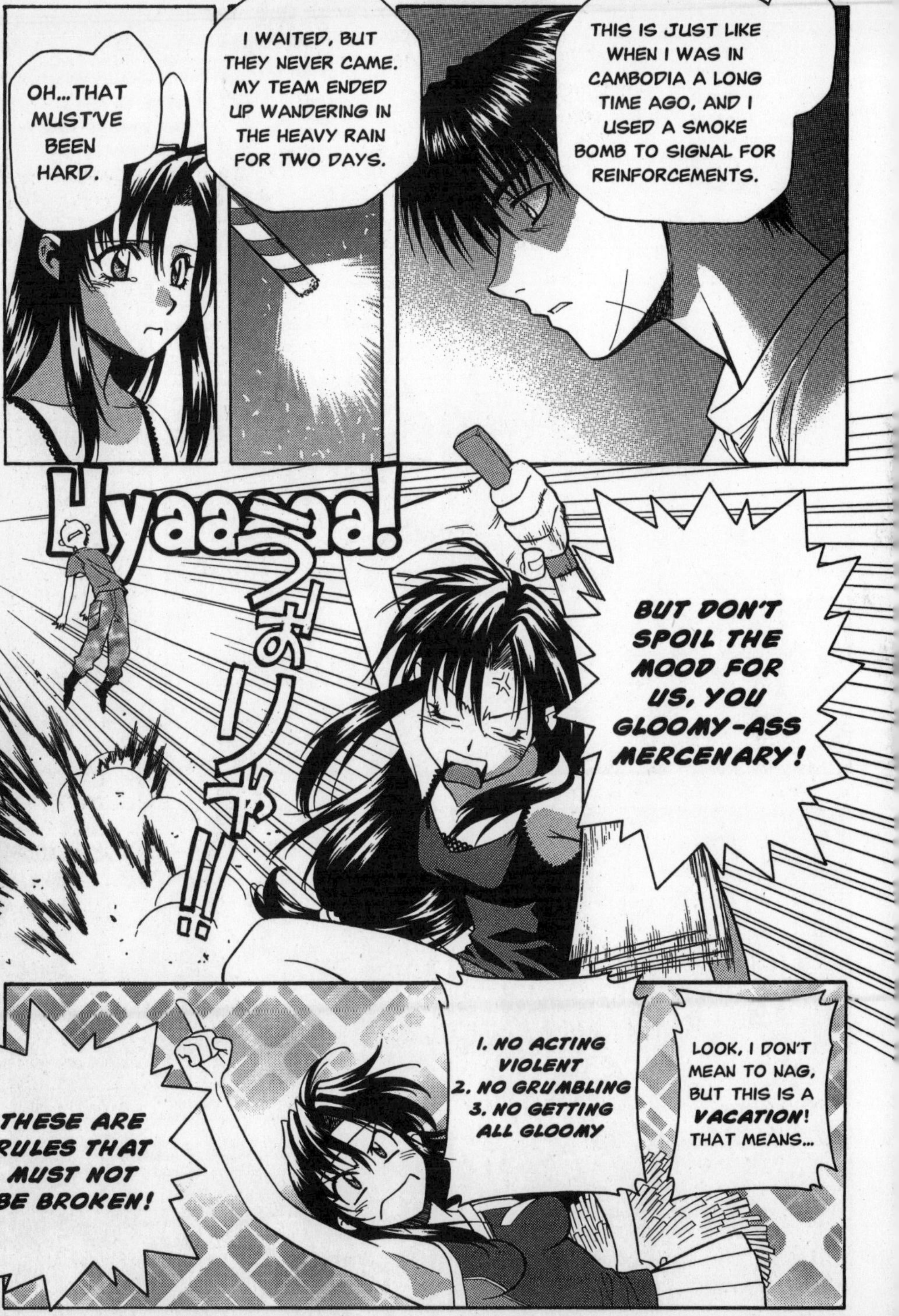
THIS IS JUST LIKE WHEN I WAS IN CAMBODIA A LONG TIME AGO, AND I USED A SMOKE BOMB TO SIGNAL FOR REINFORCEMENTS.
I WAITED, BUT THEY NEVER CAME. MY TEAM ENDED UP WANDERING IN THE HEAVY RAIN FOR TWO DAYS.
OH...THAT MUST'VE BEEN HARD.
BUT DON'T SPOIL THE MOOD FOR US, YOU GLOOMY-ASS MERCENARY!
Hyaaaaa!
LOOK, I DON'T MEAN TO NAG, BUT THIS IS A VACATION! THAT MEANS...
1. NO ACTING VIOLENT 2. NO GRUMBLING 3. NO GETTING ALL GLOOMY
THESE ARE RULES THAT MUST NOT BE BROKEN!

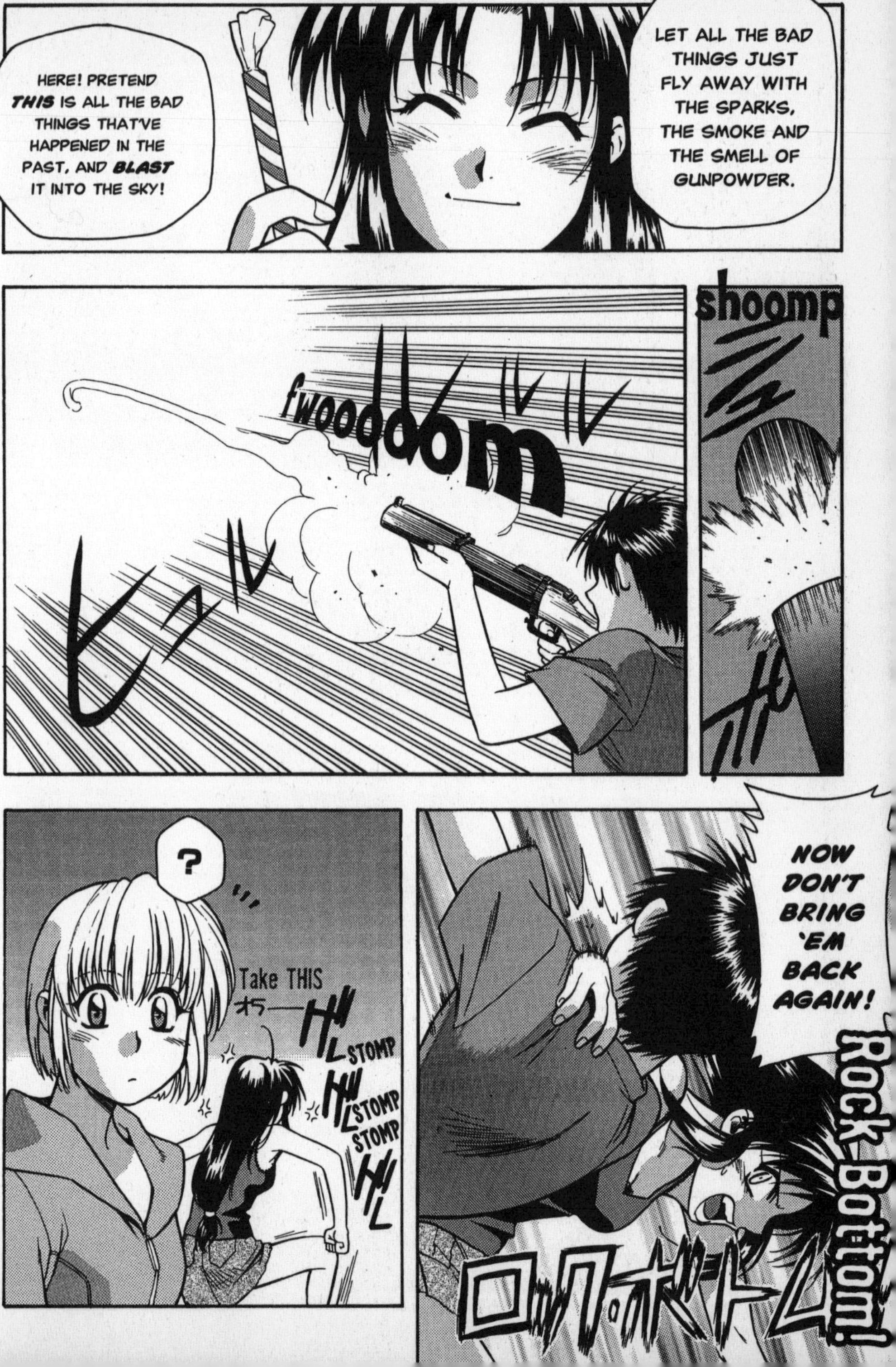

LET ALL THE BAD THINGS JUST FLY AWAY WITH THE SPARKS, THE SMOKE AND THE SMELL OF GUNPOWDER.
HERE! PRETEND ***THIS*** IS ALL THE BAD THINGS THAT'VE HAPPENED IN THE PAST, AND ***BLAST*** IT INTO THE SKY!
shoomp
fwooodom
NOW DON'T BRING 'EM BACK AGAIN!
Rock Bottom!
ロック・ボトム!
?
Take THIS
オラー
STOMP
STOMP
STOMP

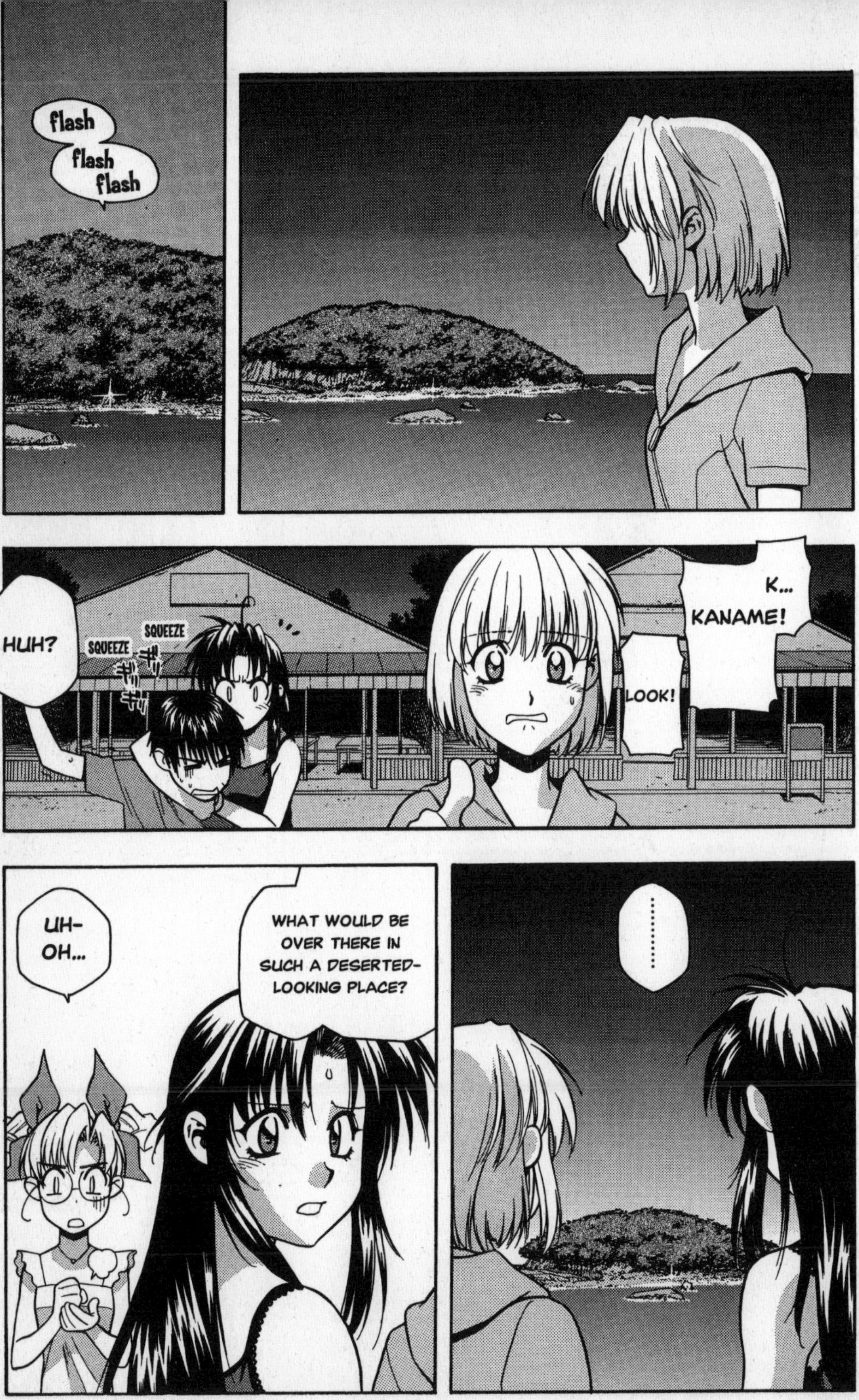
flash
flash
flash
K... KANAME!
LOOK!
SQUEEZE
SQUEEZE
HUH?
......
WHAT WOULD BE OVER THERE IN SUCH A DESERTED-LOOKING PLACE?
UH-OH...

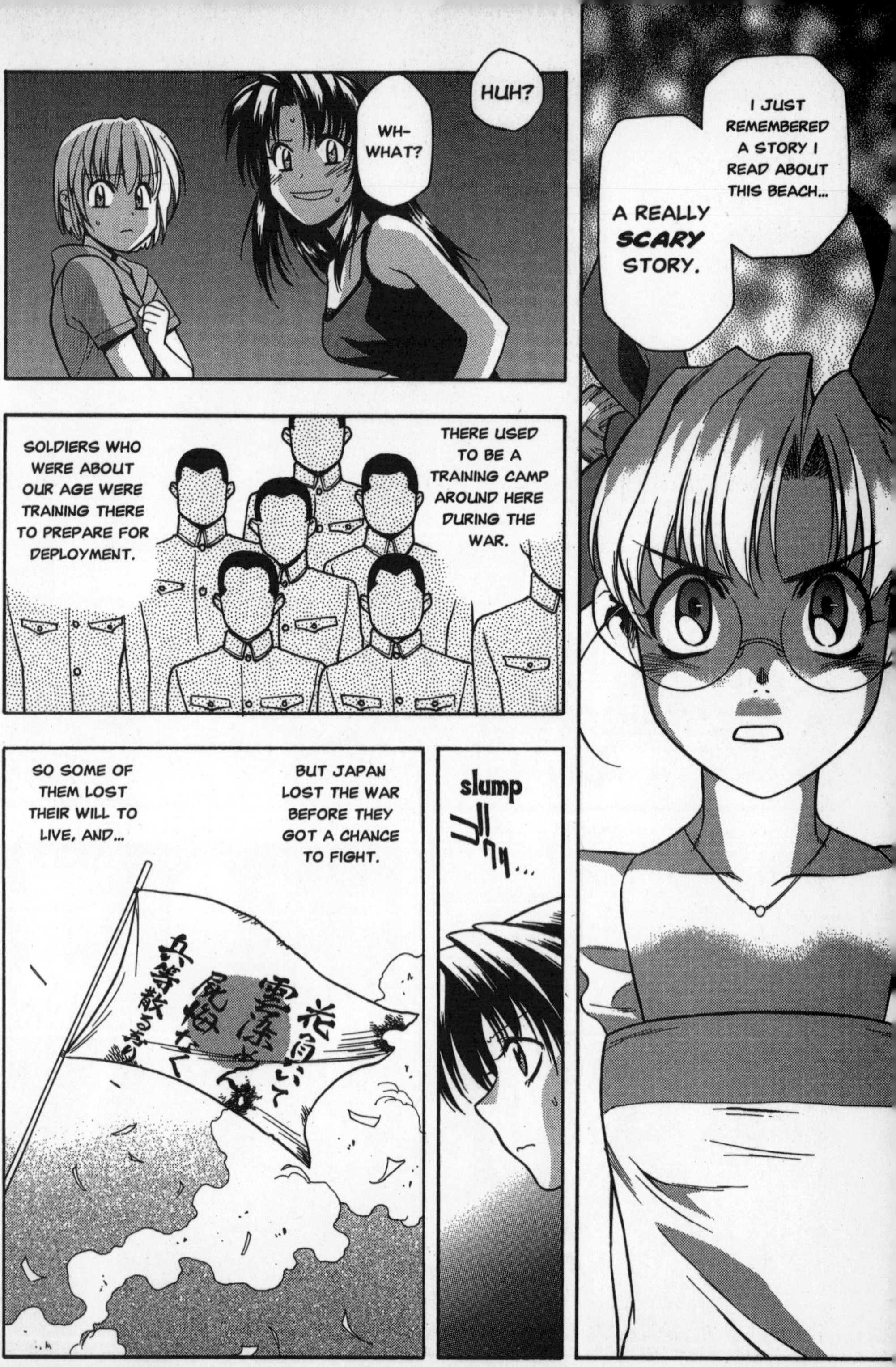
I JUST REMEMBERED A STORY I READ ABOUT THIS BEACH...
A REALLY SCARY STORY.
HUH?
WH- WHAT?
THERE USED TO BE A TRAINING CAMP AROUND HERE DURING THE WAR.
SOLDIERS WHO WERE ABOUT OUR AGE WERE TRAINING THERE TO PREPARE FOR DEPLOYMENT.
slump
BUT JAPAN LOST THE WAR BEFORE THEY GOT A CHANCE TO FIGHT.
SO SOME OF THEM LOST THEIR WILL TO LIVE, AND...

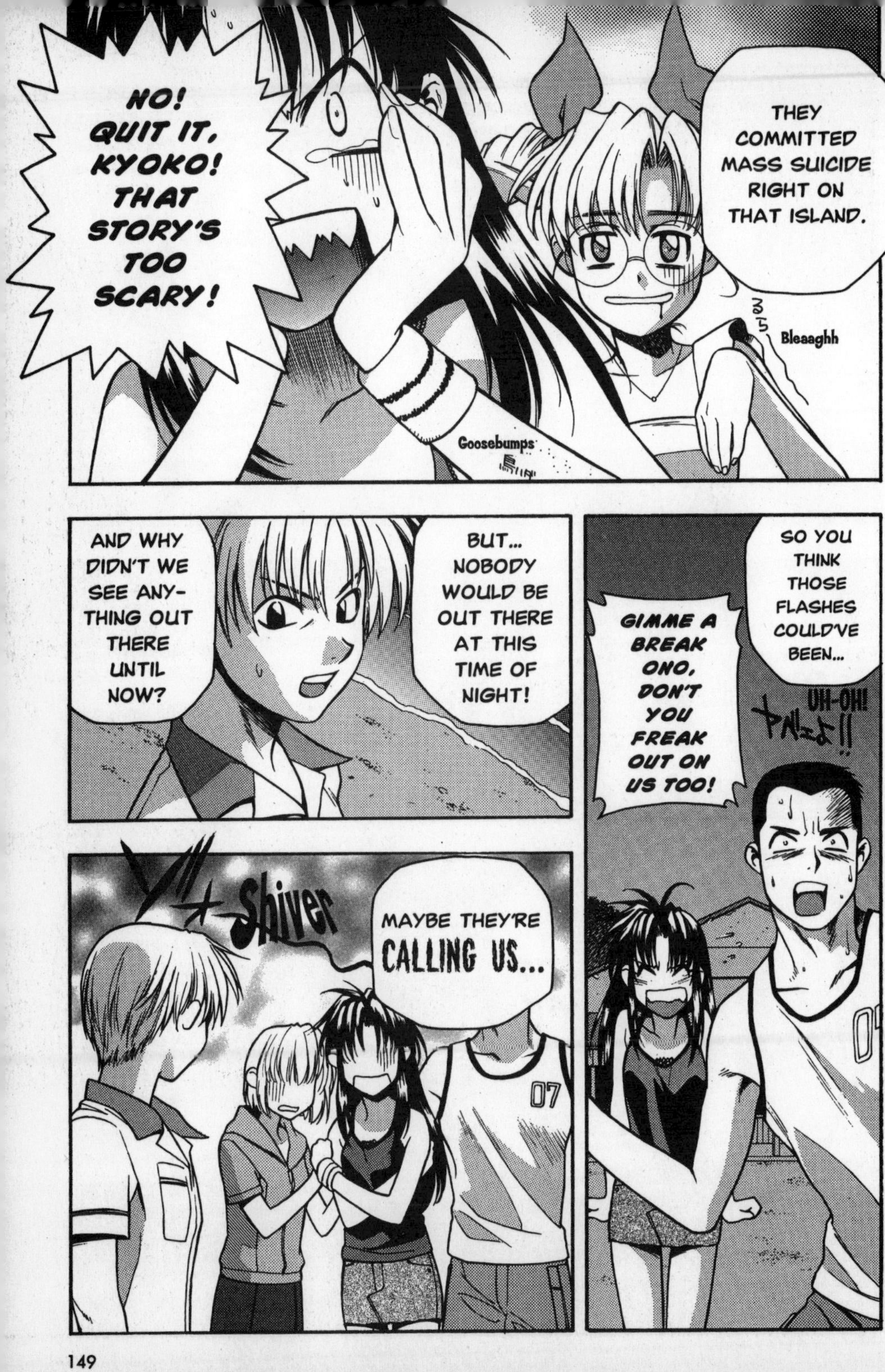
THEY COMMITTED MASS SUICIDE RIGHT ON THAT ISLAND.
Bleaaghh
NO! QUIT IT, KYOKO! THAT STORY'S TOO SCARY!
Goosebumps
SO YOU THINK THOSE FLASHES COULD'VE BEEN...
UH-OH!
GIMME A BREAK ONO, DON'T YOU FREAK OUT ON US TOO!
BUT... NOBODY WOULD BE OUT THERE AT THIS TIME OF NIGHT!
AND WHY DIDN'T WE SEE ANY-THING OUT THERE UNTIL NOW?
Shiver
MAYBE THEY'RE CALLING US...

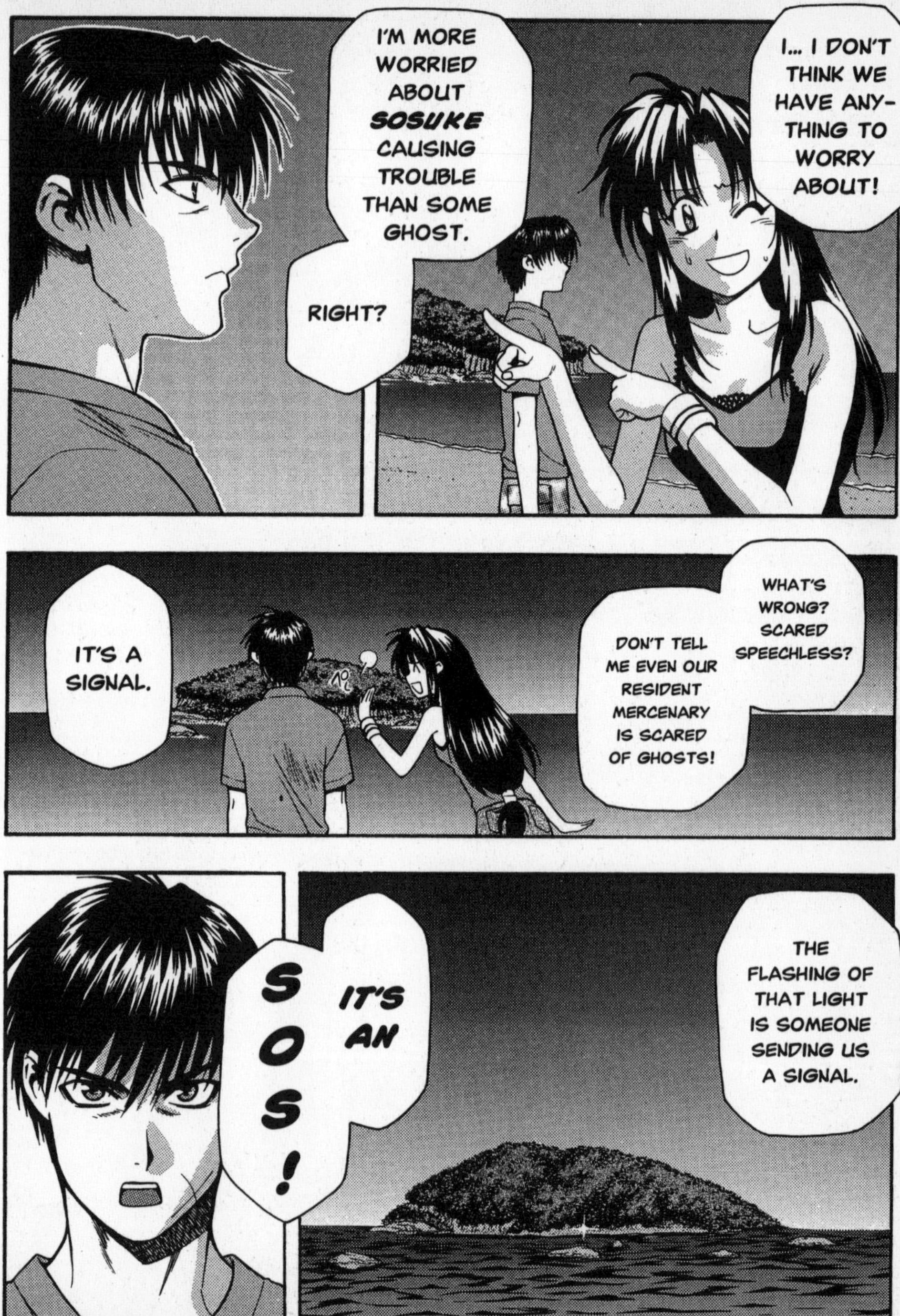
I... I DON'T THINK WE HAVE ANY-THING TO WORRY ABOUT!
I'M MORE WORRIED ABOUT SOSUKE CAUSING TROUBLE THAN SOME GHOST.
RIGHT?
WHAT'S WRONG? SCARED SPEECHLESS?
DON'T TELL ME EVEN OUR RESIDENT MERCENARY IS SCARED OF GHOSTS!
IT'S A SIGNAL.
THE FLASHING OF THAT LIGHT IS SOMEONE SENDING US A SIGNAL.
IT'S AN SOS!

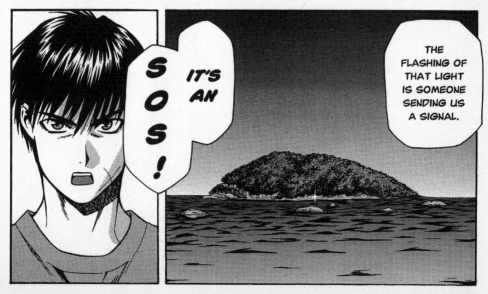

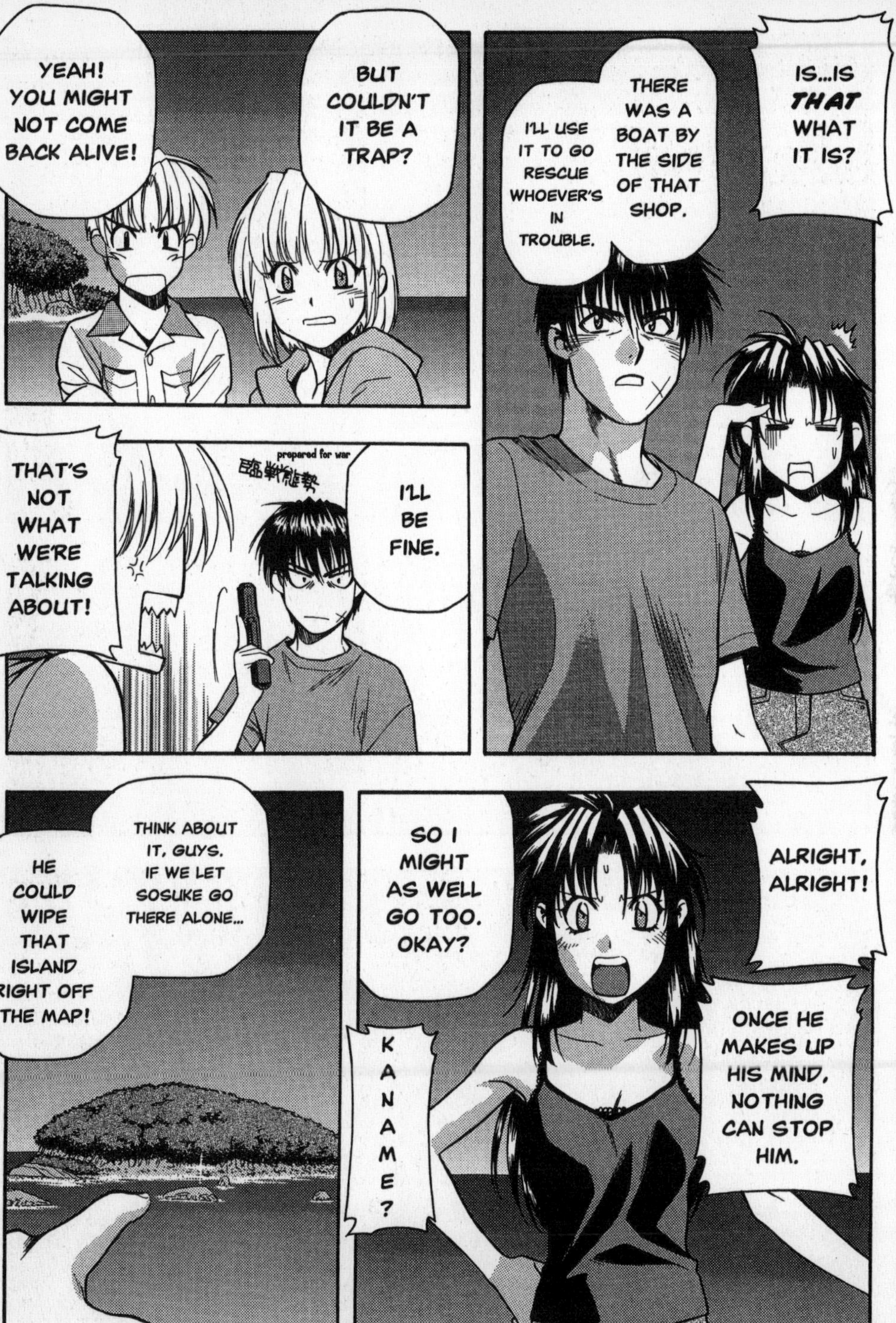
IS...IS *THAT* WHAT IT IS?
THERE WAS A BOAT BY THE SIDE OF THAT SHOP.
I'LL USE IT TO GO RESCUE WHOEVER'S IN TROUBLE.
BUT COULDN'T IT BE A TRAP?
YEAH! YOU MIGHT NOT COME BACK ALIVE!
臨戦態勢
prepared for war
I'LL BE FINE.
THAT'S NOT WHAT WE'RE TALKING ABOUT!
ALRIGHT, ALRIGHT!
ONCE HE MAKES UP HIS MIND, NOTHING CAN STOP HIM.
SO I MIGHT AS WELL GO TOO. OKAY?
KANAME?
THINK ABOUT IT, GUYS. IF WE LET SOSUKE GO THERE ALONE...
HE COULD WIPE THAT ISLAND RIGHT OFF THE MAP!

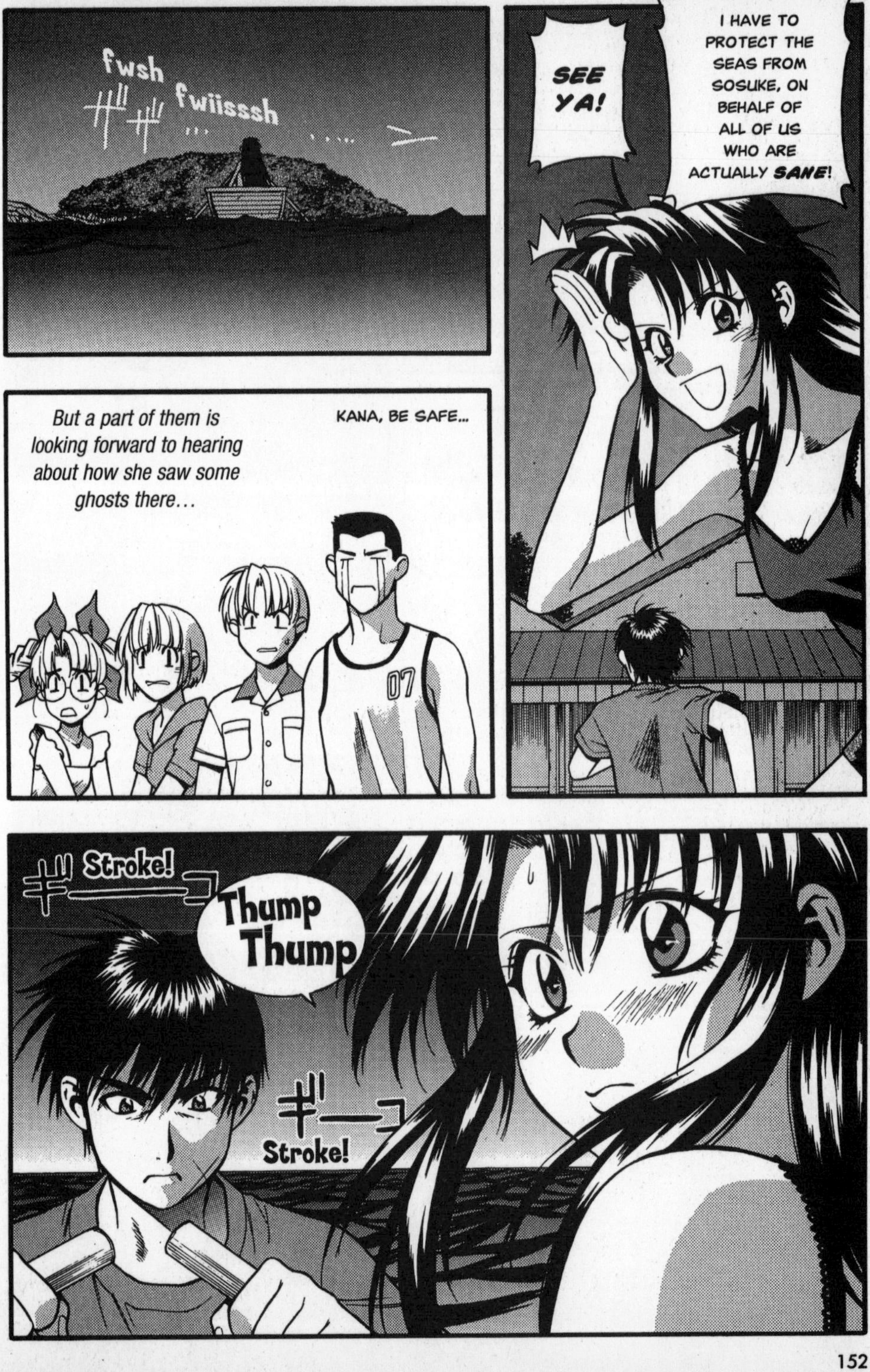
I HAVE TO PROTECT THE SEAS FROM SOSUKE, ON BEHALF OF ALL OF US WHO ARE ACTUALLY SANE!
SEE YA!
fwsh
fwiisssh
KANA, BE SAFE...
But a part of them is looking forward to hearing about how she saw some ghosts there…
Thump Thump
Stroke!
Stroke!

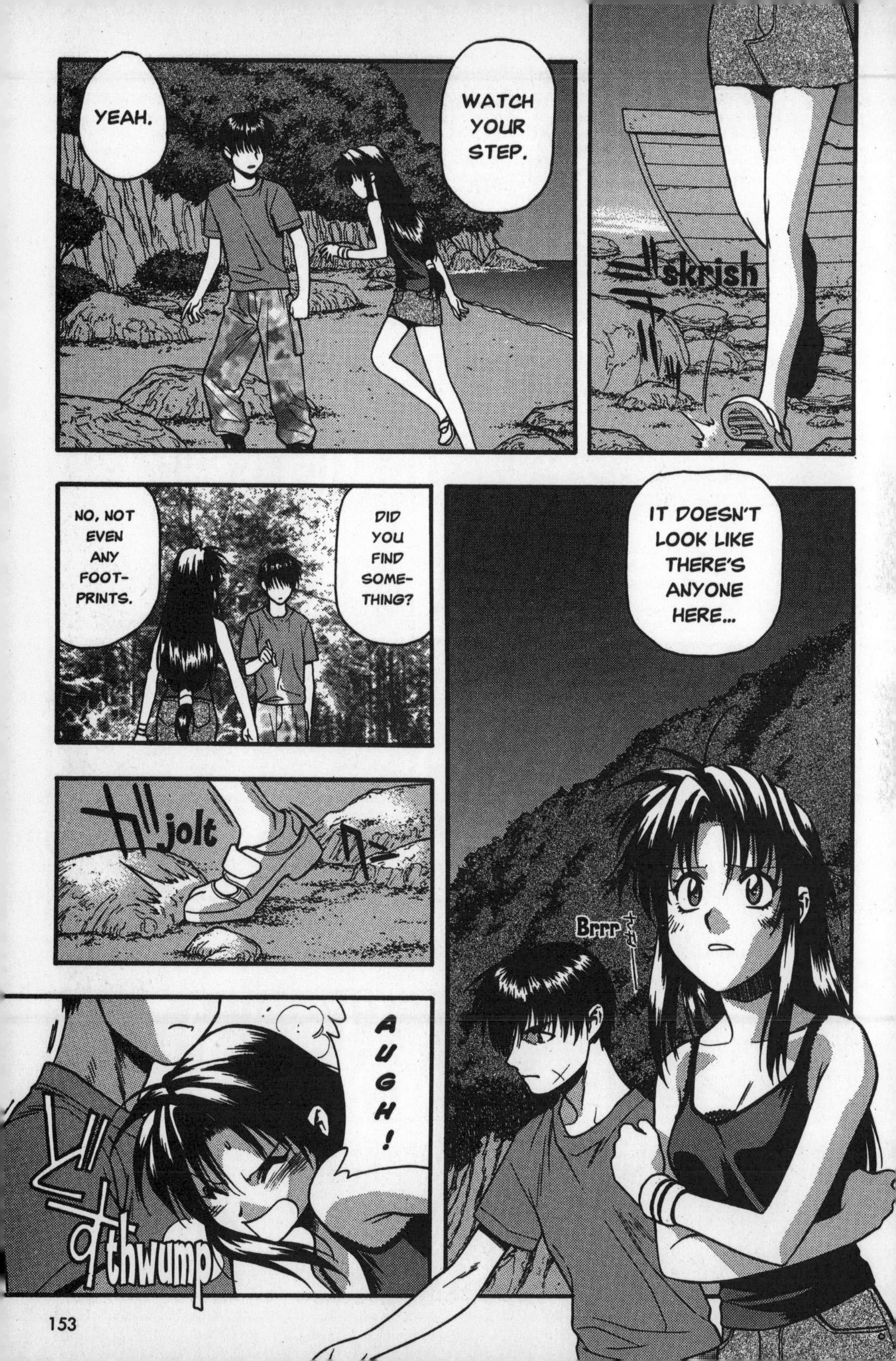
skrish
WATCH YOUR STEP.
YEAH.
IT DOESN'T LOOK LIKE THERE'S ANYONE HERE...
Brrr
DID YOU FIND SOME-THING?
NO, NOT EVEN ANY FOOT-PRINTS.
jolt
AUGH!
thwump

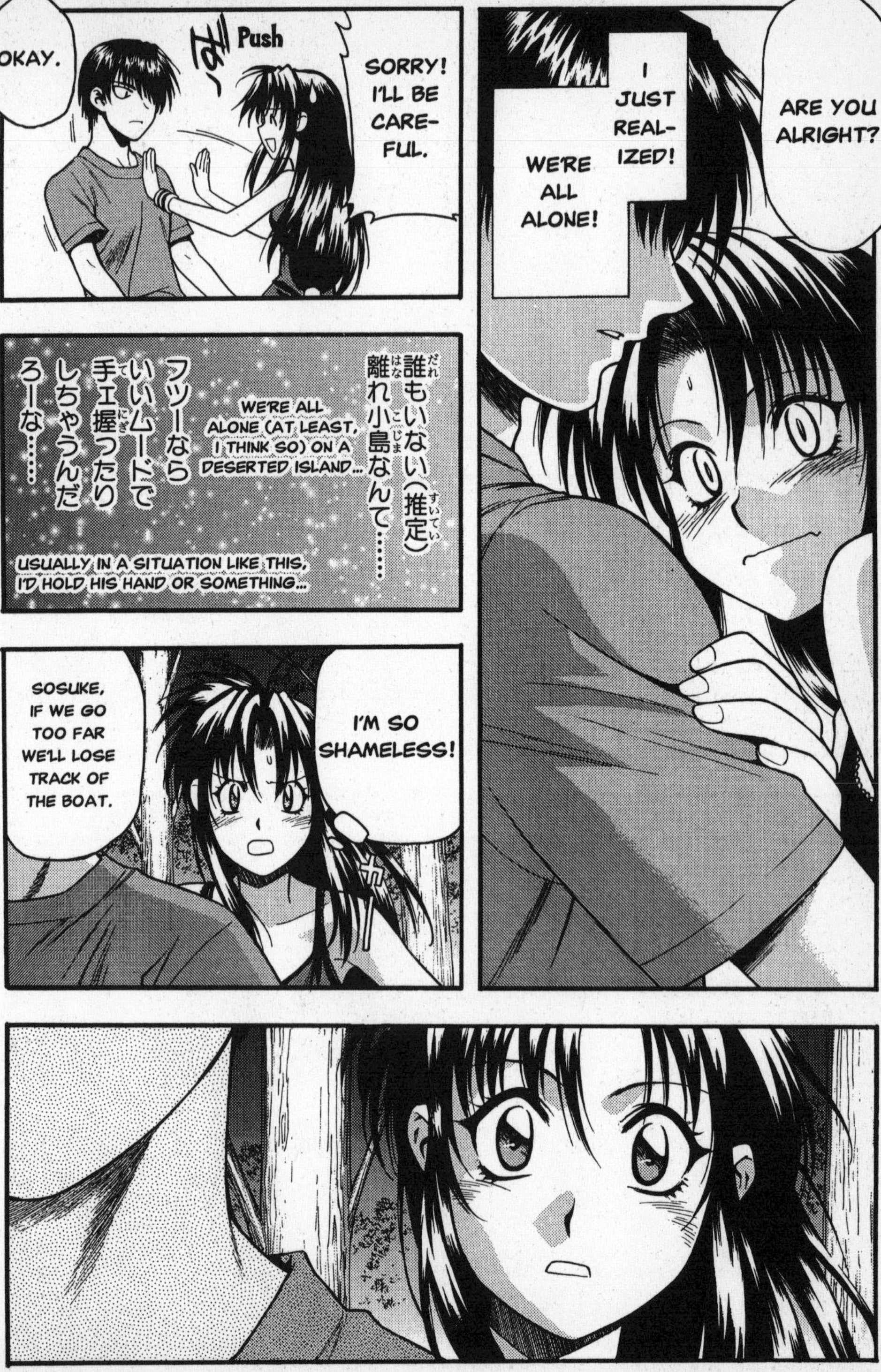
ARE YOU ALRIGHT?
I JUST REAL-IZED!
WE'RE ALL ALONE!
SORRY! I'LL BE CARE-FUL.
Push
OKAY.
誰もいない(推定)離れ小島なんて……
WE'RE ALL ALONE (AT LEAST, I THINK SO) ON A DESERTED ISLAND...
フツーならいいムードで手ェ握ったりしちゃうんだろーな……
USUALLY IN A SITUATION LIKE THIS, I'D HOLD HIS HAND OR SOMETHING...
I'M SO SHAMELESS!
SOSUKE, IF WE GO TOO FAR WE'LL LOSE TRACK OF THE BOAT.

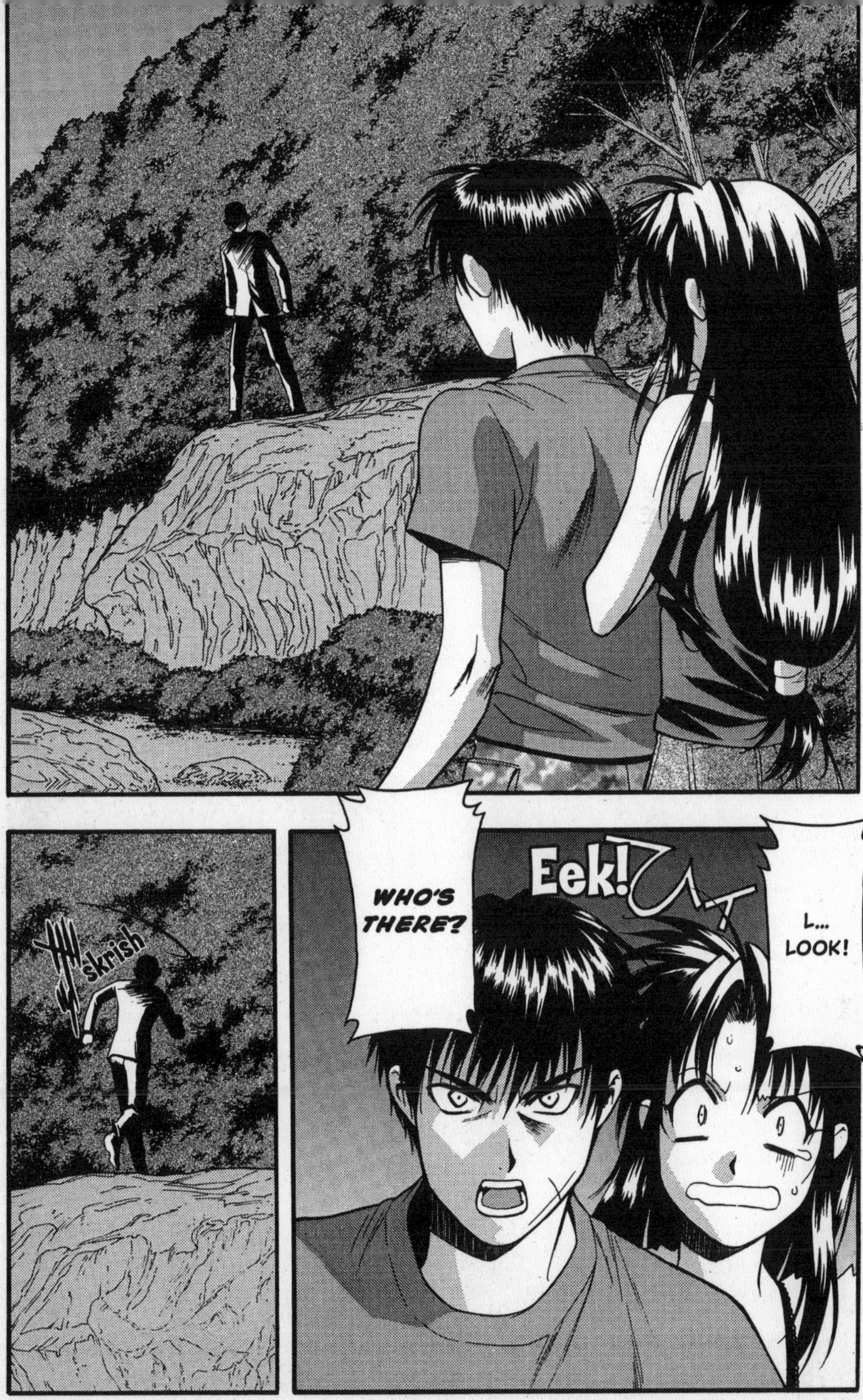
L... LOOK!
Eek!
WHO'S THERE?
skrish

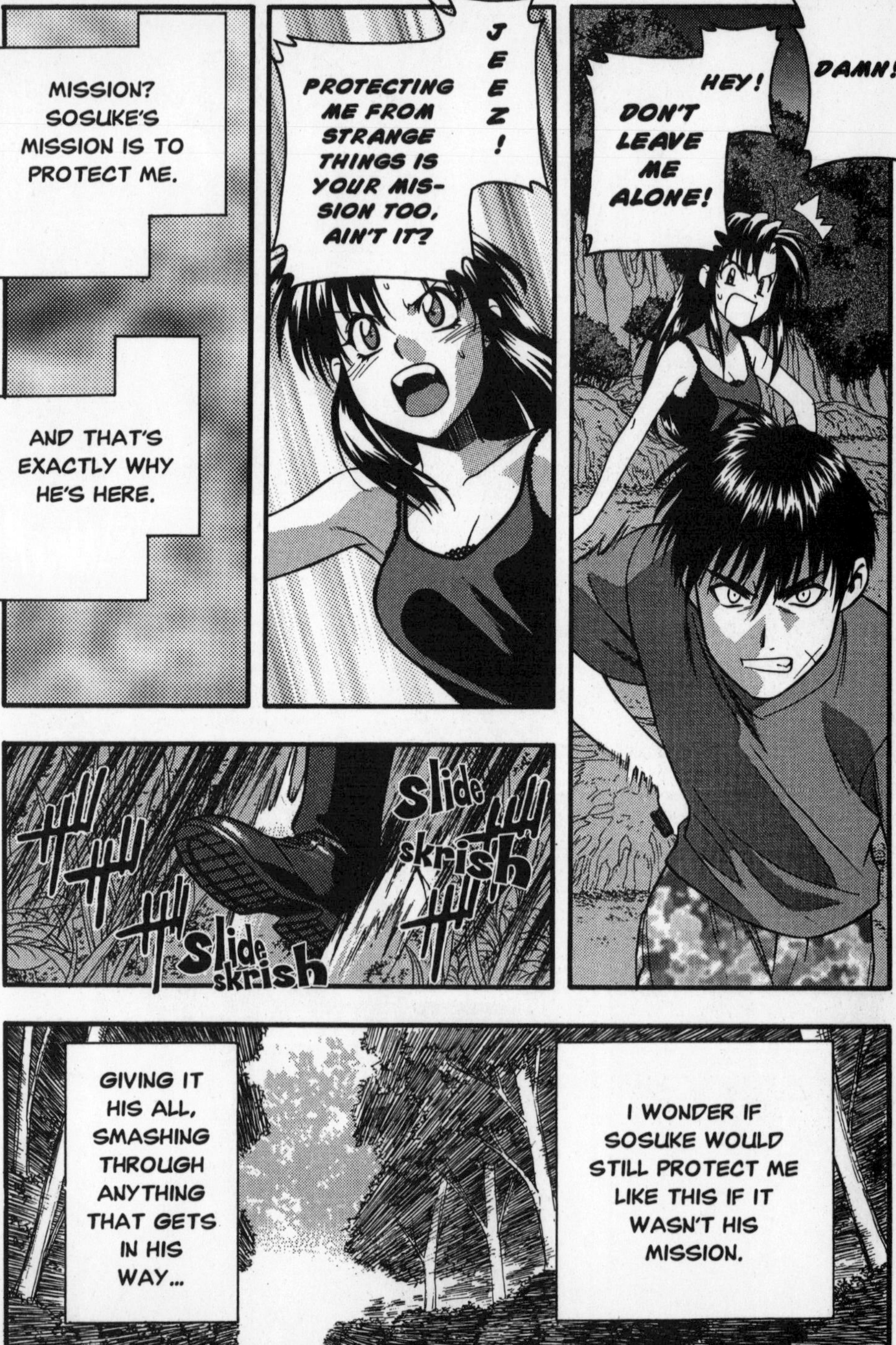
DAMN!
HEY! DON'T LEAVE ME ALONE!
JEEZ!
PROTECTING ME FROM STRANGE THINGS IS YOUR MISSION TOO, AIN'T IT?
MISSION? SOSUKE'S MISSION IS TO PROTECT ME.
AND THAT'S EXACTLY WHY HE'S HERE.
slide skrish
slide skrish
I WONDER IF SOSUKE WOULD STILL PROTECT ME LIKE THIS IF IT WASN'T HIS MISSION.
GIVING IT HIS ALL, SMASHING THROUGH ANYTHING THAT GETS IN HIS WAY...

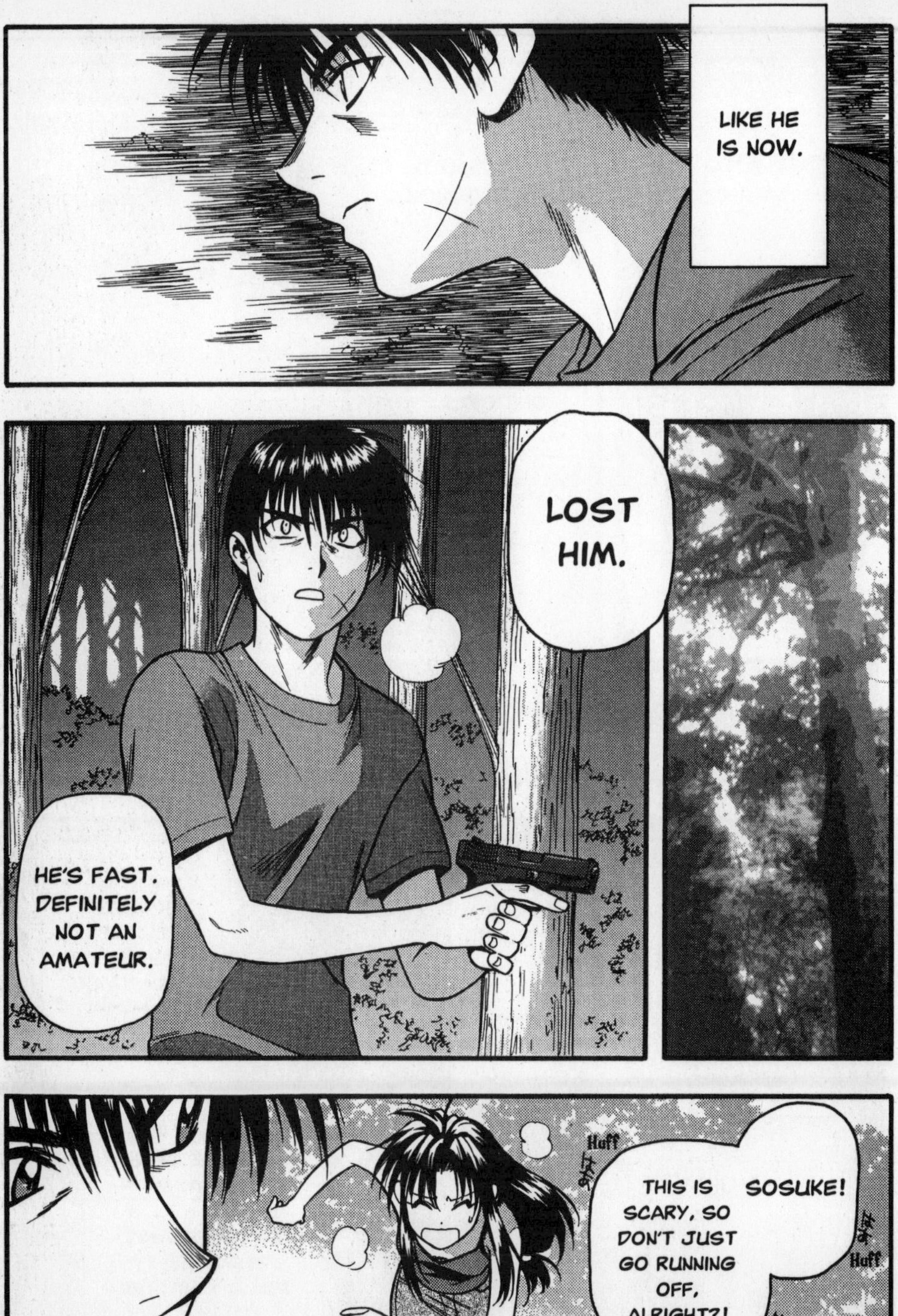
LIKE HE IS NOW.
LOST HIM.
HE'S FAST. DEFINITELY NOT AN AMATEUR.
Huff
SOSUKE!
THIS IS SCARY, SO DON'T JUST GO RUNNING OFF, ALRIGHT?!
Huff
Huff

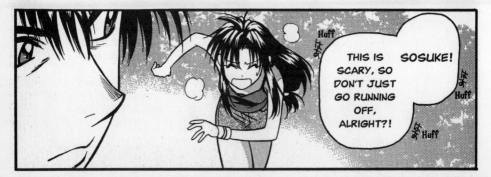

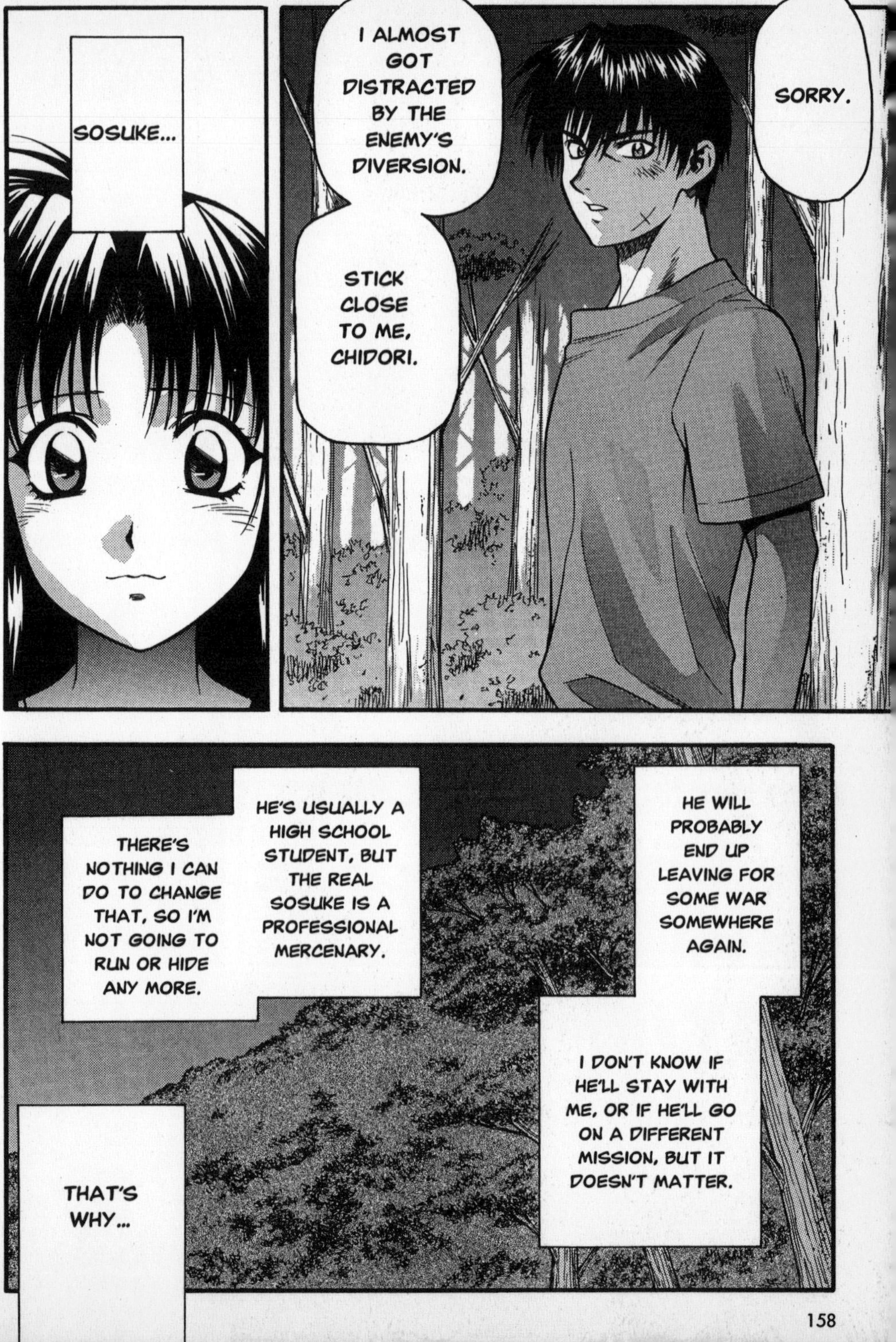
SORRY.
I ALMOST GOT DISTRACTED BY THE ENEMY'S DIVERSION.
STICK CLOSE TO ME, CHIDORI.
SOSUKE...
HE WILL PROBABLY END UP LEAVING FOR SOME WAR SOMEWHERE AGAIN.
HE'S USUALLY A HIGH SCHOOL STUDENT, BUT THE REAL SOSUKE IS A PROFESSIONAL MERCENARY.
THERE'S NOTHING I CAN DO TO CHANGE THAT, SO I'M NOT GOING TO RUN OR HIDE ANY MORE.
I DON'T KNOW IF HE'LL STAY WITH ME, OR IF HE'LL GO ON A DIFFERENT MISSION, BUT IT DOESN'T MATTER.
THAT'S WHY...

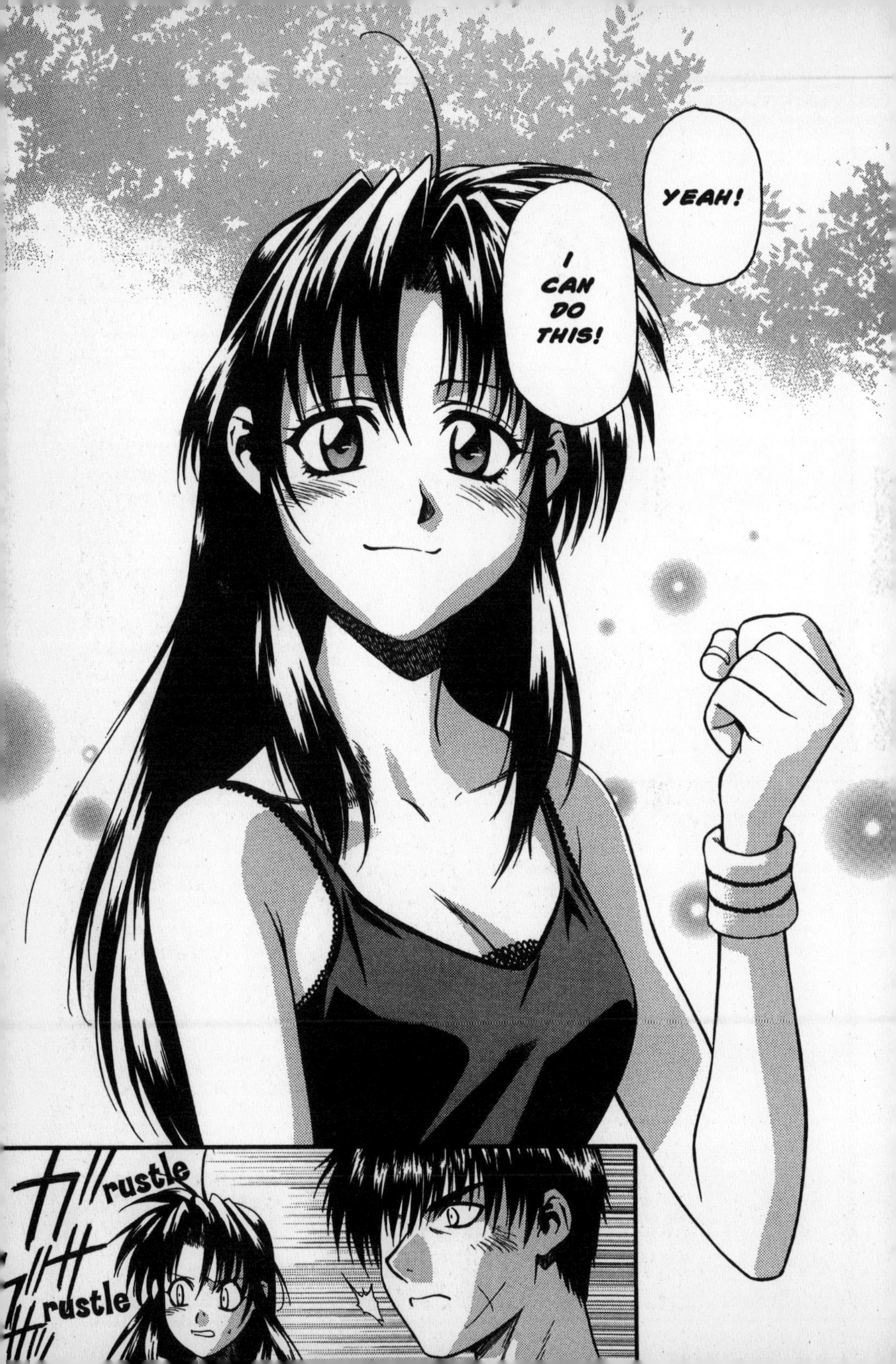
YEAH!
I CAN DO THIS!
rustle
rustle

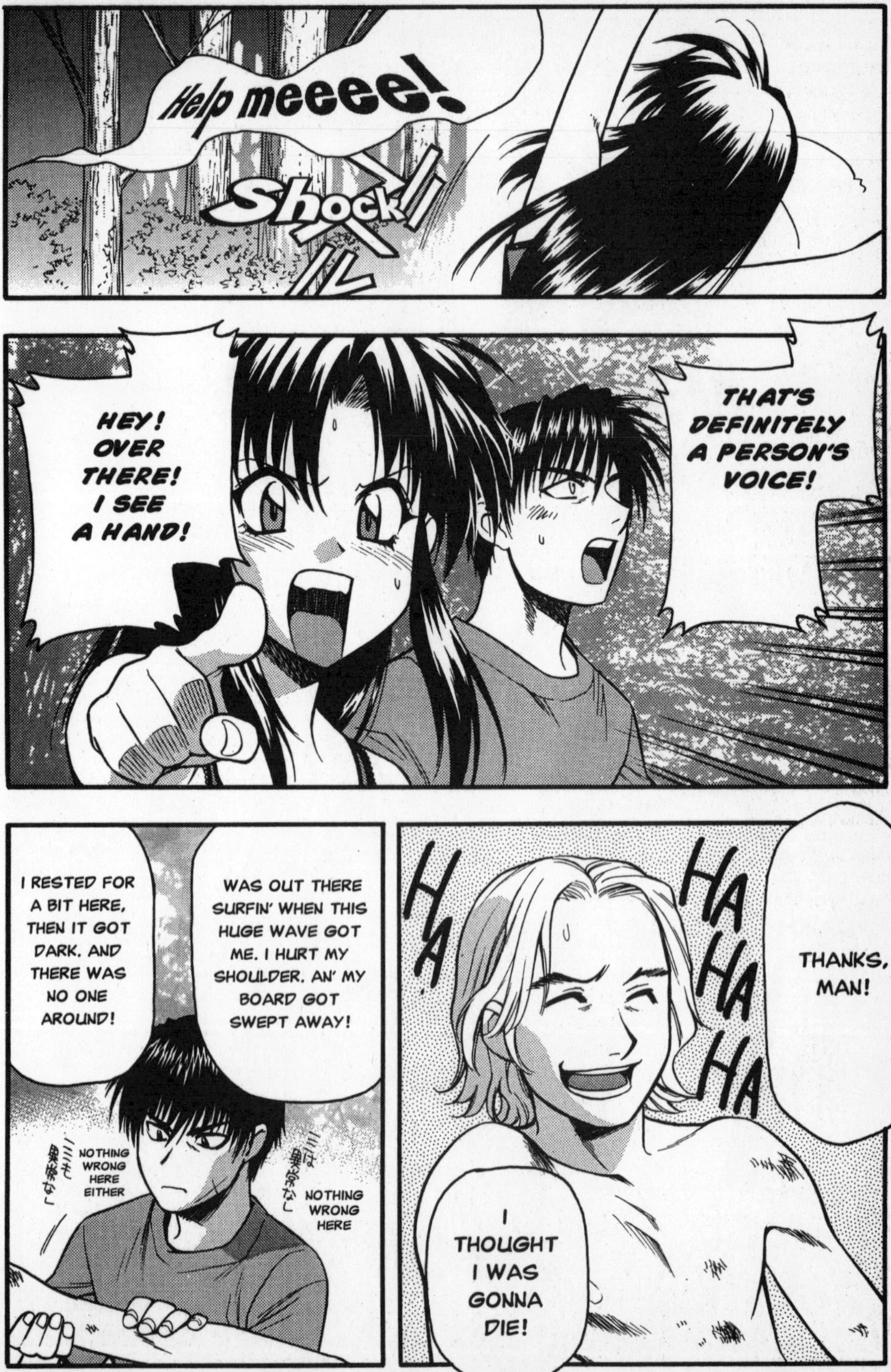
Help meeeee!
Shock
THAT'S DEFINITELY A PERSON'S VOICE!
HEY! OVER THERE! I SEE A HAND!
HA HA HA HA HA
THANKS, MAN!
I THOUGHT I WAS GONNA DIE!
WAS OUT THERE SURFIN' WHEN THIS HUGE WAVE GOT ME. I HURT MY SHOULDER. AN' MY BOARD GOT SWEPT AWAY!
I RESTED FOR A BIT HERE, THEN IT GOT DARK. AND THERE WAS NO ONE AROUND!
NOTHING WRONG HERE
NOTHING WRONG HERE EITHER

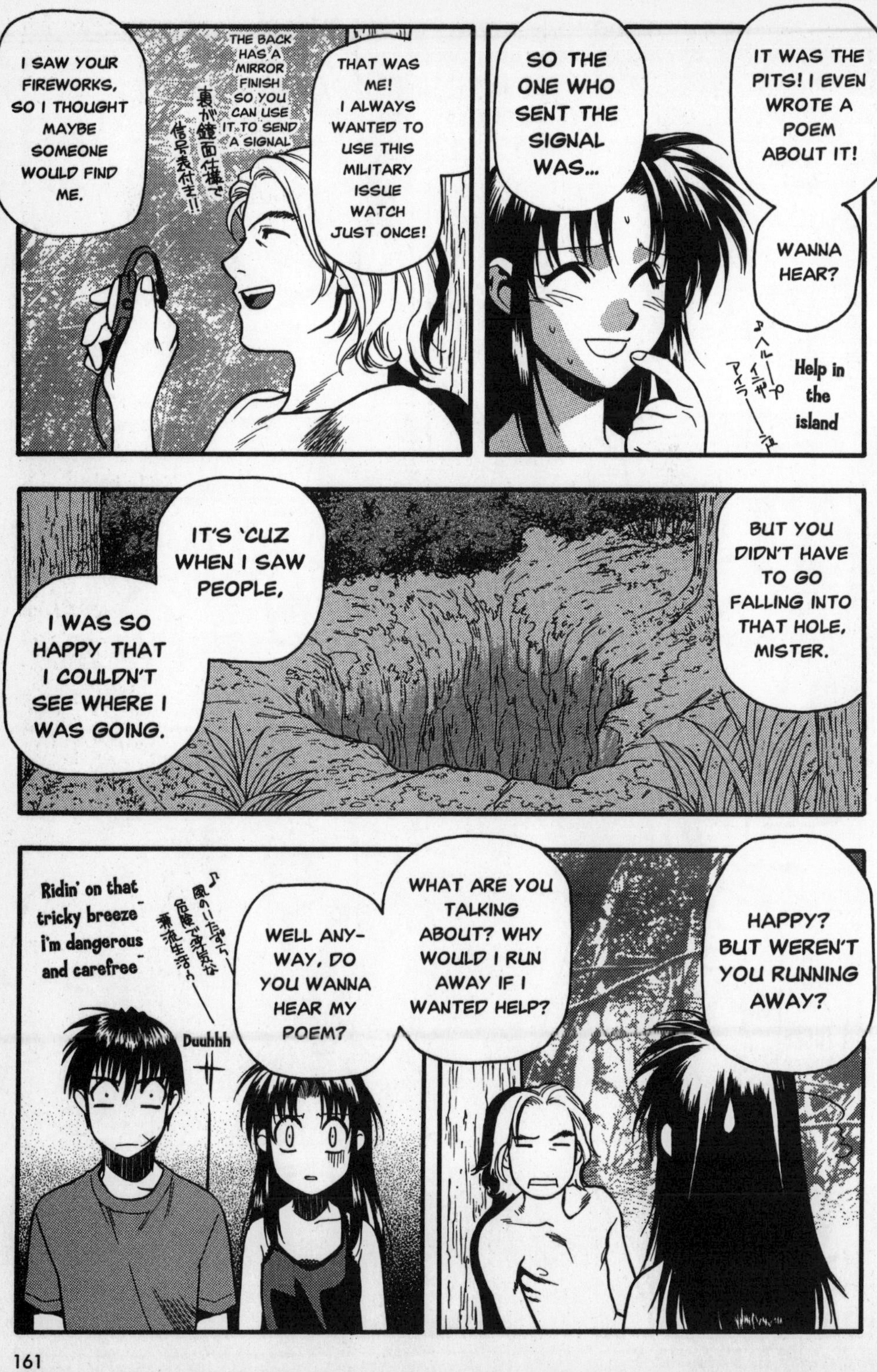
IT WAS THE PITS! I EVEN WROTE A POEM ABOUT IT!
SO THE ONE WHO SENT THE SIGNAL WAS...
WANNA HEAR?
♪ヘルーープ
Help in the island
THAT WAS ME! I ALWAYS WANTED TO USE THIS MILITARY ISSUE WATCH JUST ONCE!
THE BACK HAS A MIRROR FINISH SO YOU CAN USE IT TO SEND A SIGNAL
裏が鏡面仕様で信号表付き!!
I SAW YOUR FIREWORKS, SO I THOUGHT MAYBE SOMEONE WOULD FIND ME.
BUT YOU DIDN'T HAVE TO GO FALLING INTO THAT HOLE, MISTER.
IT'S 'CUZ WHEN I SAW PEOPLE,
I WAS SO HAPPY THAT I COULDN'T SEE WHERE I WAS GOING.
HAPPY? BUT WEREN'T YOU RUNNING AWAY?
WHAT ARE YOU TALKING ABOUT? WHY WOULD I RUN AWAY IF I WANTED HELP?
WELL ANY-WAY, DO YOU WANNA HEAR MY POEM?
♪風のいたずら 危険で多感な 漂流生活♪
Ridin' on that tricky breeze - i'm dangerous - and carefree -
Duuhhh

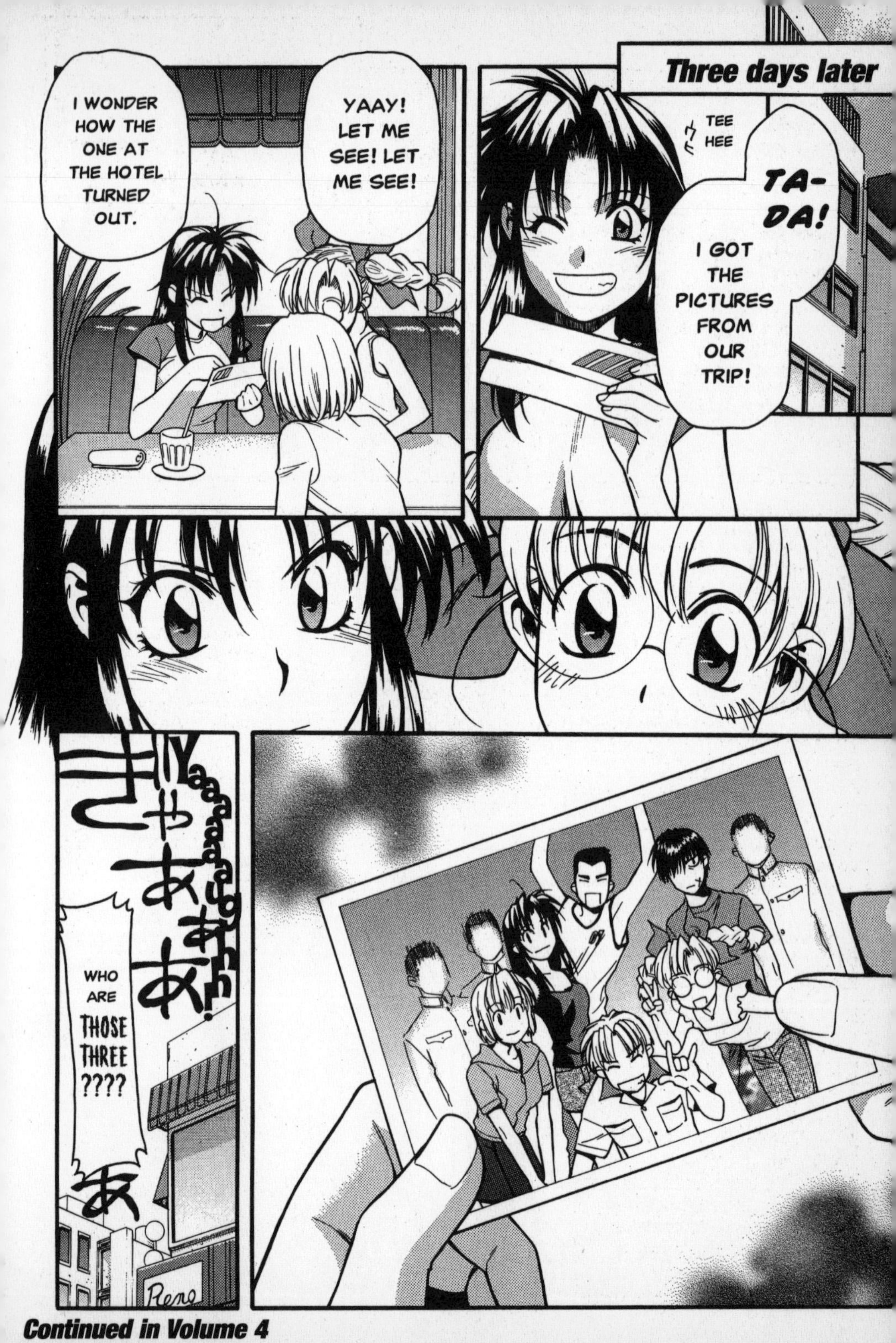
Three days later
TEE HEE
TA-DA!
I GOT THE PICTURES FROM OUR TRIP!
YAAY! LET ME SEE! LET ME SEE!
I WONDER HOW THE ONE AT THE HOTEL TURNED OUT.
Yaaaaaaaaaaaugh!
きゃあああ!
WHO ARE THOSE THREE????
あ
Rene

Continued in Volume 4

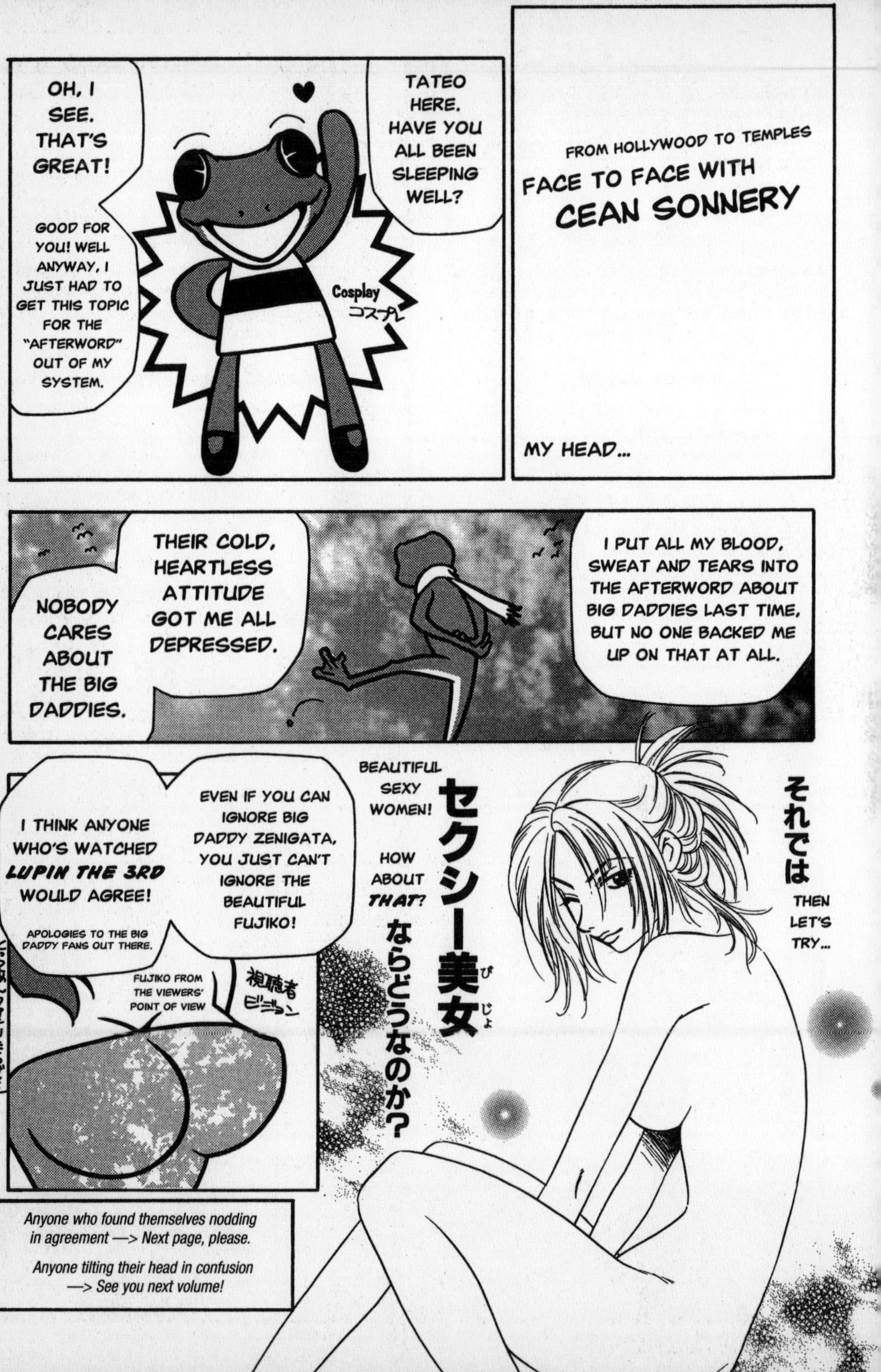
FROM HOLLYWOOD TO TEMPLES
FACE TO FACE WITH CEAN SONNERY
MY HEAD...
TATEO HERE. HAVE YOU ALL BEEN SLEEPING WELL?
OH, I SEE. THAT'S GREAT!
GOOD FOR YOU! WELL ANYWAY, I JUST HAD TO GET THIS TOPIC FOR THE "AFTERWORD" OUT OF MY SYSTEM.
Cosplay
コスプレ
I PUT ALL MY BLOOD, SWEAT AND TEARS INTO THE AFTERWORD ABOUT BIG DADDIES LAST TIME, BUT NO ONE BACKED ME UP ON THAT AT ALL.
THEIR COLD, HEARTLESS ATTITUDE GOT ME ALL DEPRESSED.
NOBODY CARES ABOUT THE BIG DADDIES.
それでは
THEN LET'S TRY...
セクシー美女ならどうなのか?
BEAUTIFUL SEXY WOMEN!
HOW ABOUT THAT?
EVEN IF YOU CAN IGNORE BIG DADDY ZENIGATA, YOU JUST CAN'T IGNORE THE BEAUTIFUL FUJIKO!
I THINK ANYONE WHO'S WATCHED LUPIN THE 3RD WOULD AGREE!
APOLOGIES TO THE BIG DADDY FANS OUT THERE.
視聴者ビジョン
FUJIKO FROM THE VIEWERS' POINT OF VIEW
Anyone who found themselves nodding in agreement —> Next page, please.
Anyone tilting their head in confusion —> See you next volume!

セクシー美女 In ハリウーッ!!

Beautiful Sexy Girls in Hollywood!!

これだけ見りゃキミもメロメロ！な作品を挙げてます♡ *They'll rock your world!*

Read this, and you too can fully appreciate these shows!

JANE FONDA

BARBARELLA WAS A SEXY SCI-FI MOVIE, BUT ANY BOY LESS THAN 18 YEARS OLD WOULD PROBABLY THINK IT WAS OUTRAGEOUS. BUT SHE'S CUTE! AND SHE DOES COSPLAY!

PAM GRIER

THE WAY SHE LOOKS AS A STEWARDESS IN **JACKIE BROWN** IS JUST...WHOA. SHE'S BEAUTIFUL AND QUEENLY.

SALMA HAYEK

SHE'S THE MOVIE QUEEN WHO PLAYS IN **FROM DUSK TILL DAWN** AND **DESPERADO**. SHE WAS GOOD IN BOTH, BUT WAS CRAZY SEXY IN **DAWN**. I WANT HER TO GRIND HER HEELS INTO ME LIKE SHE DID TO QUENTIN TARANTINO.

MONICA BELLUCCI

THE WAY SHE FIRES OFF THAT HUGE GUN IN **DOBERMANN** HAD ME SPELLBOUND. I'M SO JEALOUS OF HER HUSBAND! DAMN YOU, VINCENT CASSEL!

PENELOPE CRUZ

JUST WATCHING **WOMAN ON TOP** WAS ENOUGH FOR ME TO GET SUCKED IN BY THIS SPANISH BEAUTY. HER BIGGEST ALLURE IS THAT SHE'S SO CUTE YOU'LL FORGIVE HER FOR ANYTHING.

PAMELA ANDERSON LEE

SHE PLAYED IN THE **VIP** TV SERIES. SHE CHANGED HER OUTFIT FIVE TIMES IN THE FIRST EPISODE. EVEN BARBIE WOULD BE STUNNED BY THIS PRETTY PLAYMATE. SHE HAS TWO CHILDREN, BUT HAS SUCH A SEXY BODY! THAT'S GOTTA BE SOME SORT OF SUPERNATURAL PHENOMENON!

LIV TYLER

SHE PLAYS IN **PLUNKETT & MACLEANE**. SHE WEARS A C-CORSET! AND HER EYES ARE SO SHINY! SHE'S TOO SWEET FOR THAT "NOBLEMAN." CURSE HIM!

ANGELINA JOLIE

THE STAR OF **LAURA CROFT TOMB RAIDER**, AND THE SEXIEST ACTRESS IN HOLLYWOOD. OF COURSE! SHE'S STRONG, AND SHE'S GOT THE BOOBS TO BOOT!

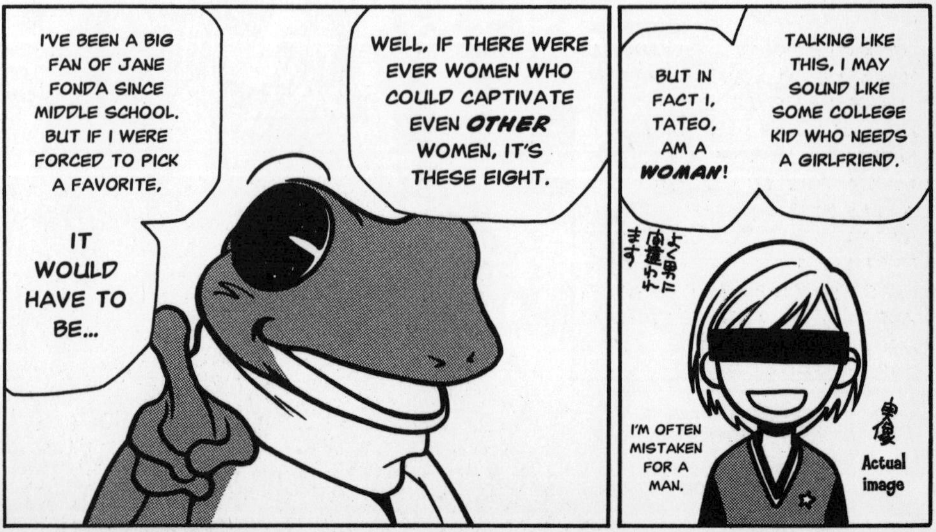
TALKING LIKE THIS, I MAY SOUND LIKE SOME COLLEGE KID WHO NEEDS A GIRLFRIEND.
BUT IN FACT I, TATEO, AM A WOMAN!
よく男に間違われます
I'M OFTEN MISTAKEN FOR A MAN.
実像
Actual image
I'VE BEEN A BIG FAN OF JANE FONDA SINCE MIDDLE SCHOOL. BUT IF I WERE FORCED TO PICK A FAVORITE,
IT WOULD HAVE TO BE...
WELL, IF THERE WERE EVER WOMEN WHO COULD CAPTIVATE EVEN OTHER WOMEN, IT'S THESE EIGHT.

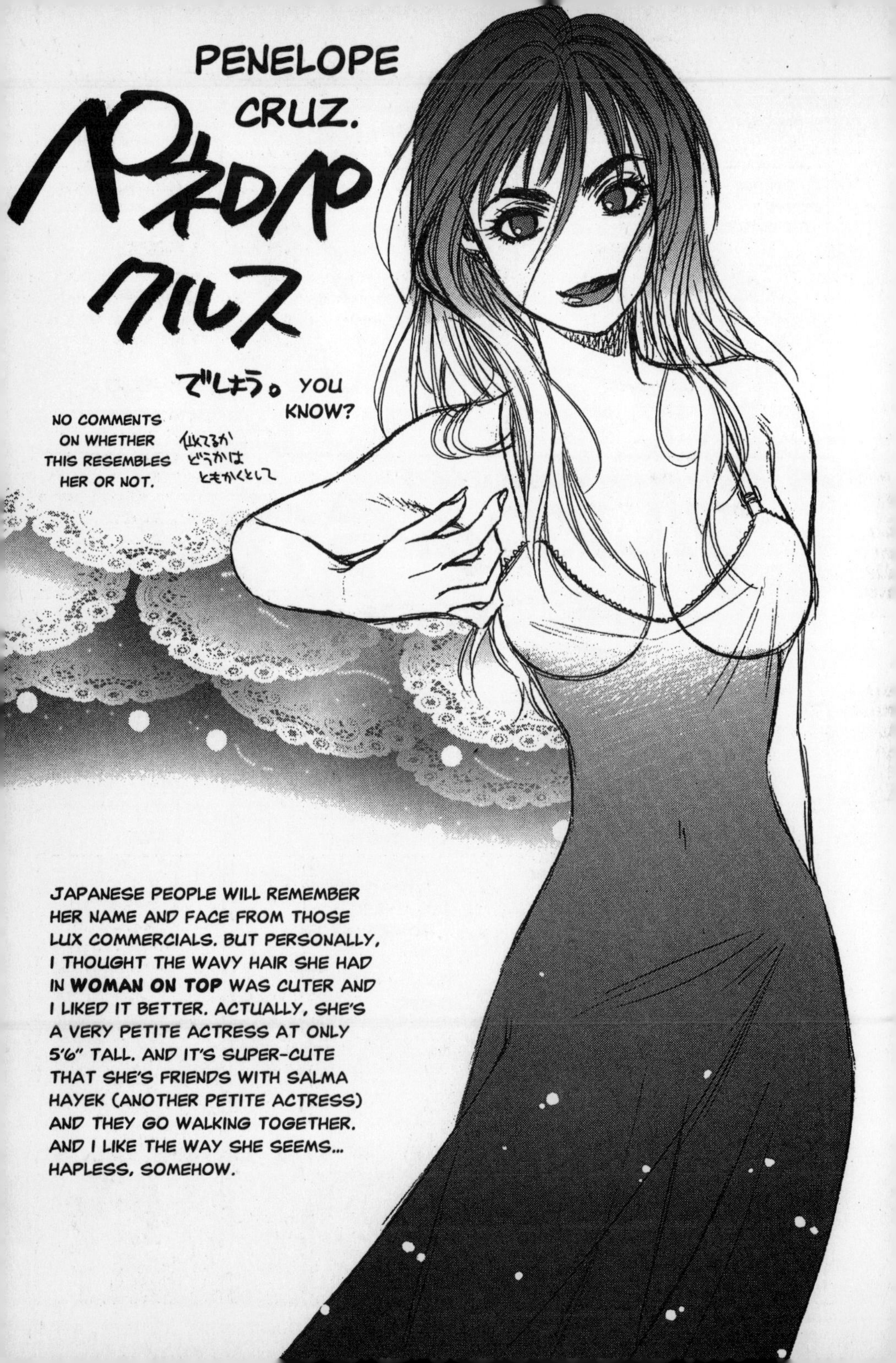
PENELOPE CRUZ.
ペネロペ
クルス
でしょう。 YOU KNOW?
NO COMMENTS ON WHETHER THIS RESEMBLES HER OR NOT.
似てるかどうかはともかくとして

JAPANESE PEOPLE WILL REMEMBER HER NAME AND FACE FROM THOSE LUX COMMERCIALS. BUT PERSONALLY, I THOUGHT THE WAVY HAIR SHE HAD IN **WOMAN ON TOP** WAS CUTER AND I LIKED IT BETTER. ACTUALLY, SHE'S A VERY PETITE ACTRESS AT ONLY 5'6" TALL. AND IT'S SUPER-CUTE THAT SHE'S FRIENDS WITH SALMA HAYEK (ANOTHER PETITE ACTRESS) AND THEY GO WALKING TOGETHER. AND I LIKE THE WAY SHE SEEMS... HAPLESS, SOMEHOW.

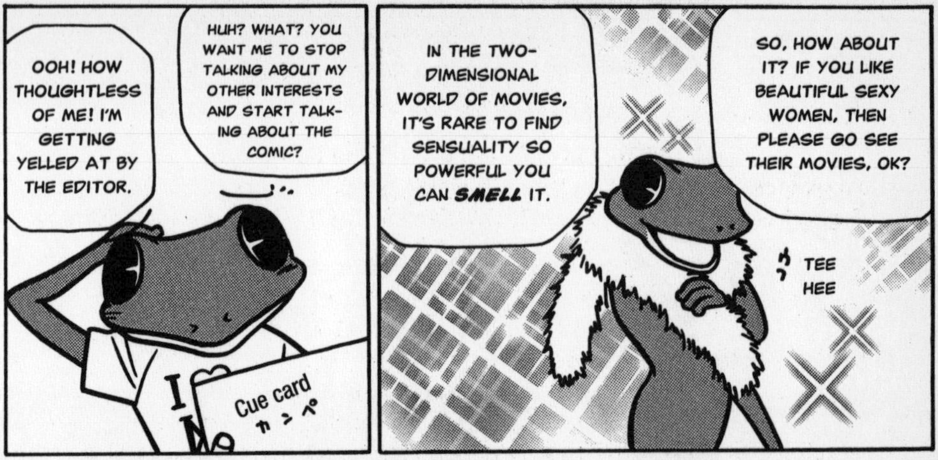
SO, HOW ABOUT IT? IF YOU LIKE BEAUTIFUL SEXY WOMEN, THEN PLEASE GO SEE THEIR MOVIES, OK?
IN THE TWO-DIMENSIONAL WORLD OF MOVIES, IT'S RARE TO FIND SENSUALITY SO POWERFUL YOU CAN SMELL IT.
TEE HEE
HUH? WHAT? YOU WANT ME TO STOP TALKING ABOUT MY OTHER INTERESTS AND START TALKING ABOUT THE COMIC?
OOH! HOW THOUGHTLESS OF ME! I'M GETTING YELLED AT BY THE EDITOR.
Cue card
カンペ

What's going to happen in the next FMP?

フルメタの今後はどうなるのか!?

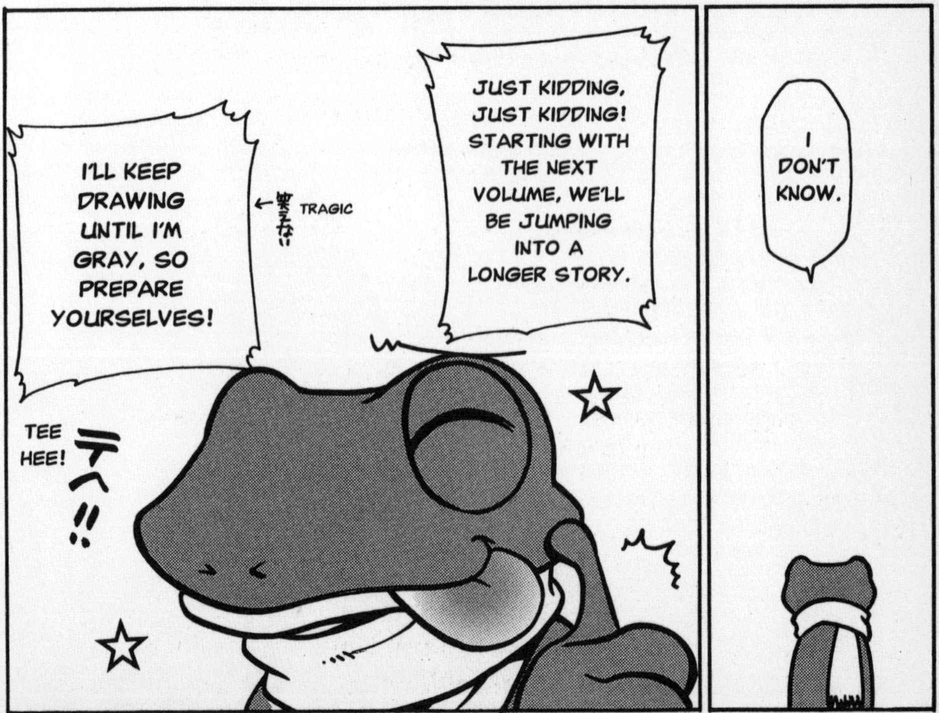
I DON'T KNOW.
JUST KIDDING, JUST KIDDING! STARTING WITH THE NEXT VOLUME, WE'LL BE JUMPING INTO A LONGER STORY.
I'LL KEEP DRAWING UNTIL I'M GRAY, SO PREPARE YOURSELVES!
笑えない
TRAGIC
TEE HEE!
テヘ!!

今回のヘルパー様→庭谷っち・荒海っち・綾っち・夜神っち 皆 肉を食べよう。

Helper gang for this volume: Niwaya, Arakai, Aya, Yagami. Let's all eat some meat.

Full Metal Panic! Volume Three

Author **SHOUJI GATOU**

Illustrator **RETSU TATEO**

Character Creation **SHIKIDOUJI**

© 2002 RETSU TATEO • SHOUJI GATOU • SHIKIDOUJI

Originally published in Japan in 2002 by KADOKAWA SHOTEN PUBLISHING CO., LTD., Tokyo.

English translation rights arranged with KADOKAWA SHOTEN PUBLISHING CO., LTD., Tokyo.

Translator **AMY FORSYTH**

ADV Manga Translation Staff **JAVIER LOPEZ, KAY BERTRAND, BRENDAN FRAYNE, EIKO MCGREGOR**

Print Production/Art Studio Manager **LISA PUCKETT**

Graphic Designer **GEORGE REYNOLDS**

Graphic Artists **JORGE ALVARADO, WINDI MARTIN, RYAN MASON, NATALIA MORALES, KRISTINA MILESKI, SHANNON RASBERRY, LANCE SWARTOUT**

Graphic Intern **IVAN CURIEL**

International Coordinator **TORU IWAKAMI**

International Coordinator **ATSUSHI KANBAYASHI**

Publishing Editor **SUSAN ITIN**

Assistant Editor **MARGARET SCHAROLD**

Editorial Assistant **VARSHA BHUCHAR**

Proofreader **SHERIDAN JACOBS**

Research/ Traffic Coordinator **MARSHA ARNOLD**

President, C.E.O. & Publisher **JOHN LEDFORD**

Email: editor@adv-manga.com
www.adv-manga.com
www.advfilms.com

For sales and distribution inquiries please call 1.800.282.7202

ADV MANGA is a division of A.D. Vision, Inc.
10114 W. Sam Houston Parkway, Suite 200, Houston, Texas 77099

English text © 2004 published by A.D. Vision, Inc. under exclusive license.
ADV MANGA is a trademark of A.D. Vision, Inc.

ISBN: 1-4139-0007-0

First printing, February 2004

10 9 8 7 5 4 3 2 1

Printed in Canada

LETTER FROM THE EDITOR

Dear Reader,

Thank you for purchasing an ADV Manga book. We hope you enjoyed the hilarious antics of Sosuke and Kaname.

It is our sincere commitment in reproducing Asian comics and graphic novels to retain as much of the character of the original book as possible. From the right-to-left format of the Japanese books to the meaning of the story in the original language, the ADV Manga team is working hard to publish a quality book for our fans and readers. Write to us with your questions or comments, and tell us how you liked this and other ADV books. Be sure to visit our website at www.adv-manga.com and view the list of upcoming titles, sign up for special announcements, and fill out our survey.

The ADV Manga team of translators, designers, graphic artists, production managers, traffic managers, and editors hope you will buy more ADV books – there's a lot more in store from ADV Manga!

www.adv-manga.com

Publishing Editor
Susan B. Itin

Assistant Editor
Margaret Scharold

Editorial Assistant
Varsha Bhuchar

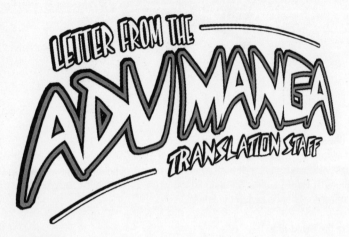

LETTER FROM THE ADV MANGA TRANSLATION STAFF

Dear Reader,

On behalf of the ADV Manga translation team, thank you for purchasing an ADV book. We are enthusiastic and committed to our work, and strive to carry our enthusiasm over into the book you hold in your hands.

Our goal is to retain the true spirit of the original Japanese book. While great care has been taken to render a true and accurate translation, some cultural or readability issues may require a line to be adapted for greater accessibility to our readers. At times, manga titles that include culturally-specific concepts will feature a "Translator's Notes" section, which explains noteworthy references to the original text.

We hope our commitment to a faithful translation is evident in every ADV book you purchase.

Sincerely,

Javier Lopez,
Lead Translator

Eiko McGregor

Kay Bertrand

Brendan Frayne

Amy Forsyth

ADV MANGA™

www.adv-manga.com

Full Metal Panic Vol 03

PG. 122 It's like something out of a fairy tale!
The word that Kaname used in the original Japanese was *botchan*, which conjures up images of a handsome, well-bred young boy from a rich family (but who is also frail and/or sheltered). Famed author Natsume Soseki wrote a novel called ***Botchan***, but this particular reference is unrelated to the book.

PG. 143 We're the Genki Kids!
In Japanese, *genki* means healthy, energetic, active, etc. (all of which certainly fit Kaname and the others in this scene). "Genki Kids" here may be a pun on "Kinki Kids," a Japanese pop duo that has also branched out into television acting.

PG. 146 Rock Bottom
This is the name of the finishing move performed by professional wrestler The Rock.

PG. 148 The flag
The writing on this flag is based on the following anonymous poem (minus the second line). It was found written on the wall of a sugar factory in San Fernando where troops lodged in the battle for Leyte Gulf (Oct. 23-26, 1944):

hana maite	Following (=obeying) the flower
	(seems to be a patriotic phrase)
sora uchi yukan	We will head into the skies
kumo somen	We will stain the clouds
(shi)kabane (kou)kai naku	A corpse has no regrets
warera chiru nari	We are scattered (=fallen in battle)

PG. 163 Cosplay
In the first panel, the author is cosplaying as a Powerpuff Girl.

PG. 166 LUX
A brand of shampoo which Penelope Cruz advertised in a series of commercials.

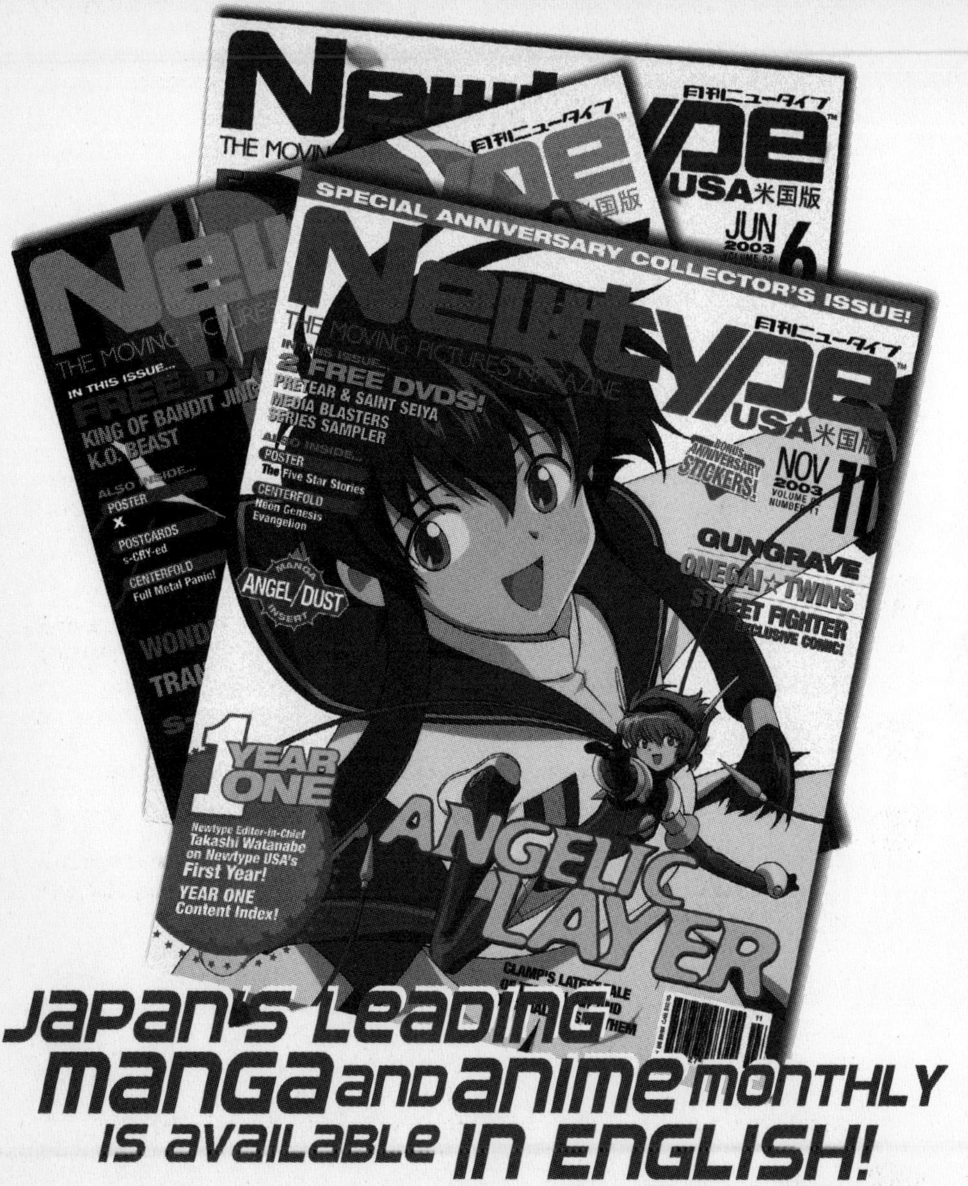
Newtype
THE MOVING PICTURES MAGAZINE
USA 米国版
JUN 2003 6
IN THIS ISSUE...
KING OF BANDIT JING
K.O. BEAST
ALSO INSIDE...
POSTER
X
POSTCARDS
s-CRY-ed
CENTERFOLD
Full Metal Panic!
SPECIAL ANNIVERSARY COLLECTOR'S ISSUE!
月刊ニュータイプ
2 FREE DVDS!
PRETEAR & SAINT SEIYA
MEDIA BLASTERS SERIES SAMPLER
POSTER
The Five Star Stories
CENTERFOLD
Neon Genesis Evangelion
MANGA INSERT
ANGEL/DUST
BONUS ANNIVERSARY STICKERS!
NOV 2003 11
GUNGRAVE
ONEGAI☆TWINS
STREET FIGHTER
EXCLUSIVE COMIC!
1 YEAR ONE
Newtype Editor-in-Chief Takashi Watanabe on Newtype USA's First Year!
YEAR ONE Content Index!
ANGELIC LAYER

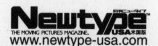

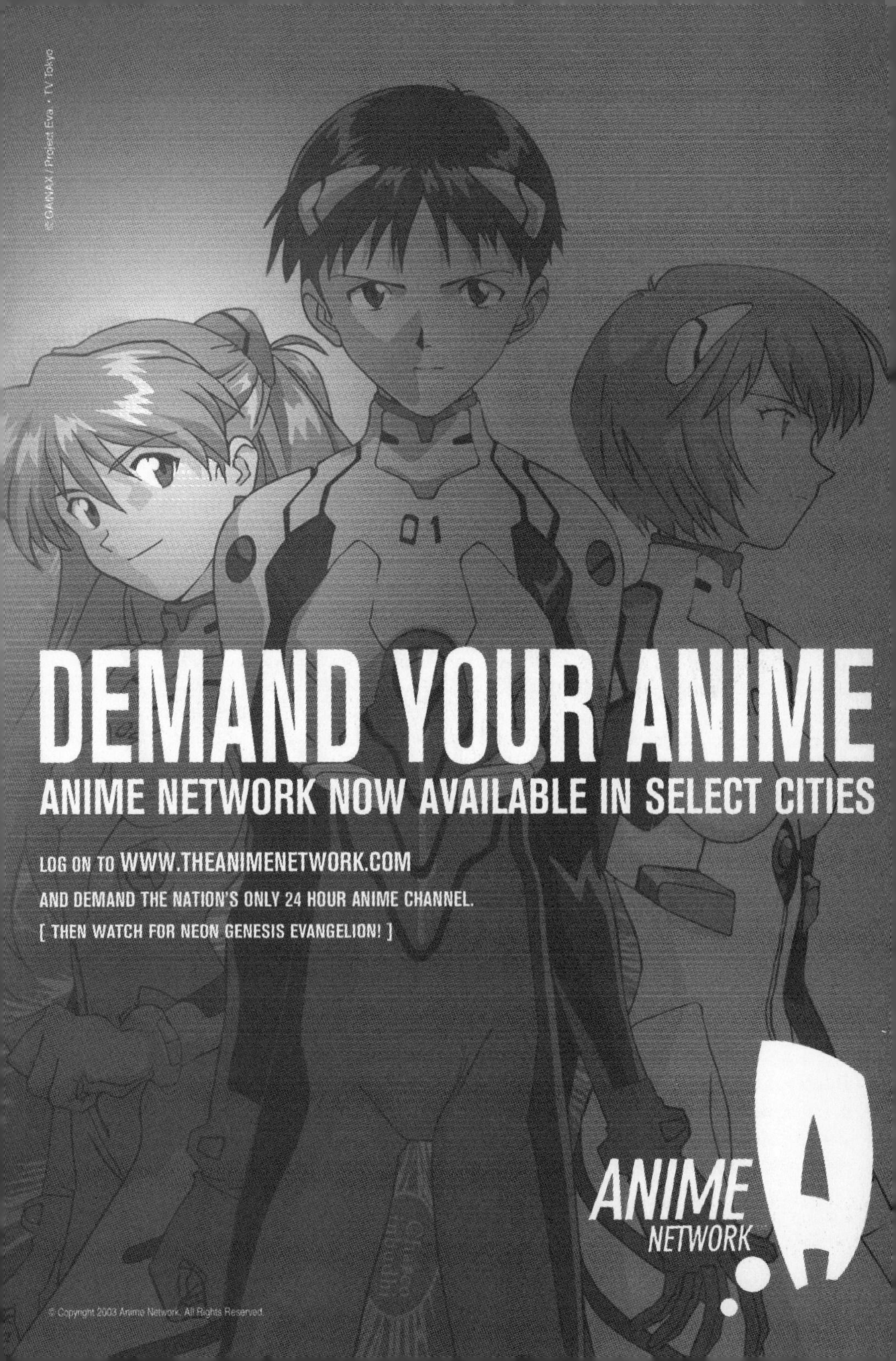

DEMAND YOUR ANIME
ANIME NETWORK NOW AVAILABLE IN SELECT CITIES

LOG ON TO WWW.THEANIMENETWORK.COM
AND DEMAND THE NATION'S ONLY 24 HOUR ANIME CHANNEL.
[THEN WATCH FOR NEON GENESIS EVANGELION!]

ANIME
NETWORK

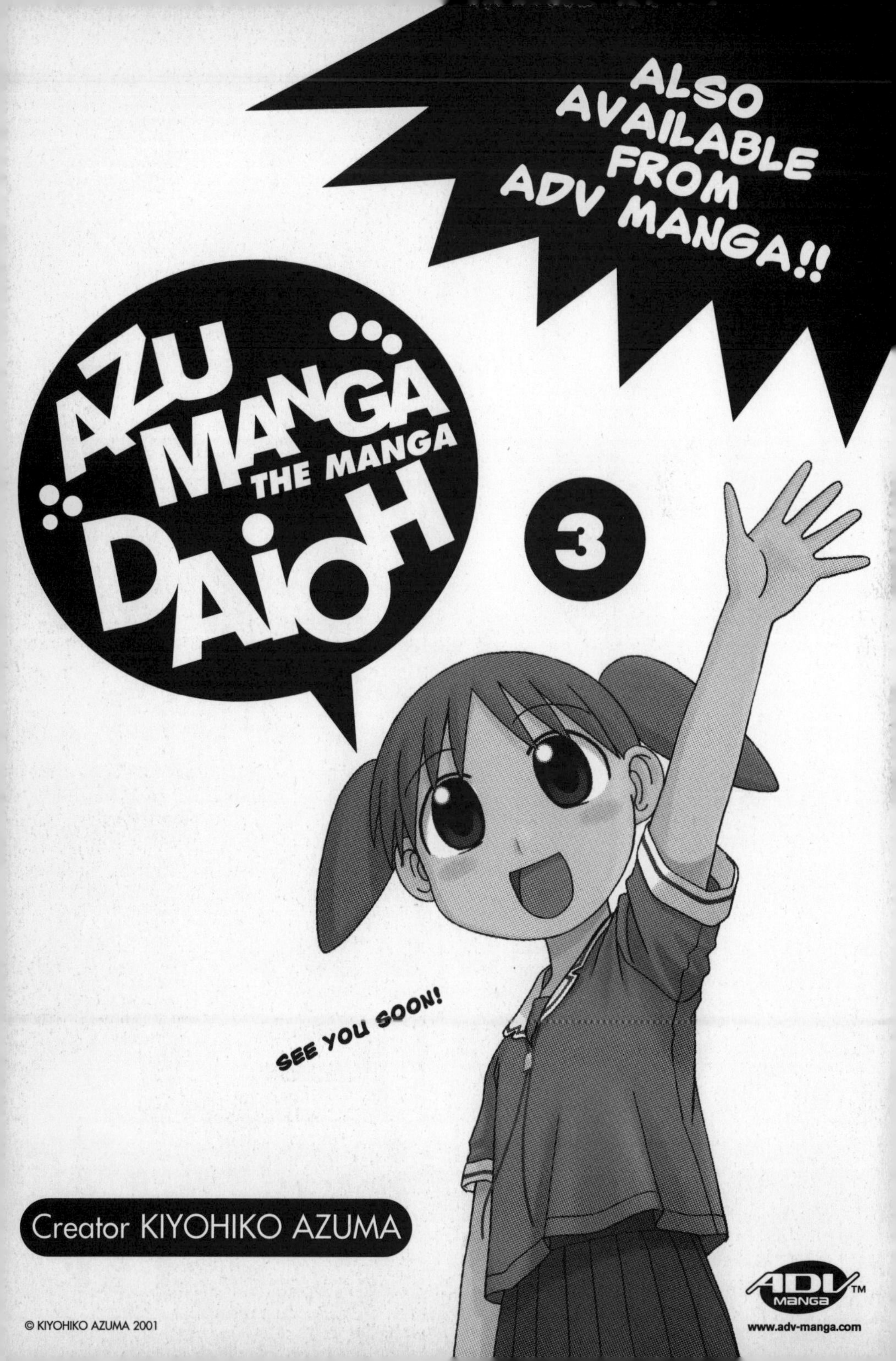
ALSO AVAILABLE FROM ADV MANGA!!
AZUMANGA DAIOH
THE MANGA
3
SEE YOU SOON!
Creator KIYOHIKO AZUMA
ADV Manga TM
www.adv-manga.com
© KIYOHIKO AZUMA 2001

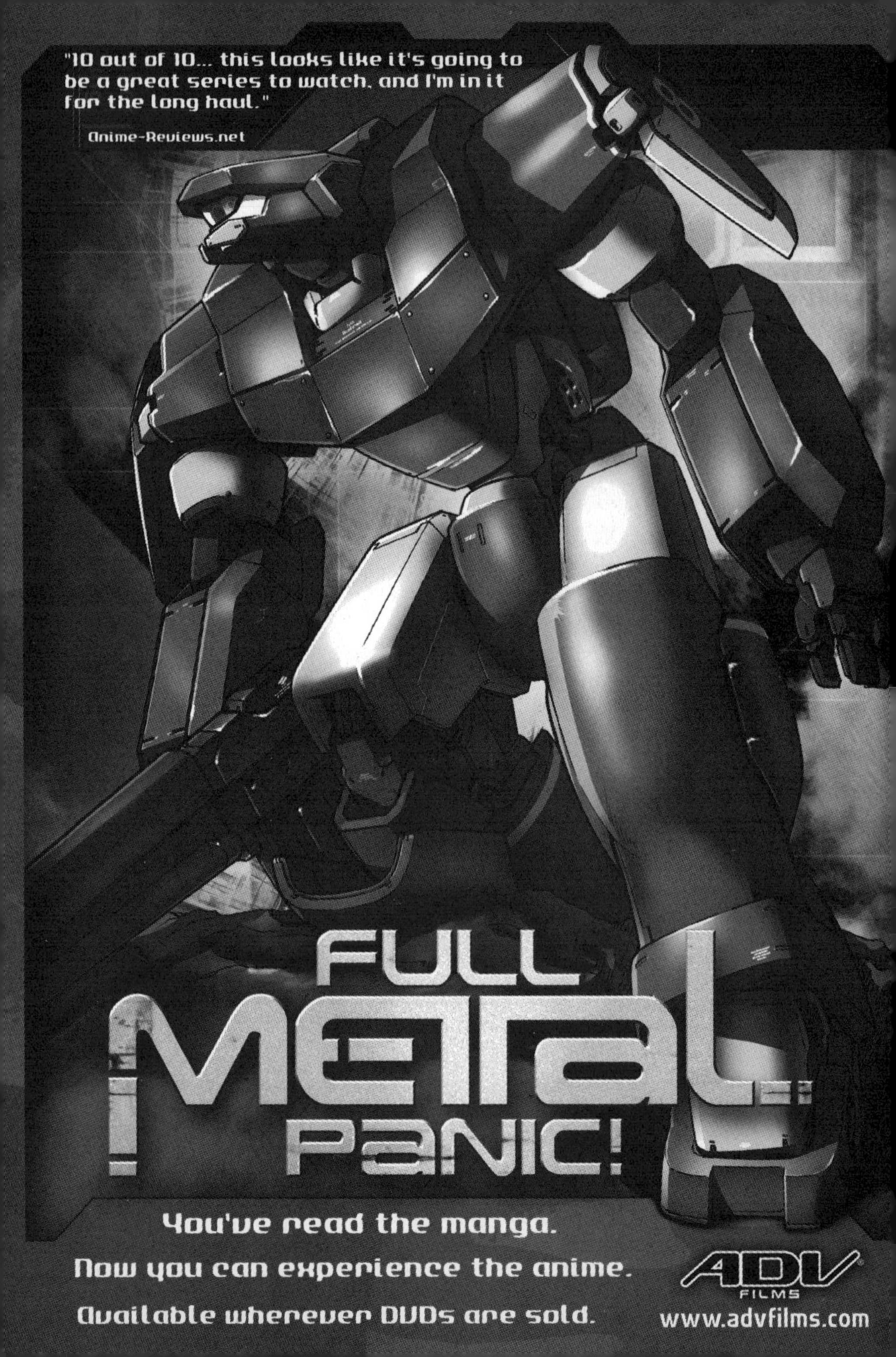
"10 out of 10... this looks like it's going to be a great series to watch, and I'm in it for the long haul."
Anime-Reviews.net
FULL METAL PANIC!
You've read the manga.
Now you can experience the anime.
Available wherever DVDs are sold.
ADV FILMS
www.advfilms.com

QUESTION #1:
When can I get more Nana?!

ANSWER:
NOW!!
Only from ADV Manga!!

Story
Yasuhiro Imagawa
Art
Azusa Kunihiro

ADV
MANGA™
www.adv-manga.com

More Panic!

FULL METAL PANIC! 04

AUTHOR
SHOUJI GATOU

ILLUSTRATOR
RETSU TATEO

AVAILABLE APRIL 2004!

www.adv-manga.com

 **ANIME SURVEY**

PLEASE MAIL THE COMPLETED FORM TO: EDITOR – ADV MANGA
℅ A.D. Vision, Inc. 10114 W. Sam Houston Pkwy., Suite 200 Houston, TX 77099

Name:_____

Address:_____

City, State, Zip:_____
_____

E-Mail:_____

Male ☐   Female ☐   Age:_____

Cable Provider:_____

☐ **CHECK HERE IF YOU WOULD LIKE TO RECEIVE OTHER INFORMATION OR FUTURE OFFERS FROM ADV.**

1. Annual Household Income (*Check only one*)
- ☐ Under $25,000
- ☐ $25,000 to $50,000
- ☐ $50,000 to $75,000
- ☐ Over $75,000

2. How do you hear about new Anime releases? (*Check all that apply*)
- ☐ Browsing in Store
- ☐ Internet Reviews
- ☐ Anime News Websites
- ☐ Direct Email Campaigns
- ☐ Online forums (message boards and chat rooms)
- ☐ Carrier pigeon
- ☐ Other:_____
- ☐ Magazine Ad
- ☐ Online Advertising
- ☐ Conventions
- ☐ TV Advertising

3. Which magazines do you read? (*Check all that apply*)
- ☐ Wizard
- ☐ SPIN
- ☐ Animerica
- ☐ Rolling Stone
- ☐ Maxim
- ☐ DC Comics
- ☐ URB
- ☐ Polygon
- ☐ Original Play Station Magazine
- ☐ Entertainment Weekly
- ☐ YRB
- ☐ EGM
- ☐ Newtype USA
- ☐ SciFi
- ☐ Starlog
- ☐ Wired
- ☐ Vice
- ☐ BPM
- ☐ I hate reading
- ☐ Other:

4. Would you subscribe to digital cable if you could get a 24 hour/7 day a week anime channel (like the Anime Network)?
- ☐ Yes
- ☐ No

5. Would you like to see the Anime Network in your area?

- ☐ Yes
- ☐ No

6. Would you pay $6.99/month for the Anime Network?

- ☐ Yes
- ☐ No

7. What genre of manga and anime would you like to see from ADV?
(*Check all that apply*)

- ☐ adventure
- ☐ romance
- ☐ detective
- ☐ fighting
- ☐ horror
- ☐ sci-fi/fantasy
- ☐ sports

8. How many manga titles have you purchased in the last year?

- ☐ none
- ☐ 1-4
- ☐ 5-10
- ☐ 11+

9. Where do you make your manga purchases? (*Check all that apply*)

- ☐ comic store
- ☐ bookstore
- ☐ newsstand
- ☐ online
- ☐ other: ______________
- ☐ department store
- ☐ grocery store
- ☐ video store
- ☐ video game store

10. What's your favorite anime-related website?

- ☐ advfilms.com
- ☐ anipike.com
- ☐ rightstuf.com
- ☐ animenewsservice.com
- ☐ animenewsnetwork.com
- ☐ animeondvd.com
- ☐ animenation.com
- ☐ animeonline.net
- ☐ planetanime.com
- ☐ other:

All information provided will be used for internal purposes only. We promise not to sell or otherwise divulge your information.